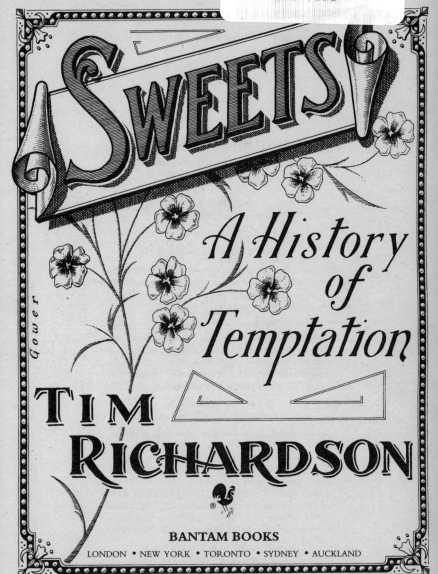

SWEETS

A History of Temptation

TIM RICHARDSON

BANTAM BOOKS

LONDON • NEW YORK • TORONTO • SYDNEY • AUCKLAND

SWEETS
A BANTAM BOOK : 0 553 81446 X

Originally published in Great Britain by Bantam Press,
a division of Transworld Publishers

PRINTING HISTORY
Bantam Press edition published 2003
Bantam edition published 2003

1 3 5 7 9 10 8 6 4 2

Set in 11/13pt Bembo by
Falcon Oast Graphic Art Ltd.

Bantam Books are published by Transworld Publishers,
61–63 Uxbridge Road, London W5 5SA,
a division of The Random House Group Ltd,
in Australia by Random House Australia (Pty) Ltd,
20 Alfred Street, Milsons Point, Sydney, NSW 2061, Australia,
in New Zealand by Random House New Zealand Ltd,
18 Poland Road, Glenfield, Auckland 10, New Zealand
and in South Africa by Random House (Pty) Ltd,
Endulini, 5a Jubilee Road, Parktown 2193, South Africa.

Printed and bound in Great Britain by
Cox & Wyman Ltd, Reading, Berkshire.

Papers used by Transworld Publishers are natural, recyclable products
made from wood grown in sustainable forests. The manufacturing processes
conform to the environmental regulations of the country of origin.

Tim Richardson is the world's first international confectionery historian. He also writes about gardens, landscape and theatre, and contributes to the *Daily Telegraph*, *Country Life*, *House and Garden* and *Wallpaper**. He lives in north London.

For Claire and for George –
my sweets

Boys and girls are my best customers, sir, and mostly the smallest of them; but then, again, some of them's fifty, aye, turned fifty; Lor' love you. An old fellow, that hasn't a stump of a tooth, why, he'll stop and buy a ha'porth of hard-bake, and he'll say, 'I've a deal of the boy left about me still.'

'A sweet-stuff man, formerly a baker', quoted in
London Labour and the London Poor (1851) by Henry Mayhew.

CONTENTS

ACKNOWLEDGEMENTS

First I would like to thank my wife Claire for her forbearance in the face of my overwhelming interest in small sugary objects. I apologise to my small son, George, for telling him that my extensive sweets store was 'Daddy's pills', and for allowing him to feed me sweets while still in a state of ignorance about them.

Tif Loehnis of the literary agency Janklow & Nesbit was the person who encouraged me to write the book in the first place, gave me the confidence to put in the preliminary work, and has provided me with support, friendship and wise editorial counselling throughout. Thank you, Tif. Thanks also to Tif's colleagues in the New York office, Tina Bennett and Dorothy Vincent. Doug Young of Bantam Press had faith in the book and has prevented me from becoming wrecked on the wilder shores of the Isle of Discursiveness. Thanks also to Colin Dickerman and Bloomsbury for their backing as publishers in the USA, and especially for making small chocolate bars in the shape of the book.

Since this is a book without footnotes, I would particularly like to thank all those authors whose excellent work I have used – see the bibliography, but notably Sidney W. Mintz, Martin Levey, Joël Glenn Brenner, Anil Kishore Sinha, Catherine Brown, Laura Mason, Harold McGee, Nicholas Whittaker, J.H. Galloway, Karen Hess, Maguelonne Toussaint-Samat, A.W. Logue, Gilda Cordero-Fernando, Mary Simeti and Alan Davidson. The quotation from Ronald Melville's translation of

Lucretius, *On the Nature of the Universe* (1997), is reprinted by permission of Oxford University Press. The staff in the Rare Books Reading Room at the incomparable British Library have been professional, helpful, interested and a pleasure to work with.

During my research I benefited from co-operation and help from many people in the confectionery business, and I would like to thank Tony Bilsborough of Cadbury, Wilson Deyermond of Penguin Confectionery, Paul Gandar of the magazine *Kennedy's Confection*, Daniel Hencke and Paul Richardson of Haribo, Elizabeth Müsteli at Toblerone, Pamela Whitenack at the Hershey Community Archive, Susan Fussell at the National Confectioners Association (USA) and John Newman of the Biscuit, Cake, Chocolate and Confectionery Alliance (UK).

Many friends provided help and information, and I thank Stefan Stern for reading the sections on business, Noël Kingsbury for bringing back Anil Kishore Sinha's book from India, Gordon Taylor for various press clippings and also information on liquorice, Bronwen Riley for information on Fisherman's Friend, and Stewart Lee for accompanying me to Cadbury World and sustaining me with cups of steaming Bovril. In addition, many friends brought back sweets for me from foreign climes, and I thank Mary Creagh and Adrian Pulham for chocolates from Brazil, Chris and Kazuko Flook for sweets from Japan, Mark Giles for a big bag of sweets from Saudi Arabia, Dorothy Vincent for maple candies from Vermont, Miraphora Mina for Italian violet cachous, Janice Acquah for Ghanaian chocolate, Felicitas Rost for Mozart balls from Germany, Eleanor Church for Mormon chocolate, Catherine Max for more chocolate, and Juliet Summerscale and Daniel Noguez for Uruguayan *dulce de leche*.

Finally I would like to thank the sweets inventors. Keep it up!

PROLOGUE

My grandfather worked for a toffee company. My father was a dentist. So I have always had strong feelings about sweets. But I have never been confused. I like sweets. I like them a lot. And that is why I set about writing this book, the first-ever world history of sweets. I wanted to find out more about my favourite things – and yes, I did want to eat a whole lot of sweets in the process. The world was my gobstopper.

As I delved deeper into the subject, discovering the sweets cultures of other nations and poring over ancient pharmaceutical and cookery manuals, it soon became apparent that a love of sweets has been a part of almost every gastronomic culture. The history of sweets goes back a long, long way, right back to the earliest human civilisations, and (until the late twentieth century) mankind always associated this love of sweetness with goodness and pleasure. I was embarking on an historical, geographical and gastronomic excursion into an extraordinary world of invention, secrecy, eccentricity, obsession and happiness.

The sweets of a country are, in fact, the one aspect of a cuisine that can almost always be enjoyed and understood by foreigners. I say 'almost' because there will always be exceptions in the world of confectionery – there are millions of sweets out there and (as we will see) some of them are rather strange. But most of them are just really nice, wherever they are from.

Sugary sweetness is often maligned as an unsophisticated, unsubtle, childish taste, but for those of us who are attuned to its nuances and are able to suck or chew or lick without prejudice, the variations of flavour and texture in sweets, and all the gradations of sweetness as it mingles and enhances other flavours, are one of life's great sensual pleasures. This is not to say that we should all aspire to be sweets gourmets. With the sorry exception of fine chocolate, sweets have so far escaped the clutches of connoisseurship; they remain democratic, unpretentious and, for the most part, cheap. After all, it is children who are the best judges of sweets.

No, my approach has been primarily one of description, per- haps enthusiasm on occasion, but there should be no suggestion that my taste is better than anyone else's. With sweets, it all depends on where you grew up and what your favourite sweets were in childhood: sampling hundreds of different sweets from around the world has been a vital part of the research process, but when it finally came to the crunch and I had to decide on my personal top ten sweets, I found that if I was honest, most of them were the sweets from my home culture that I would have chosen before I embarked on this sweets odyssey.

But what fun it has been finding that out. In the process of writing this book I have been transformed into an international confectionery historian – the world's first. My study is crammed with sweets from all round the world, and as I wrote the book I frequently broke off to sample some rare delight which suddenly took my fancy. The history of sweets is a footnote to a footnote of official world history. Sweets are really not very important amid the drama of wars and empires and social upheaval. But they can improve our everyday lives, providing an innocent moment of pleasure and respite. If you offer someone a sweet, the chances are they will smile. And perhaps that is worth something.

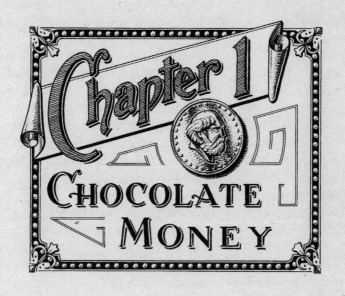

Chapter 1

CHOCOLATE MONEY

My trousers were in the trouser press. My hand was in the minibar. At last, I was an international fancy foods delegate. I had just flown in for the four-day orgy of confectionery flesh-pressing that is the Internationale Süsswaren Messe, or ISM, held every January in Cologne's multiple, apparently never-ending, purpose-built exhibition halls. There are a dozen other international sweets fairs in the sweets industry calendar – including the Fancy Food and Confectionery Show and All Candy Expo (both held in Chicago, by rival organisations), Intersweets in Moscow, or Confitexpo in Mexico – but this is the big one. Buyers, wholesalers and manufacturers, ranging in size from multinationals to small family businesses, all converge on Cologne to taste new sweets, make deals and eye up the competition. The city's trouser presses are running at full pelt, hotel breakfast buffets are bereft of the good stuff by 8.30 a.m., and the discos are full of dodgy dancing. ISM attracts 33,000 visitors.

It is a seriously businesslike show – the showcase of the world confectionery industry, certainly, but also the place where the biggest deals are brokered, while the destiny of hundreds of smaller companies is decided through smaller deals worked out in huddles around tiny tables at the backs of the stands. The delegates are there to sell sweets, wholesale, to all comers, as I discovered when I introduced myself to scores of them in an attempt to talk candy. I had imagined that the sweets industry would be delighted to welcome its first international confectionery historian; that I would spend my time garnering insider information, listening to curious anecdotes and fending off over-eager sweetmakers desperate to be a part of my chronicle. But the reality was different: many of the small- to medium-sized manufacturers are never very far away from ruin, and the sharp-eyed delegates were there to fill their order books. In sales, tunnel vision is a prerequisite. My trouser creases were as crisp as anyone else's, yet I was generally treated with polite condescension, and occasionally pitiful puzzlement, before being quietly moved aside in favour of more lucrative possibilities. It was all rather galling at first, but I was soon resigned to my fate – after all, any business successful enough to have a history will be, by its nature, more interested in the future than the past – and I resolved to visit every stand at the show, however briefly, over the next four days.

It was a crazy idea. A sweets fair sounds like heaven on earth, perhaps, but there are eight massive halls at ISM, and each is crammed with stands that are only vaguely grouped by theme or nationality. One second you are examining Chinese chews, then all of a sudden it is Trinidadian lollipops. It is most discombobulating. And it is not helped by the extreme parsimony of the sweetmakers when it comes to dishing out free samples. I was expecting to leave the fair every day with sackfuls of sweets (for professional tasting, later), but most of the 1,500 companies – if they offered anything at all – had put out a derisory bowl of their cheapest wrapped sweets, and I felt slightly embarrassed pocketing them without at least some pretence of interest in the business. In fact I did leave the show with sackfuls (or plastic-bagfuls) each day, but they were weighed down more by paperwork than by sweets. This did not lessen the humiliation when one of my bulging bags exploded and I was forced to scrabble around on the floor for rolling gobstoppers like the sweets urchin I had so quickly become.

By mid afternoon on the first day I was pleased to have negotiated three entire halls, only to discover that two of them had upper floors which were nearly the same size again. But I continued with my mission, visiting tiny stands of family sweet-makers, where the same recipe has been passed down through the generations, as well as the huge conglomerates like Chupa Chups of Spain or Baci of Italy, whose displays required teams of hostesses, giant model sweets, mock retail displays, video presentations and special restaurants and bars where valued contacts could be cultivated. Then there were the surprises, like Fisherman's Friend, the quaint Lancashire manufacturer of strong medicinal lozenges in old-fashioned packaging. I was expecting a tiny stand, staffed by some sterling Lancashire types, but of course Fisherman's Friend is now big international business, and the family-owned company boasted one of the largest and certainly the most decorative displays at the show, complete with a full-size trawler staffed by a uniformed 'crew'. They were expensively and successfully marketing the product by distributing large bags displaying the Fisherman's Friend logo. Long gone are the days when these cough sweets were sold only to wheezing trawlermen on the quayside at Fleetwood, in tablet form because a spoonful of medicine was impractical at sea.

For the international confectionery historian, the fair was a succession of hundreds of such short, sweet encounters: a Mexican delegate forcibly squirted bright blue and in-determinately flavoured candy breath spray in my mouth; I had a long and mutually incomprehensible dialogue with a pleasant Chinese lady who sat me down and showed me several books of bright pink candy designs; I was treated with suspicion by a Russian lollipop maker; patronised by several French chocolatiers; dismissed by a German marzipan artist; refused entry to the Mozart-ball stand; charmed by at least four members of an Italian liquorice dynasty; technologically dazzled by a Belgian pastille maker; fascinated by a Pakistani inventor of candied paan mixes; indulged by a charming Turkish Delight magnate; almost adopted by an elderly Chilean chewing gum pioneer; and astonished by a British fudge and toffee maker. This last because my late grandfather used to work for the firm,

Bristow's of Devon, as a sales representative, and when I approached the stand with some diffidence and asked if anyone remembered him, both the Bristow brothers (Plymouth Brethren) immediately recalled him with affection and even named the exact year of his death, some twenty years previously. The show rolled on and I rolled with it. Back in my hotel room, I solemnly munched through the sweets of nations, trying to cultivate a connoisseurial air. One day, during a pause for a frankfurter lunch, I was perplexed by the sight of two children among the milling crowds of suits and stilettos. These were the only children I saw during the four days at the show – a ratio which seemed somehow unreal, when so many of the products were directed at them as consumers.

A few conclusions about the state of the industry could be drawn. The difference in national sweet tastes (explored in chapter eleven, The Himalayan Gobstopper), while still notice-able, is being eroded quickly as multinational sweets companies aim to create global brands. The main trends in the sweets industry at the beginning of the twenty-first century are the unstoppable rise of chewing gum (particularly sugar-free); the burgeoning and as yet unexploited Asian sweets market; the popularity of 'nutraceutical' sweets which cross over as healthy products (through vitamin supplements, for example); the massive increase in sales of gummy sweets and sour or fizzy-sour (acidulated) sweets; and the emphasis on marketing sweets to suit specific occasions and lifestyles, rather than simply the endless search for new flavours and textures. Marketing is now just as important as invention.

But the Cologne show is no place to discover the secrets of the industry; it is a gargantuan sales pitch for thousands of finished products. The entrepreneurial nature of the business, and the originality and sometimes unalloyed eccentricity of confectionery products, means that each and every sweets com-pany has its own private philosophy and guards its secrets carefully. There is a lot of money to be made out of con-fectionery – as a business, it is far bigger than steel, for example

– and there are hundreds of sweets millionaires out there, many of them running small family firms that depend on a handful of product lines, or even just one celebrated sweet. Doreen Lofthouse of Fisherman's Friend, the matriarchal head of this old family company who in the 1950s saw the potential of the Victorian medicinal lozenge and began marketing it, is consistently rated one of the richest women in Britain.

Confectionery brands are extraordinarily durable: the top twenty bestselling sweets and chocolate bars of any country have generally remained almost the same since the 1960s, and many bars date back to the 1930s or even earlier. It is true that the big companies like Mars, Cadbury, Nestlé, Kraft and Hershey dominate sales in terms of overall percentages, but even the smaller brands, which do not make it into the top twenty bestselling sweets lists – makers of sugar confectionery, rather than chocolate bars, in the main – can be extremely profitable. People develop emotional bonds with sweets that date back to their earliest memories of childhood, locality and the family home. Sweets are the memorials of our innocence. They remind us of the time when the world could be measured out in sweet little objects of desire. Particular brands can conjure up memories of specific moments of childhood in a way nothing else can. It is a truism that smell is the sense most intimately connected with memory, but perhaps sweets are the objects connected most closely with our childhoods. The extraordinary brand loyalty of confectionery customers over decades and, in many cases, lifetimes, is commercial testimony to this resonant quality. With sweets, the distinction between adulthood and childhood is blurred. We joyfully regress when offered a sweet – just for a moment your boss can look like a five-year-old. Sweets are one of the best conduits of communication between grown-ups and children – we all like them, and we all know what is good about them. Sharing sweets, a grandfather and a grandson can be united in olfactory heaven-on-earth, a quality exploited by advertisers. There is also a sense that some sweets have been around so long they are immortal, and that quality can be conferred on us: the world is all right if your favourite sweet tastes the same now, at the age of ninety, as it did when you were five.

The sense of security that sweets can bring is reflected in the way sweet sales rise in times of war or economic or social unrest. After the terrorist attacks on New York on 11 September 2001, confectionery sales in North America rose appreciably and (for the industry) slightly embarrassingly, prompting the president of the Confectionery Manufacturers of Canada to reflect: 'It is a trend confectioners see every time the economy goes down or stress levels go up, and it happens right across the continent.'

When a large sweets company takes over a small one and acquires some well-known brands, which has happened a lot in the past few decades, they are well advised to leave the name, logo, packaging and recipe alone. A photograph of a rack of sweets in a 1950s shop contains a surprising number of familiar packages, and the recipes change remarkably little over the years (although in most cases the bars will have got bigger). Mars gambled when it finally 'harmonised' its international brands, Snickers and Starburst, and ditched the old British names for the sweets, Marathon and Opal Fruits. There was a sustained and heartfelt outcry over these changes which the company could never have anticipated, and it still reverberates today: it is not uncommon to find British people who will not relinquish the old Marathon name, and some even refuse to buy Snickers bars on the grounds of confectionery imperialism. The apparent blunder was surprising because Mars, with its Slough operation at the emotional heart of the business, has always been alive to British sensibilities as well as American. But the company's policy was ultimately justified in that sales of both products rose despite the name-change.

Tinkering with a recipe is more dangerous, as Coca Cola found to its cost when it altered its product, but Mars again gambled in Britain with a new look for Mars in 2002: smaller, lighter and less heavy on the caramel. The classic strengths of the Mars Bar – its big 'American' size, energy levels to help you work, rest and play, and pure satisfaction – are now outmoded, with the consumer demanding a lighter, less demanding snack. Since the 1980s, the sweets industry has been battling against the influx of health and granola bars, as well as new sweet snack alternatives (particularly ice creams and biscuits), and the aim has been to reposition confectionery made for the adult market as a healthier proposition. Mars' instinct about the new Mars Bar formula is probably right, and the company has been careful to retain the old logo and colour scheme, with a lighter typeface to suit the product. It is a blander bar, but sales will probably be higher.

Nostalgia may be a key emotion in the mind of the public, and it can ensure a long life for a product, but the consumer base will inevitably grow older, probably dwindle and perhaps eventually die off altogether, so a forward-looking company will have been continually launching new ideas in the intervening years, creating in the process the old-fashioned favourites of the future. Indeed, ever since the time of small-scale sweetmakers working in kitchens and backrooms to produce their own inventions, the economic advantage of originality has been decisive in the confectionery business. The classic bars prevail, it is true, but otherwise it is a fast-moving business, with a very sharp end in terms of retail. Today, Mars and other global sweets companies identify innovation as the key to continued success, a lesson Hershey had to learn in the 1980s when it suddenly began to launch or acquire new products after relying on the enduring appeal of a dozen brands for seventy-five years – to the detriment of its market share. (Reliance on consumer loyalty to a limited number of brands was traditionally a feature of the American confectionery industry, whereas in Britain there has always been a mania for new launches.)

Of the hundreds of new sweets launches that hit the confectionery racks every year – about 150 in the United States, for example – only a handful will remain in circulation, and every manufacturer has to be sanguine about its sweets graveyard of great ideas unappreciated and unbought by the sweet-eating public. Even the best companies make big mistakes which, fortunately for them, tend to sink without trace. Whoever heard of the pineapple Mars Bar? It was Forrest Mars' second British launch in the 1930s, proving that great ideas do not always come in twos. Cadbury could boast (but it won't) of the ill-fated Aztec Bar, subject of an expensive advertising campaign in the late 1960s, but which only lasted eight years. Banjo was another British bar that was fairly popular in the 1980s, but never quite cut it commercially and was eventually withdrawn, as was Amazin Raisin (1971–78). The much-loved Spangles eventually died a natural death. The American Marathon, an extra-long caramel chocolate bar launched by Mars in 1973 (nothing like the British Marathon, or even Snickers), with calibrations on the packaging to emphasise its eight-inch length, lasted just eight difficult years. Failed Rowntree bars from the 1930s include Cokernut, Three Aces, Brunch Bar and Barcelona Caramel, and its oddly named Kassidic Assortment floundered early in its life. There are hundreds more examples of lower-profile, less ambitiously marketed sweets that disappeared after a few years or even months. Some of them were on a kamikaze mission, launched simply to profit briefly from a passing fad, or even to act as a 'spoiler', designed to scupper the launch of an opponent's product.

Given the hyped-up, competitive atmosphere of the confectionery industry, and the absolute necessity for originality and innovation, the secrecy that surrounds sweets companies is perhaps more understandable. Recipes are locked away in safes or memorised by a chosen few, and key workers must sign confidentiality clauses as part of their contracts of employment. There are many stories of companies despatching spies to work in their rivals' factories, and not all of them are fiction. The respectable end of chocolate spying is the practice of sweet-company executives visiting competitors' factories under the auspices of a machinery manufacturer, ostensibly to see the machines in action in an industrial setting. But they are well aware that this is an excellent way of gleaning valuable information about competitors' working methods.

There is good reason for all this secrecy: it is weird but true that it is generally impossible for a company to create an exact copy of any familiar classic sweet without inside information: there are just too many variables in the manufacturing process. Even as an industry outsider, I found it difficult to obtain permission to visit any sweets factories: Lindt was one of several companies who categorically refused, and Suchard cancelled my visit after initially agreeing, ostensibly because of fears of terrorist attack. But where I did gain access, even a tiny glimpse at the research and development laboratories was denied. Hygiene is the usual reason proffered, which is curious, when the rest of the food industry is not as fastidious, provided visitors are properly clothed and covered. The only really frustrating example of industry secrecy which I encountered concerned Swizzels, the old family firm based in Derbyshire that makes Love Hearts, Fizzers, Parma Violets and other delicious yet cheap tablet-form sweeties, as well as flavoursome chews like Drumstick Lollies. I wanted to see how these sweets were pressed out, and how the strange 'romantic' phrases which befuddled me as a boy and bufuddle me still get imprinted on the Love Hearts. It is fascinating how no other fizzy sweets have quite the same perfumed yet chemically sharp snap of Swizzels' Love Hearts, which are undoubtedly the superior article. But I had no interest in or motive for stealing the recipe from the factory: a packet of Love Hearts cost just 15p in 2002, so the effort of purloining the recipe, purchasing machinery and making my own Love Hearts would hardly seem worth the outlay. But in spite of my best efforts, I was never allowed access.

All this secrecy is not designed simply to protect a company's recipes: its machines and methods are just as important. Technology is kept under wraps – literally, in the case of Mars, who reportedly shrouded their machines in white sheets when guests were invited into its Slough factory for a rare on-site product launch. But again, this is not simple paranoia: although confectionery machines are made to standard specifications by respected companies such as Lehmann and Loesch, manufacturers will eagerly customise them, or even design and make their own contraptions for specific processes, all to gain an edge over the competition. Many sweets can be made only by one type of machine, with special modifications. So it is important not to underestimate the power of machinery in the modern sweets industry, in comparison with the more romantic considerations of taste, texture and packaging ideas. From its beginnings in the early nineteenth century, new machines for mass production and packaging have been crucial to the success of even the most intrinsically delicious new sweet. As Henry Weatherley remarked in his seminal and hitherto overlooked *Treatise on the Art of Boiling Sugar* (1864):

> The large increase in the consumption of sweets, made from boiled sugars, in the United Kingdom, during the last quarter of a century, has arisen principally from the cheapness and facility of manufacture, derived from the introduction of machinery [...] Twenty years since it was considered rather a clever thing (with a pair of scissors, the principal tool a sugar boiler used) to cut a seven pound boil of acid drops to size, and, with the help of a practised boy, make them round and press them flat, with the hands, in half-an-hour. The same quantity may now, with the machine, be made into drops, by the boy alone, in five minutes.

Weatherley was hardly impartial, since his London showroom was filled with confectionery machines: lozenge cutters, paste cutters, jelly moulds, drop machines, African forcers, cracknell cutters, Coburg pans, Devonshire pans and his most famous invention, the currant dressing machine, which 'will thoroughly cleanse from all grit and refuse 20lb of currants or sultanas in three minutes'.

Innovative use of machinery has often accompanied success

in the confectionery business. The example of Samuel Born and the Just Born company illustrates this. A Russian immigrant to San Francisco, Born founded his candy company in 1910 and six years later was awarded the keys to the city for inventing the Born Sucker Machine, which mechanically inserted sticks into lollipops. Later, in the 1950s, the company again displayed its astute appreciation of the value of technology with the acquisition of the Rodda Candy Company, which specialised in marshmallows and jelly beans. By capitalising on this technology base, Just Born was able to create bestselling lines including Marshmallow Peeps, the bullet-shaped and zesty Mike'n'Ike fruit candies and Hot Tamales.

Traditionally, innovations in chocolate technology came from continental Europe, while sugar confectionery machines were invented by the British or the Americans, but by the late twentieth century these old divisions had been broken down. Machinery is a crucial aspect of the industry even today, and product innovations are frequently driven by new technical possibilities.

It was time to penetrate the wall of secrecy and visit some sweets factories. What would they be like? Would they be magical, unpredictable places, like Wonka's factory, with its steaming and chugging machines? Or perhaps they would resemble the serious-minded Victorian edifice that produces Toot Sweets in *Chitty Chitty Bang Bang*? The reality was far better than any of this. I visited half a dozen sweets factories, and every time I entered one I was delirious with joy, ecstatic that the machines were exactly as I hoped they would be − long conveyor belts crammed with little sweets being prodded and poked, coated and dried, and extraordinary cauldrons and pipes and pushers and packers and printers and stampers and choppers and scrapers, all working away to produce super-fresh examples of super sweets, which were left lying around in vast piles, trays and buckets, as if one had stumbled on a candy Eldorado.

The first factory I visited was the Haribo plant in Pontefract,

Yorkshire, birthplace of all English gummy bears, and I nearly fainted with deranged pleasure at first sight of what was going on in its chambers of delight. I just could not believe that sweets are really made like this. The liquorice allsorts mix was being created as I watched: long thin pipes of pink cream being propelled along conveyor belts, and churning vats of swirling creams in different colours. It seemed incredible that thirty-foot-long conveyor belts are really necessary in a sweets factory, and that you pour a mix in one end of a machine and sweets come out of the other. Scores of different machines are needed in any general sweets factory, although it is a curious fact that chocolate and sugar are rarely made side by side at the same establishment – they require quite different technologies.

A lean master confectioner with a glint in his eye showed me round the plant, including a room called 'the cream kitchen', but the combination of protective earmuffs and the fact that I am half deaf made his commentary difficult to gauge. We saw huge all-in-one heating and cooling machines (the secret of much industrial sweetmaking lies in sudden temperature changes), watched as great palette moulds of different-coloured jelly beans were filled and solidified, marvelled at the way the browny black liquorice curled out of the end of a great machine to fall with a plop onto trays, and looked at thousands of tiny mints tumbling over and over and round and round inside the panning machines.

One contraption was siring hundreds of midget jelly babies in pristine white moulds by means of six colours and six flavours ejaculated from six buckets of swirling gum mixture at the top of the machine, the consistency, flavour density and colour of the mixtures regulated by computer. My guide occasionally broke off to consult a readout that had disgorged from one of the adjacent computers, and this – coupled with all the men in white boilersuits – gave the plant the air of a villain's hideaway in a 1970s James Bond movie. But the last thing I wanted to do was throw a villain into a chocolate vat, remark 'Don't get too browned off, old chap' and turn the Haribo factory into a burning fireball of destruction, as Bond would have done. All I wanted to do was jump in the machines and swim around in the cauldrons with my mouth open, eating sweets as I went, or place my head beneath one of the pipes and swallow whatever came out. I could live in the sweets factory, I reflected, sleeping in a cranny by day and emerging by night to gorge on sweets until dawn. But I tried to look calm and businesslike, and only took a sweet or two from the many buckets when offered, and even then maintained a quizzical and, I like to think, professional and detached air. Nevertheless, every sweet I ever ate in this way – fresh off the machine – tasted better than it ever had before. It was surprising to discover that most sweets, like fruit, taste that much better after they have just been plucked (although some sweets, such as Starburst or Skittles, start their lives as unpalatably hard and soften with time).

After my tour, I had an interview with Daniel Hencke, a friendly young German Haribo executive, and as I left he gave me a whole bag full of Haribo sweets and merchandise, including a Haribo cap, tee-shirt, stickers and watch, which I wore for several months until I gave it away to a child, as I should have done at first. I was very pleased with my booty and we parted with great bonhomie and salutation. We were going to meet up for a drink at the next ISM show. Where was the ruthless investigator of the sweets industry now? A novelty watch and a load of free sweets had made me the media patsy of the gummy guys.

What about a state-of-the-art chocolate factory? I had been conducted round Cadbury's Bournville plant, clad in regulation white coat and hat, and marvelled at the precision and vastness of the machines, as well as anachronistic touches like the old wooden clocking-in machines, which were still in use. I had toured an old-fashioned English boiled-sweets factory (see Lucky Dip: Rhubarb and Custards, page 190). But I wanted to see the latest technology. In Britain, the best place would have been the new Nestlé factory, wholly dedicated to KitKat production, but surely Switzerland, home of the science of *chocologie*, would provide the best insight.

The Toblerone factory, built in 1985, is sited inside a vast, anonymous steel box by a motorway on the outskirts of Bern, in German-speaking Switzerland. The old factory in the city centre is now a university library, but it is still known as the Toblerone building. The new factory has one word on its exterior, Kraft, the name of the German multinational which acquired the company (itself now part of Philip Morris). Mysterious wisps of smoke emanate from the top of the building, and a barrier checkpoint for cars, complete with a uniformed sentry in a kiosk, lend it the air of a Soviet research station. Then the smell of chocolate hits you. Other factories producing food and drink often exude slightly disconcerting odours, redolent more of the raw materials than the finished product, but all chocolate factories smell of fresh chocolate, which is very nice, if potentially cloying over a long period. (I once drove to the Mars factory, which is on a large industrial estate in Slough, and found my way there guided by smell alone.)

The amazing thing about the Toblerone factory is that it does not just smell of chocolate, it smells of Toblerone chocolate. Every single bar of Toblerone in the world is made here. The brightly-lit factory is fully computerised and sparsely staffed, but it is still laid out as a classic production line. Henry Ford would have approved of the long, straight banks of machinery: ingredients in one end, finished chocolate bar – fully wrapped and boxed for despatch – at the other.

Full employment in Switzerland means that Toblerone relies mainly on immigrant labour to staff its factory, which I was told employs people of thirty-three nationalities. Yet the pristine machines, overarched by gangways and hemmed by computer screens, seem to get on with the job unaided. Machinery so dwarfs humanity in this factory that it seems that the people one sees flitting between them are somehow in thrall to the machines. But a world ruled by chocolate machines might not be so bad; perhaps some of us already live in that world. Each section of the factory is kept at a specific temperature, rather like a Roman bath: the first room is warm and comforting, the place where the smooth milk chocolate is mixed up with the gritty little pieces of honeyed nougat that lend the bar its characteristic texture and flavour. The second room, where the bars solidify, is of course much colder, and it is quite a shock to the system. I saw a little relic of humanity, in the shape of a picture of a funny hedgehog, hanging by one of the computer terminals. 'It's internal,' explained my guide. 'Oh,' I replied. It appeared to be some kind of safety message.

Some of the machines in the Toblerone factory are a little bit frightening, with their unpredictable, jerky movements and massive strength. Huge boxes of Toblerone were being wrapped in cellophane by an odd spinning machine that moved with deliberation and extreme speed, and one orange robot with suckers on its arms was lifting small boxes into a yellow cage, placing cards between layers and straightening the boxes with all the fastidiousness of a tyrant. It was the apparent lack of human control that was disconcerting. A brand new, bright red machine was churning out thousands of individual pieces of Toblerone, specially designed for the British market, and the sight of all these little brown chunks jostling for position on the conveyor belt as they entered the wrapping machine reminded me of the crowded entrance to a ski-lift (we were in Switzerland, after all).

Humanity loomed reassuringly in a small area where cheerful Fräuleins were making by hand the giant Toblerone bars, popular as Swiss wedding gifts, that weigh 4.5kg, forty-five times the size of a normal bar. (There used to be a 7kg bar, but it was abolished.) There was a terrible moment when one giant bar, fresh out of the mould, was being carried across the room and suddenly broke in half and fell to the floor. Without a second thought, the lady put the two huge chunks of chocolate in the bin. It was a tragedy.

The Toblerone factory was a highly impressive operation, and if it did not contain quite the joy and variety of the Haribo plant, there was no doubt that the quality of the product was in no way affected by high-tech production methods. (Plus, the nice lady at Toblerone gave me a free chocolate coat-of-arms of the city of Bern.) On my way out I was shown that the factory was not quite the anonymous steel box it had appeared to be. 'Look up,' said my guide, and there, fifty feet above us, was a gigantic replica of a Toblerone bar smashing into the side of the building. It looked as if it had been fired at the factory from outer space, but I was told that the idea was that it should appear to be bursting out of the factory.

High technology has seen the end of many of the old customs of the sweets factories. In the world of chocolate, factories used to be divided into a 'wet end' and a 'dry end', with men employed with the wet chocolate – heavy-duty churning and carrying duties – and women with the dry – handling, quality control and packaging. It is a well-known industry fact that the fingers of women and children are more nimble, careful and faster working than those of men, and in the case of chocolate it was reckoned that women's hands were also cooler and less likely to melt the product. There are many late-nineteenth-century photographs of workrooms filled with women and girls in white bonnets, doing everything from packing bars in boxes to cracking Brazil nuts with hammers to inspecting chocolate soldiers.

Later, this kind of handiwork was restricted to chocolate-box packing, and the Cadbury workers on the Milk Tray line, for example, were renowned as the fastest packers in the world, with their special slanting conveyor belt which for some reason made packing the chocolates in their trays so much easier. Even with the most repetitive jobs, sweets work was still quite convivial, with all the talking and even communal singing that went on to relieve the monotony. In the 'longitude' section of the Hershey factory in the 1940s, where the chocolate was blended, the big practical joke was to submerge your colleague's bucket into one of the mobile tubs of chocolate – which must have been funny at the time, and taken the mind off the high temperatures (up to 108 degrees F), the closed windows (to keep insects out) and the fact that every inch of your body and hair was covered in cocoa and that you could never get rid of the smell. And there is always the time-honoured perk of being able to eat as many sweets as you like while on the premises.

Production lines can be extremely boring: in *Jobs in Baking and Confectionery* (1985), the ideal modern confectionery worker is described as practical, flexible, imaginative, numerate, able to get along with others, punctual, tolerant of unsocial hours and aware of the need for stamina. This would have meant little to the night worker mentioned in *Reshaping Work: the Cadbury Experience* (1990), who came off the production line and found he could not stop repeating the packing motion with his arms. But it is good to know that workers do actually eat the sweets as they go. At every sweets factory I visited I asked people what it was like to be able to scoff as many sweets as you want, all day. They all said exactly the same thing: to start with, you go a bit mad and eat them all the time; then you go off them completely; finally, you get a sense of proportion and only eat them occasionally. The sweets worker would offer this conclusion wisely and warily, like a lion tamer describing his job. But I never quite got over the fact that eating sweets could be a part of someone's professional duties.

It seems whimsical of the sweets companies that while guided tours of their factories were available and extremely popular back in the days of (wo-)manned production lines and difficult working conditions, now that everything is clean and automated, they are banned. The reason given is hygiene. The visitor centre has now superseded the classic factory tour, although at Cadbury World – Europe's biggest visitor-centre attraction – you are allowed a brief foray into part of the working factory.

This is not the case at Chocolate World in Hershey, Pennsylvania, which is some distance from the factory. These visitor centres, and the various chocolate museums one finds throughout the world, tend to concentrate on the process of harvesting cocoa beans and making them into chocolate: lots of pictures of cocoa beans, crouching West Africans brandishing machetes and long, technical descriptions of the conching process. They are highly informative, but do miss some of the joy of sweets. Hershey's Chocolate World, however, has an excellent gimmick: a train in which you are encouraged to imagine that you are a cocoa bean going through the process of being made into chocolate. First, you are roasted by being blasted with hot air in a red tunnel, then you are winnowed by being shaken and manoeuvred about. Presumably health and safety regulations curtailed an interpretation of the final stages of the process, in which the beans are mashed up and the chocolate liquor is pressed out of them. One would never have anticipated it, but Chocolate World is actually a superbly informative and entertaining facility, with its huge replica machines and interesting film footage of processes, like the way special tree-shaking machines are employed during almond harvesting. Compared with this, the converted Ghirardelli factory on the San Francisco docks is a disappointment: it is basically a shopping mall.

During my forays into the sweets factories, I was never allowed to see inside a lab, but insiders say they look like pharmaceutical research establishments: product development is conducted ever more scientifically, and even large companies now outsource part or all of this aspect of their business to flavour houses such as IFF, Bush Boake Allen and Virginia Dare, whose job it is to develop new tastes and textures. There is even an inter-nationally known sweets research and tuition establishment in California called Richardson Researches, run by an English con-fectionery guru called Terry Richardson. I could not quite believe that there was another sweets enthusiast out there called T. Richardson. I emailed him and made some chummy comments about how it was all an amazing coincidence and so on, and he sent me a polite and extremely brief reply. Perhaps the world of confectionery is not big enough for two T. Richardsons?

★ ★ ★

Companies like to imagine that they can cleverly spot niches in the market and fill them with successful new products, but in the history of confectionery many of the best sweets were either invented haphazardly – the result of some sweetmaker just adding a little bit of this and that to see what might come out – or entirely by accident. The best sweetmakers never tire of trying to make new sweets from the same old ingredients: in his last years, Milton Hershey became obsessed with tinkering around in his sweets laboratory, to the exasperation of staff, who knew that he had lost his sense of taste after years of smoking Havana cigars. Among his inventions at the time were onion- and beetroot-flavoured sherbets, which were served in his hotel restaurant.

A classic accidentally invented sweet is bubble gum: its inventor, Walter Diemer, was a 23-year-old accountant in a candy firm, and it seems he was just messing about in the lab. 'I was doing something else, and ended up with something with bubbles,' Mr Diemer explained, with the fazed obscurantism of the inspired inventor. It transpires that the lurid pink colour was also a random choice – it just happened to be at hand, said Diemer – but with hindsight it is clear that bubble gum could not possibly have been any other colour. Edinburgh Rock was another happy accident, reminiscent of the discovery of penicillin. Sweetmaker Sandy Ferguson left a batch of rock in his cellar, and it duly went soft. When he rediscovered it weeks later, something compelled him to try it. And it was nice!

Most new sweets are variations on well-worn themes, but it is amazing how new and exciting they can seem to the sophisticated and subtle sweets palate of the public. Take the Wispa chocolate bar, developed in top-secret conditions (its codename was P46) by Cadbury in the 1970s as a belated answer to Rowntree's bubbly Aero, a bestseller for half a century and more. The Wispa too contained bubbles, but tiny ones, which lent the chocolate a unique velvety texture. At its launch in 1981, Wispa was a smash hit – in fact, the bar had to be suspended until 1983 to allow time for a dedicated production line to be established – and it has sold well ever since. It is all down to bubble size: these bars may have been almost the same size and made of chocolate of very similar composition, but any chocolate bar lover will confirm that an Aero and a Wispa are entirely different propositions.

Recently, there has been more of an emphasis on diversifying existing brands – launching orange or mint versions of established bars, for example – and also a strategy of fitting new products and their packaging to specific lifestyle occasions, whether they be a formal or relaxed social occasion, watching TV, driving a car, light snacking during the day (hence mini or funsize bars) or using a chocolate bar as a meal replacement or manly snack. This last is far less common now, but the Depression era in the United States saw the launch of bars with names like Chicken Dinner, Idaho Spud and Big Eats, and of course the enduringly satisfying PayDay bar (1932). Then there are supermarket multipacks, seasonal variations, new shapes for old bars and giant versions. In the 1980s Mars scored a marketing success when it persuaded us that putting chocolate in the fridge was a good idea for the summer (and from here it was a short step to the chocolate-bar-as-ice-cream phenomenon). Few sweets are marketed specifically at either men or women – what is the point in losing half your potential market at the outset? – although advertising can send subtle messages that direct the product towards one sex while not alienating the other. The British campaign for the German sweets called Campino shows thirty-something women sharing and enjoying them in a non-girly way. My own big idea for a new sweet was based on the concept of an ice-cream flavour chew: a milky chew in the shape of either an ice cream cone or an ice lolly on a stick. Of course it could be eaten all year round, without refrigeration, and the stick would make it into a kind of lollipop. I think it is a neat idea. No sweets company has shown any interest in my ice cream chew.

The challenge for sweetmakers to innovate is driven by our retail habits. Sweets buyers hardly ever buy the same brand twice in a row, and the most recent research indicates that 80 per cent of confectionery purchases are made on impulse (perhaps it is more surprising that 20 per cent of purchases are therefore planned in advance). We have up to a dozen regular favourites, and our allegiances can change over time. The top bar in the United States generally has a market share of about 11 per cent, which leaves plenty of room for the rest, and people are not afraid to try new sweets since it is hardly a significant outlay of time or money. The average regular sweets buyer is extraordinarily knowledgeable about them, and highly familiar with scores of different products. In the retail sphere, we are all sweets experts. It is quite normal to be able to look at a rack of sweets – say, fifty different types on display – and to know exactly what each one tastes like. What other area of the retail world do we know so well? We match sweets to our mood, and faced with a rack of sweets, there is often a moment of delicious indecision.

The recipe of a new sweet will always be a variation on an established theme. In the United States, it is simple: the obsession with peanuts and peanut butter (sales of these products outstrip all others) means that the search is continually on for new ways of presenting the nut. New and exotic fruit flavours, such as mango and papaya, have been tried more recently, and the indigenous confectionery idiosyncrasies of individual nations can be exported quite successfully. It is probably easier to make an original chocolate bar than a new item of sugar confectionery, because of the greater number of ingredients and therefore greater potential complexity in flavour and texture of the latter. The appearance of a sweet will often reflect its flavour and texture, and because sweets are optional extras in terms of nutrition, they have to justify themselves to us, tempt us, through their appearance. That is why sweets are the most beautiful class of foodstuff. Eye candy.

The colour, sheen and texture of many sweets is naturally beautiful: a cube of Turkish Delight or nut-studded nougat needs no adornment, and boiled candy can be as luminous as stained glass. Blue is traditionally viewed as a difficult food colour, but it has enjoyed success in recent years in M&Ms and Smarties, and has become identified with raspberry flavour. In fact, colours linked to flavours were a relatively late innovation in sweets: the Rain-Blo (1940) was the first gumball with this characteristic, and M&M coatings are still notoriously uniform (unlike Smarties, which all taste different). Sweets in the simplest shapes can be attractive, but their malleable properties are also exploited, as they are moulded into all kinds of fantastic shapes and unlikely objects, from prawns to power tools. There is even a noticeable predilection among sweetmakers, particularly in Germany, to make confections in imitation of national foodstuffs, such as Bratwurst or spaghetti. This is the fantasy realm of sweets. Artists have been attracted by the rich colour palette and textural possibilities of sweets, and fascinated by the fact of consumption. On a decorative level, the jelly bean manufacturer Jellybelly has an in-house artist, Peter Rocha, who makes intricate collages from hundreds of these multi-coloured sweets, with their slight shine.

Sweets crop up in contemporary art, generally as a kitschy, jokey aside, but chocolate inspires deeper meditations, and takes its place in the litany of 'taboo' materials – including meat, excrement and human remains – that are now the subject of gleeful experimentation in the galleries. Helen Chadwick was an artist fascinated by the texture and associative power of chocolate: she created a bubbling chocolate fountain for one exhibit. In *Gnaw*, Janine Antoni took bites out of a huge lump of chocolate and exhibited the result as a satire on the masculinity of minimalism. And Dadaism found a friend in chocolate: the Swiss chocolate firm of Sprüngli (later merged with Lindt) sponsored the 1917 Dada gallery and exhibition in Zurich, and Marcel Duchamp found inspiration in a chocolate grinder he saw working in a shop window in Rouen, and included it as the principal motif in his major late work, *The Large Glass*, 1923. 'It fascinated me so much I took it as a point of departure,' he explained. 'The chocolate of the rollers, coming from one knows not where, would deposit itself after grinding, as milk chocolate.' It has been suggested that this is a sexual motif. Duchamp was also inspired by the textural possibilities of chocolate itself, and noticed that the shape of the chocolate form significantly changes its essential colour: 'a surface of native-chocolate colour will be composed of a sort of chocolate phosphorescence completing the moulded apparition of the chocolate object'. The shape of chocolate also affects its taste – in the case of Easter eggs and other moulded chocolates, because of the surface-to-air ratio.

The shape of certain sweets – Reese's Peanut Butter Cups, for example, or Cadbury's Curly Wurly, or even the classically simple four-stick KitKat – makes them into design classics with a commercial appeal that endures from childhood to old age. The chocolate Easter egg was of course inspired by the ancient association of Easter with eggs, and perhaps by the medieval custom of donating gifts to poor children at this time. It was really a variation on the sugar egg, popular in Eastern Europe, elaborately painted with seasonal scenes or wildflowers and braided with icing. In Verdun there was a strong tradition of decorated sugar eggs, and W. A. Jarrin noted in *The Italian Confectioner* (1820): 'They are usually filled with imitations of all sorts of fruits. In Paris they put in a number of nick-nacks, little almanacks, smelling bottles with essences, and even things of value for presents.' It is possible that the egg tradition inspired the Victorian invention of Christmas crackers, which were originally filled with sweets. At this time eggs were also made of toffee, marzipan and nougat. But the simple idea of a chocolate egg is irresistible, and they are now enjoyed all year round. Kinder Eggs from Germany (with a layer of white chocolate beneath the brown) continue the tradition of putting gifts inside eggs, and Cadbury's Creme Egg contains a bizarre and lovely fondant resembling egg white and egg yolk.

But one modern brand above all demonstrates the commercial power of shape and appearance in confectionery: Toblerone. When I visited the factory and asked about the secret of the bar's success, I was surprised to be told: 'It is because it is Swiss. Chocolates, watches and cheese are typical of Switzerland, and that is why people buy them.' I begged to disagree. The chocolate is indeed excellent, but the bar is successful because it is a triangular prism. Toblerone's distinctive shape and correspondingly invincible brand image allows it to transcend national barriers, and this has helped to make it the second most popular airport purchase (after cigarettes). It is instantly recognisable and reassuring, and one of a very few worldwide brands that are truly international. Toblerone may once have managed to fit no fewer than three flugelhorns on its package design, and it may be true that Theodor Tobler based the original shape of the bar on the peaks of an Alpine mountain range, but it is likely that a good proportion of those who buy this chocolate at airports do not know that it comes from Switzerland. I suspect Theodor Tobler would be perfectly happy at this state of affairs: one of his first priorities when he took over the company in 1900 was to establish an international sales base, as well as an effective in-house advertising department. This early emphasis on marketing was underlined by the way Tobler invested in printing and packaging machines for his factory at the same time as chocolate machines. It was a far-sighted approach that set the brand on its way, and the product has barely been changed. The original bar was smaller (Toblerone was at first vended from machines at train stations, and thus a lifestyle-marketed product), the lettering was green rather than red, a German eagle motif was discreetly dropped, and a blue Alp symbol added in 2000. But the distinctive light tan livery has always remained the same, as has the shape.

The names of new sweets can be hit upon just as haphazardly as the recipes. Theodor Tobler formulated the name Toblerone as a mixture of his own name and 'torrone', after the nougat which is its definitive ingredient. It has also transpired that the word is easily pronounceable in almost every language, and seems to belong to none, which has not harmed sales. Sweets names can be inspired by the most whimsical of whims: the celebrated American Oh Henry! bar, invented in the 1920s, was apparently named after the delightedly outraged cries of a young sales assistant when her beau came into the shop to flirt. The Tootsie Roll (1896) was named after the nickname of the inventor's daughter. Sweets can be descriptively named after what they resemble, from the gruesome bullseye to the lifebelt-shaped Lifesaver (1912), the English version of which, Polo (1939), brilliantly echoes the shape of the mint with the letter O on its minimalist green and dark blue packet, as well as the idea of polar coolness. A pack of Polos represents sweet, name and packaging in perfect equilibrium.

Sweetie names were quite often in-jokes enjoyed by the manufacturers, and this was particularly the case in the days when the commercial stakes were a little lower, and firms launched a number of sweets every season without having to pay for huge marketing campaigns. Milk Duds (1928), bite-size caramel morsels covered in chocolate, were supposed to be perfectly round, but the maker could not get the process right, so they were launched as 'duds' because they still tasted good enough to sell. Today, such whimsy is unheard of at the big-business end of confectionery: a new bar's name will be bland, brief and strangely memorable. Sugar confectionery marketed at children can still be gloriously surreal, though: there is still room for all those sweets with Zs in the name, like Zagnuts or Abba Zabba, and, as Nicholas Whittaker observes in *Sweet Talk* (1988), his history of twentieth-century British sweets, Ks still habitually replace Cs in the krazy world of sweets naming.

There is no predicting what name will stick. The Peter Paul Candy Manufacturing Company was founded in 1919 in New Haven, Connecticut by Peter Paul Halajian and five Armenian associates. Perhaps their relative unfamiliarity with English led them to hit upon the extraordinary name of Mounds in 1920 for their new coconut and chocolate bar. The word is now synonymous with coconut in the United States. Their Almond Joy (1946) also sounds like some kind of mis-translation, but it too turned out to be a brilliantly memorable name. America has always shown a particular flair for naming candy bars. There was a vogue in the 1920s and 1930s for sweets named after real food, like Boston Baked Beans or Hot Tamales, but these were superseded by more jokey or exotic names. Similarly, the popular practice of naming sweets for patriotic reasons has waned; in Britain there were Bonaparte's Ribs and Nelson's Balls in the post-Napoleonic period, Alma Drops and Sebastopol Balls during the Crimean War, and Buller's Bullets, Kruger's Favourites, Khaki Toffees and Transvaal Toffee in the Boer War.

Snobbery is a potent factor in sweets naming, particularly in continental Europe, where it seems almost every sweet has aristocratic pretensions. This is a reflection of the enduring European perception of confectionery as the work of skilled artisans rather than an item of mass production. The republic of France is particularly attached to its aristocratic candy heritage, although in recent years it has been the Italian firm of Ferrero Rocher (whose English operation is based in Watford) that most memorably promoted the idea of high-class sweets sophistication through its 1970s advertisements about the ambassador's cocktail party, which it later revived with great kitsch effect (although apparently Ferrero Rocher executives did not see the funny side and withdrew the ad in 1999). Monty Python produced a sketch based on the ridiculous pretentiousness of the chocolate assortment, with delights such as anthrax ripple and crunchy frog – 'We use only the finest baby frogs, dew-picked and flown from Iraq, cleansed in the finest quality spring water, lightly killed, and sealed in a succulent, Swiss, quintuple-smooth, treble-milk chocolate envelope, and lovingly frosted with glucose.'

If continental Europe is associated with sophistication and craftsmanship, Britain's marketing value is sturdy traditionalism, hence sweets such as America's Heath Bar (1932), which is marketed as the 'English toffee bar', and oddities such as Japan's popular Chelsea toffee brand, which is described as quintessentially Scottish despite the fact that Chelsea is in the heart of London. The endorsement of sports stars, pop stars or cartoon characters is an excellent way of shifting a candy product, and the waning of the popularity of a particular star may not necessarily see the end of the sweet, as with the Amos 'n' Andy bar (1931), which was named after a black radio show and remained popular long after the show had been forgotten. Passing fads can also be capitalised upon by the enterprising confectioner. Some really are fleeting, like the Loch Ness Monster Surprise Bags launched after the discovery of the Loch Ness monster in 1934, but others have prevailed: the Charleston Chew is still going strong in America, while the 1920s dance it was named after has become a curiosity piece. Horror, monsters and creepy crawlies are safe commercial choices in gummy and sugar confectionery. But the most reliable standby for sweets namers since the 1950s has been the idea of space travel: put an astronaut or some planets and stars on the packet, call it Atmosphere Equalizer or Space Ship Rations, and you are halfway there.

The packet is vital, of course. The marketeers say that in the shop, the customer recognises the colour of the pack first, the shape of the logo second, and the name of the product third. The actual design of the pack is less important than the overall colour, hence the graphic success of a product such as the delicate purple Milka bar from Suchard, or even the un-compromising brown of the Hershey Bar. In fact, the most successful chocolate bars are all colour-coded in this way. Today, there is a massive range of sweet packaging, but in the early days of the modern industry, the late nineteenth century, traditional designs were favoured. The Swiss opted for Alpine scenes and bonny milkmaids, the French adored Boucher-esque fantasies of the eighteenth-century aristocracy, while the British followed the example of Richard Cadbury, a quiet man who personally pioneered the idea of the chocolate box adorned with a sentimental scene, painting sunlit rural landscapes, flowers, or children and animals in cute situations. The Regency fantasy of the Quality Street assortment, based on a romantic comedy of the same name by J. M. Barrie, author of *Peter Pan*, in which Captain Valentine Brown woos Phoebe, was a huge success for Rowntree.

This bourgeois indulgence enraged the Modernists, who scorned 'chocolate-boxy' images as dishonest, bad design. In his *Inquiry into Industrial Art in England* (1937), Nikolaus Pevsner inveighed against the kitschness of chocolate boxes, arguing that no object is so humble or peripheral that it should not be subject to sound design principles, and wondering why the chocolate manufacturers should rely on such outmoded design styles when their factories and working practices were so inspiringly modernistic. But the fact was, sentimental chocolate boxes sold well and were matched to the market, who appreciated 'a touch of class': the upper classes in Britain did not buy Cadbury's wares at this time; they still favoured imported French chocolates. In any case, not all Cadbury's boxes were anathema to Modernists: the design for the Vogue chocolate assortment of 1935 sports stylish lettering that would have pleased even the sternest black-polo-necked and bespectacled guru of the Bauhaus.

Packaging can define a sweet. Think of TicTacs, or the cultish Pez. This Austrian brand features a cartoon-like character head which you press down to dispense the little brick-like sweets from the bottom of the container. The shape and plasticity of this product is ironically reminiscent of a toothbrush, or perhaps a cigarette lighter (Pez were launched in 1927 as a smoker's breath freshener). Pez has a strange effect on people. The funny dispensers with their characterful appeal are, it seems, highly addictive to anyone with the smallest streak of the collector in them, and there are dozens of fans' websites dedicated to them. In the world of Pez, there are more than 275 different heads to collect, including six eerie spirits, four safari animals, three crazy fruits and ten kooky zoo figures. One Pez dispenser sold for $4,500, so clearly things have got a little out of control.

In recent years there have been much-hyped experiments with hologram sweets wrappers, plus the launch of Holopops in

1998, in which the design on the lollipop changes as you move it around. Another gimmick was the Sound Bites Lollipop (1998), a lollipop containing a radio. But wacky design and crazy colours remain more attractive to sweets buyers, and in recent years the craze for sour (or zzour!) sweets has led to a dizzying array of cartoon packet designs showing kids' heads being blown off or their mouths turned inside out by the krazy effect of the candy.

In the more sober world of single-sweet packaging, for toffees and the like, there are, for the record, nine different types of wrap, including the classic bias or oblique overlap wrap (like an envelope, for chocolates), the pillow wrap, the roll-and-stick wrap and the bunch-fold wrap. The old problem of the noise of unwrapping sweets in cinemas and theatres has been addressed by a team of scientists, who concluded that it is futile to try to open the sweet slowly – better to get it over with quickly. And in 2001 BBC Radio 3 and orchestras including the Royal Philharmonic endorsed Sela-Coughs, cough sweets made by a Midlands firm which come in special 'quiet' waxed wrappers.

In theory, marketing consists in finding out who the consumers are, what they want, and then giving it to them. In practice, of course, consumers do not know what they want, and like to be surprised at the novelty of a new product. Nevertheless the confectionery industry was one of the pioneers of marketing strategy, before marketing even had a name. To gain an advantage over all those competitors, business-minded sweetmakers would instinctively discern a lifestyle niche for the product, and identify the target demographic group, or else some unique selling point associated with appearance, texture or taste. Hence the early development of opera assortments or motoring chocolate, the ever popular linkage of sweets with romance – Cupid's Whispers and other 'conversation lozenges' were popular in the 1890s – or even more specific associations, such as Rocket Rinking Toffee of 1910, for ice skaters. But the explosion of sweets marketing occurred in the 1920s and 1930s, and it is no coincidence that this was the time when the world's big confectionery companies were consolidating a hold on the market which they have not yet relinquished. This period saw the invention of a significant number of today's favourite brands, remarkable for their taste, quality and original design.

The old Quaker firm of Rowntree of York is an example of a company which transformed itself through pioneering marketing initiatives. By 1931, the company was in trouble, beset by a profound lack of knowledge of its consumers, apparently random product innovation and an antipathy to advertising. Cadbury's Dairy Milk, the bestselling product of its biggest rival, was trouncing sales of Rowntree's chocolates. A new approach was needed, and slowly, during the 1930s, the company turned itself round. The key to its vision was the friendly relationship between George Harris, a Rowntree director, and Forrest Mars, who had scored a runaway success a few years earlier with his Mars Bar, made at Slough. This was what the Americans called a 'combination bar' – that is, it was not just a slab of pure chocolate, but a nutty, biscuity or fruity bar core that was enrobed with chocolate. Such products were generally scorned by the high-quality British confectioners, who viewed them as short-term, novelty products. But sales of Mars Bars had continued increasing for several years, and it was clear that there was a future for these new-fangled products.

Rowntree saw how Mars had inserted itself into a position as Hershey's number-one competitor by concentrating on combination bars rather than the pure chocolate products which were Hershey's mainstay. Given the failure of its own basic milk-chocolate bar, Extra Creamy Milk, Rowntree decided to concentrate on new combination bars, chocolate assortments and sugar confectionery. The research department at Rowntree's York factory must have been a busy and exceptionally creative place in the 1930s, because it churned out Black Magic in 1933, KitKat Chocolate Crisp and Aero in 1935, Dairy Box in 1937, Smarties Chocolate Beans (later copied in the United States) in 1938 and Polos in 1939. The success of the new strategy was enhanced by the company's investment in advertising. For example, for the launch of Black Magic, a plain chocolate assortment, advertising agency J. Walter Thompson came up with a high-class 'story'. An advertisement depicted a couple looking out over Venice, with a handwritten note super-imposed: 'Sweet of Alan to think of bringing a fortnight's supply of Black Magic with us on our honeymoon.' This specific association of product with people is ubiquitous now, but it was innovative at the time. Meanwhile, Mars continued to launch its own cleverly conceived products: Milky Way in 1935, 'the sweet you can eat between meals', and the following year Maltesers, which were initially labelled low-fat 'energy balls'.

Advertising is the handmaiden of marketing (or perhaps its pushy mother). Anyone can sing a dozen jingles from television adverts, and it would be possible to list scores of them in a nostalgia-fest meaningless to anyone of a different generation or nationality to your own. Early advertising was relatively straight-forward, emphasising the qualities of the product, its potential health-giving properties, and even the grandeur and beauty of the modern factory where it was made. A particularly fruitful approach was urging the male customer to use sweets as a way of controlling wayward, reluctant or sulky women. A 1910 advertisement in *Confectionery Journal* noted: 'If he understands women he will take her to the confectioner's and when she is chock full of candy she will be a very agreeable young woman.' However, informal tests have shown that sweets do not allow men to control the minds of women in this way.

Some manufacturers relied on the old-fashioned standby of trumpeting the reputation of the manufacturer, an approach espoused most dramatically by John Mackintosh, the toffee moghul, who announced his entrance to the United States market in the 1920s with a Nietzschean advertisement that proclaimed:

I am John Mackintosh, the Toffee King, Sovereign of Pleasure, Emperor of Joy. My old English candy tickles my millions of subjects. My Court Jester's name is Appetite. I was crowned by the lovers of good things to eat. My most loyal subjects are dear little children. My throne is guarded by the Imperial Unarmed Army of Candy Makers. I am the world's largest consumer of butter, my own herd of prize cattle graze the Yorkshire hills. I buy sugar by the trainload. I am John Mackintosh, Toffee King of England and I rule alone.

Advertising developed into a more sophisticated beast. In his classic book about advertising and psychology, *The Hidden Persuaders* (1957), Vance Packard records how American candy manufacturers hired Ernest Dichter, an advertising guru (a rank that is one above account manager in advertising), who identified guilt as the main problem for consumers. The old strategy of suggesting that candy is an acceptable way of rewarding yourself – an idea instilled in childhood – was clearly not appropriate in this situation, and Dichter came up with the notion of selling bite-size pieces of candy within multipacks: indulgence in moderation. As Packard explains: 'The consumer will be left with the feeling that candy manufacturers understand him and the bite-size pieces will give him the "permission" he needs to buy the candy because the manufacturers are going to "permit" him to eat in moderation.' Today, sweets advertisements precisely reflect the lifestyle proposition the product has been created to fulfil, whether they are fantasy bars for moments of private indulgence, take-a-break bars for busy days, gifts, multipacks for 'home stock', or fun assortments for sharing out with children. Think of a situation in which sweets might be appropriate, and the chances are a product has been conceived to fit it.

The problem is, a good proportion of confectionery is aimed at children. This seems to be almost a taboo subject in the sweets business. Perhaps it is hard for a grown man to accept that he is trying to manipulate the mind of a child to make a profit. On the other hand, he is also bringing the child great joy, so it is complicated. Children, needless to say, are fickle as consumers, although they show high levels of purchase satisfaction: children like buying and owning things. Peer influence on candy choice has been noted from the age of five. It is now believed that the only way of creating some kind of brand loyalty is through character merchandising or the inclusion of 'premiums' like toys, figures, cards or games; many sweets are really edible toys. The sweets companies keep a close eye on pocket-money levels, and price their packs accordingly. Haribo recently launched a new range of smaller bags of their gummy Goldbears precisely to meet this demand. The market is only going to get tougher, as more products emerge that tempt junior consumers to part with their money, from trading cards (such as the smash-hit Pokémon range) to mobile-phone expenditure. The one area no one has ever cracked is confectionery for the teen market. Adolescence is a time when many people simply stop buying sweets, as they grow out of childhood. Does this say something about those of us who never stopped buying sweets?

Lucky Dip

TURKISH DELIGHT

It was my early memories of Turkish Delight that fired my interest in sweets. I adore Turkish Delight, and it was my grandfather who got me hooked – on the good stuff. My grandfather was neither Turkish nor did he have exotic connections; he lived in Maidenhead. But he was in the sweets business, and could lay hands on some top-class Turkish Delight. His secret store of imported lokum rahat, *to give it its Turkish name, was kept locked in a cabinet, inside a green-baize-lined drawer that was ceremoniously unlocked when my parents were out of sight.*

The packaging of Turkish Delight tells you it is something special: an octagonal wooden box with a lid that creaks and groans as you lift it off. Inside, a nest of scrunching waxed paper conceals these pink cubes of delight, entirely smothered in pure white icing sugar. My grandfather would produce this intoxicatingly exotic receptacle, spear a chunk with the box's uniquely stubby wooden fork and proffer it at arm's length, as the fine dust powdered the air around it like a comet's detritus. I would close my eyes and bite onto the fibrous stick, slide the powdery Turkish Delight off and finally sink my teeth into the delicious pink lump. The taste is unctuous and perfumed with roses, the texture a sublime and sensual concatenation of powderiness, slight resistance from the skin of the cube, and creamy gooiness within. I was only ever allowed one, so perhaps I have been catching up with my desire ever since. A strange and wonderful substance; it has required considerable effort of will to discover how Turkish Delight is made and in doing so break for ever the mystery surrounding it.

The best Turkish Delight in the world can be found among the stalls of the Egyptian Bazaar (not the better-known Grand Bazaar) in

Istanbul. This Turkish Delight is as light as a feather, and soft and bouncy on the tongue rather than gooey and creamy. The secret is freshness, above all, plus the quality and delicacy of the flavouring ingredients. The perishability of this temperamental sweetmeat is the bane in the lives of Turkish Delight manufacturers, as I discovered when I interviewed several of them at the ISM sweets fair. The Turkish entrepreneurs became quite distressed about the subject of packaging and the unavoidable firmness and chewiness (both undesirable characteristics) of the exported article.

As with many Middle Eastern sweets (halva and baklava, for example), the basis for Turkish Delight is a cereal product: cornflour starch, which is mixed with honey or sugar syrup and flavourings, then cut into cubes when cool and dusted with icing sugar. It is that texture that makes Turkish Delight so sensuous and sexy. Turkish Delight comes in a wide range of flavours as well as the standard pink rosewater, and it is often complemented with nuts – the more-ish chewability of pistachio is a particularly suitable partner.

Lokum rahat means 'throat's ease' in Turkish, and it was most likely invented by Arab apothecaries some time around the ninth century, as a species of lohoch: a gummy, slowly melting medical preparation prescribed for sore throats and other ailments. There are early records in Arabic of sweets and medicines based on starch and sugar syrup, and the Persian No Rooz (New Year's) speciality – Turkish Delight with almonds, cut in slices and threaded on long cords to dry in confectioners' shops – could be an echo of this early lokum. Specific names and dates are often erroneously associated with the invention of particular sweets, not least for commercial reasons, and in the case of Turkish Delight the name of the supposed inventor is Hadji Bekir of Constantinople, whose 'original' secret recipe, passed down the generations, is still followed by one Istanbul manufacturer. As lokum or rahat, Turkish Delight is made all over the Middle East, Russia and the Balkans, and it is hugely popular in Greece, served with strong black coffee at the end of dinner. It was sold in Britain from the late nineteenth century, where it was first marketed as 'lumps of delight'. In Dickens's last novel, The Mystery of Edwin Drood (1870), the 'wonderfully whimsical' Rosa Bud announces to Edwin:

'I want to go to the Lumps-of-Delight shop.'

'To the—?'

'A Turkish sweetmeat, sir.' [. . .]

[Which she then] begins to partake of with great zest: previously taking off and rolling up a pair of little pink gloves, like rose-leaves, and occasionally putting her little pink fingers to her rosy lips, to cleanse them from the Dust of Delight that comes off the Lumps.

Which is about as sexy as Dickens gets.

Turkish Delight remains, for Westerners, the most exotic of sweets, and the advertising slogan for a chocolate-covered version of Turkish Delight, made by Fry's, memorably sums it up: 'Full of Eastern Promise'.

Chapter 2

HEART OF SWEETNESS

The biology of sugar is disarmingly simple; white table sugar is perhaps the purest foodstuff known to man. It is typically 99 per cent sucrose, a disaccharide made up of one molecule each of two other common food sugars: fructose and glucose (which are monosaccharides). In nutritional terms, there is virtually no difference between the three – they are all simple carbohydrates, easily absorbed and converted into energy. The fructose found in fruit is no better or worse for you than sucrose, and neither is glucose, the energy sugar. It is just that sucrose tastes nicest, is the most adaptable in the kitchen or food factory, and has been exploited commercially for the longest period. (Now, however, high-fructose corn syrups account for almost half the carbohydrate sweeteners used industrially in the United States, principally in soft drinks; and glucose, which is cheaper than sugar and can often replace a proportion of it in sweet-making, is an important ingredient in the confectionery business.)

Sucrose is present in the juice of all green plants, but exists in sufficient quantities to be viable for commercial extraction only in sugar cane and sugar beet. It is the ideal repository of chemically stored energy because it has high energy values and can be absorbed into the bloodstream quickly: even complex carbohydrates are ultimately broken down into sugars in the digestive tract for this end. So although most sweets do not contain many vitamins and minerals, taken in some moderation they are indisputably good for us. Sugar is also cheap to buy, easy to transport and keeps indefinitely. It is a preservative, an aid to the fermentation of beer and wine, an activator (it encourages yeast growth) and it is added to frozen foods to prevent formation of crystals. But most importantly for our purposes, you can make sweets out of it.

What is sweetness? A scientific definition is: 'a modality of oral chemosensitivity and also the example par excellence of hedonic experience'. This means: sweet is a taste, and it tastes really good. But scientists of taste have not got very far in explaining precisely how sweetness is ascertained. Of the four basic sensations of what Western nutritionists call the taste tetrahedron – sweet, salt, sour, bitter (Eastern scientists add astringency and umami, a 'thick' flavour) – sweetness registers first, in a few seconds. Next comes sour, in four to eight seconds, followed by salt and bitter. Textural observations and scent are simultaneously transmitted through the offices of the mouth and nose. Then the brain registers recognition or, more likely, confirmation (because we have seen what we are eating) of the flavour or specific food being tried, and assigns it an emotional approval rating. Aftertaste can transform our opinion of the food being tried. Whether we like or dislike certain foods and flavours is to a large extent culturally determined, but broadly speaking, if sweetness is available, *homo sapiens* falls on it like bees. The physical basis of our response occurs via the excitement of the tastebuds when they come in contact with food. Tastebuds are elongated cells that terminate in gustatory hairs. They regenerate every two weeks or so, but our brain obviously retains memories of flavours. About fifty of these tastebuds form a papilla, one of the little nipples found all over the tongue and also in the throat (there is a lot more taste sensation in the throat than one might think). Until quite recently it was believed that different parts of the tongue registered different taste sensations – the received wisdom was, sweetness at the tip, bitterness at the back and sourness and saltiness at the sides. But now a pattern theory of taste perception is in the ascendancy, in which it is argued that while different types of papillae do indeed detect different tastes – by discerning the shape of molecules in the food, locking with them and transmitting a taste signal to the brain – they are clustered all over the mouth and throat in varying concentrations. It is possible that some people have higher numbers of sweet papillae than others, and therefore show a preference for sweetness.

According to A. W. Logue, author of *The Psychology of Eating and Drinking* (1986), sweetness exhibits one curious anomaly: 'The sweet taste continues to be pleasurable only if the sweet substance is not swallowed. Swallowing a sweet substance apparently results in negative feedback from the stomach, leading to a decrease in the perceived pleasantness of that substance (a phenomenon known as alliesthesia).' Perhaps this is why most sweets have been made as little balls to be sucked and kept in the mouth: to prolong the pleasure of sweetness by keeping the papillae in periodic contact with sweet molecules for as long as possible. The way we pass sweets around in our mouths, bringing them into contact with new papillae in different parts of the mouth, is one of the pleasures of sweet-eating; other foods are not designed for this treatment. When we have finished one sweet we are eager to replenish our mouth with another, so we can re-enliven the tastebuds and banish any negative signals from the stomach. The lollipop is custom-made for this, going in and out, refreshing our sweet sense again and again, just as it is needed.

It is notoriously difficult to describe and ascertain different flavours, so while a taste might give us pleasure, we cannot accurately describe the sense data we are receiving and explain why it is to our liking. For a scientific theory of the mystery of how we taste, one may as well turn to the Roman poet Lucretius (94–55BC), who in *De Rerum Naturum* (translated by Ronald Melville, Oxford University Press, 1997) expounds an elegant theory of mastication:

> The tongue now, and the palate, which give us taste,
> Need no more work of reasoning to explain.

In the first place we sense flavour in the mouth
When we press it out in chewing food, as a sponge
When full of water is pressed and begins to dry.
Next, what we press out is distributed
Abroad through all the passages of the palate
And winding channels of the porous tongue.
Therefore when bodies of the oozing juice
Are smooth, they sweetly touch and sweetly stroke
All the wet trickling regions round the tongue.
But contrariwise they prick the sense and tear it,
Being pressed out, the more they are filled with roughness.

He goes on to explain that smooth round atoms – found in honey and milk, for example – are sweet, whereas hooked ones are bitter. This description of how flavours rub up against the tastebuds is about as satisfying and precise as any in modern science.

The biological question of why we should like sweets and sweetness quite so much is equally vexed. The theory commonly expounded, among the small coterie of students of sweetness, at least, is that early man first learned a liking for sweetness as a way of distinguishing between ripe and unripe fruit. In this sense, taste is seen as the gatekeeper of ingestion. This evolutionary preference eventually became genetically programmed into *homo sapiens* as an inherited characteristic or species trait. Anthropological guesswork further suggests that sweetness acts as a nutrient indicator: in nature sweet things tend to be good for us – the sweetness directs us to the most useful food sources, such as vitamin-rich plant tissues – whereas bitter substances might well be poisonous (young children and pregnant women are most sensitive to bitter tastes). So we instinctively prefer life to death, warmth to cold, comfort to pain, sweetness to bitterness, sex to spinach.

Our liking for sweetness goes back further, into pre-humanoid evolutionary history: chimpanzees are partial to honey, and will direct their brainpower towards fashioning pointed sticks to prise the sweetness out of bees' nests in tree hollows. In nature, all kinds of animals seek out sweetness, from the nectar-obsessed bee and the honey-handed bear, to the inquisitive hummingbird, sipping at bright flowers in the dappled jungle. In southern Africa, honey badgers are employed to sniff out bees' nests, and, as Renata Coetzee explains in *Funa: Food from Africa* (1982), the honey bird has also learned to work alongside man to indulge a sweet tooth: 'The bird gives a peculiar call and when followed moves on to a tree some distance away. This procedure is repeated until the nest is reached, where the bird is rewarded with a portion of the honey.'

The idea that primal urges are lurking deep within us, forcing us to commit despicable acts and eat despicable foods, is seductive; the implication is that we are still cavemen at heart, noble savages at best, scavenging and foraging for food, rooting about for sex, fighting each other, eating sweet things and raising children amid the surety of robotic pre-ordainment. The irony of this is that with the mass production of sugar, pure sucrose, from just one plant, sugar cane, sweetness was isolated from the very nutrients it was designed to signpost in nature. Have we corrupted sweetness by identifying it and manufacturing it by the ton? Prime debunker of evolutionary ideas of sweetness is Sidney Mintz, the brilliant historian of sugar as a commodity. In *Sweetness and Power* (1986) Mintz has convincingly argued that evolutionary and genetic factors are only part of the story, that our liking for sweetness is historically linked to where we live, who is in control of economic and political power, and how rich we are. Humanity has become progressively more obsessed with sugar and sweetness not simply because we are naturally predisposed to it, but because of a range of complicated cultural factors. To take an example, the reason why British people eat a lot of sweets has more to do with imperialism, cheap calories, the perception of luxury and the popularity of other commodities related to sugar, notably tea, than it has to do with primitive man's fruit-eating habits.

The most extreme extension of this argument is that our sweet tooth is entirely the result of cultural programming. If so, the process starts early. Mothers' milk is naturally sweet, as is cow's milk or baby-formula milk. Milk is in fact the only effusion from the human body that tastes at all sweet, rather than salty (except the urine of some diabetics). For a little baby, a mother represents food. Later, a child will come to love milk for its flavour. I once heard a woman recall how she knew it was time to stop breast-feeding her two-year-old son when he exclaimed 'Mmmm, delicious!' while at the breast. When the flabbergasted mother asked the young gourmet what the milk tasted like, he replied: 'Butter and jam.' Perhaps we just have sweetness forced down us until we become addicted to it, and the sweetness of mothers' milk sets us up for a life-time of craving? Some work has been done on the potential for taste preferences in the womb, since it is known that tastebuds are formed early on in the life of a foetus and it is likely that unborn babies can detect flavours in the amniotic fluid that they swallow in the final stages of preg-nancy. But this research into the embryonic sweet tooth is inconclusive.

The only practical way to find the answer to the question of whether sweet preference is acquired or innate is to discover whether new-born babies have a taste for sweet things before they get anywhere near their mother's milk. This experiment – giving sweets to a large sample of brand new babies – is a difficult one to get away with, but a super scientist called Professor Jacob Steiner of the University of Pennsylvania has managed it. Somehow Steiner obtained parental permission to test seventy-five new-born babies and one hundred more who were three to seven days old. The object was to discover whether these babies, who had never tasted anything, had any innate flavour preferences. To do this, the babies were fed solutions of salt, bitter and sour, as well as plain water as the con-trol stimulus, and their facial expressions were carefully monitored. The written observations were backed up by photographs of the faces of the gurning babies, registering their approval or disapproval of the tastes.

Professor Steiner reported: 'Stimulation with the bitter fluid leads to a typical arch-form opening of the mouth with the upper lip elevated, the mouth angles depressed, and the tongue protruded in a flat position [. . .] It was often followed by spitting.' So: the babies scrunch up their faces, stick their tongues out and spit. It is safe to assume they don't like bitter. 'The sour stimulus leads to a lip-pursing [. . .] often followed by a wrinkling of the nose and blinking of the eyes.' The new-born babies are not quite ready for a lemon sherbet. 'The sweet stimulus leads to a marked relaxation of the face, resembling an expression of satisfaction. This expression is often accompanied by a slight smile and was almost always followed by an eager licking of the upper lip, and sucking movements.' Happy sugarbabies. New-borns bear no malice and love sweetness.

When the same experiment was carried out on adults, they exhibited exactly the same facial reactions – but only when they were tested in groups. Adults have learned to control their facial expressions, and barely lifted an eyebrow in private. But pulling faces at each other when trying strong tastes is, it seems, an instinctive way of communicating our feelings about food to others. We are certainly closer to chimps than gods. In fact, Professor Steiner carried out the same experiment on chimps, and their facial reactions were the same as the humans'. Then the scientist went in search of bigger game, proffering his flavoursome solutions to an elephant in a zoo: the response to bitter was 'gaping, drooling and trunk rubbing' (a negative reaction, according to elephant experts), while for sweet the elephant indulged in 'licking and trunk sucking' (positive). It has been argued that animals that display sweet preference have an evolutionary advantage, because they are able to seek out the best sources of calories. Similarly favourable reactions have been noticed in cats, dogs, chickens and rabbits, and also carp and catfish. Professor Steiner has even tested a prawn, which showed a pronounced dislike for bitter substances.

But enough of elephants and prawns. In other experiments on human babies it was noticed not only that they pull 'sweet' and 'bitter' faces from the earliest stages of life, and that they show a preference for the sweetest solutions of all (sucrose and fructose over lactose and glucose), but that although their heart-rates initially increased when they sucked at sweet liquids, when the solution was made even sweeter, the rate of sucking decreased. One would imagine that a helpless baby, never sure when the next food is coming, would drink an energy-rich solution as quickly as possible. The chief scientist's reaction: 'I have an explanation, but it is not a physiological explanation. I think the infant slows down its sucking rate to savour the substance in its mouth. The increased savouriness of food in the mouth is exciting. I think it is a joy response.' Anyone who likes sweets can understand the baby's thinking. A good sweet will always elicit a joy response.

The affinity between babies and sweetness is acknowledged in many cultures across the world, in that new-borns are often given honey or some sweet solution as soon as they are born, sometimes in a semi-ritualised way. In many cases they continue to be fed sweet things during the first week or weeks of life. Spices such as cinnamon or aniseed, or almond oil, are often part of such concoctions. The practice was first recorded in ancient Greece, and today, to take just a few examples, babies in the West Indies might be given a mixture called 'Luck', of honey, olive oil and spices; in Samoa, they are fed cane juice in the first week; in Upper Burma, muslin dipped in honey is given; while in Pakistan, a mother will put a mix of ghee, sugar and honey on her finger for the baby to suck. A version of the practice even found favour with the modern Western medical profession: until recently, many new-born babies in the United States were first given a solution of 5 per cent glucose in water. Such initiations are the start of an intense relationship with sweetness that will last a lifetime.

The practical advantages of indulging a baby's sweet tooth are clear: sugar substances are rich in glucose, which the baby finds easy to ingest and digest, and this can be converted into energy and released into the bloodstream almost immediately. So in places where food is scarce, sweetness helps keep babies alive. In addition, sweet solutions will give both mother and baby strength while the mother's milk is 'coming in', which can take several days, and allow the baby to get used to feeding routines, as well as establish from the start the idea that the world is full of interesting tastes. Throughout infancy, the porridges and mushy mixtures which babies of all cultures are fed are routinely sweetened, and manufactured baby foods are relatively high in sweetness, even if it is fruit rather than sugar that is listed on the ingredients. Conversely, anti-sweetness can be used to control a baby's feeding habits: in some countries, when the child is ready to be weaned on to solid food, a mother might rub her nipple with aloe or another bitter substance, so the baby will reject the breast.

The sense of what sweetness is varies between individuals within the same food culture. The idea of the sweet tooth, a sliding scale from sugarbabies to sourpusses, is not a myth, although the sweet tooth is not a bovine molar, as suggested by eighteenth-century meat-carving expert John Trusler, who suggested in *The Honours of the Table*, of 1791, that 'There is a tooth in the upper jaw, the last tooth behind [. . .] having several cells and being full of jelly'. The ability to sense different flavours also varies, and it has been noted that overweight people tend to have well-developed taste responsiveness. This double-edged sword of food appreciation is what one might call 'Fat Gourmet Syndrome', a condition I myself have been suffering from in recent years. The intensity of the 'sweet tooth' in an individual is no simple matter, either. People who like sweet things do not just devour sweetness wherever they find it: they tend to select particular concentrations of sweetness in certain situations. So a person who likes to eat sweets all day may not take sugar in his tea or coffee, or a person who professes not to like sweets and desserts might like to have tomato ketchup (essentially sweet) with a wide variety of savoury things. Children obviously show a strong preference for sweet things, which fades as they get older, but beyond the fact that children simply have more tastebuds than adults, the reason for this is not understood. Perhaps this is another species trait that has evolved in humankind: children need to be high-energy consumers, so their taste for sweet, glucose-rich foods is increased in the vulnerable early years. There is evidence that suggests that children, particularly boys up to about nine years old, are less able to taste strong flavours – half as sensitive to sweetness and one-seventh as sensitive to sour. So the sweets little boys like are often unpalatably sweet to adults. We tend to eat sweets when we are nervous or stressed, and at least one sweet (chewing gum) is used by adults partly for this specific purpose. The role of sweets as an oral comforter has been proven by their efficacy as a cigarette replacement for people trying to give up smoking (smokers, incidentally, tend to eat fewer sweets). It has been claimed that certain personality types exhibit different food preferences. In *Sensation Seeking* (1979), Marvin Zuckerman suggests that people who say they prefer 'wild, uninhibited parties' go for spicy, sour, crunchy foods, whereas the people who like 'quiet parties with good conver-sation' like sweet or bland food. As someone who likes all parties and all types of foods, I am not sure where I stand here. In the kitchen, perhaps.

Our personal sweet tooth is also the result of cultural back-ground and taste experiences, and sweet preference varies widely between different peoples at different moments in history. Even cultures who had a limited exposure to sweetness, such as the north Alaskan Inuit or the New Zealand Maoris, were found to have taken to sweetness immediately and quickly attained similar consumption levels to those who had been eating sugar since childhood. Where sweetness is scarce – and it was scarce globally until the expansion of the Caribbean sugar industry in the seventeenth century – it is still sought out, revered and protected. In northern Alaska, where there is no natural source of sugar and importation is expensive, people imitate bees, seeking out red and white clover and pink fireweed, and boiling it up with a small amount of sugar-syrup solution. The result, known as squaw honey, is still made by some Alaskan housewives.

Research has been carried out that suggests that girls like sweetness more than boys, and that Afro-Caribbean babies prefer all flavours in stronger concentrations than other racial types, but this evidence is far from conclusive. Cold lessens the ability to perceive sweetness, which is possibly part of the reason why colder countries – northern Europeans, for example, and notably the Scots – have a marked preference for sweet things, although Australia's high sweets consumption defies this argument. Professor Steiner himself tested a cross-section of society in his experiments, concluding: 'These reactions appeared involuntarily in all tested subjects, regardless of age, sex, ethnic, cultural or educational background, or state of health.'

Beyond the innate taste preferences found in all human beings, it appears that the specific likes and dislikes of an individual are acquired over time – in the case of sweetness, there is a big difference between ideas of what a sweet is in different cultures. The Chinese, for example, have historically used little sugar, and many Chinese 'sweets' taste unbearably sour to Europeans. Similarly, the Japanese habit of eating sour things, such as pickled *daikon* (radish), for dessert, seems eccentric to Westerners. A group of Indian labourers of the Karnatka social group habitually chew the fruit of the tamarind, which is sour enough to be unpalatable to most people, as a 'sweet'.

But sweets have been largely ignored in the literatures of nutrition, anthropology and history. Nutritionists tend to skip by sweets, because most of them are almost pure sugar, and can therefore either be dealt with briskly or attacked for the evils they are supposed to perpetrate. Anthropologists generally ignore sweets because they often appear incidental to a food culture, compared with necessary staples like the unglamorous corn or yam (although we spend far more on sweets than we do on bread). And most food historians barely mention sweets, because information about them tends to be scanty, and they do not occur at prescribed mealtimes. Sweets do not count as food, or even snacks, but exist in a category of their own, a halfway house, in culinary limbo. Perhaps this is because sweets are more about fashion and flavour than they are about nourishment. Yet sweets have been assiduously developed throughout history by all kinds of cultures, most comprehensively in the three great sweet-eating civilisations: India, the Arab countries and among the English-speaking peoples.

What is a sweet? When I first embarked on my research, it seemed simple. A sweet was a little something you carried around in your pocket to eat outside prescribed mealtimes. But that is a modern, Western idea of a sweet. In fact, every nation has its own view of what a sweet might be. My basic approach evolved to embrace anything that is considered a sweet in its home culture, even if it does not match up to Western expectations of what a sweet ought to be. Baklava is an example: this flaky, syrup-soaked pastry is found all over the Middle East, north Africa, and eastern Europe. Westerners would certainly call this a cake, or a dessert – after all, you have to eat it with a fork, off a plate – but it is not necessarily eaten as a dessert on its home territory. It exists outside the boundaries of normal food consumption, as a snack or occasional food.

Sweets have always been the currency of children. They are often the most important objects in children's lives. Roald Dahl, author of *Charlie and the Chocolate Factory*, knew this: 'The sweet-shop in Llandaff in the year 1923 was the very centre of our lives,' Dahl recalled in *Boy*. 'To us, it was what a bar is to a drunk, or a church is to a bishop. Without it, there would have been little to live for.' Sweets accompany the rites and rituals associated with belonging to groups and gangs, making friends and splitting up, sharing or hoarding. Sweets reveal both our greediness and our generosity; through sweets you can break friends as easily as make friends. They are given as rewards, and that association remains with us for the rest of our lives. They are also taken away or banned, as punishment; great injustices have been perpetrated by adults through the power of sweets. The sweets economy of children creates its own rules; it can instil a sense of the meaning and value of property. Children first learn the joys of ownership through sweets, stolidly counting out, measuring and rationalising these gorgeous little items, which are indubitably and irreversibly theirs, like nothing else in their lives. Children hunt for bargains in the sweetshop (big is usually better) and bartering or swopping sweets creates a sense of proportionate worth. In *The Lore and Language of Schoolchildren* (1959), Iona and Peter Opie note: 'It is a cardinal rule amongst the young that a thing which has been given must not be asked for again.' And that includes sweets, which are the easiest thing for a child to own, and therefore to give. Once given, however, a sweet is unlikely to be salvageable: all the recipient can do is open their mouth wide and show the sweet nestling there on the tongue, partially eroded. A valuable lesson in life.

Hygiene can be forgotten when it comes to sweets, particularly among children. The jewellery designer Fulco, Duc di Verdura, recalled his childhood in Sicily:

Another particularly Palermitan type was the candy man. This vendor, always surrounded by a group of greedy youths, stood with a stopwatch in his left hand, while from his right dangled a string about a foot and a half long, with a large oval piece of hard candy on the end. This allowed the client, who had paid an infinitesimal fee, to suck the candy for exactly one minute, after which, as soon as the stopwatch sounded, the sticky sweet was torn from his mouth and immediately inserted into that of his neighbour. Naturally there were always scenes and discussions which ended in fights. The slogan of this hygienic industry was 'a penny a lick'.

We learn about money through sweets, rationing our pennies, and many adults retain for ever a fairly accurate reckoning of sweet prices from their youth. We learn about stealing, too. How many people with no criminal history or predilections in adulthood must admit to stealing sweets on at least one occasion as a child? We confront our childhood fears through sweets: colourful versions of spiders, snakes and creepy crawlies, vampires or parts of the body. With sweets, we can be a cannibal or a tyrant or a madman or a giant or all of these things, transgressing the basic rules of society by indulging in unspeakable acts that flaunt internationally acknowledged laws, like biting the heads off babies. With sweets we can be super-humans who can bite through solid metal or stones, trolls who devour bugs, spiders, mice and insects, or pretend adults who smoke (sweet) cigarettes. In Mexico, even death is conquered, with the sugar skulls and skeletons of the Day of the Dead. Through sweets, the world is miniaturised and made palatable; all the accoutrements of the adult world, from tool kits to mobile phones, can be conquered by being consumed.

For adults, too, friendships can be made, cemented or revitalised through the ritual of sharing sweets. A gift of sweets can be neutral, anonymous, and acceptable to all sexes, ages and backgrounds. But sweets can have an unpredictable, anarchic edge: when someone produces a bag of sweets, they automatically attain temporary roguish status. Eating is not just about nourishment but enjoyment; social situations are created out of food occasions, and this is certainly true of sweets, where those occasions tend to be informal. The intimate little action that is the offer of a sweet creates a sense of surprise, of novelty, and of anticipation, even in the most serious-minded of people.

We are charmed by sweets because curiosity is one of the main pleasures of sweet-eating. When someone offers you one, the day seems brighter and hardships are slightly easier to endure. In this sense sweetness is a kind of anaesthetic, a barrier to mental pain. As William Gunter, eccentric author of the 1830 manual, *The Confectioner's Oracle*, inimitably put it: 'We are perhaps never in such good-humour as when we are eating a delicious morceau of confectionery: compared to the violent gesticulation with which we attack a ragout.' Sweetness complements other flavours, but it can also bludgeon them into oblivion or obliterate their subtlety (a danger with salt, too). The nineteenth-century French magistrate and gourmet Anthelme Brillat-Savarin described sugar as 'the universal condiment, which never spoils anything' – over-generous perhaps, and proof that even gourmets can fall into the embrace of sweetness and find it difficult to rouse themselves.

Sweets are perfect companions for journeys, one of the oldest practical uses of sweets. And they are unique in that they can hang around a person for hours or days or weeks or – if left in a drawer or an old jacket – for years, and still be eatable and enjoyable at any time. (There is a limit, as I discovered at a tender age, when trying to consume a packet of pre-war Spangles in a late uncle's chest of drawers: they were supposed to be clear and hard, but were disconcertingly – and memorably – opaque and chewy.) In the workplace, sweets are ritually shared out, and they can cement office relationships by making them temporarily informal. Sweets can lead to more. A gift of chocolates, in particular, can amount to a formal declaration of amorous intentions, although the chocolates must be of the right sort. Sweets can stickily bind together a whole community, as they do throughout Europe, where specific sweetmeats are often associated with a particular town or region.

Citizens are, generally without realising it, extremely patriotic about their national sweets. The difference between the English and the Americans over chocolate is a case in point: both nations have an extraordinarily sweet tooth, but the English find a Hershey Bar gritty and harsh, and the Americans think Cadbury's Dairy Milk is too sweet and cloying for a chocolate bar. Both are right and both are wrong.

There is also the secrecy factor. Adults spend the most money on sweets. Where do the sweets go? Presumably into the mouths of these adults, but where and when? It happens, of course, but it is rare to see someone actually scoffing a sweet or a chocolate bar. People like to ferret their sweets away and eat them on the sly, in the car or at the desk, in the park or standing up in the kitchen. Eating sweets can be as private as going to the lavatory. The sweets manufacturers have latched on to lifestyle, as opposed to flavour, as the key selling point for new brands – sweets for travelling, as gifts, healthy sweets and so on. But no one has managed to create a sweet specifically for the secret muncher. Perhaps it is too close to the bone. The small reverie induced by a sweet blurs the senses just enough to cushion the eater, taking a break, against the prospect of imminent work, or simply against the uncertainties of the day ahead. And of course a sweet can be enjoyed, in the background, as you go about almost any daily task – with the exception of speaking.

You don't exactly eat a sweet. A sweet is not food. You put it in your mouth and it kind of happens to you. Indeed, the sweetie is eating you, through the good offices of a marauding tribe of dental caries. And a sweet can also have its revenge by radically altering your appearance – turning your mouth black or red or green or yellow, just in time for that job interview or first date.

Sweets are plural. Not only do they come in bags or packets of ten, twenty, thirty or more, even solid sweets, such as a bar of chocolate, can be formally broken into pieces. Sweets are for sharing – with others, or with yourself (which is done by saving the unfinished packet and returning to it later). We are all object fetishists when it comes to sweets. Everyone has a different way of eating different sweets, a whole repertoire of munching, biting, sucking and chewing activities, tailor-made for each specific sweet. Some sweets demand a decision: with a human-shaped sweet like a jellybaby, are you going to eat it whole, bite the head off or nibble at the legs? We are allowed to play with sweets, and break the taboo of taking food out of our mouths to inspect it. Lollipops go in and out scores of times, and half-eaten gobstoppers or even aniseed balls are objects of curiosity for young and old alike. Adults play, too: a box of chocolates is also a toy, the plan inside treated with mock seriousness.

Sweets mean all these things to us. While we have been taking them for granted, they have sneaked up and gained a place in our affections. That is not to say that sweets are important in the general scheme of things: a sweetie will not change the world. It is the very humility of the sweet which is its secret strength and one of the reasons for its enduring popularity. All a sweet wants you to do is suck it and see.

Lucky Dip

LIQUORICE

The colour is black and the rich, full taste is somehow black, too. The flavour of liquorice seems to have its own special texture – a dark, almost alcoholic savour that pastes the mouth and teeth, imbued with its own special sweetness. This is not like the powerful yet strangely anonymous attack of sugar sweetness, but an aromatic, vegetable sweetness that comes into its own only when you swallow. The aftertaste of liquorice is stronger, if anything, than that first taste – a scirocco of sweet flavour that whirls into being as if from nowhere and hotly lingers in the mouth. More than any other sweet, liquorice can stay with the eater and the flavour can be reproduced time and again simply by closing the mouth and inhaling the fragrance. Liquorice seems to live and breathe, itself, in this moment of the spirit; the flour paste or gum that is the vehicle for the sweet juice is an immaterial, temporary vessel for the essence. Perhaps this is partly why liquorice is habitually moulded into so many unlikely shapes, from pipes and cigars to buttons and cats, because the flavour itself triumphantly transcends any such physical interpretation.

Liquorice is not just liquorice. There are about a dozen edible varieties of the fiendishly difficult to spell Glycyrrhiza glabra, *a small shrub whose long fibrous roots and rhizomes contain a liquid that is fifty times sweeter than sugar, offset by various bitter tastes and aromas. It grows wild throughout Asia and in southern Europe, and has been a popular flavouring and medicament since ancient times. It is still valued in the West as a balm for coughs and stomach ulcers, and it remains a staple of Chinese medicine, where it is valued as a tonic for heart and spleen, ulcers, colds and skin disorders. It is also said to be good as an anti-inflammatory, for menstrual cramps and as a laxative. An Icelandic* scientist — liquorice is unfeasibly popular in Iceland — discovered that a liquorice sample dating back to AD756 still had active medicinal properties. And in all my researches, liquorice is the ONLY sweet which has produced in me unquenchable cravings for immediate satisfaction. It is a powerful confection.

Liquorice grown in different places has different flavours. Spanish liquorice (var. glabra) is the name given to the variety most commonly grown today, and connoisseurs (of which there are few) claim to be able to tell the difference between crops harvested in Spain, Italy, Turkey and France. A mid-nineteenth-century advertisement by London liquorice wholesaler Robert McAndrew gives different prices for Anatolia, Anchor, Caserta and Canessa liquorice sticks. Even today, liquorice sticks are wrapped in bay leaves for transportation, and when the brown (not black) juice is extracted and diluted with water, each country has its own preferred methods of making sweets with it. (It is weird sucking on a woody liquorice stick; I was first given one by a friend when I was 12 — he told me it was cannabis and I believed him and became quite high on it.)

In Britain, Australia and America, a sweeter taste is preferred, so quantities of sugar are mixed with the liquorice extract and thickeners, such as flour and gelatin, which give the sweet its pliable texture and make it ideal for modelling. Aniseed or its derivative anethole is frequently used as a flavouring, since its lip-pursing sweetness naturally complements the darker tang of true liquorice, and it is easy to confuse the two flavours. The black colour is artificial, so red liquorice is not fake liquorice in the way white chocolate is fake chocolate. Bootlaces, pipes, cigars and wheels are popular shapes in the English-speaking world, although the most traditional liquorice, made in Pontefract in Yorkshire (where it is said Dominican monks first planted this 'sweet root' in the sixteenth century), is a conservative disc. Liquorice is no longer grown in Yorkshire (or Surrey, the other old English liquorice centre), and the town's factory was bought by Haribo in 1972. But Pontefract still holds its annual liquorice carnival, with a liquorice queen who might be dressed in liquorice clothes and adorned with liquorice jewellery, and Haribo has continued making the Pontefract cakes. In the United States, popular brands include Twizzlers and Y&S, both now owned by Hershey, Gimbal's Black and White Mix and, of course, Good and

Plenty, which are old-fashioned comfits. There was a furore when Hershey acquired the old Saint Louis, Missouri, firm of Switzer and toned down the uncompromising flavour of its liquorice rectangles. In Australia, a soft liquorice is made by famous firms such as Kookaburra, and liquorice pipes filled with colourful pastes are popular. Australia's classic Apricot Allsorts (perhaps they should be called 'Onesorts'?) are a take on the celebrated Liquorice Allsorts made by the firm of Bassett of Sheffield in Britain (now owned by Cadbury). The firm had been making 'liquorice sandwiches' since the 1840s, and the story goes that Allsorts were only invented half a century later when a sales rep accidentally muddled up his samples and simply offered the random selection to a Leicester confectioner – with fantastic commercial results.

Liquorice is quite a different matter in the Netherlands, Germany and Scandinavia (except Norway), where it is usually not sweet, but salty. Finnish liquorice is rated saltiest of all, although its Panda brand is benign enough to be sold throughout Europe (in chemists and health food shops). Another Finnish speciality is Skolekridt Liitulaku: liquorice school crayons. It is often fish-shaped in Sweden, and in Denmark there are fun brands like Trollendrop (troll sticks), filled with sweet liquorice paste, Graffitydrop (with a crunchy shell) and Stimorol liquorice chewing gum. Iceland is mad for liquorice – either small, very strong pills, such as those from the popular Opal or Topas brands, or the chocolate-covered, caramelly Lakkris Kulur. Olsen Olsen is a popular Icelandic chocolate-covered marzipan bar with a liquorice centre.

But the Netherlands has the most sophisticated liquorice culture of all – it is something of a national obsession. Dutch liquorice comes in a huge range of saltiness and sweetness and in all kinds of shapes, each one suggestive of a specific flavour. The popular Boerderij Drops are salty farm animals, while the classic Katjes Kinder (cat-shaped) have a slight ginger flavour. Haring Drops, shaped like herrings, are really salty, although 'double-salt' liquorice, available in various formats in Europe, is the one reserved for seriously salty liquorice lovers. There are liquorice hats, witches, keys, ships' ropes, buttons, beehives (honey-flavoured) and coins, each with its own particular flavour. Not all Dutch liquorice is salty: Zaanse Drops, made in the Zaan region, are soft and sweet, and Trekdrops are sweet bootlaces. There is even banana-flavoured liquorice in *the shape of a gorilla – ask for 'Katja Apekoppen met Banaansmaak'. Animals are the classic shape: the Pond Box by Venco is available in a 'zoo' mix or a sweet and salty mix. In Germany liquorice comes in a hot, 'Turkish pepper' flavour, and in the South of France the ZAN company (now owned by Haribo) has been turning out its salty liquorice wafers since 1862. Needless to say, anyone who is used to sweet liquorice finds the salty article a dreadful abomination, a crime against confectionery. But as always with sweets, it is what you are used to.*

An excellent median in the world of liquorice can be found in Italy, where since the eighteenth century there has been a market for small liquorice pellets that have a very strong flavour but are not too salty for those not used to the taste. The Calabrian family firm of Amarelli (a noble house) grow their own liquorice in fields around the factory, and they produce gorgeous sweets, like the minty, sugar-coated Bianconeri, violet-scented Senatori and jolly Amarellini, which look like beach pebbles. These come in traditional little tins that are, for me, the most beautiful sweets packaging in the world. The designs are old-fashioned, but elegant rather than kitsch. On top of this, the Amarelli family must be the most charming and solicitous sweets manufacturers of all. There are a number of other traditional liquorice brands surviving in Italy: Puntini and Chipurnoi, for example, and the big chewing gum concern, Perfetti of Milan, also makes Golia Nera liquorice and fruity Morositas liquorice.

Historically, liquorice has perfectly straddled the divide between confectionery and medicine. Most ancient cultures mention it as a medicine (the ancient Egyptians were particularly keen, and had a liquorice drink called mai sus*) and Theophrastus in the third century* BC *noted its sweetness and its efficacy against coughs and asthma, and also its ability to stave off thirst. This quality has made liquorice a useful addition to the soldier's ration pack: it is said that Roman legionnaires chewed liquorice on the march, and more recently it was issued to both French and Turkish soldiers in the First World War (the British were surprised to find liquorice on the bodies of dead Turkish soldiers at Gallipoli). Napoleon's valet, Constant, recalls in his memoirs: 'When his toilet was completed I gave him his handkerchief, snuff-box and another little tortoise-shell box containing small pieces of liquorice.' These would have been eaten to refresh and sweeten the tyrant's breath, however, not to* *allow him to march without drinking. The first reference to liquorice in English is in the early thirteenth century, when it was noted for its sweetness (sugar was hardly available in Europe at this time). An early fourteenth-century poem contains the aside, 'His love is al so swete, y-wis, So, ever is mylk or licoris!' and Chaucer himself describes the 'pore scholar at Oxenford' as 'himself so swete as is the roots of licorys'. It is curious that unicorns were reputed to have a hunger for liquorice.*

Liquorice imported from the Middle East and Spain quickly became an essential part of the medieval pharmacopoeia, first in the infirmaries of monasteries, where it is mentioned in medieval accounts (at St Mary's Hospital in Chichester, for example), and later among the professional physicians. It began to be blended with gum in order to make it dissolve slowly in the mouth, and therefore ease a sore throat more effectively. The Rosa Medicinae, a standard medieval medical manual, includes a remedy for scrofulous glands made from snails and liquorice. The medicinal overtones of liquorice have never been lost: George Dunhill of Pontefract, the man who first started adding sugar to liquorice in 1760, was himself a chemist, and even in the nineteenth century the name for a length of liquorice was a Bath pipe, named after the spa town, and Bath lozenges were liquorice-flavoured.

There is a most revealing mention of liquorice in a medical treatise of 1657 by Richard Tomlinson: 'Children delight herein, for which end they demerge small pieces of Liquorice in water in a glasse bottle, which when it is flave with Liquorice-juice they drink off, and put more water thereunto; which they agitate for more potions. The Cappadocians [from central Turkey] and Spaniards bring us every yeare Liquorice-Juice, condensed into Pastills.' This is an early reference (perhaps the first) to children enjoying sweetly-flavoured soft drinks. Liquorice water, or Spanish liquorice water as it was often known (liquorice has been called 'Spanish' since the nineteenth century), derived from the Middle Eastern original called sous, and it was a popular and cheap children's 'potion' even into the mid twentieth century, so strong and rich that it was described as an 'intoxicating fluid' by Dickens. It was known as 'sugar ally' to a mid-twentieth-century generation.

Chewy, sticky, pliable liquorice; black as pitch, oozing juice like a rope oozes tar. We should all eat more of it – for medicinal reasons, of course.

Chapter 3

THE FIRST SWEETS IN THE WORLD

What was the world's first sweet? This is the perfectly reasonable question continually asked of the international confectionery historian, and it is most vexatious. It all depends on how you define a sweet. And since most ancient sweets exist now only as fleeting references in manuscripts, inventories and early books, we have to speculate as to what they were really like.

Did cavemen eat sweets? There is a Stone Age cave painting near Valencia, dated to about 8000BC, that depicts a sweet-toothed caveman hanging on to vines, or a rope, while raiding a bees' nest for honey. A companion waits nearby for the honeycomb to be tossed down, while the insects buzz round them, caught in the image like a constellation of rage. Perhaps the honey hunters rewarded themselves with pieces of honeycomb, made piquant by throbbing stings? It was honey that first taught us that sweetness is good, but a piece of honeycomb does not count as a sweet. A sweet has to be made by human hand – it can't just be plucked from the tree or picked up from the ground.

There is evidence in the caves of the Dordogne from about 8000BC that early man was harvesting cereals with stone sickles, and throughout the northern hemisphere, by the neolithic period (5000BC on), humans had progressed from gathering to farming. So prehistoric man may have used homegrown flour and stolen honey to fry up a version of the little honey cakes or dumplings that are still a basic sweet food in many parts of the world. But this would be more of a cake than a sweet. Another prehistoric contender for the title of earliest sweet is a ball of sap heated and hardened in the sun. As we have seen, all plants contain a certain amount of sugar in their green blood, and although only sugar cane and beet have enough for commercial exploitation, several other species, notably sorghum grass, have appreciable amounts, as do the reeds that were often used as prehistoric thatching material. If the green stem of such a reed is broken in spring, when the sap is rising, a globule of the sticky, sweet substance will solidify at the broken end. In primitive cultures this is simply broken off and eaten, just like a boiled sweet. But this is foraged food: a sap ball simply does not have the feel of a real sweet. The native North American peoples took the process a stage further, by harvesting the reeds in spring, drying them, then crushing them between stones over a fine cloth. The white sap powder was then separated from the shards of stem, mixed with a little water, rolled into small balls and placed over the fire, where they swelled up to double size. But although these cooked sap balls might well count as sweets, they were not the earliest ones.

To find the first sweets, it is necessary to follow the progress of the twenty-foot-high, bamboo-like swaying reed that is the sugar cane, *Saccharum officinarum*, the source of the most readily available sugar hit on the planet. Botanists agree that this species was developed in human cultivation from another cane species – either *Saccharum sinense*, carried south from China by the Austronesian peoples in the fourth millennium BC; or *Saccharum robustum*, taken to Papua New Guinea from Indonesia; or from another, now extinct species. Whatever the identity of this ancient cane, it appears that plants with chewier, juicier, sweeter stems were continually selected by their discerning cultivators in Papua New Guinea, until the super-sweet and super-juicy sugar-cane reed developed. It is believed that *Saccharum officinarum* was first domesticated some time between 8000 and 4000BC (evolutionary botany is an inexact science) and from Papua New Guinea it was carried to the rest of south-east Asia and the Pacific Islands, and then on to China and India, where it gradually supplanted any less succulent native species of cane.

In the modern era, sugar would make the transition from luxury commodity to staple food, but there is a chance that it may have made the reverse transition in early times. It has been suggested that sugar cane and bananas were the staple diet in Papua New Guinea right up until the introduction of the sweet potato (cassava) in the seventeenth century. In the 1930s, anthropologists came across tribes on the island for whom sugar cane was still a staple food. And Alfred Russel Wallace, Darwin's eccentric rival as creator of the theory of natural selection, noted the importance of sugar cane during a visit to the Aru Islands, off New Guinea, in 1869:

> Here they eat it continually, they half live on it, and sometimes feed their pigs on it [. . .] Whatever time of the day you enter [a house], you are sure to find three or four people with a yard of cane in one hand, a knife in the other, and a basket between their legs, hacking, paring, chewing and basket filling, with a persevering assiduity which reminds one of a hungry cow grazing, or a caterpillar eating up a leaf.

The juice of the cane contains up to 17 per cent sugar, and the process of extracting, or refining that sugar takes considerable technological expertise. (Sugar beet contains an identical substance to cane – pure sucrose – but the tortuous method by which the sugar is extracted was not formulated until the late eighteenth century.) It is, of course, possible to eat raw sugar cane: it is a delicacy still enjoyed, by children especially, in cane-producing countries all over the world. A slice of raw cane, so evocative of the tropics, possesses one of the characteristics of many sweets: you have to work at it. It is immensely satisfying to draw out the sweetness enmeshed in the bundle of tough fibres. Like a sweet, a length of sugar cane is portable, refreshing, comforting, keeps for a while and is the ideal companion on a journey.

But raw cane is not quite a sweet. To make sweets, you need

sugar, and to make sugar, the canes must first be squashed, pressed or milled until all the precious juice is squeezed out of them. The simplest method is to pound the canes with stones. This must be completed within a day of the canes being cut, because they deteriorate quickly. The fibrous waste-matter left over from this process was used after the seventeenth century as fuel to fire the next stage: the boiling down of the juice until it crystallises into a solid. What is left is raw sugar: brown and unappetising, resembling dirt. Not at all like pure white sugar. It contains 'cane trash': soil, bacteria, moulds, live sugar lice and other detritus. So the refining process continues, with the sugar being reboiled and reduced time and again to separate the impurities from the intended end product, pure sucrose. The technique of using lime to help coagulate any impurities on the surface of the sugar liquid is recorded in Persia in the sixth century BC, and later bullocks' blood and the more appetising egg white were used for this purpose. The refining process has been vastly improved over time, but the principle of repeated evaporation is the same. Refineries are often sited far away from the plantations – usually in the port cities where the raw sugar is unloaded – and sugar is always transported in a raw or semi-refined state from its country of origin. This is not due to a lack of technology in the tropics, but because the humidity of the journey tends to spoil the refined article.

Any of the Asian societies cultivating sugar cane in prehistory could have discovered how to refine sugar from sugar cane. But the earliest record of any form of sugar manufacture, and of sweetmaking to accompany it, occurs in Sanskrit literature. Thus, India is the cradle of sweeties, the birthplace of the first sweets in the world. The people of India had exploited sweetness early: cave paintings in Madhya Pradesh, dated to about 6000BC, show men attacking bees' nests. The Aryans of ancient India, the people who dominated the sub-continent from 1200BC to 600BC, were famed in later literature for their liking for milk (they enjoyed a range of rice puddings) and honey. They are thought to have introduced bees and beekeeping into

India, and consequently a taste for sweetness. The favourite sweet dish of the Aryans was the *apupa*, a small circular cake of barley meal or rice flour, baked in ghee and sweetened with honey. One passage from the *Rigveda*, the earliest Sanskrit text (written down in about 1200–1000BC but the product of a much older oral tradition), describes how the Aryans would 'drive their chariots around in a leisurely way while drinking honey, listening to the beautiful humming of the bees, with their chariots also humming like bees, drinking milk laced with honey'. It was the Aryans who introduced the enduring tradition of always offering a sweet something to guests – in their case *madhuparka*, a mix of honey, curds and ghee – and this is the first recorded incarnation of a hospitality rite common to many cultures, from the tea and biscuits of the English to the syrupy *zolba* sweets of modern Iran. Perhaps the ancient Aryans' penchant for sweet, milky foods led to the evolution of the essentially milk-based Indian sweets tradition.

The very name of sugar derives from the Sanskrit *sarkara*, meaning gravelly, and the first account of sugar cane dates back to the *Atharvaveda*, the last in the quartet of ancient Sanskrit *Vedas*, which scholars now believe were created some time between 2000BC and 500BC. In this very first mention, sugar is equated with amorous passion, as a lover describes how he is filled with the sweetness of honey and will plant a ring of sugar cane around his love 'to banish hate, That thou may be in love with me, my darling, never to depart'. Sugar cane is mentioned quite often in ancient Sanskrit literature, but references to sugar itself are rare (although we do learn that it was given to elephants), and to specific sweets, even rarer. The Hindu epics – the *Mahabharata* and the *Ramayana*, written between 600BC and AD200 but again from a much older oral tradition – contain passing references to several sweets, particularly milk-based ones such as the round *laddu* and simple *kheer* (sweetened condensed milk). In the *Ramayana*, a sweet dish is a focus of the early part of the story, because Vishnu magics over some divine *kheer* to King Dashratha and his three childless wives. The king is described as holding the golden dish just as a man cradles his beloved wife in his lap. It is not hard to guess what effect this ambrosial dish has on the fertility of the king's wives. In the Saundarkand, or 'beautiful chapter' of the *Ramayana*, honey is used to mask the bitter taste of medicine, one of the most ancient uses of sweetness.

The early Jain literature of about 500BC mentions sugar candy, or recrystallised sugar (*matsyandika*), and it may have been especially important to the vegetarian Jains because they do not eat honey for fear of inadvertently consuming bee embryos. In the Sutra period (500–200BC) several new sweets are described in the literature. The celebrated Panini, the grammarian of ancient Sanskrit (who lived some time between the seventh and fourth centuries BC), incidentally provides much information on ancient Indian life in his learned discourse on linguistics. He mentions fields of cultivated sugar cane, and that the people enjoy *guda* (boiled and thickened cane juice, used in cooking and for drinks) and *phanita* (juice boiled down even more, from which sugar can be crystallised). Sugar refined in the ancient way is still commonly available in India, where it is known as *jaggery* or *gur*. Panini also writes of *sarkara*, granulated sugar, and of *palava* (a sesame-based sweet) and *samyava* (a milky sweet similar to the modern *churma*).

References to sweets and to various forms of solid and liquid sugar occur in all kinds of ancient Sanskrit works. In medical treatises, sugar consumption is linked with digestion and increased semen production. Perhaps the most promising sugar-based health drug is an elixir from the *Charaka*, a standard Indian medical book of the second century AD. The remedy is a mix of ginger, liquorice, long pepper (more aromatic than black pepper), gum arabic, ghee, honey and sugar. If a soup of this is eaten every evening for three years, it has an effect like spinach on Popeye: 'One remains young for a hundred years, improves one's memory, and overcomes all diseases. In such a man's body even poison becomes innocuous; his limbs grow hard and compact like stone; he becomes invulnerable to creatures.'

Sugar also gets a mention in the notorious *Arthasastra*, by Kautiliya, first minister to a fourth-century BC emperor. This is a Machiavellian manual of cynical statecraft that advocates spying on the populace and political assassination. It also deals with more mundane subjects, including seven different ways to greet a neighbour, a description of the different types of forest and the five varieties of sugar – at least one of which, from the description, has to be a solid.

One of the difficulties with ancient Indian literature is that the dating of even the major works is extremely imprecise, so that it is impossible to be sure of the exact meaning of any technical term for sugar at a given moment in history. Take *guda*, or thickened cane juice. The name is derived from an Indo-European word meaning 'to make into a ball', which implies this cane 'juice' may have been more solid than liquid, or at least viscous. But we cannot be sure. Indian scholars tend to be gung-ho about early Indian sugar-making – convinced that sugar was in circulation in northern India by 500BC and probably much earlier – whereas most Western academics prefer to stick to a date of about AD500. But given the wealth of references to sugar-cane cultivation in early literature, and the development of early sweets as codified by Anil Kishore Sinha in his remarkable *Anthropology of Sweetmeats* (2000), it seems reasonable to agree with the Indian scholars and go for an early date. One discernible trend in the mazy mass of Sanskrit literature is the way coconut sweets became notably more popular in India by the second century BC, and coconut is still the principal flavouring for sweets in the south of the country. What we do know is that an astonishingly rich sweets culture evolved in India from these beginnings, a whole universe of soft, milky, gently spiced delights that we will enjoy later. For now, suffice to say that in ancient times, sugar and sweetness were considered to be of Indian origin.

The sweet dishes of other ancient cultures cannot be conclusively described as sweets, but equally they should not necessarily be dismissed out of hand. What about fruit, particularly figs and dates – can these become sweets in some circumstances? Figs and dates were the most ancient sweet-fruit staples, and they figured largely in the diet of the ancient Egyptians, a civilisation that is recorded back to 3200BC. Baskets of figs have often been found in ancient Egyptian tombs. Melons and pomegranates were other popular sources of sweetness, and a jar that had contained grape syrup was found in Tutankhamun's tomb. The sweetness of dates and figs was also treasured in the ancient Mesopotamian cultures – the Greek historian Herodotus said that to the ancient Assyrians, dates were 'food, wine and honey' and the Greek Xenophon in the fourth century BC noted the size, succulence and colour of the dates in the region, and how they were dried and eaten as occasional foods. But fruit is not a sweet. Reay Tannahill, however, author of *Food in History* (1973), suggests that Mesopotamian dates were dried in winter, chopped up, mixed with barley paste and shaped into bite-sized pieces. These are serious sweets contenders.

The ancient Greeks and Romans were similarly enthusiastic about figs and dates. In Greece, junior priests called sykophants ('fig revealers') were charged with announcing the start of the fig season, and the word took on its pejorative meaning when it was used to describe informers who reported the illegal export of figs from Attica. In both Greek and Roman theatres, dates wrapped in gilded paper were sold like choc ices. The first-century AD Roman agricultural writer Columella states that dried figs were a staple winter food for the Roman people, and even cites a recipe for fig sweetmeats: tread the figs into a pulp, mix this with toasted sesame, aniseed, fennel seed and cumin, form into little balls and wrap in fig leaves. Store in jars. These certainly sound like they should count as sweets. The Romans were also fond of sweet varieties of acorns, but these are nuts, of course. It seems reasonable to suppose that many of these sweets or quasi-sweets were on sale in the streets as occasional fare.

Pastries are more difficult to categorise. It appears that in any ancient culture where both honey and flour were available, people have made sweet honey cakes. If we are to count modern baklava pastries as sweets, why not these honey cakes? It is a problem, but in the absence of any evidence about how most of these sweets were eaten, we cannot reasonably conclude that they were treated as sweets and eaten casually, outside meal-times. But first, a few examples. Ancient Egyptian pâtisserie was something of a speciality. There are hieroglyphyic carvings of industrious bakeries making *ta*, the standard loaf, shaped like a naval tricorn hat, and several other types of loaves and pastries have been identified. Some of these were made with date flour, or sweetened with honey. There is even a hieroglyphic representing a stack of pancake-like offerings, which is trans-lated as 'piled up sweets', and in the tomb of Rameses III (1194–1163BC) in the Valley of the Kings there is an inscription of a bakery that works like a strip cartoon, showing the making of what might be a *jalebi*: a long, thin, honey-drenched pastry similar to the kind eaten as a sweet in the Middle East and India today. Much later, in 158BC, the accounts kept by a pair of brothers, minor priests at the temple of Serapeum at Memphis, contain references to honey cakes, sesame cakes, pancakes and milk cakes. It appears that Egyptian temple priests, like all vicars since the dawn of time, enjoyed holding tea parties. Honey and dried fruits are also among the essential articles listed in the ancient Mesopotamian baker's store, so perhaps small, sweet, decorated cakes were also part of the cuisine there. In Ancient Sumer, in the third millennium BC, honey, dates and cakes were offered up to the gods, and in the archives of the Babylonian kingdom of Mari of 1780BC there is mention of a kind of honeyed cake bread baked in the oven. Honey cakes certainly feature in the records of the Carthaginian and Phoenician peoples of the first millennium BC.

The ancient Greeks enjoyed an array of honey cakes and breads. The best hunting ground for honey was Mount Hymettus, near Athens, where the honey had (and still has) a savour of thyme. Honey obtained without smoking the bees out, and therefore with an uncontaminated flavour, was best of all. It was called *akapniston* ('unsmoked'). In his unequivocally aspirational lifestyle manual, *The Life of Luxury*, Archestratus (*c.* 330BC) recommends a thin pancake drenched in honey from Attica. Athenaeus, in the invaluable third-century BC compilation called *Deipnosophists*, or 'The Philosophers at Dinner', includes a great glossary of cakes made of honey and flour in various pancake or ball shapes, including *basyma*, a bread of flour, honey, nuts and dried figs, which we would probably call a cake. Athenaeus also records *itria* – thin, cakey sweets of sesame and honey, which were later described as either dry or wet – and *gastris*, an early form of nut brittle, in which the honey is boiled to a hard caramel.

In the large, square dining room of a wealthy ancient Greek friend, one would recline on one of the couches – there were usually seven of them – perhaps with a companion at the other end, and enjoy a big banquet brought in on little tables. The third and final course was wine accompanied by *tragemata*, or 'what one chews'. The *tragemata* consisted of cakes, 'sweets', fruit (fresh and dried) and nuts. The best description of a Greek meal is the banquet of Philoxenus (which ends in disarray and bad temper), related by Athenaeus. Philoxenus was a character, the court poet in about 400BC at Syracuse in Sicily. The island was destined to play an important role as a conduit of sweets from the Middle East into Europe, and even then it was associated with sweet things (at this time Xenophon noted the import to Athens of *hedysmata*, sweet things, from Sicily). Philoxenus's pudding:

At last we had our fill of food and drink. The servants cleared away, and brought in warm water, soap and oil of orris to wash our hands. They gave us muslin towels, divine perfumes, wreaths of violets. Then the same polished tables, loaded up with more good things, sailed back to us, 'second tables' as men say: sweet pastry shells, crispy flapjacks, toasted sesame cakes drenched in honey sauce, cheesecake made with milk and honey, a sweet that was baked like a pie; cheese and sesame sweetmeats fried in hottest oil and rolled in sesame seeds were passed round.

Even in the sweet course one finds the sour-sweet combination beloved of the Greeks (and later the Romans). The final stage of the meal was, as ever, the most social, with guests lingering to chat and nibble at tidbits at their leisure. As the Greek poet Alexis put it: 'The man who first discovered *tragemata* was clever. For he found a way to prolong the party and never have our jaw bones idle.'

The Spartans were known both for their toughness and for a quite despicable cuisine epitomised by their national dish, an evil black broth which everyone else found quite uneatable, and which added to their reputation as fearless fitness fanatics, unmoved by hardship. But even the Spartans had a sweet tooth, evinced by Alcman's seventh-century BC account of a banquet with 'seven couches and as many tables crowned with poppy-seed bread, with linseed-bread and sesame bread and, for the girls, buckets full of honey sweets'. This mention of honey sweets – called *khrysokolla* (literally 'inlaid with gold'), made of honey and flax-seed – is the first in which sweets are explicitly and patronisingly linked with women.

Roman sweets, called *dulcia*, were also based on honey, and Roman bakers, who made a variety of honey breads, turned their hand to making pastry dainties with names like *liba*, *spira* and *savillum*. Jars with holes in the bottom, recovered from archae-ological sites, are believed to have contained honeycomb; the honey seeped into receptacles beneath the jars. And in the ruins of Herculaneum, in the suburbs of modern Naples, it is possible to stand in the ruins of a baker's shop where the remains of potential sweetmaking utensils, including moulds and a ladle, were recovered. It is amazing to stand at the counter of possibly the oldest sweetshop in the world and imagine what Roman sweets were like.

Some of them sound quite disgusting. Apicius, who wrote the only surviving classical cookbook in the first century AD and, according to Seneca, eventually committed suicide because he had spent all his money on food and good living, is most famous for his recipe for dormouse pie, which has been an in-joke in academic circles for hundreds of years. The flesh of the little fellows may have tasted sweet, because they were fattened up on figs. But a dormouse is not a sweet. That way, madness lies. Apicius lists several types of Roman sweets. The most palatable is a type of stuffed date, with a filling of either nuts, pine kernels or ground pepper, which is rolled in salt and then fried in honey. A modern version of this could perhaps be called a 'Roman dormouse', in the gruesome spirit of many sweets, if you imagine the date is the dormouse's body, the nuts are its crunchy bones and the honey is its blood. In any event, the classical historian Phyllis Pray Bober says this is 'delicious if one toasts the pignoli, uses Kosher or canning salt and the rosemary honey the Romans favoured'. Another of Apicius's sweets is a flour concoction, boiled to a hard paste in water, cut in pieces, left to cool, fried in oil and then drenched in honey and sprinkled with pepper.

It is sometimes supposed that the Greeks and Romans did not know of sugar, because Apicius mentions only honey as a sweetener. In fact, sugar was known to classical cooks, but it must have arrived in small quantities and been prohibitively expensive. Classical cooks valued pepper more than any other spice from the East, and while these empires rose and fell or blundered along, the gourmet remained contented with honey. The first reference to sugar in classical literature is attributed to the Greek general Nearchus of Crete, who commanded the returning fleet of Alexander the Great's army in 327BC, and came across sugar cane in what is now the Punjab, as he sailed from the mouth of the Indus river to the mouth of the Euphrates (although recently some scholars have suggested this may have been a type of sweet sorghum grass – a suggestion that bedevils all early references to sugar cane). The first-century Roman geographer Strabo records the description of 'a reed in India [that] brings forth honey without the help of bees, from which an intoxicating drink is made, though the plant bears no fruit'. He also describes what was probably rock sugar, or *khand*, as 'stones the colour of frankincense, sweeter than figs or honey'. (Nine hundred years later, when sugar cane had spread to the Middle East, other soldiers on campaign – the Crusaders – would also come across sugar cane and tell of it back home with the same curiosity.) Strabo also cites the observation, by Eratosthenes, the polymathic third-century BC librarian of Alexandria, of an Indian plant – 'a big reed, sweet both by nature and by the sun's heat' – and the first-century Greek physician and naturalist Dioscorides was able to describe sugar with accuracy and, probably, first-hand knowledge: 'There is a kind of solidified honey, called saccharon, found in reeds in India and Arabia Felix, of a similar consistency to salt, which crunches when in the mouth, just like salt.' The idea that sugar was a kind of salt persisted into the medieval period, when it was occasionally called 'Indian salt'.

So for the Greeks and for the Romans, honey was the sweet delicacy par excellence, while sugar was considered primarily as a medicament (the Roman Pliny, like the Greek Dioscorides, notes it as a curative alone). It is only very recently that the medical authorities have decided that sugar is bad for us. Mesopotamian medical records, for example, include preparations designed to cure diseases, the nature of which we can only guess at: one involves honey mixed with river clay, water and hot cedar oil, spread over dried apples. It sounds like something you might be given for breakfast in Finland, but was probably meant as a poultice.

Sugar cane was introduced to China early in the first millennium BC but, unlike India, China did not develop a sugar-based sweets culture. In fact, it developed hardly any sweets culture at all. Despite the presence of cane, maltose remained the Chinese sweetener of choice in ancient times. This is a jelly extracted from grains and the green reeds of the sorghum grass. It is mentioned in Chou Dynasty scriptures of 1100BC and is still produced commercially on a small scale in the southern United States. There are no extant records of honey in China dated prior to the third century BC, at which time the poem 'The Summons of the Soul' was written, which mentions a variety of luxury foods enjoyed by rich Chinese: 'Fried honey cakes of rice flour, and sugar-malt sweet-meats; Jadelike wine, honey-flavoured, fills the winged cups.' For some reason – lack of demand, or technological difficulties with sugar cane – the Chinese relied on imports of sugar-cane juice and, later, sugar from India and Indo-China. By the third century AD, solid 'stone honey' from Indo-China, in cake-form and shaped like men or animals, began to be imported. Such a reliance on importation is economically inadvisable and culturally embarrassing, and in AD647, the Emperor T'ai Tsung persuaded a delegation from the Indian state of Maghada (in modern Bihar) to take a group of Chinese research workers back with them to India, to learn the secrets of sugar refining. Thereafter, possibly with the aid of one Tsou, a sweet-toothed monk from the Umbrella Mountain of Szechuan, who reputed-ly advanced sugar-refining methods, China was able to produce good-quality crystalline sugar, known as 'sugar frost'. Another Buddhist monk, Jian Zhen, is credited with introducing sugar to Japan in 754, to mask the bitter taste of his herbal medical preparations.

During the Sung Dynasty (960–1279), ping (cake) shops in China, as well as itinerant vendors, produced sweets for children: preserved or candied fruits, thick jelly sweetmeats, and sugared and honeyed jujubes. These last are round fruits, reminiscent of dates, and the prototype, some scholars believe, for the narcotic consumed by Odysseus and his lotus-eating companions. The luscious sounding name, jujube, has certainly seduced Western confectioners, and since the early nineteenth century the term has been used for a fruit-flavoured gummy lozenge that is a balm for a sore throat (or an excuse for a sweetie). Real jujube is never used to flavour these sweets, of course. Itinerant hawkers or pedlars would sell sugar cane, honeycomb, jujubes and also hollow, crisp, semi-transparent figures of animals, birds, flowers and people, made out of sugar mixed with soya, cane, barley or sesame. Chinese sugar-refining was given a boost in 1280, when Kublai Khan, no less, called in experts from Egypt to reveal how to make truly white sugar. But sugar never entirely supplanted maltose and the other sweet alternatives in China, as it was to do so spectacularly with honey in the West. In fact, China's sweets culture, like its dairy culture, has always been paltry in relation to the size of its populace and the potential market for the product.

The taste for sweets spread very gradually, as sugar cane entered cultivation westwards, but the next explosion of sweet-making can be dated precisely to the Arab conquest of the seventh century. The Arab tribes took their culinary lead from ancient Persia, where sweetness was accorded a high place in gastronomy. So as the territory brought under the control of the Caliphate of Baghdad expanded, a taste for sweets followed. The Islamic-Arab empire was to become, after India, the second great sweet-eating civilisation.

After the death of Mohammed in 632, the tribes of Araby – taking their lead from the Prophet himself – immediately set about the task of promoting Islam by conquering and occupying as much territory as possible. These original evangelical Muslims were strikingly successful, first defeating the Roman emperor Heraclius in Syria in 636, then quickly hitting Persia, Egypt and Cyprus before expanding into north Africa and invading Morocco. In 711 a Berber army from Morocco under Arab leadership invaded Spain via Gibraltar, so in a mere seventy-five years, the Arabs had established an empire, and a religion, that stretched across the Middle East and into parts of north Africa and Europe. Sicily, Crete and Malta were overcome by the end of the ninth century, although Sicily had been under nominal Arab control since 655. The empire did not overrun Christian Byzantium, however, nor its capital, Constantinople.

The Bedouin Arab taste for sweetness was, by necessity, limited almost entirely to dates – deserts do not yield desserts, however just they may be. But this was not the case with the regions they had conquered. The Arab empire was to be remarkably fluid in terms of the diffusion of culture between distant regions, and the food culture was no exception. This is why the food of the Middle East has long been characterised by a certain homogeneity, with scores of dishes being made, with only slight variations, in several countries at a time (and usually claimed as a national invention by the patriotic cooks of each of the countries concerned; see Lucky Dip: Baklava, page 168).

By far the most important culinary culture to be absorbed into this new Arab empire was that of Persia, a land that occupied the whole of what is now Iran, plus parts of Iraq, Pakistan and Afghanistan, and the eastern half of Turkey. Prior to the Islamic conquest, the Persians under the Sassanian kings, who had ruled the empire bequeathed by Alexander the Great since about AD226, created what was perhaps the most magnificent cuisine ever devised, a consolidation of a tradition that stretched back at least as far as the seventh century BC.

Food for the ancient Persians was to be savoured as much for its appearance and scent as for its taste, which was gloriously subtle, a delicate admixture of flavours in which sweetness was by no means confined to the final course. Echoes of this cuisine survive in Middle Eastern cuisine, and modern Iranian food from the towns of Yazd and Kerman, in the salt deserts of the south and west of Iran – where Allah has never entirely supplanted Zoroaster – is supposed to be closest to it. For many who taste it today, Iranian food is the most delicate and pleasing, with beautiful dishes such as jewelled rice, and creamy stews called *khoresh* that suspend soft and tender meat, vegetables and fruit in a sublime balance of sweetness and sour citrus. The sweet dishes are just as subtle, delicately perfumed with rosewater and offset with the chewy fragrance of cardamom and pistachio.

At the time of the Arab conquest of Persia in 637, sugar cane had been in cultivation there for at least a century. One story has it that Darius of Persia discovered cane in the valley of the Indus in about AD500 and brought it back to the Persian Gulf, from whence it was taken to Assyria and the rest of the Middle East.

Sugar cane is mentioned in Sassanian literature as one of the plants included in the medicinal botanic garden of King Khusrau (531–78) at his hospital at Jundi Shapur. The king's sweet tooth was also recorded: a liking for *ghotab*, sweet pastries stuffed with almonds and sugar or meat. The serious emphasis placed on food in ancient Persia is evinced by King Khusrau's declaration that gastronomy was to be one of the essential subjects his son should study. It appears that 'domestic science' is not the upstart subject some claim it to be.

Persia had been famed for its cuisine, and for its generosity with sweetness, since classical times. When Herodotus visited Persia in about 500BC – assuming that we believe he actually did – he was intrigued by the sweet things (*shireeni*, in Persian) served after the meat course. Indeed, later Persian writers would criticise the Greeks' lack of a dessert course; ancient Greek *tragemata* must have been deemed essentially nibbly. A century later Xenophon, in his history of the invasion of the Persian king Cyrus II, called *Anabasis*, recorded how contemporary Persians were in the habit of sending representatives abroad specifically to track down new foods, including 'cooked dishes, sweets, incenses and perfumes'. And the Roman Apicius evidently considered the food of Persia worthy of a namecheck, as he includes a dish of Parthian (Persian) lamb, stuffed with prunes and herbs, in his cookbook.

The sweetness of sugar, and the liberal use of spices, milk and nuts, were facets of ancient Persian cuisine enthusiastically assimilated by the Abbasid Dynasty, the caliphs of Baghdad who ruled the Arab empire from 750 to 1258 and claimed kinship with Mohammed, and these tastes were to spread slowly westwards and northwards to the rest of the Middle East and into north Africa. The Arabs introduced a few culinary innovations, such as camels' milk and camels' hump, and a taste for dates, into the lands they conquered, and such delicacies prevailed, but rich Arabs tended to emulate the cultural mores of the aristocratic class which they supplanted, as well as that of Persia. The influence of Persian cuisine, and particularly that of the city of

Isfahan, on the empire was enhanced by the fact that many high-ranking Abbasid officials were in fact Persian converts to Islam.

As the hub of the empire, Baghdad was the recipient of startling culinary riches, and by the early medieval period the city was home to a thriving new-wave culinary culture. The historian David Waines has provided a snapshot of Baghdad as a nexus of cosmopolitan taste:

> From Syria came apples, pomegranates, plums, figs and apricots as well as fine olive oil; an oil made from violets and roses came from Kufa; saffron came from Yemen and Isfahan, honey from Mosul [. . .] Tabaristan provided citrus fruits, Herat yielded currants; cane sugar came from Ahwaz; salted fish and butter-milk from Khwarizm, cloves, spikenard and nutmegs from India; quinces from Nishapur, figs from Hulwan and pears from Nihawand.

The Arab empire was astonishingly rich in resources, not least culinary ones. But fruit was easier to produce than sugar, and the early development of sweets was hampered by technical challenges. Sugar did come to have a profound effect on the cuisine of the Middle East, and this is important globally because it was the fashion for Eastern exotica that would introduce spices, and sweets, to Europe – and from there to the rest of the world. But the successful cultivation of sugar cane depended on the use of unfamiliar irrigation techniques, and these took time to become established. Even then, when the irrigation problem was solved, there was the mystery of refining. So, like other crops from India grown in the Arab empire – cotton and bananas, for example – sugar cane entered cultivation in the Middle East very gradually. After the conquest, it took centuries for cane to become established in most areas: sugar only emerged as an important cash crop by the tenth century – in Egypt, Persia, Syria, Cyprus, Sicily, southern Spain and north Africa. It took nearly three hundred years of

Arab occupation for a sugar industry to gain a foothold in Andalusia and Sicily. Cane was also taken west and south, via Oman, to east Africa, and by the year 1000 there were sugar industries in Yemen, Ethiopia and, most importantly, Zanzibar. The Middle East, however, remained the main conduit for sugar, as it did for all spices (as sugar was classed), until the 1600s. Sugar became more and more important in the Arab world, although at this time it was emphatically not the staple food, manufactured and transported in bulk, that we know today.

There are few early cookbooks surviving to give us an idea of the role of sweets and sweetness in the Middle East from the time of the seventh-century Arab conquest and into the medieval period. The earliest source is a cookbook known as the *Kitab al-Tabikh*, compiled in Baghdad by Ibn Sayyar al-Warraq in the late tenth century. Two copies exist: one in Oxford and one in Helsinki. Sweet confections figure as a part of this cuisine, as remarkable for their appearance and perfume as for their taste. In Arabic gastronomy, sugar was appreciated almost as much for the glittering lustre it gave food when sprinkled over at the last minute before serving, as for its flavour. So in the *Kitab al-Tabikh* there is *aruzza*, a rice dish, with 'sugar sprinkled all over, so it flashes and gleams like light itself'. The most interesting sweets reference in this cookbook is to a type of *lawzinaj*, an almond sweet which al-Warraq says was made for kings while travelling. This is the antecedent of the diamond-shaped pastry sweets of the Middle East, which appear to have given their name to the fruit-based, often medicinal lozenges of European confectionery (also diamond-shaped traditionally). Al-Warraq is careful to note the scents which should be added to this *lawzinaj*: a heady conflagration of musk, amber and mastic.

Another sweet named by al-Warraq is the *khabi*, a domed pastry confection which was adorned with almonds dyed red and yellow. Small pieces of nuts, vegetables and spices were habitually sprinkled over the dishes, savoury and sweet, in this cookbook: pomegranate seeds, fresh coriander, pieces of cucumber, celery, rue, pistachios or almonds. In addition to their decorative role — colour, often supplied by saffron, is discussed in every recipe — these sprinklings probably fulfilled a medicinal purpose. This is of interest to the international confectionery historian because the idea was later taken up in medieval Europe, when sweets in the form of comfits — small, sugar-coated seeds — were used to decorate both savoury and sweet dishes in the same way. The almonds, the basis for so many Middle Eastern sweets, are the clue. It sounds a tortured comparison, but the practice of sticking glacé cherries, angelica, chocolate Smarties or M&Ms on cakes really can be traced back to this Arab example. Another invention that has been attributed to the Arabs, on somewhat flimsier grounds, is caramel: in Arabic it is *kurat al milh* (say it quickly) or 'ball of sweet salt'. This probably does not refer to the soft toffee we know today, but simply sugar that has been high-boiled until it turns brown and slightly bitter. One of the early uses of this Arabic caramel was not sweet-related: it was a depilatory for harem ladies.

Almonds were the basis for a large number of Arabic sweets, from the simple sugared almond to that mysterious and maligned, waxy and sweet putty, marzipan (see Lucky Dip, page 145). The almond offers an irresistibly pliable chewiness, a delicate and distinctive flavour and a strange perfume that lingers on the palate and in the nose, and it was exploited to the full by Arab confectioners in an array of sweets based on almond paste. Nougat, *turron* or *torrone* are foremost among them today. Rosewater, too, emerged as a vital ingredient for Arabic pastry sweets, and the perfume and flavour it lends to sticky confections is still the most distinctive aspect of Middle Eastern sweets, although Westerners unfamiliar with using this liquid in cookery often find it difficult to place (and to find). This preparation must be the most romantic ingredient in the confectioner's pantheon: a distillation of thousands of rosepetals, picked just before dawn for the best flavour — usually by maidens, as it happens. Pastry sweets dipped in honey and steeped in rosewater are not so easily transportable as dry sweets, but the *k'ak*, or doughnuts of the Arab empire, were associated with travellers: even sticky sweets can provide succour on a journey. In Andalusia in southern Spain, one of the last strongholds of the Arabs, a favourite doughnut of this sort was the *majabbanat*, stuffed with white cheese.

Egypt made a fortune from sugar, and the early medieval period saw some conspicuous consumption. By the tenth century, the amount of sweetmeats consumed, sold or given away by the households of a grand vizier could exceed 500kg per day – if records are to be believed. The tables at feasts would be adorned with large-scale sugar models of trees, buildings or animals (a custom that would be replicated in medieval Europe), and there was a tradition of giving sweets and sugar to the poor. It was reckoned that sixty or seventy tons of sugar could be consumed (or, more likely, distributed) at a single banquet. In his *History of Sugar* (1949), Noel Deerr reports that a particularly grand fifteenth-century banquet was held to celebrate the annual re-opening of the irrigation canals of the Nile Delta, which were vital to the cane fields:

> Over 100 cooks were engaged in using up 400 cantars of sugar (20 tons), which was distributed among the guests according to their rank, in quantity from 25lb to 1lb. Among these delicacies were young hens boiled in syrup, and the tables were adorned with statues of elephants, lions, giraffes and deer, all made of sugar. Two castles, each requiring 17 cantars of sugar, were on display, which the beggars were invited to carry away at the end of the feast.

A cookbook written in Arabic in Spain in the thirteenth century contains a variety of sweets recipes that call for different syrups, or jullabs (from which the word julep derives), some of them flavoured with rosepetals. These multi-coloured syrups were an important basis for sweetmeats, and mixed with ice or cool water they became *sharbat*, the refreshing drink of the East. There is a recipe for a whole chicken cooked in sugar syrup and rosewater, so it becomes encased in candy and looks, as the recipe specifies, like a lemon – which must have been amusing to eat amid the juicy groves of Andalusia. But this chicken is not a sweet, of course. Several recipes refer to *fanid*, the Arabic word for sugar cooked to what later became known as the 'hard crack' stage. The simplest of these *fanid* recipes is for hard-boiled sugar sweets which are formed into ring and disc shapes while the sugar is soft. Variations on this sweet incorporate crushed and sweetened almonds; one of them, called *ma'asim*, or 'wrists' – possibly referring to the action needed to make its twisted shape – is toasted in flour and then 'laid aside and the children are allowed to play with it'. The sweet called *qasab hulw* is a mixture of milk and sugar thickened and left to set on a slab, then rolled up and cut into segments so that it resembles sugar cane. We have always wanted sweets to disguise themselves, to mock reality, and this is an early example of such a novelty.

The shape and appearance of Arabic sweets was highly important. In the *Kanz al-fawa'id fi tanwi' al-fawa'id*, an anonymous compilation of some 800 medieval recipes, possibly made in Egypt, the only recipes in which shape and appearance are specified are those for sweets, such as the finger-shaped *sha'biya*, or sweets shaped as figures.

The taste of many of the sweets of the Arab empire was dictated by what was locally available. In the deserts of the south, dates and milk puddings (*muhalabieh*) were the speciality. One thirteenth-century recipe for stuffed dates, called *rutab mu'assal*, uses rosewater, almonds, musk, camphor and hyacinth. When a date is thus transmogrified, it becomes a sweet. In the east, towards India, there was an emphasis on rice, saffron and cardamom. And in the mountains of the north, honey and fruit (dried and fresh) were exploited. Fruit preserved in sugar or sugar syrup was to become a speciality export of the Middle East.

The Ottoman Turks, who overwhelmed Christian Byzantium

in 1453, inherited the food culture established by the Arabs, fellow Muslims, and re-assimilated the cuisine of Persia, extending its influence even further under Suleyman I in the sixteenth century, to embrace Russia, the Balkans, Romania, Greece and Turkey. Thus the *moussaah* of the Abbasid Arabs becomes *mussaka* elsewhere. It is likely that the range of small, sticky, baklava-like pastries was significantly extended by the Ottoman Turks from the fifteenth century. Even Vienna was infused with the culinary spirit of the Ottomans – that city's famous predilection for sticky cakes, eaten with a fork and accompanied by coffee, is descended from the honey-soaked Turkish precedent.

These Eastern sweets were generally pastry confections: flaky ones which delicately explode in the mouth, the pastry shards tickling the palate; or succulent ones, oozing honey and rose-water, that engorge the senses with luscious sweetness. But an important element of the Western sweets tradition is that of hard sweets that you suck or bite. These sweets also came from the Middle East, but they did not arrive officially, as part of the cuisine. That is too straightforward for sweets, the anarchists of gastronomy. As we shall see in chapter six, some of them came disguised, and the disguise was medicinal. But first let us sample the delectable variety of Eastern sweets made for export to Europe.

Lucky Dip

ROCK

I have never met anyone who actually enjoys eating rock. More than with any other confection, one has the sense that this sweet is physically attacking the teeth, clinging indefatigably to the molars so that when you finally prise it away, fraught and distracted, you can never be quite sure that you have not detached a tooth with it. No, rock is not really a sweet to be eaten; it is the ritual of buying it at the seaside that is important. And to add to the fun, over the years a panoply of silly shapes for rock has been developed: false teeth and babies' dummies that laugh in the face of tooth decay; bacon and eggs on a plate, sometimes with sausages, peas and chips or even a fishcake; hot dogs made of rock; trays of iced cakes; bags of pebbles; and now a frog on a stick, which is an appealing idea because such a thing would be a rare and unwelcome sight in nature. The surreal, drunken sense of humour in rock perfectly matches the devil-may-care anarchy and gaudy tackiness of the British summer holiday resort.

The word rock today describes a stick of peppermint-flavoured white candy, coated in a lurid pink colour, with letters running through it. The letters generally spell out the name of whatever seaside resort the souvenir was purchased in, and within the cellophane wrapper is a photograph of said resort, either in vivid Technicolor or in the cheapest and grimiest black and white imaginable. Of course it is possible to have any letters or symbols put into the rock, and several firms now specialise in manu-facturing bespoke sticks for corporations and events. There is a story that a rock worker in Blackpool in the 1970s, incensed at a decision by management to lay off seasonal workers, made up a valedictory batch of rock with a message to his employers, expletives included.

Rock has to be handmade; this is one sweet that cannot be made at home. But unlike other breeds of confectioner, rockmakers have never tried to keep their methods secret. What would be the point, when the stuff is so difficult to make, yet so cheap to buy? Professional rockmaking requires experience and skill, and rock specialists tend to concentrate on this one sweet and renounce all others – 'once a rockmaker, always a rockmaker', goes an old saying. In many ways rockmaking is a ridiculous, arcane and difficult process, but we are very glad for it. A stick of rock may be hard to eat, but it looks so pink and smart and right at the seaside, lying next to its confederates, that it is difficult to resist. Rock is the classic holiday impulse food buy: a good idea at the time, when one is infused with holiday bonhomie, but not so nice at home.

The process of rockmaking can be viewed up close in several seaside towns, where white-coated rockmakers knead and pull their elastic ropes of pliant candy in full view of the public. It is surprising, therefore, that some people still believe the pink letters are put into the white rock by being pushed into it manually, or fired from a special gun. The letters are in fact made by moulding them to quite a large size, perhaps six inches high, from a long piece of pink rock, and then surrounding them with white sugar candy. This makes a huge sausage in which the letters are illegible; it is impossible to imagine that this gigantic, disordered roll of colour might become an elegant stick containing legible words or patterns. The sausage is then pulled and pulled until the long rock pipe is the desired diameter, the letters can be read, and it can be chopped into sticks of any length.

But where did rock begin? The name comes from 'rock candy', which was not rock as we know it but just another name for sugar candy – crystallised sugar – in medieval times. The phrase is still current, if somewhat old-fashioned, in the United States today, and it means exactly the same thing; there is even one surviving rock-candy specialist in America (Dryden & Palmer), helping to fulfil a demand for simple, coloured but unflavoured sugar candy. The popular 1906 song 'Big Rock Candy Mountain' celebrated this type of rock candy (as well as bees, cigarette trees and soda-water fountains). In fact, the word rock has been used to describe all kinds of sugar confectionery, and not necessarily candy that is hard. In Scotland, for example, taffy rock bools ('toffee rock balls'), later renamed Hawick balls, are indeed hard boiled sweets, whereas glessie is a soft toffee of brown sugar and golden syrup, mistily recalled by a writer in the Scottish

Magazine *for December 1925: 'But the glessie! Who that ever tasted it can forget the stick of sheeny golden rock which stretched while you were eating it to gossamer threads of silver glistening like cobwebs in the sun?'* Gibraltar rock, or jib, a sweetie standard in nineteenth-century Britain and America, was another type of semi-soft to hard pulled candy, named after the igneous British dependency in the Mediterranean.

The truth about the genesis of rock proper is the Holy Grail for the international confectionery historian. That quest awaits an Arthur capable of penetrating the Avalonian mists of confectionery rumour and counter-rumour, a fog fuelled by municipal patriotism. I can humbly offer only the following speculative and partial account. If this slim addition to the world of rock scholarship advances its study one iota, aiding stronger, more diligent minds to come, I will be able to lay my head on my pillow at day's end and know that I have, in a small way, helped assuage mankind's insatiable curiosity about this mysterious pink stick.

Rock in stick form, with letters inside, appears to have emerged some time in the early to mid nineteenth century. The first reliable mention appears in London Labour and the London Poor *(1851) by* Henry Mayhew, who notes of the city's street confectionery industry:

> The man who has the best trade in London streets, is one who, about two years ago, introduced – after much study, I was told – short sentences into his 'sticks'. He boasts of his secret. When snapped asunder, in any part, the stick presents a sort of coloured inscription. The four I saw were 'Do you love me?' The next was of less touching character: 'Do you love sprats?' The others were, 'Lord Mayor's Day' and 'Sir Robert Peel'. This man's profits were twice those of my respectable informant's.

The strange message 'Do You Love Sprats?' may well have been designed as a ready-made smart riposte from a young man who found himself the recipient of a stick reading 'Do you love me?' from a girlfriend. (Treat 'em mean, keep 'em keen.) It appears that romance was the watchword with rock in its earliest incarnation: another early reference occurs in Henry Weatherley's Treatise on the Art of Boiling Sugar *(1864),* who describes it as 'Love Rock', because the word LOVE was what was generally encased in the sweet.

It is possible that lettered rock was not the invention of Mayhew's enterprising street confectioner. One story suggests it was invented on the Isle of Man in 1847 by a local confectioner called Bill Quigeen. However, the name which keeps cropping up in rockology is that of Dynamite Dick. This sweetmaker from the Lancashire seaside town of Morecambe, credited as inventor of rock and honoured in the way all rockmakers tend to be by being nicknamed Dynamite Dick, was said to have earned his moniker after a gold-rush veteran, fresh back from the Klondike, noted the resemblance of his sticks of rock to high explosive. This would date the invention of rock to some time between 1896 and 1914.

The story needed checking out, so I travelled up to Morecambe on a midsummer's day, when it was raining hard and freezing cold. Paul Hart of Morecambe's premier rock shop, accurately named The Rock Shop, said: 'Yes, I have heard about Dynamite Dick. We all know the name. But I don't know anything about him.' I bought a cardboard plate of rock fish fingers and chips from the shop. My advertisement in the excellent Morecambe Visitor *yielded some fairly interesting reminiscences about the town's rock trade, particularly its huge popularity in former days. The half-dozen letters and emails from readers also indicated that Dynamite Dick's real name might be Dick Taylor, and that he was not a character from the mid nineteenth century, but the early twentieth. The librarian of Morecambe Library said Dynamite Dick made something called TNT, or Taylor's Noted Toffee, and further delving revealed that he died in 1955, aged 76, having been known as Morecambe's 'Rock King' for thirty years. It appears that the Klondike story may have arisen because there had been a shanty town nicknamed 'The Klondike' in Morecambe in 1900, to accommodate workers during the construction of an artificial harbour. But Dynamite Dick probably earned his nickname after an escapade in 1917 when he heroically manoeuvred trucks out of a munitions dump that was in the process of exploding (an action for which the rockmaker was later awarded an* OBE*). Nothing was what it seemed about Dynamite Dick. Whatever the derivation of his nickname, he was obviously not the inventor of lettered rock – he was born twenty-eight years after Mayhew's first mention of the sweet.*

Perhaps Blackpool might supply the answer? The jaunty seaside town is the rockmaking centre of the world, and there are still a dozen or so companies turning out rock that is the best there is: flavoursome, brittle and sticky only in extreme heat. Blackpool, of course, has more hours of sunshine than anywhere else on earth, barring Paignton, so the town's rock is often tested to the limit. According to Margaret Race, author of The Story of Blackpool Rock (1990), the concept of seaside rock occurred to a Burnley miner-turned-sweetmaker called Ben Bullock, during a holiday in Blackpool in 1887. So Mayhew's 1851 reference to London rock is still the earliest, although it is worth speculating whether rock was developed piecemeal by several confectioners through the 1830s and 1840s, as the skills of the sugar boilers and pullers were competitively honed in response to demand for cheaper, mass-produced sweets for the general populace.

But Ben Bullock's idea of marketing rock as a seaside souvenir sparked a craze that would sweep Britain in the first half of the twentieth century. During the boom years (for rock) of the 1930s to 1950s, rock hawkers would wander up and down the beaches selling rock illegally, or even knock on the windows of bed-and-breakfast establishments, to sell to people having their dinners. Margaret Race, who comes from a rockmaking dynasty herself, says that these rock sellers were a rough bunch: one Blackpool woman called Maggie Bishop was known for getting very drunk and hitting the arresting policemen on the head with her sticks of rock.

When sweets rationing ceased in 1953, there was a nationwide craving for the uncompromising sugariness of rock, and a local newspaper reported long queues of panic-buyers outside Blackpool rock shops at 5.30 a.m. Locals still talk about these queues. There was a thriving black market for rock, and London criminals would travel up by train to secure illegal supplies to sell at a premium in the capital. There were stories of female workers pushing prams, filled with rock sticks, out of the factory gates, and headlines of the West Lancashire Evening Gazette read 'Relentless War Opens on Rock Racket − Special Ministry Squad Here' and 'Bolder Type of Rock Spiv'.

Rock does not inspire such hysteria today, but it still represents a valuable little aspect of Britain's culture. If someone brings back a stick of rock from the seaside for you, it will make you smile and perhaps behave in a raffish manner, temporarily. Just don't try to eat it.

Chapter 4

JUICY FRUITS AND SPICY CENTRES

The sweets imported from the East, in tandem with sugar, are the wellspring of modern confectionery. The whole sweets tradition of the West stems from two basic confectionery models, imported from the Middle East: preservable sweetmeats made for the early-medieval long-distance export market, and the medical example of the use of sugar in combination with various drugs and vegetable extracts. Most modern sweets, except chocolate and toffee, can be traced to these beginnings, and in many ways it is remarkable how little they have changed.

The preserving qualities of sugar – it draws out moisture from the seeds or fruits or roots it coats, and in the process prevents micro-organisms flourishing – made sweets a suitable commodity for long sea journeys, and this keeping quality is still one of the defining characteristics of Western confectionery. Conversely, baklava-like pastries deteriorate fairly rapidly, and they did not make the transition to Europe until they accompanied mass immigration and consequent consumer demand in the twentieth century. This chapter traces the journey of sugar from East to West and chronicles the sweets that became popular in the medieval period. We shall see how some of them are still on sale today in almost identical form, and the descendants of all of them can be found in any sweets department. Chapter five examines when, where and how these sweets were eaten. And chapter six explores the close parallels between pharmacy and confectionery.

History books generally announce that the first Europeans to come across sugar were the Crusaders. It is true that during their wars with the Arabs (1096–1272) the Crusaders found sugar cane in Israel, Syria and Lebanon. There are several explicit mentions of sugar cane in Crusader memoirs. Fulcher of Chartres, a chaplain travelling with a starving Frankish army in the Holy Land on the First Crusade in 1099, recalls: 'In those cultivated fields through which we passed on our march there were certain ripe plants which the common folk called "honey cane" and which are very much like reeds [. . .] In our hunger we chewed them all day because of the taste of honey. However, this helped but little.' Another account occurs in the collection of Crusader reminiscences gathered by Albert of Aix:

> In the fields of the plains of Tripoli can be found in abundance a honey reed called zuchra; the people are accustomed to suck enthusiastically on these reeds, delighting themselves with their beneficial juices, and seem unable to sate themselves with this pleasure in spite of their sweetness. The plant is grown, presumably and with great effort, by the inhabitants [. . .] It was on this sweet-tasting sugar cane that our people sustained themselves during the sieges of Elbarieh, Marrah and Arkah [Acre, 1104], when tormented by fearsome hunger.

This is evidence that the Crusaders themselves resorted to using sugar cane as rations in dire circumstances.

There are no references to the Crusaders enjoying Arab sweets, however, although one must assume that they did, since they are known to have enjoyed other novelties, such as citrus fruit. The nearest thing to a sweet encounter in the records involves the two most eminent personages of the Crusades: Saladin and Richard the Lionheart. On Richard's first day in the Holy Land, in June 1191, when he had just arrived to take command at the siege of Acre, he and the King of France tried to arrange a parley with Saladin. Saladin refused the offer, but instead displayed his customary chivalry by sending over a gift of sherbet. This was not the fizzy powder beloved of modern children, but *sharbat*, its noble antecedent, the non-alcoholic, fruity and sweet drink still enjoyed in the Middle East and southern Spain. (I remember the excitement of being served this classic sherbet, in liquid form, for the first time in a restaurant in Cordoba; the tears in my eyes were not fizz-induced.) At its best, *sharbat* was cooled by the addition of snow and ice transported from the mountains, even in summer (hence sorbet and American sherbet), and this is what Richard received at Acre.

It is romantic to imagine that sugar, together with tales of incredible sweet delights such as snowy *sharbat*, wended its way back to the cool green valleys and forests of northern Europe in the saddlebags of the returning Crusaders. This was certainly one route – James Traeger, author of *The Food Chronology* (1996), has found a specific reference to Crusader knights returning to Europe in 1148 with spices, including sugar. But an eye for a profit will quickly succeed initial curiosity, and traders – both Arabic and European – would have been alive much earlier to the wider economic potential of this curious substance and the joy that accompanies it. Alexandria could still lay a claim to being 'the greatest emporium in the inhabited world', in Strabo's phrase, since it was the gateway to the East for many European traders. The Arabs had been trading sugar for 400 years and had strong links with producers in India; sugar was also being traded out of the Byzantine Empire – Constantinople – in the tenth century. And right at the start of the Crusades, Christian Europeans regained control of two important and accessible sugar-producing centres, Toledo and Sicily.

To find Europe's first sweets, it is necessary to follow the progress of sugar, because wherever sugar was exported, refined or traded, sweets are found in its shadow. To begin with, sugar, or variations on sugar – powdered sugar and sugar candy (of which more later) – was imported from the East on its own. Sweetmeats followed, in the form of candied and preserved citrus fruit, called sucket in England. Of the Europeans, it was the Venetians who got to sugar first. The modern view of beautiful, sinking Venice, the epitome of faded grandeur, belies the truth that this voracious city state, once an appendage of the Byzantine empire, operated amorally in its dogged pursuit of riches – and very successfully so after 1100. Venice had culti-vated trade links with the Middle East for centuries, and there is a record of a new sugar warehouse being built in the city as early as 966. The sugar from that warehouse was exported to central Europe, the Black Sea and the Slav countries. Given Venice's status as a hub of trade, it would be remarkable if the taste of sugar had not attained an even wider orbit by this date.

It was during the period of the Crusades that Venice, always in competition with Genoa and Pisa, took decisive control of the export market for spices, via the ports and permanent 'factories' it controlled at the eastern end of the Mediterranean. The trade worked both ways, since Venice also acted as a supplier of cereals, metals, wood, cloth, arms and other products to the crusading armies. The nature of this relationship is exemplified by the way Venice provided the funds and logistics for an attack on Constantinople by forces of the fourth Crusade led by the Count of Champagne in 1203; Venice's reward was control of the city's docks, and therefore its sea trade, including the lucrative sugar connections. Similar canny investments at this time secured control of ports on the Greek coast. And Crete, where the Arabs had established sugar plantations, was simply bought for cash (its old name, Candia, became the term for a large-crystalled grade of sugar, and later formed the root of the word candy). Venice was officially a crusading state, but it spent more time fighting the forces of Pisa than those of Islam. Its most serious rival, Genoa, though possibly even more ruthless and cynical than Venice, was so riven with political infighting and changes of government that it was never able to mount a lasting challenge to Venetian supremacy.

So, as part of its portfolio of money-making schemes, Venice helped create and then responded to the explosion in demand in post-Crusades Europe for sugar and other new spices ('old' spices were pepper and saffron, long known in Europe). Sugar converged on Venice from all points of the compass in the Mediterranean: from Spain and Morocco in the west, Tunisia and Sicily in the south, Damascus and Antioch in the east, and of course from Constantinople. Venice also had strong links with Egypt via the port of Alexandria, one of the destinations of the caravan routes from China and India. Traders from the Italian city states would travel north across the Swiss Alps with their stocks of spices, join the Rhine for the journey through Germany into France, and so on to the fairs at Champagne, where they traded with Flemish wool merchants who had come south. The price of the Venetians' exotic cargoes would steadily rise on the journey, as each staging point charged its own toll. They would then return to the East, where there was a great appetite for textiles. In Alexandria, Venetian entrepreneurs traded metals, textiles and slaves for alum, wheat, sugar and – as a lucrative sideline – sweetmeats.

Sugar itself was exported in solid conical loaves of various sizes, since a cone-shaped mould was in standard use wherever sugar was refined. We tend to think of sugar as a pure, white and unvarying substance, but the difficulty and expense of refining meant that until the mid nineteenth century there were many more grades of sugar than today, and that a batch or loaf of sugar was by no means always white – and if it looked white on the outside, it may have been brown within. Given that it took mankind more than two millennia to perfect the science of sugar refining, it is ironic that brown sugar and 'unrefined' sugar (that is, partly refined sugar) are now more expensive than pure white sugar, and that the cheaper 'brown' sugars are simply white sugar dyed with molasses, with little alteration to the flavour, because we believe it looks more natural that way.

Balducci Pegolotti, an early-fourteenth-century Florentine trader, listed various types of sugar in his handbook, which is full of savvy tips for fellow merchants. Pegolotti dealt in a dizzying array of commodities, and under the heading of spices comes everything from mercury to wax, indigo to cotton, glue to olive oil, as well as five kinds of loaf sugar, in order of quality: mucchera, cafetino, bambillonia, musciatto and dommaschino. The colour and cost of these loaves varied widely. A sugar loaf looks a little like a bomb, which is apt, given the incendiary effect sugar was to have on the palate of Europe. The historian Carole Shammas has suggested: 'The English population was quite familiar with [sugar] long before the sixteenth century. Their acquaintanceship, however, took the form of small lumps received as gifts or as special treats.' This is a guess, but it is a persuasive one: the implication is that the sugar loaf, as a luxury, was naturally suited, at the retail end, to be sold in small quantities with relative ease on the part of the shopkeeper.

A loaf of sugar was a common sight in grocers' shops into the twentieth century, where it would be scraped or attacked with special sugar cutters until the requisite amount of sugar was detached in granules and uneven lumps, and then ground down to a powder if necessary – just as it had been since medieval times. The only modern echo of this form of sugar is the knobbly brown or white sugar lump served with coffee in smartish restaurants and cafés. (The French brand À La Perruche proudly labels its individually packed, vacuum-sealed sugar lumps, printed with an excellent picture of a parrot, as 'pure cane'.) The historical connection is hardly a selling point, since few people today can recall the sound of sugar being scraped, although one Margaret Thatcher fondly recalled the sugar loaves in her father's grocer's shop.

In the final stage of refining, the loaves would be suspended in racks, the tapered end pointing down, and any remaining impurities and moisture would drip out. That was the theory. In practice, sugars from different places had reputations which fluctuated wildly over time. The medieval sugar merchant needed to know the quality to expect, and the market value, of at least ten different grades of sugar. When judging a batch of sugar loaves, a good rule of thumb was its apparent whiteness and hardness. Egyptian sugar (known as Alexandrian or Babylonian sugar) was of consistently good quality during the

Middle Ages: the traveller Simone Sigoli praised the sugar of Cairo as 'the best in the world, white as snow and hard as stone', which became something of a benchmark. Even in 1820 a confectionery manual specifies: 'Loaf-sugar should be fine, white, dry, and difficult to break, and present a sparkling appearance when broken.' The Arab chronicler Ibn Battuta travelled up the Nile in 1336 and poetically claimed that the very walls of the port of Damietta were made of sugar, and noted how: 'At Cairo at the serais every Friday travellers were served with sweetmeats, and at Maulaway, where there were eleven sugar factories, the poor people came into the boiling house without interference to soak their bread in the hot syrup.'

When a consignment of sugar arrived in Venice from the Middle East, north Africa or the southern Mediterranean, it might be black with impurities, so it was often necessary to refine it again to make it saleable. This practice was known as double-refining, although for sweetmaking it was generally the best treble-refined (or royal) sugar, almost white, that was called for. This third refinement was usually accomplished in the destination city of the sugar. There were sugar refineries in Venice from 1470, and soon afterwards at Bologna, and the technology was eventually exported to all the major port cities of Europe – the first refinery in London is recorded in the 1540s. (A century later John Evelyn, touring the light industry of Bristol, as you do, enjoyed 'a collation of eggs fried in the sugar furnace'.) With typical opportunism, the Venetian coppersmiths dominated the market for the large cauldrons needed in the refineries.

Medieval Venice had to share the spoils of sugar brokering with Genoa and the port of Pavia, and later its inland neighbour Milan and the northern European centres – notably the ports of the Hanseatic League. So although Venice dominated the scene, sugar found its way into Europe via hundreds of other trade routes; the southern French ports, such as Marseilles, were important conduits, and the Catalans had established their own lucrative links with sugar traders in northern Europe (one of the earliest sweets manuals, a treatise on comfit-making, was written in Barcelona in the 1470s). But there was still a lot of money to be made in Venice. The Cornaro (or Corner) family emerged as the dominant Venetian sugar-trading dynasty, and one of their coups, in the fifteenth century, was taking control of the sugar island of Cyprus by marrying into and financially supporting the royal family. The island's sugar industry had been consolidated in the thirteenth century by the crusading Knights Templars and Hospitallers, retreating from Syria, but the Cornaros had since established a lucrative monopoly on the island's sugar. When the family palace overlooking the Grand Canal burned down (or caramelised; the fire started in the sugar store in the attic), the Cornaros were able to pay for the best and commissioned Jacopo Sansovino, the Doge's architect, to rebuild their new palace in the magnificent form of the Palazzo Corner della Ca'Grande.

Early medieval accounts and inventories show that ready-made sweets often accompanied sugar exports from the Arab lands – Spain in particular. Sugar made up the bulk of the cargo, but sweetmeats, mostly in the form of preserved fruits, commanded an even higher price. The earliest reliable mention of sugar in Britain is contained in the late-twelfth-century accounts of the household of Henry II, where it is listed among spices as part of the kitchen expenditure. His grandson, Henry III, is on record in 1226 as having instructed the Mayor of Winchester, one William the Spicer, to obtain for him three pounds of Alexandrine sugar, 'if so much is to be had'. Clearly it was a rare and highly expensive commodity at this time. However, by 1288, the household of Edward I was using more than 6,000lb in one year, including a large amount of sugar candy in the form of rose and violet sugar (of which more in a moment). It is reasonable to suppose that most wealthy households in England had a store of sugar by the mid thirteenth century, although honey must have continued as the everyday sweetening agent. The first recorded bulk sugar import to England – 10,000lb of sugar and 1,000lb of sugar candy – into

Southampton from Venice, was in 1319, although this did not turn out to be an auspicious start for the sugar trade: the ship's Venetian captain, who had traded his sugar for English wool and was heading to Flanders to sell it, was murdered by the treacherous English crew and thrown overboard.

So what were these early medieval sweets? There were preserved fruits, pastes and suckets (candied orange or lemon peel), comfits (little seeds or roots coated in sugar), marzipan and other almond sweets, gummy pastilles, lozenges, candied flowers and also *manus christi*, the most mysterious sweet of all time. Nougats and nut brittles, or *croccantes*, were favoured in southern Europe. We shall examine all of these sweets later in this chapter.

The arcane secrets of the Arab sweetmakers were gradually discovered by European artisans, and the precise chronology of the emergence of a European confectionery industry is difficult to gauge. With most medieval sweets, we are left guessing whether the finished article had been made 100, 1,000 or 2,000 miles away from where it was eventually scoffed. A comparative study of the inventories and feast menus of the twelfth century onwards, when sweets first began to appear in Europe, and of the cookbooks and professional manuals of some 500 years later, reveals that very few sweets introduced at an early stage later fell from favour entirely. Although their relative popularity may have waxed and waned, and recipes, names and ingredients varied slightly according to time and place, the basic forms of sweets remained essentially unchanged after their first introduction. The first confectioners of Venice are recorded by 1150, and during the medieval period the city's master confectioners became famous throughout Europe. It appears that sweets were being independently manufactured on a significant scale in Sicily and Venice, and perhaps in other northern Italian cities, by about 1200. At this time the confectioners concentrated mainly on the art of preserving and candying fruits; hard, sugary sweets were the province of the apothecaries. The idea that confectionery was really an Italian skill endured into the nineteenth century, and hundreds of Italian artisans reaped the benefit of the reputation that preceded them in the rest of Europe. (It has even endured in the respectable literature of food history: one Italian academic, writing in 1994, described a mention of sugar in a fourteenth-century Anglo-Norman work as 'precocious' – which is itself a precocious assertion.) It is true, however, that the influx of Italian culinary artistry resulting from the arrival of the Medicis into France after the marriages of Catherine de'Medici to Henri II in 1533 and Marie de'Medici to Henri IV in 1600 did have a serious impact on French confectionery skills, and specifically the art of moulding sugar into ornate sculptures and table decorations. It has also been suggested that the verdancy of fifteenth-century Piedmont, and the consequent abundance of high-quality fruit and vegetables, led to a blossoming of cuisine, including confectionery, in northern Italy, especially when compared with France, which was recovering from the ravages of the Hundred Years War.

Sugar candy was the most basic sweet to be exported from the East, and it accompanied the earliest cargoes of sugar. On the cusp between sugar and sweet, sugar candy was at the very top end of the sugar price scale. The method was simple: sugar was dissolved in water, boiled down and allowed to crystallise slowly into lumps that could either be sucked, like a boiled sweet, or used as a concentrated sweetener in the kitchen, where it was considered superior even to treble-refined sugar for sweetmaking purposes. This sugar candy does not sound like much of a sweet, but it was highly favoured in Europe, particularly in the versions known as rose or violet sugar: small, fragrant crystalline nobules flavoured with flower essences. A ninth-century Arabic treatise on trade, the *Al-Tabassur bi-l-tigara*, incidentally mentions various Persian sweet products made for export with sugar, and it includes sugar candy from Ahwaz in the Persian Gulf. There were also fruit syrups, rosewater and candied capers (which do not appear to have caught on in Europe). In medieval household inventories the amount of rose sugar or violet sugar listed is often considerably more than that for normal white sugar. It is a testament to the power of sugary sweetness that sugar candy, the simplest sweet of all, remained popular for some 900 years after it was introduced to northern Europe in about 1100. To take an example from about the midpoint of this timeframe, the 1685 inventory of the travelling chest of a young undergraduate, fresh up to Oxford, includes not only oranges, lemons, raisins and nutmegs, but also one pound of brown sugar candy and a quarter pound of white sugar candy, with which to make new friends. In the United States recently, coloured and flavoured sugar candy on traditional wooden sticks has been undergoing a renaissance.

Another simple confection, and one of the earliest to find favour in Europe, was the pennet, also known as penned, penyde or penid – a word derived from the Persian *fanid* via the Arabic *penid*. This was a simple stick of soft, pulled white candy, sometimes formed into a twist. Pennets were supposed to be good for colds and consumption, and at the close of the thirteenth century they were prescribed to Edward I's six-year-old son in the last months of his little life, along with liquorice and sugar candy. All to no avail, alas. An echo of these associations remains in the fact that sticks of rock are usually flavoured with peppermint or oil of wintergreen, both of which have medicinal connotations.

The most evocative and obscure medieval sweet was *manus christi*, which translates as 'the hand of Christ'. It dates from the time when it was believed that a sweet could save a life, and it crops up time and again in medieval European account books, inventories and medical handbooks, although every description is slightly different. This confusion, coupled with the esteem in which it was held and the way it had vanished completely by the early nineteenth century, makes *manus christi* perhaps the most mysterious sweet of all.

Manus christi is usually described as a stick of hard sugar candy flavoured with violets, cinnamon or rosewater. Its special nature and potentially miraculous power are reflected in the not infrequent addition of gold leaf to many *manus christi* recipes. There was a strong belief that flakes of gold and silver, or even crushed gemstones, would prove medicinally efficacious in most circumstances. But only if one could afford such extravagance: a gold-flecked and translucent sugar stick, delicately flavoured, was a sweet that was generally reserved for the rich. *Manus christi* was treated as a cordial rather than as an emergency measure, taken occasionally or regularly, depending on a person's general level of hypochondria, much as we might take vitamin pills today. Henry VIII's apothecary regularly restocked his *manus christi* supply (as well as rhubarb pills to keep the royal hawks in health), and in 1516 a pound of *manus christi* was a solicitous gift from Thomas Allen to the Earl of Shrewsbury. This healing hand of Christ in sweet form also crossed the Atlantic early on: it is mentioned, complete with a smattering of gold leaf, in the late-seventeenth/early-eighteenth-century cookbook bequeathed to Martha Washington (the president's wife). But there are bewildering anomalies in the history of *manus christi*. Sometimes it is a liquid cordial; apothecaries invented versions containing crushed pearls (*manus christi perlata*); and in one late-fourteenth-century Parisian recipe book it becomes a type of marzipan. The truth about *manus christi* is that the name was used for a variety of expensive medicines based on crystallised sugar, and very few of them had appreciable healing properties. What united them all was their expensiveness and their deliciousness.

Preserved or candied fruits, together with fruit pastes and syrups, were the most decadent sweet exports from the East in the early medieval period. Fresh oranges, lemons, limes and tamarinds all fetched a premium in Europe, but citrus fruits boiled in water and then preserved in sugar also gained in popularity as more people tried them. Of course they did: they were delicious, expensive, exotic and unnecessary. The sugar made the fruit taste sweet and sexy in its syrup, and also preserved it so it could be consumed in winter – a luxurious perversion, a frisson of which is experienced today when one enjoys imported out-of-season fruit.

At his coronation at Avignon in 1344, Pope Clement VI enjoyed 'candied fruits of many colours' for the eighth and last course of the feast held in his honour. The colour of preserved fruits was extremely important to the confectioners: rich reds, greens, golds and oranges, enhanced artificially if necessary, that make the pastel tones of nature insipid. But the appeal of these sweetmeats was not always decorative and gastronomic, it could be medicinal, too. Nostradamus, the healer and seer, produced a book filled with discursive recipes for fruit preserves and other remedies which we would call sweets; his most tempting recipe is for pumpkin sweets, preserved in syrup and coated in sugar. In the introduction to this work, published in 1555, Nostradamus stresses the medical application and decorative quality of preserved fruits: 'If they are preserved in sugar, that will protect them against decay and they will acquire a very desirable sweet taste. In cases of necessity the human body receives more strength from a small quantity of such fruits than from many other foods [. . .] And when you have made something beautiful, its attractiveness, goodness and taste will be all the greater.' Nostradamus knew many things, and one of them was that for the confectioner, as for the pâtissier, appearance is as important as flavour.

Even homegrown fruit is unavailable for part of the year, so the technique of candying was soon applied to all kinds of fruit, and also flowers. Brillat-Savarin, the eighteenth-century 'philosopher of the kitchen', noted that candying allows us 'to enjoy the fragrance of those fruits and flowers long after the period fixed by Nature for their duration' – a piquant triumph over the elements for this rational man of the Enlightenment, and a pleasure it is easy to overlook in these days of canning, freezing and refrigeration. The triumph of this technique is echoed in the title of one early-seventeenth-century recipe: 'Clusters of Grapes kept till Easter', and confectionery manuals often included an almanac of the year, with monthly reminders of those fruits that will be ready to preserve. A preserved clementine wetly glistens and the bitter tang of the peel can be discerned through the sugar carapace. A gentle bite, and the sealed sweetness of the pulp seeps out, a perfect balance between fruit flavour and lucent syrup. With a preserved pear, it is the graininess of the flesh, suspended in syrup but grating against the tongue, that is the main pleasure.

Preserved fruits must have been irresistible to the English, whose enduring love for fruit was noted by visitors such as a Venetian ambassador who in 1618 marvelled at the way Londoners consumed raw fruit in the streets, 'like so many goats'. Fresh fruit was considered digestively detrimental in the early medieval period, possibly because too much of it can lead to an upset stomach, and that minor ailment was mistakenly linked with fatal cases of diarrhoea, particularly in infants, that were in reality caused by contaminated water supplies. But by the sixteenth century, fruit was seen as an innocent but virtuous pleasure, with the healthful overtones of the countryside that the English have always found irresistible. Dairy products enjoyed the same reputation, so a dish of fruit and cream was the epitome of simple, healthy living. In the late sixteenth century, the poet Michael Drayton described just such a fruity, creamy convocation in a rustic setting, as a feast for a shepherd king:

> Green plumbs, and wildings, cherries chief of feast,
> Fresh cheese, and downsets, curds, and clouted cream,
> Spic'd syllabubs, and cyder of the best.

The process of candying is an investiture that makes even an apple majestic. The fruit is repeatedly bathed in an increasingly strong mixture of glutinous syrup – perhaps augmented with the fruit's pulp, or a white wine – until it is entirely suffused with sweetness. Then it is basted with sparkling sugar that hardens into a frosty coat, or else a shiny, smooth patina. The colour of the fruit deepens, and its flavour is enriched and transformed by the sugar. The friable flesh of a crunchy confection is the result of this sugary transubstantiation.

There is not much evidence of the consumption of preserved fruits in the medieval Islamic world – any that were produced were perhaps intended primarily for the export market. In any event, it appears that preserving was one of the skills quickly transmuted and developed by the first European confectioners. It was the most practical – if not the cheapest – way of enjoying exotic fruit, either whole, or in the case of pineapples and other large items, in chunks. Many modern sugar-coated boiled sweets, devised for the mass market in the nineteenth century, are astonishingly close imitations or cheaper versions of these high-class medieval fruit preserves: the ever-popular boiled sweets called pineapple cubes, for example. Dried figs, dates and raisins – universally known as raisins of Corinth – were not sweets, of course, but they were transported and sold in company with sugar and sweets. Dried fruits were cheaper than sugar and sweets, and as such were an important alternative new source of sweetness for the many who could not afford the sugary luxuries. They are still a useful 'healthy' alternative to sweets for very young children, who develop a great passion for them. The Arab method of making delicious sweets out of fresh dates by stuffing them with marzipan was echoed in the medieval French sweet known as 'Capuchin nougat': a dried fig with a green walnut inside.

The sucket was the humblest member of the noble family of fruit preserves. These little sweets, known as *succade* in France and *succata* or *zuccata* in Italy (where they were most often made with pumpkin), were usually shards of orange and lemon peel, boiled in water, reboiled in sugar syrup, sometimes with rosewater, and then coated in sugar. The name survives as *sucette*, modern French for a lollipop. The peel of the citron, a type of huge, coarse lemon, was (and is) considered the best for candying, and a strange five-lobed variety, called *fo shu kan* or Buddha's Hand, is grown specifically for candying today in China. In 1420 an Italian galley at the Port of London is recorded as offloading eleven jars of 'sitrenade' – the sitren refers to citron – which was the lemon variety of the sweet known as sucket. A version of sucket is still a perennial favourite in England: this is not made of real peel, but consists of a sweet fruit jelly, sugared and made in imitation of slices of orange and lemon. It is still made by hand, as it has to be, in a factory in Carlisle: I saw a team of ladies stand at immensely long tables rolling out a long snake of sugary orange and lemon jelly, which then has a layer of yellow 'pith' and another layer of orange or yellow 'rind' painstakingly added to it (all sugar), before it is sliced up and packaged.

The sucket is an excellent example of a sweet that has endured the vicissitudes of the centuries almost without change. Parings of oranges or lemons were either boiled up in sugar syrup or, as in Gervase Markham's recipe in *The English Hus-Wife* (1615), boiled in water and then coated in a syrup that had been repeatedly boiled and augmented by egg whites. One recipe in *The Complete Confectioner*, of 1789, 'by a person late an apprentice to the well known Messrs Negroni and Witten, of Berkeley Square' – in fact one Frederic Nutt – is for 'lemon prawlongs', no relation to the sweet known today as a praline. The name may have changed, but this prawlong of Berkeley Square is a sucket: 'Take some lemons, and peel the rind off in four quarters; take all the white off from the inside of the rind; cut the yellow rind in pieces, about one inch long and about the tenth part of an inch wide; have a pan of boiling syrup on the fire, and let it boil till it comes almost to carimel, then put the prawlongs in, and stir them very much with a large wooden spoon till they are cold; put them in a large sieve, and shake them just to let the sugar that does not stick to them go through the sieve; lastly put them in your box, and keep them in a dry place.' These precise instructions smack of years of first-hand experience, a quality which is by no means always the case with confectionery or other cookery manuals, in which plagiarism was rife.

A variation on the sucket theme in Mr Nutt's manual is the

recipe for Seville orange jumbles: discs of rind first dried, then boiled in syrup, then dried again on top of the stove for two or three days. (Jumbles, also known as jumbals, later came to refer to nutty, ring-shaped biscuits.) Another member of the sucket family is described in an elaborate recipe for 'millefruit rock candy', a mass candying of fruit that requires an extraordinary utensil, one of the boxes of which Mr Nutt is fond. This box is one foot long and eight inches wide, made of tin, with a plug-hole at the bottom and wires stretched across it. Fruits and roots were placed across the wires and the box was filled with syrup. This was placed in a hot oven for three hours and then the syrup was let out of the plughole. The box, with the dripping fruits, was put back into the stove for half an hour and, as Mr Nutt explains in the coup de grâce, 'then take them out and you will find it will be candied all round them'.

A similar piece of apparatus was developed for the manu-facture of sugar candy. John Nott's *Cook's and Confectioner's Dictionary* of 1723 explains that to make it, you must pour a sugar solution 'into an earthen Pot, in which small Sticks are laid across; set the Pot into a Stove, and the Sugar will coagulate about the Sticks'. A mid-seventeenth-century medical manual promises that after fifteen to twenty days of this process, the sugar candy will be 'shining like Crystal' (though it also 'hurts the teeth'). Other recipes require even more time: the one in Martha Washington's cookbook suggests leaving it in the stove for three weeks followed by a week's drying out. The idea was that when enough sugar candy had precipitated, it was broken off the sticks and placed in a box for munching and crunching later. But surely even a skilled confectioner would have experi-enced problems getting all the sugar candy off the sticks? If the sticks were 'laid across' or placed upright in the jar, the ends would have remained clean, and the only thing to do would have been to grasp the stick and lick the sugar candy off. Here we probably have the genesis of the lollipop or popsicle – supposedly invented in America in the nineteenth century and not on commercial sale before that date, but most likely an updated, mass-produced version of sugar candy on a stick.

Suckets were standard sweetmeats into the nineteenth century, and the healthy associations of citrus fruit, pulp, juice and peel were enduring. This may provide a clue to the truth behind an inconclusive anecdote regarding Dr Johnson, as related by Boswell:

> It seems he had frequently been observed at the Club to put into his pocket the Seville oranges, after which he had squeezed the juice of them into the drink which he made for himself. Beauclerk and Garrick talked of it to me, and seemed to think he had a strange unwillingness to be discovered. We could not divine what he did with them, and this was the bold question to be put. I saw on his table the spoils of the preceding night, some fresh peels nicely scraped and cut into pieces. 'Oh, sir,' said I, 'I now partly see what you do with the squeezed oranges which you put into your pocket at the Club.'
>
> Johnson: 'I have a great love for them.'
>
> Boswell: 'And pray, Sir, what do you do with them? You scrape them, it seems, very neatly, and what next?'
>
> Johnson: 'Let them dry, Sir.'
>
> Boswell: 'And what next?'
>
> Johnson: 'Nay, Sir, you shall know their fate no further.'

The mystery of Dr Johnson's orange peel remains. It is hard to imagine Johnson indulging in the womanly art of candying and easy to see him heeding the wisdom of the Ancients, so the most likely explanation is that he followed Pliny the Elder's example and ingested the raw orange peel, either suffused in water, or nibbled raw before bed, as an aid to digestion.

The story of confectionery is one of enterprise and continual innovation, so naturally the art of candying was not long confined to citrus peel alone. One of the earliest pieces of evidence for such diversification is a gift of *zuccata* from one Messer Datini, a fourteenth-century Prato merchant, to a crony. Datini's accompanying note announces, 'There is no finer gift today than a box of zuccata, for a sponge cake is fit for woman in childbirth, but a zuccata is for gentlemen.' This is an early example of male embarrassment about sweets, viewed as a weakness of women and children. But the macho Datini could hardly argue that his gentlemen friend lacked a sweet tooth, when his gift of candied pumpkin weighed no less than ten pounds.

Confectioners attempted to candy almost any vegetable matter they could lay their hands on, particularly cheap and plentiful local produce, or roots, stems, flowers and fruits that were supposed to have medicinal properties. Soft fruit was generally avoided, because if you push it you'll mush it and that candy ain't dandy. Unripe soft fruits could withstand the process, however, and preserving them was a useful way of using up windfall plums, damsons or apricots; sometimes the stones were left inside them – for the ease of the cook, and to help the fruit retain its shape. This is the sugarplum, although the term was never confined to preserved plums alone, but came to refer to almost any sweetmeat. The name was perhaps a reference to the little 'stalks' of wire sometimes inserted into preserved fruits, as decoration and also to make them easier to handle. Green walnuts were another popular candying subject; the botanist John Gerard, in his *Herball* (1597), says that made into a succade, they are 'a most pleasant and delectable meat, comfort the stomach and expel poison'.

The likely suspects for candying from the fruit garden were just waiting to be plucked out of the air – apples, pears, apricots, peaches, plums, damsons, quinces, gooseberries, cherries, barberries and so on. But the confectioners dug deeper. Into the earth, in fact. All kinds of roots and stalks were being candied in England by the sixteenth century: root ginger had been available for some two hundred years and was a hugely popular flavouring, and there was parsley and fennel root, elecampane (a bitter medicinal root made palatable through candying, and still on sale as an asthma treatment in the mid nineteenth century, in the form of flat candy cakes), angelica (the only stalk still regularly candied; it is used as a cake decoration) and sea holly, or eringo.

This last, a root which tastes a little like parsnip, was generally believed to be a powerful aphrodisiac, a notion that has been traced back to the Romans. In *The Merry Wives of Windsor*, Shakespeare has a lusty Falstaff exclaim: 'Let the sky rain potatoes, let it thunder to the tune of Greensleeves, hail kissing comfits and stone eringoes: let there be a tempest of provocation.' The world centre of eringo – or 'ringo' – cultivation was the Essex town of Colchester, which enjoyed a thriving trade in this candied root right up until the mid nineteenth century. Unfortunately the sexual connotations of the town waned as the demand for eringo did, and Colchester today does not have a particularly erotic atmosphere. Orchid roots also had aphrodisiacal associations: they were collectively known as satyricons, after the rutting fauns of mythology, and were also candying subjects. Among other suckets, candied lettuce stalks sound rather appealing, especially if given their French name, *gorges d'ange* (angels' throats). And there was always medical authority to turn to as an excuse for eating sweets. The ex-monk Andrew Boorde, in his *Dyetary of Helth* of 1542, justifies some really obscure sucket ingredients: 'The roots of borage and bugloss sodden tender [boiled] and made in a succade, doth engender blood and doth set a man in a temperance.'

The majority of these fruit sweetmeats were available in two guises. They could be wet, swimming in rich syrup, stored in jars and eaten with a spoon or (later) a fork. Or they could be dry, in lumps or little chips, coated in sugar and kept in boxes between thick sheets of paper. The number of fruits available to be preserved or candied, wet or dry, meant there was a wide range. In Rabelais' *Gargantua et Pantagruel* (1552), the greedy god Manduce is presented with 'preserves dry as well as liquid, 78 kinds'. This wet/dry distinction is rigorously maintained in the confectionery manuals, and remained important until the late nineteenth century. A nice example of the demarcation can be found in a description of a food fight involving Oliver

Cromwell. This is related in an anti-Cromwell treatise of 1664, *The Court and Kitchin of Joan Cromwell*, ungallantly couched as a sly attack on the domestic failings of 'the wife of the late usurper' (all the recipes attributed to her are boring and dated). The incident, which is supposed to have occurred at the end of a banquet given by Cromwell in 1656, could easily be dismissed as mischievous propaganda, but there is something odd about the precision of the narrative that gives it a ring of truth. The public were allowed to attend such feasts as spectators, and one such,

> a Big Bellied Woman, a Spectator, neer Cromwell's table, upon the serving thereof with Sweetmeats; desiring a few dry candies of apricocks, Col. Pride sitting at the same, instantly threw into her Apron a Conserve of Wet, with both his hands, and stained it all over; when as if that had been the sign, Oliver catches up his Napkin and throws it at Pride, he at him again, while all that Table were engaged in the Scuffle.

At this point, all the other Parliamentarians at the feast rise and crowd round to get a view of the commotion. The implication seems to be either that Cromwell and his parliamentary colleagues were yobboes, chucking these wet sweets and napkins around, or that the parsimonious Cromwell was upset at the waste of expensive sweets given away to the commoners he lorded it over.

There were other fruit sweets devised in the medieval period, the ancestors of multi-coloured modern fruit jellies. The names for these sweets make them sound more like breakfast or teatime delicacies, but it is necessary to forget the modern meanings of these words for a moment. Take marmalade. Today, this is a jam-like condiment made of oranges and sugar, semi-liquid and flecked with strips of peel that look like deep-sea creatures swimming in an orange ocean. But the name is derived from the medieval Portuguese *marmelada*, a stiff paste that was cut in slices rather than spread. The word derives from the Portuguese *marmelo*, or quince, since this fragrant yet knobbly item was originally the favoured fruit for preserving, and it became the term used by the mid sixteenth century to describe all kinds of fruit preserves, not glutinous and syrupy as they are today, but stiff enough to be made into individual sweets if so desired. The Portuguese gained a reputation as the masters of the art of preserving fruit, and oranges were known as portyngales in England in honour of this link. The art of preserving appears to have been quickly mastered by artisans in most European countries, taking their lead from Portugal and Spain, but it is hard to discern precisely when and where these developments occurred. The most common modern version of *marmelada* is the membrillo (quince jelly) of Spain, eaten with manchego cheese, but this is rougher in texture than the medieval version would have been. A clear version of quince *marmelada* was (and is) called *cotignac* in France and quidonny in Britain, and the word came to be applied to a wide variety of fruit conserves, made with pears, peaches, apples and damsons as well as oranges and lemons. Spreadable marmalade, made from oranges specifically, was devised only in the eighteenth century, probably in Scotland. It is possible that the technique of making these marmalades and other conserves, by boiling up equal amounts of fruit pulp and sugar in water, was inherited from the Levant, where confectioners were skilled at melding fruit with sugar largely because of the ubiquity of sherbet. This is the beverage from which all modern soft drinks and all syrups are descended (and also a lemony alcoholic drink called shrub, popular in the eighteenth century and still made commercially in Bristol). The main ingredients of sherbet were sugar syrup or sugar candy – in Turkey a dark pink substance called *gul sekeri* – and any one of scores of fruit juices and pulps (usually lemon). However, a seventeenth-century visitor to Turkey described this base sherbet flavour not as a liquid but as a type of fruit paste. And Francis Bacon, writing in 1626, notes: 'They have in Turkey and the East certaine Confections, which they call Servets [sherbets], which are like to Candied

Conserves and . . . these they dissolve in Water, and thereof make their Drinke, because they are forbidden wine by their Law.' Perhaps fruit pastes were used in a variety of ways in the East. It is possible, however, that there were existing recipes for such things in England, before the influx of Eastern ideas, since the 'mosses' which are mentioned in recipe books by the seventeenth century – fruity mixtures of varying consistencies – sound typically English and may descend from medieval dishes such as 'apulmoss', which was made of apples, honey and almond milk.

Marmalades and other conserves should really be classed as wet sweetmeats. They were sometimes called fruit pastes in the early confectionery manuals. A large dish of such a marmalade or conserve could be simply cut in pieces, or individual sweets could be shaped with moulds, or impressed with mottoes or heraldic crests. Edward, Duke of Guelders, departing for war against Prussia in 1369, took with him no less than forty-six pounds of sweets, including quantities of pinenut and ginger comfits, and also five pounds each of red rusen and white rusen, which were stiff conserves moulded into the shapes of various fruits. Paste of Genoa became the generic term for high-quality fruit paste, whether made in Italy or not. The food historian Maguelonne Toussaint-Samat has suggested that Genoa became known for fruit-paste confectionery because it was one of the principal destinations of the early refugees from Spain, fleeing the Inquisition (southern Spain had been the last stronghold of the Arab empire, and confectionery skills endured).

Stiff fruit jellies, coated in sugar, as well as the wobbly ones for the pudding table, were greatly in favour during the eighteenth century, when the thickening agent used was sometimes isinglass, that strange substance garnered from the swim bladders of sturgeons and less glamorous fish, such as cod and hake. Fruit or flower syrups became an important aspect of European confectionery, either as versions of sherbet – cooling drinks for hot days – or, more commonly, as a mask for medicines. Another type of conserved fruit sweetmeat persists as the unappetisingly named 'leather', thin layers of fruit paste, made of fruit and sugar in equal parts, which are hung out to dry like linen if it is hot enough. This leather is known as *armadine* in the Middle East, and it is found across the Balkans and in some more unlikely places: a peach leather is a speciality of Charleston, South Carolina.

Candied flowers were another irresistible delicacy. Violets and rosepetals were the most popular candidates for this floral frostification, although blue borage, rosemary, pinks (dianthus) and marigold flowers were among other flowers deemed suitable. Candied flowers have a kind of archaeological appeal: petrified, brittle yet somehow representing the very essence of themselves. These petals were not just used for decorating food, as they are today (the exquisite candied violets of Toulouse are the best), but eaten as sweets in their own right or used as an ingredient in other sweets. Marigold petals were candied 'in wedges, the Spanish fashion', and in fact any sweet containing flowers was delineated 'Spanish'.

Rosepetals candied on the bush, outdoors in the garden, are perhaps the most epicurean of sweets. Sir Hugh Platt, in his delightful *Delightes for Ladies* (1602), suggests simply pouring sugar syrup over the living flowers of a rose bush and leaving them to dry in the sun. A floral barbecue. William Rabisha's recipe in *The Whole Body of Cookery* (1661) is more precise. He suggests candying the petals on a sunny day: 'Turn them often in the sun, sometimes sprinkling Rosewater, and sometimes searsing [sieving] sugar on them, until they be enough, and come to your liking, and being thus done, you may keep them.' If that is not decadent enough, Elizabeth Grey, Countess of Kent, in *Secrets in Physick and Chyrurgery* (1653), gives instructions for spotting the candied flowers with real gold leaf.

The aristocratic confectioner was by no means a contradiction in terms. Candying or preserving fruit and flowers and jam- and comfit-making were considered dainty occupations for the leisure hours of a lady. Sir Hugh Platt's is perhaps the most charming of the early cookbooks, packed with confectionery recipes for the genteel lady. Sir Hugh gallantly refers to his female readers in his verse dedication:

> Of sweetes the sweetest I will now commend,
> To sweetest creatures that the earth doth beare:
> These are the Saints to whome I sacrifice
> Perfumes and conserves both of plum and peare.

A talent for confectionery in a woman, therefore, indicates a sweet disposition and a practical nature. These attributes, coupled with the prospect of a supply of free sweets for the husband, would surely transform any woman into a sugary siren irresistible to any man. One unlikely fringe benefit for a lady confectioner might be the possibility of sweet spicy scents perfuming the person – but this is a fantasy from the fevered imagination of a poet too shy to speak to a woman in person. The subject of Robert Herrick's 1648 poem, 'To the Most Fair and Lovely Mistress Anne Soame', was his cousin.

> So smell those odours that do rise
> From out the wealthy spiceries;
> So smell the flower of blooming clove,
> Or roses smothered in the stove . . .
> Thus sweet she smells, or what can be
> More liked by her, or loved by me.

Presumably a kissing cousin.

The professional confectioners must have used such books as well, for most of them are exhaustive compendia of previous works, filled with technical detail. It was not until the mid eighteenth century that artisans began to acknowledge that they were revealing the secrets of this gentle art for the benefit of the professional as well as the amateur. By that time, a proficiency with confectionery was considered a desirable or even necessary skill for a young wife to acquire. Herrick's fragrant pot-stirrer had been superseded by a virtuous utilitarianism. In Samuel Richardson's *Pamela* (1740), the young heroine lists sweetmaking among her wifely duties: 'I will assist your housekeeper, as I used to do, in the making of jellies, comfits, sweetmeats, marmalades, cordials; and to pot, and candy, and preserve.' This is also evidence that the art of confectionery was considered as much the skill of preserving fruits and making jam as it was of concocting the dry suckets and sweetmeats which we would today label exclusively as sweets. As late as 1760, Hannah Glasse was crediting various noble ladies with sweets recipes in her *Complete Confectioner*. Lady Allen and Lady Hewet are given a namecheck, and Lady Leicester has no fewer than three recipes, including 'Lady Leicester's Hollow Gumballs', made with a kind of lemony fondant.

What of fruit gums? Pastilles, lozenges, jellies, gums – all these choice chews were made with gum arabic or its cheaper substitute, gum tragacanth, generally called gum dragon (a much better name, and one worth sticking with). Gum arabic is obtained from the wounded bark of the acacia tree, which grows in north Africa, Arabia, north India and the Middle East, and gum dragon is from *Astragalus gummifer*, a tree found in Turkey and the Middle East. Gum dragon was a standard ingredient in the confectioner's store from the seventeenth century, although it was the French who became masters of the art of making gums, a process that was accelerated following their colonial incursions into north Africa (land of gum). Journeymen gum specialists from France were employed by sweetmakers throughout Europe; in England, it was Frenchmen who worked on the prototypes for fruit pastilles and fruit gums. At Rowntree in York, a roving confectioner called Claude Gaget called with a sample of his gums in 1879 and he was taken on immediately, with his pot and his boy. His sweets sold like wildfire. The quality of the gum has always been a problem, however. In *The Practical Confectioner* (1822), James Cox advises: 'Take some gum dragon, pick out all the dirt and black pieces from it . . .' And the same advice is being offered in *Skuse's*

Complete Confectioner of the 1950s, although a sieve rather than fingers is suggested.

The concept of chewy sweets was exported, of course, from the East, whence the gum came. The food historian Charles Perry has tracked down a reference to an early-medieval Arab sweet called *faludhaj*, which sounds like a chewier version of Turkish Delight. This is made from sugar, honey, nuts, oil, starch and gum arabic dissolved in rosewater; it is divided into squares when cool. This sweet, or indeed anything like it, does not appear to have been known in medieval Europe. Gumminess arrived in medicine. Preparations containing sugar and bound up in gum, called electuaries or lozenges, became commonplace in medieval pharmacy, after the Arabic model. (Versions of these preparations had crossed into the domain of pure confectionery, in the form of fruit pastilles, by the seventeenth century.) The presence of the gum means that the sweet dissolves slowly, which allows whatever herb or drug it contains to do its good work on one's throat at a leisurely pace. It appears that the word lozenge is related to *lauzinaj*, a kind of almond paste cake that is mentioned in a cookery book written in Baghdad in the twelfth century. But this delicacy contained no gum and was not cut into diamonds, so the relationship is obscure, beyond the etymological.

Pastilles are not so tricky as lozenges for the international confectionery historian, or his trainees. They are first referred to in the mid seventeenth century as useful vehicles for perishable medicaments. For example, the physician Richard Tomlinson states in 1657: 'The Cappadocians [from central Turkey] and Spaniards bring us every yeare Liquorice-Juice, condensed into Pastills.' It is not clear whether these pastilles were supposed to be eaten, or dissolved for use in other preparations. In the pharmacy, a pastille could also be a small pellet which gave off aromatic smoke when lit. There is an enduring story that pastilles were invented by one Giovanni Pastilla, a famous Italian confectioner who accompanied Marie de'Medici to France when she married Henri IV in 1600, but it is more likely that the word is descended from the Latin 'pastilla', meaning little cake. The one thing that is certain about pastilles is that they are always round. Otherwise, they can be made in a wide variety of flavours, and the word also came to be applied not just to gums but to all kinds of sweets. In François Massialot's *Nouvelle Instruction pour les Confitures* (1698) there are recipes for 'white' pastilles (lemon), as well as cinnamon and fennel pastilles, coloured red and white. In this book, a pastille can be long as well as round, a unique distinction in the literature, which spoils my earlier definition. The French continued to push the boundaries of pastille flavouring through the eighteenth century, with chocolate, saffron, coffee, violet, cachou, orange, cedar, musk, amber, violet, clove, raspberry and currant flavours added to the pantheon in books such as *Le Parfait Limonadier* (1705) by Pierre Masson. By 1838 and *Le Confiseur Moderne* of J.-J. Machet, we have snazzy pastilles made with rare and fine liqueurs: *Pastilles au Maraquin de Zara*, *Pastilles au Rossolis de Turin* and *Pastilles à l'Esprit de Vénus*.

The most evocative old-fashioned sweet is the comfit. The name is redolent of the sweet's own qualities: just as a sucket is nice to suck, a comfit is comforting. William Gunter, an eccentric London confectioner of the 1830s, used this wordplay (and liberal use of italics) to criticise French sweets as inferior to British: 'I have been exceedingly surprised to hear it asserted, that the French make *better* comfits than the English; they decidedly fail in this compound and would appear [. . .] to know as little of *Comfits* as *comfort*.' But there is no connection between the words comfort and comfit; as with sucket and 'suck it', their relationship is just a happy semantic collision.

The best definition of a comfit is that of the historian of early British confectionery, Laura Mason: 'A comfit is a little something, traditionally a spice or a nut, covered in a layer of hard sugar.' The key here, again, is the preserving qualities of sugar. It is possible that the comfits mentioned in the earliest records, imported from the East, were made up by Arab apothecaries and considered to be medicaments. The sugar coating preserved and enhanced the drug. But we will pay a visit to the chemist's in chapter six.

The 'little something' in a comfit could be whole seeds of fennel, coriander or aniseed, cloves, pieces of ginger or cinnamon, juniper berries, almonds, walnuts, dates, pine kernels or caraways – anything flavoursome and/or medicinal which could withstand the discomfiture of the comfiting process. Citrus peel or flesh were not suitable, but there is a reference to lemon pip comfits in the mid sixteenth century, and even comfits of melon, celery and cucumber seeds in mid-seventeenth-century France. These do not sound nice, but probably were. Mint and peppermint, so popular today, are not mentioned until the eighteenth century as suckable sweet flavours, and only became really popular in the mid nineteenth century – probably because of difficulties in making a strong enough mint-essence flavouring.

Comfit-making was seasonal, and the almanacs in confectionery manuals noted what ingredient would be ready when: François Massialot's *Court and Country Cook* (1702), for example (itself a translation of the *Nouvelle Instruction Pour Les Confitures* of 1698), notes that March is the season for violet comfits, and October is the time for comfits of must or sweet wine. Certain comfit flavours could become fashionable for a time: Pierre Pomet, in his *Compleat History of Drugs* (1712), mentions in passing that 'what is much in vogue in Paris is your green anise'. Sometimes a comfit was simply built around a piece of sugar candy – rather than a seed or root – or even made using the sugar in the pan alone, flavoured with rosewater, rose or violet essence, or musk. Musk comfits were also known as kissing comfits or muscadinoes, on account of the alluring aroma of musk, a reddish-brown substance obtained from the scent glands of male deer. Mixed with gum tragacanth, the aroma of musk was also captured in gummy lozenges. Caraway seeds, those warmly aromatic little items that crack on the teeth, were a favourite medieval flavour (they are still popular in Germany), and they also came to be used as the centres for kissing comfits. Together with musk-flavoured comfits, these were the cannonballs in the armoury of Elizabethan flirtation.

Early comfits were either coated in sugar syrup and repeatedly shimmied in a pan, up to ten times, until the exterior was hard, white and knobbly, or simply dipped in egg white and rolled in sugar. Medieval Dutch sources speak of making comfits by covering the seeds and roots in hot syrup, putting them in a box with sugar and shaking it vigorously, like a cocktail shaker. These relatively crude methods meant that the comfits came out in all shapes and sizes. As the skills of confectionery were honed, it became possible, through continual agitation of the seeds in a hot, sugary pan, to build up over a period of hours or days a much smoother, rounder, smaller and harder confection. The French confectioners made this their speciality, using a large wok-like pan suspended from chains above the fire so that it could be manoeuvred easily. The modern machine used for this process, which is known as panning, resembles a cement mixer, with hundreds of little white balls tumbling crazily around inside the vat, each one growing steadily fatter as it is repeatedly coated with hundreds of infinitesimally thin layers of sugar. No one ever fretted about the perversity of a confectioner going to such lengths to encase the toothsome kernel of a nut in a hard new sugar shell that also preserved it, in place of the one already designed by nature. Gobstoppers, hard mints and aniseed balls are the heirs of panned medieval comfits, just as a modern boiled sweet is imbued with the spirit of the medieval sucket.

The gastronomic appeal of the comfit was acknowledged in 1475 in the first printed book to contain recipes, *De Honesta Voluptate et Valetudine*, or *On Right Pleasure and Good Health*, by Bartolomeo Saachi, known as Platina, the librarian at the Vatican. In the section on sugar, Platina comments: 'By melting it, we make almonds [. . .] pine nuts, hazelnuts, coriander, anise, cinnamon, and many other things into sweets. The quality of sugar then almost crosses over into the qualities of those things to which it clings in the preparation.' Platina has astutely surmised that with a comfit, the sugar is not just a coating: it transforms that which it encases. One of the attractions of the comfit is the way it contains something real at its core, as the source of its flavour and the key to its identity. The seed is the soul. Everyone loves to discover treasure, even if it comes as no great surprise; we experience a small frisson of triumph when we finally reach the almond or the pure white core of the aniseed ball. That final crunch is a tiny victory, not moral but molar – secret, and not always entirely insignificant in the context of a difficult day. Even now, sweets that contain prizes, or more sweets – Kinder Eggs, Easter eggs or lucky bags, for example – are especially prized by children, and adults relish the randomness of raiding an unfamiliar chocolate tray without a map. A surprise inside is indisputably good value.

Sir Hugh Platt's dinky *Delightes for Ladies* provides an excellent description of the art of comfit making, and of the sweetmaker's discretion with ingredients. 'Take for every two pound of sugar, a quarter of a pound of annis seedes, or coriander seedes, and your comfits wil be great enough, and if you will make them greater, take halfe a pound more of sugar, or one pound more, and then they will be faire and large. And halfe a pound of Annis seeds, with two pound of sugar will make fine small comfits.' This passage explains the standard pre-eighteenth-century distinction between small and large, or *grosse*, comfits: the cost of sugar meant that the thickness of the coating affected the price of the sweet – almost an irrelevance in modern confectionery, now that sugar is a mass-produced staple and factors like packaging are more important commercially. (Small white comfits can be seen, spilled from the table, in one of the panels of Botticelli's 'Story of Nastagio degli Onesti' (1483) in the Prado.) Sir Hugh also describes comfits of cinnamon, almonds, caraways and fennel, and – unusually – gives instructions on how to dye the comfits red, green and yellow by adding to the sugar 'the juice of beets', 'brasell' (iron pyrites) and saffron.

In France, the larger comfits were called dragées – the name is possibly derived from the ancient Greek word for sweets, *tragemata*. Grosse dragées are often listed alongside comfits in English sources, and usually refer to sugared almonds. The dragées of the town of Verdun, in the north-east of France, were most celebrated of all, and are first mentioned in the thirteenth century. This sweet evolved into a Verdun praline, a confection of chopped almonds rolled in lightly caramelised sugar. Metz, Nancy, Toulouse and of course Paris also became known for the quality of their dragées, which were available in two forms: with a coating that was either smooth and shiny (*perlée*) or somewhat rough (*lissée*). Chopped nut comfits in white sugar were known as *dragées blanches*. After 1650 the Ursuline nuns of Flavigny became celebrated internationally for the delicacy of their hard little aniseed balls and violet-flavoured comfits (the brand survives today), and juniper comfits were a speciality of St-Roch. Varieties of comfit are the cachou, which is specifically designed for smokers and flavoured with liquorice, mint or violet (like Lajaunie cachous of France), and nonpareils, which is a big word for a little sweet, since these are sprinkles, or hundreds and thousands. Just to add to the complexity, the generic name of comfit itself was, by the eighteenth century, applied to almost any sweetmeat, whether encased in sugar or not.

There are a few intriguing references to the practice of putting sweets into drinks in Europe, although in this case it is not fruit preserves but comfits. In the *Itinerary* of the traveller Fynes Morison, published in 1617, he notes of the Scots: 'They drinke pure Wines, not with sugar as the English, yet at Feasts they put Comfits in the wine, after the French manner.' (The British habit of sugaring wine, commonplace into the eighteenth century and not unheard of in the nineteenth, was a source of some hilarity to visitors from the Continent.) John Evelyn, in the manuscript of his late-seventeenth-century recipes in Christ Church, Oxford, provides us with the very first reference to liquid lemonade, adding that his recipe would be improved by the addition of an amber comfit. This would have been a sugared grain of ambergris, a waxy intestinal secretion of the sperm whale that is treasured for a scent which has been described as a mixture of hay and violets.

The mystery of how to create a smooth, hard texture for comfits and dragées was the preserve of patient nuns and skilled craftsmen: they panned by hand for days on end, and kept their secrets close. Most sugar-coated sweets were large and knobbly, though still attractive, and such sweets appear on the well-appointed tables of Dutch still-life paintings of the seventeenth century, notably in the work of George Flegel (1566–1638). These comfits are brittle-looking, crystalline and gnarled, made in a variety of shapes that echo their subjects: round fruits, long roots, little nuts, rings of sugar candy, and so on. It seems strange, in these times of multi-coloured confectionery, that they are all snowy white, elegant against Chinese bowls or silver salvers. The size of sugar crystals clearly varies from sweet to sweet, so it is likely different grades of sugar were used, either to obtain different decorative effects, or to make the panning process easier. The art historian Norbert Schneider has convincingly argued that the confectionery in these pictures is an allegory for the sweetness of Christ's redemptive power, and that their shape and arrangement have symbolic significance; in one picture the comfits seem to form an 'A' and an 'O' shape, for Alpha and Omega, to illustrate the pleasant idea that God's love has no beginning and no end.

It was the sugared almond that emerged as the apogee of the dragée. Today, throughout western and southern Europe, almond dragées, often encased in a shiny silver-leaf coating that is added at the very end of the panning process, are an essential part of the ritual of weddings, christenings and other cele-brations. These usually take the form of a demure little bag left for each guest on the wedding table, but in southern Europe into the mid twentieth century, these dragées were enthusi-astically thrown around on special occasions, to the amazement of visitors (including Goethe, who realised that the sweets thrown at a Roman carnival were actually plaster imitations; the real things were too expensive). Little sweets are called *confetti* in Italy and in Russia. In his *Confectioner's Oracle* (1830), a scandalised William Gunter writes (his italics and exclamation marks): 'In Italy, they pleasantly pelt each other with these trifles, as they move along the Corso. The Italians pelt gently enough, but an English country gentleman threw *his* comfits with such savagery, that he actually *put out one of the eyes of his young bride!!!*'

Comfits were always extremely popular sweets among those who could afford them, and many people could, because from the fourteenth century sugar was not an astronomically expensive commodity for the nobility and the richer class. Almonds imported from Spain during peacetime were positively cheap, and these formed the basis for many sweets, and also marzipan (see Lucky Dip, page 145). Wealthy aristocrats on the move bought sweets in bulk: when Count William IV of the Netherlands joined battle against the Bishop of Utrecht in 1345, he took with him 176lb of comfits: 33lb of grosse dragées, 33lb of royal comfits, 33lb of white comfits, 22lb of anise comfits, 10lb of white tragien, 10lb of chitron and 2lb of coriander comfits. (The 'tragien' were dragées.) This is not to say that sugar and sweets were a daily or even monthly experience for the majority; a record of two hundred honeycombs taken aboard one ship in 1463 indicates that honey was still the standby sweetener for working people.

In England, however, sugar was a commonplace commodity by the sixteenth century, and the sugar loaf and cutters had become a standard sign hanging above the door of a grocer's shop. By this time, sweets were almost a part of everyday expenditure for the moderately wealthy, a status indicated in a poem by Thomas Newbery called 'The Names of All Kynd of Wares'. This is an inventory of goods on general sale at that time (1563). The sweetmeats – 'I have Suckets, Sirrups, Grene Ginger and Marmalade/Biskits, Cumfects and Carawayes, as fine as can be made' – are listed alongside basic household items such as basins, ewers, towels, pot hooks, knives, milk, butter, eggs, mutton and rat poison. Sweets were luxuries, certainly, but by this time they were becoming everyday luxuries for a significant section of society.

London did not monopolise the retail sweets market, and confectionery was sold in England at regional centres such as Bristol and York. That the mark-ups may have been high is suggested by a letter to a metropolitan friend from Margaret Paston of Norwich in the mid fifteenth century – quoted in Joseph Aubrey Rees's ambitiously titled *The Grocery Trade: Its History and Romance* (1932) – which indicates that bargains might be found in London and sent on. 'Send me word', she writes, 'what price a pound of pepper, cloves, mace, ginger, almonds, rice, galingal, saffron, raisins of Corinth, greyns and comfits.' (Galingal is an aromatic root, most likely tasted in a Thai restaurant today, and greyns were grains of paradise, an aromatic peppercorn related to cardamom which was more popular than pepper for a time.)

The household accounts of Ingatestone Hall, Essex, in the 1550s, provide another revealing insight into the relative cost of sweets. The steward visited the village grocer's and noted: 'Laid out for sugar candy bought at Ingatestone for my lady, 2*d*.' The exact amount of sugar candy is not specified. Twopence was also the price of a pound of raisins at the same shop. The same household inventory records the relative amounts spent on foodstuffs for a feast given at the house for Elizabeth I, who was calling in with her retinue during one of her progresses round the country. 'Comfits of sundry sorts' came to 28*s* 6*d*, while far more – £7 15*s* – was spent on 'sugar, cloves, mace, pepper and sundry other kind of spice'. A Tudor feast would be incomplete without a swan, and the cygnets on this occasion were ten shillings each, while a dozen quails were four shillings and a dozen chickens three shillings. From this we might deduce that sweets were expensive compared with poultry, but quite cheap compared with other spices.

Perhaps the most vivid insight into sweets consumption in the medieval period can be found in *Le Ménagier de Paris*, the name applied to a fourteenth-century treatise on how to run a household properly written by a French nobleman for his young wife (but apparently completed after she had already borne him several children). This practical-minded aristocrat, identified as one Guy de Montigny by historian Nicole Crossley-Holland in *Living and Dining in Medieval Paris* (1996), was so embroiled in the workings of his household and kitchen that one feels sorry for young Mme de Montigny, having such a perfectionist hovering at her shoulder, his grey hairs falling into the marmalade cauldron. The ménagier certainly had a sweet tooth: the household made walnut and almond comfits in large quantities, possibly using nuts from the de Montigny estate in Champagne, and he also mentions an old-fashioned confection of parsley and fennel roots in honey. Other homemade sweets were *condoignac*, a spiced quince paste preserved with honey (the equivalent of modern *cotignac*, a speciality of Orléans and reputedly a favourite of Joan of Arc), and *orengeat* in honey (sucket, or crystallised orange peel), confusingly called orangeade in English.

Among the other sweets enjoyed by the ménagier and his guests were comfits of aniseed, rose sugar, hazelnuts and coriander seed – all dipped in egg white, rolled in sugar and left to harden. These were eaten at the *voidée*, the final course of either the main midday meal or early evening supper. It was customary at this point to clear away completely all the other food, and sometimes for the diners to quit the table – hence the later term for it, dessert, from *desservir*, to clear away. It is strange that these puddingy words are so negative, referring only to the disappearance of the remnants of food and not to the positive joy that will shortly be inspired by the appearance of freshly made desserts and sweets. This is a moment in a meal when the last thing most of us want to do is desert the table. The placement of sweets at the end of a meal was a medieval innovation, because although sweets were humble pleasures, they were not yet cheap enough to be treated casually. Instead, they were absorbed into the ritual of the feast. It is time for dinner.

Lucky Dip

MARZIPAN

I never liked marzipan much. But then, I was used to the English version – bright yellow, cloying, stiff and generally found beneath the icing on fruit cakes, particularly the dreaded Christmas cake. Real marzipan is quite different: a light, moist and deliciously fresh tasting paste of sugar and almonds (both sweet and bitter), filled with the perfume of the nuts and with the ghost of a crunch of sugar. Nowadays, I really like marzipan. By itself, it cannot be called a sweet – it is a sweet material – but it can be moulded and toasted and otherwise manipulated to form all kinds of dainty confections.

The invention of marzipan, and the derivation of its name, have inspired more outlandish stories than any other sweet. In Germany, where the marzipan is slightly coarser and stronger in flavour than the French version (which is not to say it is inferior), there is a ridiculous story that marzipan was invented by a man named Marzip in 1671. This Marzip was the cook of a wealthy Brandenburg doctor, who one evening asked him to invent some special almond dish for his guests, to be served after dinner with white wine. The resourceful Marzip invented marzipan, the story goes, and went on to become cook to the Elector of Hanover. Marzip later retired to his hometown of Lübeck, opened a marzipan factory and thus began the town's famous association with the sweet paste.

Marzipan is, of course, much older than this. Almost any sweet with almonds can be traced back to Arabia and the Middle East, and marzipan is no exception. Pastes of ground almonds and sugar have been popular sweetmeats in the Arab world since the early medieval period, and they are mentioned in northern Italian accounts by 1300 (although they had probably been known at least 150 years earlier). Marzipan was certainly not a European invention, but solid proof of this is impossible to find. Everything would be much easier if an old Arabic word could be found as the source of the word marzipan, but none has been forthcoming. There is one reference to 'massipan' in a twelfth-century Arabic manuscript from Cordoba, but this is relatively late in this context and could conceivably be an Arab version of a European word. Karen Hess, editor of Martha Washington's Booke of Cookery, a late-seventeenth-century or early-eighteenth-century American manuscript, has through her notes incidentally provided a superb reference work on wider culinary history, including a comprehensive discussion on all the theories around the etymology of marzipan. Hess maintains that the earliest Western reference to a marzipan-like substance can be found in a fourteenth-century Catalan cookbook called Libre de Totes Maneres de Confits, which provides a recipe for 'mersepa'. There is a persistent idea that the word derives from the Latin phrase Marci panis, meaning St Mark's bread, and it is thought that that is how the Italian marzapane became German Marzipan, which became English marchpane and later marzipan. One French source even claims it was invented by an Italian chef called Marco, hence the name, and the Milanese also claim that they were the inventors. Then there is the medieval Latin word massapanis, which Hess suggests just might be related to marzipan, because a massapanis was a small reliquary casket that could also contain consecrated wafers – which would conceivably be made of marzipan. There could even be some crossover here with the sweetmeat manus christi, which is marzipan in at least one reference. That is not all. Another theory suggests that the word may derive from the Arabic 'marzaban', a unit of measure in Cyprus and Armenia which came to refer to the light wooden boxes used to transport various commodities, including sweets. In time, the name of the boxes – which were often reused as handy receptacles for paperwork – became the name of the sweets, too. I will not even bother you with speculation about the Indian name for marzipan: màss plow.

It appears that marzipan is never going to give up the secrets of its name, and we shall just have to take it on trust that it was the Arabs who had planted the almond groves in southern Europe who brought the recipe with them. Does this etymological confusion matter one jot to the person munching on a marzipan fruit from Sicily, or a marzipan potato from Lübeck? Somehow, I suspect not.

Chapter 5

FROM ARABY TO
SUBTLETY

From the first, sweets came last. Today we can eat sweets at any time, or even all the time, but the medieval custom of handing sweets round at the end of a meal has also endured, especially when guests have been invited. The English used the word 'voidee' for this final course until the sixteenth century, when it became known as the banquet or banket course. It is not uncommon to find the word banket being used at this time to describe the food itself collectively, rather than the course, and the word banquet was also used to mean a feast as a whole – its sole meaning today.

The tradition of clearing everything away after dinner for a banquet of sweets is recorded in the very earliest sources, including the first detailed menu for an English feast, which is contained in the late-thirteenth-century Anglo-Norman *Treatise of Walter of Bibbesworth.*

> *Et quant la table fu oustée,*
> *Blanche poudre oue la grosse dragée,*
> *Maces, quibebes, clougilofrez,*
> *E dautre espiecerye assez,*
> *E oubleie a fuisoun.*

> And when the table was cleared,
> [There was] white powder with large dragées:
> Mace, cubeb, clove gillyflower
> And other spices to try,
> And not forgetting the wafers.

A cubeb is a type of aromatic peppercorn, still in existence but now almost obsolete in cookery, and clove gillyflower was the clove-scented dianthus (pink) flower. These were heady and rare spices to be enjoyed in sweetened form in small quantities. When a medieval bill of fare mentions 'spices' or 'spicery' to be consumed at table rather than used in the kitchen, what is meant is sugar-coated spices, or comfits. The 'blanche poudre' would have been a spiced sugar bought ready-mixed from the grocer; another type was called powdour marchant. These powders were made up of finely ground sugar sophisticated with ginger, cinnamon or nutmeg, and were generally confined to the kitchen, for sprinkling on apples, quinces and pears before they were roasted. (It appears that ready-made spice powders without sugar were also available, for convenience.) Wafers are always mentioned in descriptions of the medieval banquet. These are not the thin and slightly depressing little biscuits that are served with ice cream today, but thick, waffle-like items cooked on a griddle and served hot. They were sometimes described as 'wafer cakes' and were popular as street food, sometimes with a cheese filling. But a large medieval household would employ a full-time waferer, wholly dedicated to the art of . . . wafering.

The spiciness of medieval comfits can be seen in the menu for Henry IV of England's wedding feast of 1403, which included 'sugar plums, sugar made up with roses, comfitures of fruit, sage, ginger, cardamom, fennel, anise, coriander, cinnamon, powdered saffron'. The 'comfitures' here are certainly comfits in the case of the dry seeds and herbs, and probably so with the ginger, fennel and fruit, since any preserves or wet suckets would probably have been covered by the term 'sugar plums'. Sugar confectionery's early identity as sweetened spice, rather than spice-flavoured sweet – a small but important distinction – is reiterated in the description of paradise in Chaucer's *Romaunt of the Rose* (1366):

> Ther was eke wexying many a spice,
> As clowe-gelofre, and lycorice,
> Gyngevre, and greyn de parys,
> Canell, and setewale of prys,
> And many a spice delitable
> To eten whan men rise from table.

Ginger (gyngevre), grains of paradise (greyn de parys), cinnamon (canell), and valerian (setewale) were among the 'delectable' spices Chaucer mentions, and they must have been eaten in comfit form at the banquet – when everyone rose from the table, in this case. At small gatherings, as opposed to ceremonial feasts, the host would repair with his guests to a chamber, where they could recline in comfort, chatting and eating sweets at their leisure. This is why these after-dinner sweets (sugar and spice and all things nice) became known in French as *épices de chambre*, 'bedroom spices'. It did not mean guests were supposed to lounge around on the host and hostess's bed, simply that the most comfortable room to retire to was the chamber, which was not so much a bedroom as a room with a bed in it. It was quite acceptable to entertain guests in such a room (a tradition formalised in the royal levée, or getting-up and getting-dressed ceremony) and the bed was not an embarrassment in this context.

Comfits, preserves and conserves of fruits, suckets wet and dry, fresh fruit and stiff paste sweets would be proffered from ornate gold or silver dishes or passed around in compartmentalised boxes (known as *drageoirs* in French), exactly as we circulate a box of chocolates after dinner today. On special occasions in great houses, guests might be given a *drageoir* loaded with sweets to take away with them, as they were at the marriage of Charles the Bold of Burgundy to Margaret of York at Bruges in 1468. This agreeable custom has never fallen from favour. John Nott, in *The Cook's and Confectioner's Dictionary* (1723), painstakingly describes the correct form and table arrangement for sweetmeats at the banquet, adding: 'And these baskets are commonly adorned with small Ribbands, and Taffaty Covers, and fill'd up with all sorts of Sweet-meats, Biskets, Marchpanes, Orange and Lemon Faggots, dry'd Fruits, &c. So that the most delicious Comfits may lye at the Top; and every Person eats only the liquid Sweet-meats, and shuts up, and takes away his Basket to carry home.' This practice has its echoes today in the lacy pouches of sugared almonds given to wedding guests. There are other medieval vestiges in modern sweets customs. At Oxford colleges, for example, and in English upper-class households (or pretentious ones, like mine), one of the sweets produced after dinner is identical to the medieval original: stem ginger in syrup, lifted from the jar with a fork. This bracing sweetmeat is the final incarnation of the wet sucket. The dry version – candied ginger – is also readily available.

There was even a special drink to enjoy with the comfits, fruits and wafers of the banquet. It was called hypocras. This spiced wine – probably served hot, or mulled – was reputedly named in honour of the Greek physician Hippocrates, father of humoral medicine, to further underline the idea that the banquet course was an indulgence to be enjoyed for good medicinal reasons, and not just because it was full of things that taste good. (The French tradition of the digestif of cognac works on the same principle.) Hypocras was a comforting concoction flavoured with a variety of spices, including ginger and nutmeg, but chiefly cinnamon; it was the forerunner of mulled wine. Ready-made mixtures of hypocras could be purchased from the apothecary, since the complexity of the recipe would have been offset annoyingly, for any cook, by the ease with which the hypocras spices could be stirred into a flagon of heated wine.

By the middle of the sixteenth century, the practice of retiring to a bedchamber for comfits and hypocras had become old-fashioned, and a more varied banquet began to be taken at the table, as a course in itself. The banquet course at a dinner for the Skinners' Company in London, in 1560, consisted of 'spyse-bred, comfets, sukett, marmelade, cheres, straberes' (the last two items are cherries and strawberries, which may seem obvious but took this international confectionery historian quite a long time to work out). The 'spyse-bred' was a type of spiced honey cake made with breadcrumbs, the ancestor of gingerbread. The English liking for spicy cakes and breads can be traced back even further, to the honeyed feast-day loaves and buns of the Anglo-Saxon period, and a cake called 'anne cicel', made of finely sifted flour and cumin, kneaded with milk or cream, and perhaps sweetened with honey or dried fruits. That Anglo-Saxon cake sounds like a heavier, spicer version of Italian *panettone*.

Gervase Markham provides us with an excellent rundown of the pomp and circumstance of an early-seventeenth-century dessert, in *The English Hus-Wife* (1615): 'Your preserved fruits shall be dished up first, your pasts next, your wet suckets after them, then your dried suckets, then your Marmalades and Cotiniates [stiff fruit jams], then your Comfets of all kinds; Next your Pears, Apples, Wardens [large pears], bak'd, raw, or roasted, and your Oranges and Lemons sliced; and lastly your Wafer-cakes.' Markham emphasises that each of these delights should be served singly, and cleared away before the next one arrives; 'this will not only appear delicate to the eye, but invite the appetite with the much variety thereof'. From the 1590s sweets and other edibles deemed fancy were often called kickshaws, pronounced (at first) ke-ke-shaws, since the word is a corruption of the French *quelquechose*, meaning 'something'. These kick-shaws might have been eaten at times outside the banquet course, too – when important guests or valued friends paid a surprise visit, for example. One such informal, spontaneous event occurs in the memoirs of Felix Fabri, a German Dominican brother on pilgrimage to the Holy Land in 1488, who was delighted to be served 'a collation of Cretan wine and comfits from Alexandria' by a sea captain on board his ship in Venice. We know that spice comfits were consumed just before bed in the medieval period, as an aid to digestion and as a sweet goodbye to the day, and there is a sort of continuation of this indulgence in hotels where a chocolate is left on one's pillow.

The banquet course, at first removed to the bedchamber and then taken back to the table, was finally taken outside in the early eighteenth century. It became fashionable to enjoy a lavish convocation of sweets, fresh fruit, jellies and puddings in a specially built garden building, a banqueting house, where a sumptuous dessert would be laid out, glittering in candlelight, to greet guests as they arrived on foot, or even by coach or on horseback, fresh from the main dinner in the big house. The deeply polished, reflective mahogany of the table and the flickering light would have made the sugar confections all the more sparkly and inviting. And what could be more beaut-iful than a jelly by candlelight? By the time of the heyday of the banqueting house in the mid eighteenth century, fresh fruit and puddings, such as syllabubs, were just as important as the sweets, and the banqueting course had become an extended entertainment, a midnight feast which might continue until dawn, often without the restraining influence of servants.

Even within the meal, sweets were not confined to the final course. There are many medieval references to comfits, particularly caraway comfits, being added to savoury dishes and cooked fruits as decoration and flavouring. Pears with caraways and apples with pistachios are mentioned in the menu of a 1533 dinner given for Henry VIII by the Marquis of Exeter, and the botanist and herbalist John Parkinson recommends in passing that a roast warden (a large pear) might be studded with comfits. Buns and cakes were generally improved with caraway comfits rather than currants even into the eighteenth century. One medieval recipe suggests improving the flavour and appearance of a chicken dish by scattering it with 'red dragées' – aniseed, in most cases – and orange and lemon suckets as well as sugar were sprinkled over savoury dishes at the last moment before serving.

It seems entirely natural to us that puddings, desserts and sweets should come last at dinner time, but it was not always so, and there is no evidence that human beings naturally prefer this order of flavours. Many different cultures, past and present, have intermixed sweetness with savoury, and it was a basic principle of Arabic cuisine. This model was adopted in medieval Europe and, for those lucky enough to be existing above subsistence levels, sweetness accompanied every stage of the meal. A feast given for Henry IV of England in 1399 consisted of three courses. The first included various poultry and fish dishes, plus *viaund ryal* (a purée of rice, mulberries and honey), *crustade lumbarde* (a creamy pie with dates and prunes), wine and spices. These 'spices' were probably comfits, which often appeared quite early in the meal, to accompany servings of wine, although their main role was at the banquet course. The second course was venison, pies, birds, and *leche lumbard* (small spiced date cakes), and the third was small birds and rabbits, plus quinces in syrup, *doucettys* (custard tarts) and *pety perneux* (small spiced tarts of egg, cream and raisins).

Western cuisine has not entirely lost this sweet-savoury sophistication, and dishes of spiced beef, smoked ham with fruit, or roasted meat garnished with sweet fruit sauce are the residue of this tradition. The mince pie is an example of a medieval food which originally contained sweet and savoury elements intermixed, but is now all sweet. And newer culinary habits, such as maple syrup on bacon, the popularity of tomato ketchup and other sweet condiments, and even the way marmalade is often consumed before bacon and eggs at the breakfast table, are testament to a less than rigorous demarcation between sweet and savoury that has endured in modern cuisine.

To medieval Europeans, the cuisine of Araby offered a tantalising fusion of sugary sweetness with savoury. There was already a precedent for this overlap in mead and other honey-based alcoholic drinks, and in the way ale was habitually sweetened with honey and consumed with the meal. There had been a fashion for things Eastern since the time of the Crusades, when the European adoption of local styles of dress, foods and other customs enraged the clergy – one Bishop of Acre complained that European knights were wearing turbans. The Norman kings of France and England had accepted Muslim teachers and officials into their courts, although the adoption of Arabic customs in northern Europe was far less marked than it was in Norman Sicily or in Spain, where the East–West assimilation in centres such as Cordoba, even after the Arab sultans had left, meant flowing robes, harems and circumcision were a part of courtly life. The Eastern influence endured even into the late medieval period, and in the fourteenth and fifteenth centuries Eastern customs, foods and styles of dress became even more fashionable as the military threat receded. The mixing of sweet and savoury flavours remained an integral part of Western European gastronomy into the seventeenth century, when the French led the way in isolating sweetness from the main part of the meal. By this time, however, sweets were an established and inviolable part of the European food experience.

Where else could this liking for sugar as a sweetener have come from, if not from the East, the source of sugar itself? The late-thirteenth-century menu of Walter of Bibbesworth includes a large amount of meat, including '*conyns en gravee, trestout de zucre enfoundree*', or rabbits in gravy, encased in sugar. Meat dishes that included sugar as a principal sauce ingredient were often called 'Saracen' or '*Vyande Cypre*' (referring to Cypriot sugar) and coloured red, and those that mingled sweet with savoury were given or inherited Arabised names: in medieval Italy, for example, a *romania* consisted of chicken and pomegranates, and *rumman* means pomegranate in Arabic. There are many such examples of the Arab names for fruit and vegetables becoming assimilated into northern European languages as the food itself was adopted – aubergine, for example, which started as Old Persian *badangan*, then became *al-badinjan* in Arabic, *alberjinera* in Spanish, and finally *aubergine* in French and then English. Spinach is from the Old Persian, *espenaj*. (In most cases, the exotic connection was rapidly obscured as the food became domesticated. One exception is rhubarb, which is native to Asia: although grown in Britain from the seventeenth century, it was being sold, probably in powder form, alongside exotic spices by Arab street traders in London in the mid nineteenth century.) A typical fourteenth-century medieval recipe for a meat dish sounds like something one might order at a modern Lebanese restaurant. Mawmenny, for example, was a popular dish of ground meat mingled with sugar and other spices (principally ginger and cloves) and sprinkled with onions.

The relative spiciness, and therefore sugariness, of medieval cuisine has been a matter of controversy among food historians. Everyone now agrees that it is erroneous to suggest that spices were used as some kind of mask for rotting meat (a reasoning that has also been falsely applied to Indian food). And although the amount of spice listed in medieval recipes does seem large at first glance, anyone who has cooked with spices knows that it is possible, and often desirable, to use generous amounts (with the obvious exception of chilli pepper). It is extraordinary how a seemingly massive amount of spice can be absorbed and altered by the food it is designed to complement; I recently enjoyed a dish of braised celery which appeared at first to have been smothered in cinnamon by an Egyptian chef, but it was perfectly acceptable and interesting. Then there is the deterioration of the spices themselves: the amounts specified in medieval recipes may reflect a depletion of flavour, after so many months in transportation and storage. And finally there is the matter of what an individual is used to: if one has been brought up in a tradition of spicy food, strong flavouring is desirable – and the fact is, European food (and the diet of European food historians) has been largely spice-less for the past 250 years. It is unlikely, however, that medieval food would have tasted particularly sweet. Sweetness was used to temper strong flavours, such as ginger, or to offset the sourness of vinegar; it was also added habitually during the cooking process as a seasoning to enhance flavours, as we might use salt and pepper today.

So sugar was one among many spices used in the sauces for meat dishes – with the exception of tripe and innards, for which the Europeans followed the Arab example of omitting sugar to avoid an overdose of the humour of choler. Sugar became entrenched in European gastronomy as a force for good alone, a situation it is difficult to accept in the early twenty-first century, after nearly half a century of anti-sugar propaganda from various health lobbies. But Platina, in his 1475 cookbook, set the tone for the late Renaissance attitude towards sugar: 'Nothing of what one eats is such that it cannot be completed by the addition of sugar.' And the authority Guido Pancirollus confirmed its popularity in actual culinary practice by the end of the sixteenth century: 'Nothing is served without sugar: it is used in cakes and wine; instead of plain water, one drinks sugared water; meat, fish and eggs are prepared with sugar; in short, salt is not used more frequently than sugar.' The attraction of sugar depended as much on its decorative as its gastronomic qualities. In medieval cuisine, much emphasis was placed on the value of golden food. Saffron was an easy – and expensive – way of making food appear as precious as gold, but a sprinkling of sugar could also make a dish glisten in the firelight. This emphasis on presentation was by no means as marked in European cuisine as it was in Persian food, but it was an important incidental aspect of sweetness.

Until the eighteenth century, sugar, like other exotic imported spice products, such as saffron and rosewater, was a luxurious and exotic commodity that smacked of prestige and pleasure, and royalty led the way in consumption. The English in particular became known for their sweet tooth (which tended to result in a lack of teeth – sweet or otherwise). The condition of Elizabeth I's teeth was remarked upon by a German visitor:

> Next came the Queen, in the Sixty-Fifth year of her Age, as we were told, very majestic; her Face oblong, fair, but wrinkled; her Eyes small, yet black and pleasant; her Nose a little hooked; her Lips narrow, and her Teeth black; (a defect the English seem subject to, from their too great use of Sugar).

Elizabeth's grandfather had hardly been a model of dental hygiene, either. At his death in 1509, Henry VII was described as having 'small blue eyes, only a few blackish teeth, thin white hair, and a pale face'. Tooth decay could affect low, of course, as well as high, hence Thomas Dekker's 1631 mention of 'a comfitmaker with rotten teeth'. In France, Catherine de'Medici was credited with bringing from Italy a taste for sugar as a seasoning in the 1530s, and in particular a mania for sweetened fruit cordials. In 1560, La Bruyère Champier, personal physician of Francis I, stated, 'Sugar has already become an indispensable food, naturally among the upper social strata [. . .] because people of good taste will not partake of any food unless it is covered with powdered sugar.'

Almond milk, which is naturally sweet, played a leading role in the medieval European kitchen, and therefore played its part in consolidating the continent's sweet tooth. This is a strange-sounding liquid: how does one milk an almond? The answer is: the almonds are ground down into a pulp, a little water is added and the mixture is filtered. Almond milk sweetens and thickens, and glistens as it goes. It was so common in medieval cuisine as to be almost a staple ingredient, and was called for more often than cows' milk. As the cool drink *horchata*, it is sold today in bars in the almond lands around Valencia and across Spain, although the main ingredient today is the sweet tuber called *chufa*. Echoing Arab precedent, almond milk was used for chicken and lamb dishes especially, as well as sweet puddings such as the popular standby called frumenty, made of grain, almond milk and sometimes egg and saffron. Almond-milk butter was a kind of superior peanut butter, made from curds in some recipes. It sounds rather tempting.

One advantage of almond milk over cows' milk was that it did not sour, but more important was its availability as an ingredient on fast days, when dairy products were proscribed by the Church as 'white meats'. Sweet things appear to have an innate ability to escape religious sanction, and are often incorporated into rituals and customs supported by otherwise dogmatic spiritual leaders. We shall see how sweets became part of Hindu ritual, but in the context of medieval Europe it was the intervention on behalf of sweets of Thomas Aquinas in the twelfth century that proved decisive. Aquinas was faced with the difficult problem of whether sweets counted as food, and should therefore be banned during periods of fast. His ruling was: 'Though they are nutritious themselves, sugared spices are none the less not eaten with the end in mind of nourishment, but rather for ease in digestion; accordingly, they do not break the fast any more than taking of any other medicine.' Perhaps this celebrated divine also had a sweet tooth. Almond milk was one of the ingredients of blancmange, or blank-manger (literally: white food), perhaps the most widespread sweet dish in the Western hemisphere during the medieval period. The first known recipe for it is dated about 1290, and it turns up in almost every European culinary list and feast menu of the next 350 years.

But the provenance of blancmange need not detain us, since it is not really a sweet. Marzipan, however, is. This sweet, made of sugar and ground almonds, has been exploited more than any other for its plastic qualities, and it can be considered the earliest vehicle for the zany, surreal characteristics of sweets that are moulded in unlikely or amusing shapes. Even liquorice must take second place to marzipan in this respect. The term marzipan refers to a substance rather than a specific sweet, which is a reflection of its abstract, malleable properties, and it was used for decorative purposes from its introduction – the first European record is in the thirteenth century, but it was most probably around for several centuries before that.

Medieval marzipan, known as marchpane in English until the nineteenth century, was utilised most dramatically in the making of movable table decorations known as subtleties. In France they were called *entremets*, and in Italy, *intermezzi* – both words mean 'between courses'. Subtleties were allegorical or symbolic models that provided entertaining diversions as they were carried around the hall and set on the table. They were also called warners in England, as they were sometimes used to herald a new course. A subtlety often made some serious point about the occasion, the guest of honour or a date in the religious calendar, but they could be light-hearted, too. A different subtlety would be placed on each table for the duration of a course, or for the whole meal, depending on the extravagance of the host, and sometimes they were intended to be understood as a continuous narrative, with the climax of the story illustrated at the high table – the Nativity, for example.

Subtleties were made from a variety of materials. Some were edible and some were not, but pliable marzipan and sugar plate (sugar mixed with gum tragacanth and water, called *pastillage* in French) were well suited to the purpose. Some subtleties were heraldic, religious or descriptive devices – crowns, eagles, saints, military heroes, mythic figures, coats-of-arms, the Virgin and child, a tiger looking in a mirror, a peacock with a golden beak – and some were even more elaborate: hunting scenes, skirmishes, dances, complex religious tableaux, church interiors, ships in full sail. Strangest of all were the miniature replicas of ceremonies which had just taken place and which the feast was celebrating, incorporating recognisable models of the most important individuals. One such was constructed by order of Archbishop Wareham for the feast celebrating his creation as Chancellor of Oxford University in 1503: this was a stylised building that symbolised the university, with eight towers each graced by a model of the king. Eating the king out of such a tableau would presumably be frowned upon. Although they were not always edible, subtleties were advertisements for the skills of the confectioner or cook, and for special occasions painters and goldsmiths might be drafted in to confect a temporary masterpiece.

The themes of the subtleties at an important feast would contain celebratory (or propagandic) political meaning. The coronation banquet of the eight-year-old Henry VI in 1429 was filled with symbolic meaning expressed through sweetmeats. His father, Henry v, had trounced the French at Agincourt, married Catherine, the King of France's daughter and ratified the Treaty of Troyes, which stipulated that young Henry VI should be crowned King of France as well. The subtleties carried in to the feast were intended to reinforce Henry's claim to both thrones: first, a depiction of him placed between the saints Edward and Louis to confirm his ancestry. Then a subtlety of him placed between his father and Emperor Sigismund (an ally). Then one of the Virgin Mary holding the infant Christ and a crown (Henry was nine months old when his father died). We know that the poet John Lydgate provided explanatory verses to help explain the significance of each subtlety, and it is possible that such commentaries were the usual custom, and perhaps even presaged the practice of travelling players providing running entertainment at feasts in the form of plays themed to fit the occasion.

Not all subtleties contained serious political messages, however. Richard Warner, rector of Chelwood and Great Chalfield, in his *Antiquitates Culinariae* of 1791, records the existence at medieval feasts of 'representations of the membra virilia, pudendaque muliebria, which were formed of pastry, or sugar, and placed before the guests at entertainments, doubtless for the purpose of causing jokes and conversation among them'. He also notes the tradition of making lewd wafers for Easter Day Communion, an echo of a pagan fertility rite that was understandably quashed by the Church. There was an emphasis on such fun at medieval banquets, with musicians, singers, dancers, conjurors, acrobats, mummers and, of course, minstrels. The food echoed the slightly anarchic sense of fun and holiday atmosphere of the feast, where nothing was what it seemed and surprises abounded. Everyone knows about the practice of stuffing an apple or orange into the mouth of a suckling pig roasted whole, but herrings might be formed to look like a man on horseback, balls of minced pork could be coloured and made to resemble golden apples, and minced beef was formed into the shape of a bird. A cockentrice was a very strange thing: the top half of a pig attached to the lower torso of a chicken, cooked and presented to diners as an ungainly mythical beast. Today, such playfulness with food is considered distasteful, except in the case of sweets and cake decorations.

It was the subtleties that provided a focus and set the tone for the feast. One important aspect of their role was that they provided an opportunity for vows of allegiance to be sworn to king or master; these were usually made before sugar or marzipan images of birds (swans in particular). Subtleties could also be quite large: one example, recorded in Savoy in 1403, was a castle made of meat, pea and bean paste, which contained a posse of musicians. An over-ambitious subtlety could go badly wrong: at a royal feast in Paris in 1389, a model tower wheeled in was so large that it caused claustrophobia and panic among the guests, and a barred door had to be broken down for air.

Subtleties themselves appear to have been inspired by Arabic example. We have seen how elaborate sugar table sculptures were popular in the East, and they must have inspired northern European versions. For example, an eleventh-century sultan of Egypt ordered the construction of a full-size tree made of sugar for Ramadan, and another eleventh-century caliph oversaw the creation of seven sugar palaces and no fewer than 157 smaller subtleties for a feast. Architectural models in sugar were a speciality. The poor were often allowed in to devour these constructions once the guests had departed, a tradition not unknown in Europe. An anonymous thirteenth-century Spanish cookbook contains practical instructions (in Arabic) for making models in sugar from moulds: 'If you want to make a tree or the figure of a castle, cut it piece by piece, then decorate it section by section and stick it together with mastic until you complete the figure you want.'

It appears that subtleties were at first intended for consumption at table, either at the banquet course or throughout the meal. The latter is perhaps more likely, because feast menus specify a new subtlety for each course. Presumably diners simply leaned forward and cut pieces from the model with their knives. In the commentary to a feast given at York by

Archbishop Neville in 1467, there is the direction: 'and of all Suttleties or Leches, with your brode knyfe cut a litle of, and give it to the Sewer [server] and Bearer'. It must have been delightful to smash up sugar castles in this way. Sometimes subtleties were only partially edible. The marriage in 1468 at Damme near Bruges, of Charles the Bold, Duke of Burgundy, and Margaret of York, sister to the future Edward IV, went on for days and was one of the most sumptuous nuptial celebrations ever seen. One series of subtleties consisted of thirty platters, each with a golden hedge surrounding a different fruit tree, each tree bearing the name of an abbey. Gambolling around the trees were figures of peasants picking fruit or holding baskets filled with comfits and fruit. These were the edible element of the subtlety, a sweet harvest for the charmed diners.

By the sixteenth century, however, an edible subtlety was a rarity, and the skills of the carpenter with pasteboard, canvas or even painted wood had eclipsed those of the cook with marchpane, pastry or sugar plate. Gervase Markham, writing in 1615, avoids using the word subtlety altogether (perhaps it was too old-fashioned), describing instead 'a dish made for shew only'. By this time, ornate subtleties had been superseded by marchpane models which were plainer, smaller in size and edible only in theory. They were in fact slowly evolving into the decorative marchpane, a large circular cake entirely made of or covered with marzipan, brought out for festive occasions. John Partridge provides clear instructions for marzipan making in *The Treasure of Commodious Conceites* (1584), and notes as a finishing touch: 'Ye may while it is moysse [moist] stiche it full of Comfets of sundry colours, in a comely order.' He writes that marchpane is good food for the sick, but also hints that these models were reusable: 'If it be thorough dryed, and kept in a dry and warm air, a Marchpane will last many yeares.'

In his dedication to *Delightes for Ladies* (1602), Sir Hugh Platt provides a useful inventory of the confectionery of the time, which indicates the place of sugar moulding in the pantheon of the confectioner's art:

Of marmelade and paste of Genua,
Of musked sugar I intend to wright,
Of Leach, of Sucket, and Quidinea,
Affording to each Ladie, her delight.
I teach both fruites and flowers to preserve,
And candie them, so Nutmegs, Cloves, and Mace;
To make both marchpane paste, and sugred plate,
And cast the same in formes of sweetest grace,
Each bird and foule, so moulded from the life,
And after cast in sweet compounds of Arte,
As if the flesh and form which Nature gave,
Did still remaine in every lim and part.

Perhaps the enduring custom of keeping a tier of wedding cake to celebrate the birth of a first child is a dim echo, via the marchpane cake tradition, of the medieval subtlety. In England, after all, a wedding cake is a fruit cake covered in marzipan and icing, decorated with figures of the bride and groom. A more than passable subtlety, passynge fine.

By the eighteenth century, subtleties were falling from favour as table decorations on grand occasions, replaced not only by the marchpane but also by hard-paste porcelain figures from factories such as Meissen. The aesthete and antiquary Horace Walpole noted: 'Jellies, biscuits, sugar plums and cream have long since given way to harlequins, gondoliers, Turks, Chinese and shepherdesses of Saxon china.' Walpole was himself present at the banquet to celebrate the birth of the new Duke of Burgundy, scene of a most extraordinary, automotive variation on the subtlety theme. 'The dessert', says Walpole in a letter about the occasion, 'concluded with a representation, by wax figures moved by clockwork, of the whole labour of the Dauphiness, and the happy birth of an heir to the monarchy.'

In the shadow of the magnificent subtlety was the delicate art of sculpting with sugar. Early-medieval Venetian confectioners were famed for their skills with spun sugar, which was accepted as a decorative art in its own right. This is the technique whereby a sugar syrup is boiled very hot, to 160 degrees C, or 320 degrees F, two forks tied back to back are dipped in, and the sugar mixture is flicked off to create (in theory) long, thin strands of sugar. These harden quickly but not immediately, so it is possible to prepare a bundle of these strands by draping them over a wooden broom handle, and then working them up into whatever outlandish shape is desired.

During the Renaissance in northern Italy the subtlety tradition was not discarded, but made elegant and up-to-date in *trionfi*, sugar versions of celebrated contemporary bronze sculptures, that formed the centrepiece at fashionable tables. Venice was particularly fêted for the skills with sugar of its confectioners, who moulded it into fantastic tableaux of animals, mythic figures, buildings, birds, fruits or pastoral scenes, and tiny replicas of everyday and not-so-everyday objects that littered the table for the amusement of guests. Henri III of France was treated to a banquet in Venice at which everything, including the tablecloth, was made of spun sugar − 1,286 items in all, by Nicolò della Cavalliera, copying models designed by Sansovino − and at a reception in the Doge's palace in honour of Beatrice d'Este, Duchess of Milan, there was a spread that consisted of 'divers items all made of gilded sugar, to the number of three hundred'. In humbler, more domestic vein, the Englishman Sir Hugh Platt lists 'Buttons, Beakes, Charms, Snakes, Snailes, Frogs, Roses, Chives, Shooes, Slippers, Keyes, Knives, Gloves, Letters, Knots'. Edible cutlery and tableware was an extremely popular branch of sugar confectionery, the more realistic the better. Even an alchemist, Alexis of Piedmont, did not think edible tableware beneath him, and he included a recipe in a 1562 manual. The confectionery tradition of sweets and chocolate made in the shapes of tools or other unlikely items derives from this aristocratic model. Similarly, sugar-plate models of real food were popular (and enduringly so in Germany); at Cardinal Wolsey's installation in the early sixteenth century, one guest was amazed to find a perfect likeness of a cheeseboard among the display of subtleties.

With a few magnificent exceptions – such as the Duke of Albemarle's eighteen-feet sugar tower overflowing with gods and goddesses that was too big to fit through the door of his banqueting room – the art of the sugar sculptor declined through the late eighteenth century. Until, that is, Antonin Carême, the celebrated yet boastful French chef (truly a legend in his own lunch hour), who published scores of outlandish designs for architectural conceits made in sugar. This was a revival of the kind of extravagances suggested by mid-century French confectioners such as Joseph Gilliers, whose *La Cannameliste François* (1751) was filled with exotic ideas to make the dinner table look more like the formal parterre of a garden by Le Nôtre, a pasture for a repast, punctuated by buildings of sugar and sweetmeats. Carême famously (and apocryphally) declared: 'The fine arts are five in number, one of them being architecture – whose main branch is confectionery.' In *Le Pâtissier Pittoresque* (1815), Carême provided illustrative models for sugar trophies and helmets in classical vein, windmills, boats, junks, fountains, Chinese kiosks and ruins – designs that were all fashionable, yet unoriginal. He even describes how to emulate moss with almond paste, while in other publications he provides recipes for small, portable, comfit-type sweets called *petites bouchées*, *fantaisies* and *rosaces*. Such elaborate and expensive table decorations became scarcer in Europe through the nineteenth century, but Jules Gouffé, chef de cuisine of the Paris jockey club, kept the flame alight in the latter part of the century, with his up-to-date instructions for sculpting sugar hams, swans and Mannerist trophies, and such artifices were still seen at grand dinners into the 1930s.

Sugar table decorations were the *ne plus ultra* of sweet-meats intended for conspicuous consumption. But they have vanished. The sweets that have endured are those more humble confections descended from the pharmaceutical tradition. It is these sweets – small, portable, lasting and cheap – that provided the model for today's confectionery, and it is these sweets we will savour next.

Lucky Dip

BAKLAVA

A delectable sight. The crisp golden pastry glistens with golden promise. A top-dusting of green pistachio nuts is a preamble to the anticipated luxuriance of the soft layers of pastry stacked beneath, oozing fragrant syrup. This Middle Eastern and Balkan sweetmeat is the epitome of afternoon luxuriance from Bulgaria to Bosnia, from Afghanistan to Armenia. Forty to a hundred layers of paper-thin filo pastry, each individually buttered, are stacked up in a large round tray, a few feet across, with a layer or two of nut filling (pistachio, almond or walnut) in between. The massive cake is cut into diamonds and baked in the oven, then drenched in sugar or honey syrup flavoured with rose-water. The result is a wondrous match of crisp pastry topping, soft, liquefying underside, and the interest of gritty nuts. A small cup of strong black coffee is the customary accompaniment, since its bitterness offsets the sweetness of the baklava. But it is the complex and ever-changing texture of baklava that is its chief joy, the sense one is biting down on many layers, each with their own character.

This is the most popular sweetmeat, among a large family of related pastry confections, of the Middle East and the Balkans, and almost every country where it is found claims to have invented it. The Armenians say that baklava dates back to the tenth century, since they claim the word derives from bakh *(Armenian for Lent) and* halva, *which means sweet in a number of languages – although in the West it refers specifically to a ground-sesame confection from Greece. Baklava is made in snail shapes in Bosnia, Serbia and Bulgaria, and Macedonia has a dry version, with walnuts. Turkey also favours walnuts, while the Arab countries tend to prefer pistachios and Cyprus almonds. In the*

Balkans the sugar syrup, which can also be flavoured with honey, brandy or orange-blossom water, is lighter, and might even be replaced by milk or a reduced-wine syrup. Austria's famous apple strudel is descended from baklava.

Predictably enough, the most heated arguments over the genesis of baklava are between the Greeks and the Turkish. Both adore this confection, and both dismiss each other's claim to have invented it. In his seminal essay (and there are not many seminal essays in the history of sweets), 'The Taste for Layered Bread among the Nomadic Turks and the Central Asian Origins of Baklava' (1994), Charles Perry, former Rolling Stone editor turned food historian, brilliantly speculates on the evolution of the pastry, and finally opts for the Turks − or rather, 'the Central Asian nomads speaking Turkish dialects who began invading Anatolia in the eleventh century'. He argues that these people perfected the art of baking layered bread because it was impossible to cook loaves on the portable griddles necessary for nomadic existence. Perry cites several examples of layered breads still made by the descendants of these nomadic Turks: the poshkal of the Uzbeks, and the meat-filled equivalent called yupqa. This became the yoka, a cake of Tatarstan, and also yufka, which is the word for a single sheet of filo pastry in Turkish. But these breads consist of a few fairly thick layers of bread or pastry, and Perry suggests that the missing link between them and baklava can be found in the Azarbayjani sweet called Baki pakhlavasi, which is eight sheets of dough with seven layers of nuts. Perry himself must deliver the coup de grâce of his theory:

Azarbayjan was on the nomads' path from Central Asia to Anatolia. A simple way to account for this peculiar pastry is to see it as a first fruit of the contact between nomadic Turks and the settled Iranians of the region. It seems to combine the Iranian tradition of pastries with nut fillings baked in ovens, with the layered bread of the Turks. In this view, the vastly more refined baklava familiar to the world today, made with paper-thin sheets of dough, would be a later elaboration, suited to the wealthy and sophisticated society of Istanbul after the Ottoman conquest. The likely place for the innovation would be the many kitchens of the

Topkapi Palace. In fact, the palace had a particular association with baklava. Every year, on the 15th day of Ramadan, the Janissaries of Istanbul assembled at the palace, and each regiment was given two big trays of baklava, which they slung from poles in sheets of cloth and carried through the streets of the city in a celebration called the Baklava Alayi, or Baklava Procession.

Perry's theory is impressive. Nevertheless, the Greeks will disagree with it. And so will the Armenians, and so will . . .

Chapter 6

PURELY FOR MEDICINAL REASONS

The true pedigree of sweets is not the story of a respectable culinary development at the table, but a sly and mischievously hypocritical invasion via a medicine cupboard that contained boxes of sugared seeds and roots to aid digestion. Healers have always sweetened the pill; with honey at first, but later with sugar. Sweets certainly make us feel better, at least psychologically, so all sweets are medicine of a sort, regardless of their pharmaceutical value. The Latin name for sugar cane is *Saccharum officinarum*, and the species tag *officinalis* or *officinarum* always indicates a medicinal use for the plant. Sweets can even look like tablets or pills – and vice versa – notoriously in the case of children. This link between pharmacy and confectionery has always been exploited by sweetmakers, but the first medicine men to sugar the pill, literally, were the apothecaries of the Arab empire in the ninth century.

Translations of the ancient Sanskrit medical texts were available in Persia, but Arabic medicine was most decisively influenced by the doctrine of the four humours – blood, phlegm, choler and melancholy – as expounded by the fourth-century BC Greek physician Hippocrates. The theory had antecedents in the Zoroastrianism of the ancient Persians, dating back to the seventh century BC, in which certain foods are considered suitable for certain physiological predispositions. The most influential figure in the history of humoral medicine, however, was Galen of Pergamon. It was he who summarised, expanded and popularised Hippocrates' system, intermixed with ideas from Aristotle and Dioscorides, in the second century AD, and the theory dominated European and Middle Eastern medicine for some 1,500 years. The world centre of Galenic medicine was the hospital at Salerno, near Naples, and Galen's writings were translated into Arabic and Syriac (a Persian language) in the ninth century, and into Latin in the eleventh century. The relevance of this to sweets lies in the widespread classification of foods according to their humoral properties. Sugar was regarded as 'hot' and 'moist', but not overly so. Arab apothecaries realised that it was therefore an ideal substance to use as a humoral balance when preparing a drug, either neutralising 'cold' substances, or warming them up to make them more effective. There was also an argument that the moderate 'heat' of sugar mimicked the natural status of the body. This careful humoral balancing act between warmth, cold, dryness and moistness is reflected in the very name confectionery, which comes from the medieval Latin *confecta*, via the Latin *conficere*, to put together. So the art of the confectioner was initially a medical innovation; confectionery and pharmacy were at first synonymous.

The apothecaries of the Arab empire, who began to set up shop in the ninth century, developed a medical formulary that utilised sugar in various new ways. Its supposed medicinal effects were offset and probably eclipsed by its practical usefulness in the pharmacy (honey, too, had been used as a binding agent in ancient Egyptian medical preparations). Sugar was useful to the apothecary in various practical ways: it preserved medicines by absorbing moisture and protecting them from the air; it could be used to make preparations in a range of consistencies; it coated or bound the drugs together; it enhanced (it was believed) the effects of the remedy in almost every case; and of course it made a bitter pill taste nice. Thick syrups (*shurba*), sweetened with sugar or honey and flavoured with petals or fruit, were central to Arabic medicine, as were robs (*rubb* in Arabic) – concentrated preparations of fruit or raisin juice – and julabs, light syrups. A *lohoch* was a paste or thin jelly, often made with boiled-up roots mixed with honey and almond oil, that was good for throat and chest complaints. Gum arabic was used in this preparation, and an especially thick version might be seen as the precursor of the cough pastille. Robs and *lohochs* endured as standard medical preparations in Europe into the nineteenth century.

Some drugs were prescribed in powder or pill form. Crystalline sugar was frequently added to electuaries or 'confections' taken in this way, as with an aloeswood confection mentioned in a thirteenth-century medical formulary by al-Samarqandi. This powder 'strengthens the stomach and warms it quite well. It is mixed with a *ratl* [anything between 1lb and 4lb] of sugar, two *dirhams* [six grams] of pulverised Indian aloeswood. It is placed over a fire. To it are added saffron, clove, cardamom, and so on, one after another. The sum total depends on the need. It may be mixed with lemon *rob* in a quantity to make it pleasant. Lemon juice may be used instead. It is yellow and pretty.' It also sounds like something you could bag up and sell as a sweet.

Western medical tradition was based almost entirely on classical theories obtained via the medical texts of the Arab empire. If the Arab apothecaries used sugar, then so must we, reasoned the Europeans. The eleventh-century Persian Avicenna (a convincing latinisation of his real name: ibn-Sina), the 'prince of physicians', was − as his nickname implies − universally respected, like Galen, and his writings remained standard works of medical theory in Europe until the seventeenth century, when a medicine founded on anatomical dissection began to find favour. Avicenna prescribed cordials as the best medicine for the heart, which was in turn good for one's essential *spiritus*, or sense of well-being, and prevented melancholy. Sugar was not one of these cordials (egg yolk, meat juice, spices, rosewater, gold, silver and citrus peel fell into that category), but sugar and a cordial together were an unstoppable combination. And where was such a combination frequently found? In sweets. Avicenna made a pronouncement dear to the heart of the international confectionery historian: '*Apud me in eis, quae dulcia sunt, non est malum*', or: 'It seems to me that when it comes to sweets, none is bad.' With such an unequivocal endorsement from this respected authority, sweets and sugar were ready to take Europe by storm.

Like other spices, sugar was imported into Europe as a sophisticated medicine, to be combined by apothecaries with other ingredients in the confection of expensive medical preparations. But as well as its important status in pharmacy its medicinal properties were also exploited in cookery. All medieval dishes for convalescents contained sugar, and it was seen as a desirable, health-giving addition to most everyday dishes, too. It is easy to imagine pre-twentieth-century European medicine as a litany of bleedings, purgings and other unpleasantnesses, but – following Arab precedent – the doctors rather liked sweets, since sugar was believed to be an active ingredient in simple medical preparations designed to ease digestion and balance the humours. The pleasure of sweetness was enhanced by a sense that it was also virtuous: the burgher whose stomach was so well lined with capon could reach for that twenty-fifth comfit without need of an excuse. Sweets were health food. The practitioners of humoral medicine did not recognise a formal distinction between foods and medicines – each acted upon the body, and menu and dosage alike were adjusted to suit the physiology of each individual.

Let us believe in humoral philosophy for a moment, and examine its relationship with medieval European food. The four humours – blood (associated with a sanguine personality), choler (yellow bile), melancholy (black bile) and phlegm – are found in each person in different proportions according to their constitution. Every foodstuff is also possessed of a humoral makeup, with the strength of each humour contained within it graded from the first to fourth degree, and described as hot, cold, moist or dry. Consumption of any food affects the humoral balance in the diner, for good or bad. An excess of any one humour might lead to a humoral overdose and cause illness or even death, so the health-conscious individual must avoid foods which exacerbate their dominant humoral predisposition, or else temper them with foods that have the opposite effect.

The sanguine or bloody personality is ruddy-cheeked and passionate, with a hearty appetite and a propensity later in life to heart attack, and should avoid foods that are hot and moist (including sugar). The melancholic needs no description, and should not exacerbate the problem by indulging in foods that are cold and dry. Quick-tempered individuals of choleric disposition must deny themselves foods that are hot and dry, including onions and garlic. And the phlegmatic character, pale and listless like a wet fish, should abjure anything deemed cold and moist, such as lamb. The effects of the humours could be controlled within the makeup of individual dishes. For example, fish, which are cold and moist, should be served with spices or sauces that are hot and dry, to counteract an excess of phlegm. Plump and moist young male chickens were castrated into capons to prevent them from maturing sexually, a process which would increase blood and therefore make their meat dry. This belief in the idiosyncratic effects of food on individuals is not dissimilar to the fashionable modern malaise of food intolerance. The humoral properties of food mirror their culinary qualities: balancing the humours in a dish not only makes it safe for the majority of diners, but also more palatable – it makes sense to 'warm up' cold foods like lettuce with olive oil or nuts, or to cool hot foods like chilli with yoghurt. Even today we temper the unwanted effects of certain foods – fresh parsley to counteract garlic, for example.

In humoral terms, sugar was hot and moist, although according to Jane Huggett in *The Mirror of Health: Medieval Food, Diet and Medical Theory 1450–1660* (1995), the contemporary belief was that the whitest, best-quality sugar was dry rather than moist. The use of sugar in cookery was simultaneously culinary and medicinal; the cook, however, would have perceived no distinction at all, instinctively adjusting the seasoning until it tasted both pleasant and healthy. So sugar was used both as a seasoning and as a humoral counterbalance to the other ingredients of a dish. In concentrated form, in the shape of sweets, it was believed to be an excellent digestif – an idea that was traced back to Dioscorides – and also a way of enhancing or regulating the health-giving properties of the various spices, nuts, seeds, fruits and roots it was amalgamated with or coated. The idea was that comfits rewarmed the stomach at the end of the meal, and so aided digestion, and this heating quality was also part of the reason why caraway or aniseed comfits were strewn over the meat dishes of preceding courses.

In accordance with the medical tradition inherited from the Arab world, sugar was treated as an essential element of the European pharmacopoeia and used in the preparation of a wide range of medicines, liquid and solid. Some of these were inherited directly from the Middle Eastern apothecaries: electuaries, syrupy concoctions that could be as stiff as a jelly or liquid; *lohochs*, linctuses to soothe the throat and stomach; and cordials, fruit drinks that strengthened the heart. Then there were more conventional sweets which also benefited from a medicinal reputation: sugar candy, comfits and conserves and preserves of fruit. These preparations had a significant sugar content, and many of them were adopted by the confectioners, who certainly borrowed the technological expertise and even purchased their ingredients direct from the chemist.

The earliest shipments of sugar to Europe were sold on by the medieval pepperers, a profession first mentioned in 1180 in England. By the end of the thirteenth century the medical connotations of the spices they sold were reflected in the new appellation of apothecary or spicer-apothecary – although traders calling themselves spicers, pepperers, apothecaries and spicer-apothecaries all continued to operate throughout the Middle Ages, selling almost identical products. The pepperers of the city of London were gathered near the docks in the Spicery of Westcheap, and it was from his shop here in the 1240s that one Robert de Montpellier, spicer-apothecary to Henry III, supplied powders for spiced wine (hypocras), electuaries, spices, medicines and confections to the court. In the *History of the Society of Apothecaries* (1998), Penelope Hunting estimates that by the early fourteenth century these pharmaceutical entrepreneurs were supplying a range of more than fifty different spices to wealthy houses. The versatile, honest and successful medieval spicer-apothecary had to act as a shopkeeping spice specialist, pharmacist, international trader, artistic confectioner and alchemist.

Some spicers and apothecaries were itinerant merchants who followed the courts or sold their wares to the rich and not-so-rich at the great town fairs in the provinces (events that are still associated with confectionery). By the fourteenth century, every town in England would have had a spicer's or apothecary's shop, although they varied in quality and reliability. As early as 1316 the apothecaries of Westcheap drew up regulations aimed at standardising the weighing of spices including pepper, ginger, cloves, saffron, sugar and dried fruit.

As the export trade for products from the East grew, a new type of merchant emerged: the grocer, or grosser, so named because he imported a wide range of products in bulk. In Florence the grocers were called 'speciarii', and a statute of 1300 records that they sold sugar alongside honey, wax, almonds, marzipan and other spices. The dispute between the grocers and the apothecaries, over who had the expertise to confect medicines, highlights the dual role of sweets as medicine and decorative foodstuff. For about 500 years the apothecaries and the grocers fought a running mercantile battle across Europe, with the apothecaries demanding a monopoly on pharmacy, and the grocers continually flouting the rules and in many places retaining the right to inspect the apothecaries' premises. Ultimately the apothecaries did attain guild status throughout Europe – as early as 1294 in Freiberg in Saxony and as late as 1617 in London – and they were able to enforce their monopoly. In 1432, Duke Albrecht II decreed that in Vienna, 'the merchants shall not bring any confections from Venice, neither shall they nor the shopkeepers sell them; but the apothecaries who reside here shall make such confections and trade in them'. Such restrictive practices are perhaps a root cause of why so many sweets are local specialities, made to secret recipes in a handful of factories in a particular town.

By this time, however, the term 'confection' had attained its dual meaning, and the emerging craft of confectionery was associated even more with sweetmaking than with medicine making. Confectionery was becoming an accepted culinary artform and not just the preserve of the medicos: for example, a grocer in medieval Paris had to create an impressive confection of spun sugar in order to gain entry to his guild. In places rich in the raw materials of sweetmaking, such as Sicily, Valencia and northern Italy, confectioners began to form guilds in their own right. In thirteenth-century Sicily, there was a distinction between the druggists, who dealt with items of vegetable origin only, and were called *confectionarii*, and the apothecaries, who were more nearly pharmacists, known as *stationarii*. And in England by the late fifteenth century, the official title of the king's apothecary was 'Serjeant Confectioner'.

As a retail commodity in its own right and as a new ingredient in medicine, sugar was a revelation – commercial as well as medical – to the apothecaries. Its healing qualities were confirmed by the highest authorities; it was fashionable, exotic and expensive. And it tasted so good that people kept coming back for more, regardless of whether they were ill or not. Everyone wanted a piece of this sugar. So it is understandable that the pharmacy was reluctant to relinquish it as a saleable commodity: sugar could still be bought from any apothecary up to the nineteenth century, scraped from a sugar loaf on the counter. The phrase 'like an apothecary without sugar' was in common usage, or as Richard Tomlinson put it in his *Medicinal Dispensatory* (1657): 'Sugar was unknown to the Antients; which is now so copious that to say a Pharmaopoly without Sugar, were more than an Irony.'

Among medical practitioners, honey had been used for

centuries to make bitter herbal preparations more palatable, and it remained a significant element of the pharmacy throughout the Middle Ages, particularly for the poor. Sugar quickly gained a better reputation than honey in medical circles, however, with authorities such as Roger Bacon advocating its use as early as the 1250s, and the great Albertus Magnus, in *De Vegetabilibus* (*c.*1255), providing the following full and frank definition of sugar: 'It is by nature moist and warm, as proved by its sweetness, and becomes drier with age. Sugar is soothing and solving, it soothes hoarseness and pains in the breast, causes thirst (but less than honey) and sometimes vomiting, but on the whole it is good for the stomach.' Another medieval prescription, of herbs in wine for a wounded man, suggests, 'and if the man may not drink bitterness, do sugar to the drink'. Terence Scully, the historian of early medieval French cuisine, notes that in the thirteenth-century recipes of the *Viandier de Taillevent*, the earliest source of recipes in French, the only recipes containing sugar are those specifically for the sick or infirm. Later recipes in the same manuscript specify sugar as a seasoning for all kinds of dishes, so this restriction of sugar to hospital food was short-lived, if indeed it occurred at all. Sugar was in fact one of relatively few foods that were deemed suitable as part of the cure for any kind of illness. It was one of life's unequivocal Good Things. Comfits and suckets were good presents for a man to give his pregnant wife, and after childbirth, a loaf of sugar was not only a treat but also a source of sugar to make sweetmeats to dole out to well-wishers visiting after the birth.

John of Gaddesden was royal physician in England in the early fourteenth century, and the work he compiled, called the *Rosa Medicinae*, was highly influential. It is clear that sugar was an accepted part of the medical store by this time, generally in the form of 'candi' or 'cande' – sugar candy, the simplest preparation of crystallised sugar syrup. We can probably credit John of Gaddesden with the invention of, or at least the first European reference to, the travel sweet. He advises travellers: 'In warm weather, thirst and heat are best resisted as follows. Take sugar of

roses or violets or waterlilies or diaci coreata made from conserve of chicory flowers and sugar, or else take "candi" of
tamarinds or barberry or sorrel and partake of these often on
the journey.' Sugar was not usually credited with strong healing
properties in itself, but rather as a facilitator or vehicle for other
drugs. (It crops up in some surprising places in John of
Gaddesden's book, however – as an ingredient in this bizarre
hangover cure: 'If any one have drunk too much, if it be a man
the testicles should be washed with salt and vinegar, and if it be
a woman, the breasts, also let them eat the leaf or the stalk or
the juice of a cabbage with sugar.')

The medicines described in Richard Tomlinson's *Medicinal
Dispensatory* give a good impression of the sweetworthiness of
many sugared drugs. Tomlinson has no doubts about the
efficacy of sweetness, and an aside concerning pre-natal sweet
preference – 'sweet things only nourish, and the Infant in the
womb only draws the sweetest blood' – prefigures contemporary medical speculation about whether the foetus has a
sense of taste. The jargon of the pharmacy is identical to the
confectioner's here, if a little more precise, and they must have
used the same equipment for making sweets. Careful distinction
is made between different types of sugar used – whether loaf
sugar, penides (sugar sticks) or rose sugar – which indicates that
the apothecaries were skilled in using it to make their preparations. According to Tomlinson, pills are made using an equal
amount of sugar to medicine, then taken 'in a spoon with some
syrup [. . .] involved in cherryes or the skins of dry grapes'. The
idea of being involved in cherries is appealing.

Many seventeenth-century medicines are basically sweets.
Electuaries, for example, are syrupy medicines (the word comes
from the Greek verb meaning 'to lick'), and Tomlinson gives
instructions for making them up in varying consistencies. In
other medical books, electuaries are pills, and there is good
evidence to suggest that lozenges were simply electuaries or
other medical preparations made to a thick consistency and cut
into diamond shapes – until the nineteenth century, the

primary meaning of 'lozenge' referred to its shape. 'In purging Lozenges,' Tomlinson explains, 'one dramme of powder should be mixed with an ounce of sugar cocted in water, or some juice, to a consistency somewhat more solid than a syrup in Cordiall Lozenges.' As the lozenge became an established medical confection in its own right, the shape became less important: a sugar electuary, for instance, 'may be cut into Lozenges square or round, of one, two or three dramms weight, which after they be brought to the hardness of sugar must be laid in boxes or Chests.' A predilection of confectioners and pharmacists to present mixes of sweets in two colours – white and another colour, usually red – could mean that the lozenges were laid out in a harlequin pattern. An old term for this is 'lozengeways'.

Some of these sweet preparations, such as the *lohoch* (a cough linctus, straight out of the Arabic pharmacopoeia), sound extremely medical until you learn their ingredients – in the case of *lohochs*: liquorice juice, jujubes, pineapple, sugar candy, penides and gum dragon. In *Adam in Eden* (1657), William Coles remarks: 'The juyce of Liquorice dissolved in Rose Water, with some Gum Tragacanth, is a fine Lohoch [. . .] for hoarsenesse.' This sounds like a cough drop.

Tomlinson's medical powders prefigure the dry fizzy sherbet popularised in the late nineteenth century: one recipe for a stomach salve prescribes a ground-up mixture of dill and coriander seeds, orange, cinnamon, mace, cloves and sugar candy. Delicious. The author is casual about the amount of sugar to be used by the apothecary in his preparation of drugs: 'for he may make the strength of the Medicament more weak, or more intense, as he pleases, and you shall scarce find two Apothecaryes who put the same proportion of sugar or honey to the same remedy, when the quantity is not prescribed'.

Other medicines are sweets, pure and simple, and Tomlinson nearly acknowledges this, with perhaps a hint of embarrassment and self-justification. Piniolates are pine kernels in sugar, 'as we see in many junkets which are set at the head of the table', and after giving his recipe for coriander 'biskakes', Tomlinson adds:

'But I would not put my sickle into another man's harvest, therefore I will leave these sweet breads to the confectioners.' Fruit preserves are worthy of the pharmacist, and something of a panacea – 'Condite cherries [boiled in syrup], because of their suavity and salubrity, are exhibited to the sick of any disease, and at any time' – but Tomlinson maintains that they are only suitable as wet preserves, the dry being the province of the confectioner. Sugar is listed among the vital materials of the apothecary, and syrups of violet, poppy, redcurrant, lemon and pomegranate are all deemed necessary in a professional setup.

The crossover between sweets and medicines can be found in every early pharmaceutical text, and sometimes the power of sugar seems quite exaggerated. In the mid sixteenth century, the physician Tabernaemontanus was claiming, 'As a powder it is good for the eyes, as a smoke it is good for common colds, as flour sprinkled on wounds it heals them,' and much else besides. Finally he says: 'Sugar candy has all these powers to a higher degree.' Quite the panacea. Pierre Pomet, in *A Compleat History of Drugs* (1712), repeats the claim that sugar is good for the eyes: 'Put into the eyes in fine powder, they take way their dimness, and heal them being bloodshot, as they cleane old sores, being strew'd gently upon them.' I have put sugar in my eyes by way of experiment, and it did not have this effect. I also questioned an eye surgeon (whom I encountered socially and not as a result of my experiment) on this practice, and she was stumped as to its possible efficacy. Pomet's instructions for making sugar candy, by placing sticks in a box or jar filled with syrup (the lollipop method), are identical to the confectioner's, and he says of red and white sugar candy: 'Both Sorts are better for Rheums, Coughs, Colds, Catarrhs, Asthmas, Wheezings &c than common sugar; because being harder, they take longer time to melt in the Mouth; and withal keep the throat and stomach moister than sugar does.'

It is perhaps fortunate that the medicinal practice of mixing sugar with gold, silver and ground-up gems has waned. If these sweet and extraordinarily expensive preparations had ever made the crossover from medicine to confection, we would be faced with appalling opportunities for spending huge amounts of money on our sweets. As far as Western medics were concerned, the provenance for these profligate remedies, superb money-spinners for the apothecaries, was Avicenna, the tenth-century Arab medic mentioned earlier. Various so-called 'books of secrets', medical formularies translated from the Arabic, were also respected sources in northern Europe for potions containing gold and crushed jewels. By the late thirteenth century, European pharmaceutical texts were going even further, perhaps banking on the smart notion that anyone who spent a fortune on a remedy would either be psychosomatically healed or else spontaneously combust in embarrassment and shame. Taddeo Alderotti, a physician of Bologna, lists the following concoction: 'To comfort the heart internally take one half drachma each of beryl, emerald, sapphire, red jacinth. Also two drachmas each of gold and silver. Also one drachma and a half of both kinds of pearls. Also four drachmas each of bugloss, doronicum and zedoary, white and red ben, cinnamon, clove, aloewood. One drachma each of ground silk, saffron, cubebs, cardamom, amber, camphor and musk. Also two and a half drachmas of coral, sandal, rose, dross of metals (spodium), terra sigillata, coriander. Pulverise everything which must be pulverised. To one ounce of the spices put one pound of sugar [. . .] One drachma of this electuary is taken with fragrant wine.' The amount of sugar might be noted here – sixteen times that of the powdered drug itself. Such an elixir would have been extraordinarily expensive, as Chaucer bitingly observed in his description of the Doctor of Physic:

> For gold in phisik is a cordial,
> Therefore he lovede gold in special.

The dividing line between what was a medical confection and what was a sweet consumed primarily for enjoyment was blurred right from the start, and it constituted something of a

professional crisis for the apothecaries. Despite the wide accept-
ance of sugar's medical qualities, the apothecaries' justification
for selling sweets in their shops was incoherent and inconsistent, and the problem was compounded by their scorn for
mere confectioners. Pomet mentions sugar plums in passing, only
to dismiss them as 'too frivolous for a work of this nature', and
Richard Tomlinson makes a distinction between his 'marzapane'
(good for the gut and lungs), which contains pistachio nuts,
pine kernels and sweet fruits – no almonds – and confectioners'
marzipan: 'The vulgar manner of this confecture with the
dulciaryes is most simple, as being made onely of Almonds,
rosewater and sugar.' To salve his embarrassment about sugar,
Tomlinson casts aspersions on the preserving qualities of sugary
preparations, as if to imply that 'simple' confections from non-
medical sources cannot be relied upon: 'By how much an
Electuary is more gratefull to the Palate, by so much the sooner
doth its energy and faculty decay.'

Nostradamus is a happy exception to this litany of medical
pomposity. In his book of elixirs, he cheerfully acknowledges
the gustatory enjoyment to be gained from his medicaments.
Of his marzipan cakes he notes, 'they may be used as medicine
but are very nice to eat at any time'; and of his sugared almonds,
'it is better to classify them as delicious foods which may be
enjoyed daily, rather than as medicine'. Through the eighteenth
and nineteenth centuries, confectioners happily advertised the
medicinal powers of their sweets, particularly mentholated
pastilles and anything made of liquorice or marshmallow (that
is, the herb called mallow, not the fluffy pink modern marshmallow). And the chemists were still coming up with good ideas
for sweets that the confectioners could copy, such as the
standard vehicle for powdered drugs in the nineteenth century,
the cachet, which was two pieces of dissolvable rice paper
sealed over the drug in a special machine. This item is only seen
today in the form of a 'flying saucer' sweet that contains
fizzy sherbet. On the other hand, the pharmacists were still
taking advantage of the confectioners' ingredients, since drugs

were habitually mixed with liquorice powder and liquid glucose.

There is still an uneasy relationship between pharmacy and confectionery – scientifically uneasy, that is, rather than commercially – but of course it is still possible to buy products that are essentially sweets in any chemist's shop. (Beauty products and perfumes are also good examples of quasi-medical preparations sold by chemists because of historical precedent.) A delicate distinction exists between sweets that have medicinal connotations, like cough candy twist, and medicines that are halfway towards being straightforward sweets – blackcurrant and menthol cough pastilles, for instance. Confectioners have long traded on the healing properties of certain of their sweets to help the buyer justify a purchase, and pharmaceutical companies that make cough pastilles or mentholated sweets for colds probably rely for commercial success more on how nice they taste than on their success as remedies. But although products from the worlds of confectionery and pharmacy can be almost identical, there is no confusion in the marketplace: everyone knows which packets contain sweets and which are medicine, and even if you find yourself in a foreign country, package design makes the distinction clear.

This is not a recent phenomenon. We have seen how sugar was mixed with other herbs and spices to improve their effectiveness, and sugar was itself generally regarded as an excellent cure for colds. In medical terms, it would have been immaterial whether one bought one's cough or cold sweets from the chemist or the confectioner. But good marketing by the pharmacists, coupled with the public's need for reassurance and a veneer of scientific validity when it comes to matters of health, meant that the most successful purveyors of sweet cough drops, pastilles, cordials and cold cures were those with medical qualifications, however spurious. Sweets bought from the confectioner were never taken entirely seriously as remedies. The fact that so many medical preparations contained sugar was useful to the charlatan, who could depend on an inexhaustible market for useless or almost useless remedies that nevertheless tasted pleasant.

In *London Labour and the London Poor* (1851), Henry Mayhew observes: 'Perhaps the latest mountebank in England, was about twenty years ago, in the vicinity of Yarmouth. He was selling "cough drops" and infallible cures for asthma, and was dressed in a periwig and embroidered coat, with ruffles at his wrist, a sword to his side, and was a representation, in shabby genteel, of the fine gentleman of the reign of Queen Anne.' He sounds very like the Duke and the Dauphin who trick Huckleberry Finn. Mayhew explains that the modern equivalent of the mountebank is the patterer. He counted six of them on the streets of London, of whom only two actually made the cough drops, in the form of halfpenny sticks neatly wrapped in paper. The recipes and even the ingredients of these products were kept a close secret. Their barrows, which opened and shut on one side like a piano, were painted with a picture of a distillery works, and strewn with dried herbs, notably horehound (a popular flavouring in the United States, too). The patterers attract customers with cries of, 'Long life candy! Candy from herbs!' With perseverance, Mayhew managed to secure an interview with one of these vendors, and he was struck by the man's sensitivity to imagined criticism, defensiveness and a reluctance and even refusal to answer certain questions. This from a reporter who had braved the toughest toughs of London. Mayhew did learn that in the summer, when the market for cold cures fell away, the patterer took to selling goldfish.

After the discovery of penicillin, antibiotics and other effective curatives during the late nineteenth and early twentieth centuries, and the general improvement of health provision in the West through the last century, the gap between confectionery and pharmacy widened further. People were no longer as likely to be forced into a situation where they had to seek out their own cheap curatives from street vendors and confectioners, because the alternative was to pay a doctor to receive expensive and potentially painful treatment. The confectioners realised that they could not compete with medical science, and the remedial properties of their sweets became nominal, although they continued to be sold in chemists and sweetshops alike. The crossover continues: many of the leading brands of simple cough sweets and pastilles are now made by major sweets and chocolate manufacturers, including Mars, and recently there has been a surge in sales of sweets that meld confectionery with medicine, such as sugar-free chewing gums and glucose-energy sweets. But the old-fashioned medical sweets which had already gained a good reputation tended to survive in the same form, even as they disappeared from the sweetshops and became available in chemists only. Brand loyalty, always strong in confectionery for nostalgic reasons, is even more marked in the case of medical preparations which have soothed and reassured us since childhood. The packaging of such bracingly comforting sweets is often almost identical to the Victorian original. Mummy may no longer be there to stroke our brow, but those cough pastilles she provided will probably still be available from the nearest chemist, looking and tasting exactly as they always did.

Lucky Dip

RHUBARB AND CUSTARDS

Rhubarb and custards are my favourite sweets. There are two main types of rhubarb and custard: the chewy, rectangular, wrapped version; and the boiled sweet, shaped like a torpedo, half red and half yellow, coated in sugar, and bought loose from the sweetshop. The second type is my absolute favourite sweet. A well-made rhubarb and custard is the perfect sweet (for me) because it combines the sharp, fruity savour of the rhubarb with the smooth creaminess of the custard. This sweet-sour contrast is the classic flavour dichotomy of all gastronomy. Yet a rhubarb and custard offers more: a corresponding contrast in texture, with the jagged edges of the rhubarb half and the smooth roundness of the custard half.

I eat more rhubarb and custards than any other type of sweet, and I buy them locally, from a good old-fashioned sweetshop with a whole wall of jars containing sweets to be sold by the quarter-pound in paper bags. The lady in the sweetshop stocks three different types of rhubarb and custards, each made by a different firm. She is a very shy, though not unfriendly lady, and during the first two years of our retail relationship we barely exchanged a word. On one occasion, however, the lady in the sweetshop did not reach for Bond's of London's rhubarb and custards, my preferred brand, but another, and in my opinion inferior, variety. So I asked for the Bond's instead. The lady gave me a queer look. 'They're all the same, ain't they?' she asked, but something in her tone made me realise that the question was rhetorical. She seemed to be looking at me with new eyes. 'I think the Bond's ones are nicer,' I said. The lady slowly put the other jar back and reached for my preferred brand. 'Yes, they are better,' she said quickly, almost conspiratorially. 'And they don't stick together as much.'

I wanted to see how and where rhubarb and custards were made. Why are Bond's rhubarb and custards the best? Would watching the alchemy of sweetmaking take away from the magic of consumption? Bond's of London used to be based in east London, like all the capital's sweet firms, not far from the docks and sugar refineries. It was presided over by 'Grandpa' Bond until his death in the 1960s. I came across a photograph of Grandpa Bond and his staff on the annual works outing in 1933 – a boat trip on the river. Grandpa Bond, a happy chappy wearing a beret, has his arms round the waists of no fewer than three jolly-looking girls, and everyone else in the picture looks exceptionally good-humoured and in several cases rotund. But the firm exists only as a tradename now, and my beloved Bond's rhubarb and custards have emanated from various British factories over the past decade as companies merged and split and closed down in the unforgiving and fast-moving world of the confectionery business. The current owner of the Bond's name (and of the Bond's boiled-sweet recipes) is Penguin Confectionery of Carlisle. It was a long drive from London, but I was determined to see rhubarb and custards being made. The managing director, Wilson Deyermond, said that he could not absolutely guarantee that rhubarb and custards would be 'on the slab' during my visit, but I was prepared to take that risk.

I did not see rhubarb and custards being made. But it did not matter all that much, because Mr Deyermond's general manager took me on a comprehensive tour of the operation. Sweets have been made in Penguin's sturdy, red-brick factory since 1865; before that, the building was a mill. Today's workers use the same techniques as their grandfathers would have done, with only slightly upgraded versions of machinery. Young men stretched and pulled great wedges of striped, coloured sugar while it was still hot, before feeding it into machines that stretched it even more and chopped it into sweetie sizes. They all found it highly amusing that I should be taking an interest in their work. There were big panning machines for mint imperials, and encrusted contraptions for the nut brittle. It was all most edifying.

But I was shocked to find that this one factory produced several versions of exactly the same sweets under different brand names – including rhubarb and custards. The Bond's stock made up just 20 per cent of production, and this one Carlisle factory also produced the inferior version of rhubarb and custards that I had rejected in the sweet-shop. Mr Deyermond explained that his company makes the same types of sweets to slightly different formulations for various companies, and also several major supermarkets. Any difference in price and taste is a reflection of the quality of the ingredients, of the recipe used and — crucially — the ratio of sugar to glucose in the mix. Mr Deyermond said that there are several different grades of glucose syrup, all of them are cheaper than sugar, and no boiled sweet worthy of the name should be made with a higher than 50/50 ratio of glucose to sugar. In those sweets where the proportion of glucose to sugar is high, the flavour of the sweet is impaired and they become sticky much more quickly if exposed to the air or heat. Mr Deyermond said the best boiled sweets were 60 per cent sugar and 40 per cent glucose, and Bond's were among the best.

Back in London, I reflected that visiting the factory and seeing sweets being made had not spoiled their magic. It is not as if I was under the impression they were made by elves, anyway. Bond's boiled sweets still taste just as good, and the cheaper varieties still taste just as inferior. So rhubarb and custards are still my favourites. It is said that on his deathbed, the novelist Aldous Huxley called for a dose of mescalin, the hallucinogenic drug. If ever I find myself in a similar situation I will not call for mescalin. No, a quarter of rhubarb and custards will suffice.

Chapter 7

ENSLAVED BY SWEETNESS

Any population in history which has been exposed to sugary sweetness has immediately developed an overwhelming desire to consume more and more of it. So a crisis occurred in 1453, when the Ottoman Turks, who had conquered Constantinople as part of a policy of apparently unstoppable expansion, closed down the overland caravan routes from the East into Europe. This was a most satisfying victory for the Turks over their ancient rivals, the Arabs. Even the great trading blocs, Venice included, could not find a way round the in-stransigence of Constantinople. It has been argued recently that it was the Western powers, particularly Genoa, who were partly responsible for the decrease in trade in Turkish lands, as they became fixated on the potential of the New World. But the fact remains, pepper prices in Venice multiplied by thirty times at this point, as stocks of all spices dwindled. The prognosis for sugar was not good. The Mediterranean industry, instigated by the Arabs but now presided over by Europeans, was in a state of general decline as a result of war, plague, technological stasis and mismanagement. It is true that there were periods when sugar production in the Mediterranean – in Crete or Cyprus, for example – was buoyant, but this was because the competition – the sugar industry in the Middle East – was itself in a bad state, successively weakened by the wars against the Crusaders, the Mongol invasions and Tamerlane's incursions, as well as constant friction with the Ottoman Turks. As J.H. Galloway points out in his definitive *The Sugar Cane Industry* (1989), in 1324 there were sixty-six sugar refineries in Cairo and a century later only nineteen were left, the result of agricultural slump and bad government by the Mamluk sultans. The Mediterranean and the Middle Eastern industries were doomed to play an ever diminishing role as suppliers of sugar to Europe; it appeared that anyone who could discover a cost-effective new route from India to Europe could make a lot of money. The growing European appetite for sugary sweetness had to be satisfied somehow, and a sea route to India appeared to be the answer.

It was the Portuguese who triumphed: Vasco da Gama sailed down the west coast of Africa and rounded its southernmost tip, the Cape of Good Hope, in 1497, thereby opening up a hazardous but direct sea passage to India. The Portuguese quickly consolidated their advantage on this route, and the Dutch and the English followed in their wake, literally. Meanwhile, Europe's private banking networks backed Portugal over Venice and Genoa in the control of the sugar and spice trade, and the Italian city republics began a slow but irreversible economic decline. (The most entrepreneurial dynasties prevailed, however: the Centurione family of Genoa backed the winners, became naturalised Portuguese and funded various sugar-seeking expeditions.)

Preferable to travelling thousands of miles to barter for sugar in India, however, was growing it yourself, and it happened that the triumph of the Turks at Constantinople coincided with the European powers' early colonial adventures. The Portuguese under Henry the Navigator had planted sugar cane on Madeira, a previously uninhabited island in the eastern Atlantic, about ten years after they had arrived there in 1425, and a modest supply of sugar from this new source was arriving in Lisbon by the 1450s. (The first sugar from Madeira reached Bristol in 1456.) The price of sugar traded through Venice, and now Amsterdam and Antwerp in the north, dropped through the latter half of the fifteenth century even as the new sea route to India was being sought.

Madeira became the prototype sugar colony. Portugal led the

way in exploiting the climate and workforce of its new territories, planting sugar on the tropical island of São Tomé, off the west coast of Africa, on the Azores and, later, in Brazil. Spain followed Portugal's lead and began refining sugar cane in the Canary Islands. The colonial explorers may not have discovered the Eldorados of their imaginings, but it was hot enough and wet enough to grow sugar cane. Christopher Columbus understood sugar – he was married to the daughter of a Madeiran landowner and had himself lived in Funchal, the capital of the island – and on his second trip across the Atlantic in 1493 he oversaw the planting of cane plants from the Canaries on Hispaniola (modern San Domingo), an island that was to become an important sugar producer. The Spanish also planted cane in Mexico, Cuba, Jamaica and Puerto Rico.

The European sugar market had been transformed. Until the early nineteenth century, sweets were an expensive luxury, and they would have remained so if the price of sugar had stayed as high, relative to staples such as bread, flour or cheese. But gradually, and particularly from the eighteenth and into the nineteenth century, sugar was transformed from a luxury product and status symbol of the nobility, into an everyday necessity enjoyed by all. This alteration of status was achieved with such clarity and cruelty that economists use it to exemplify the phenomenon of the commodity chain – the way in which a network of labour and production processes results in a finished commodity. In the case of sugar, it is illustrated by the way cane has been grown on plantations in poor regions with the extensive use of slave labour, to create a raw material that is used to produce a range of commodities in rich regions – not least, sweets. The key to the development of sweets as a mass-market product lies in the cheap availability of the principal ingredient: sugar. The methods used by the good capitalists of Europe, with their African patsies, to make money by providing a plentiful supply of cheap sugar, are a bitter jab at the heart of sweetness.

Slavery, while by no means endemic, was well established in

the medieval sugar industry of the Middle East and the Mediterranean (notably in Crete and Cyprus). Pope Nicolas I had given specific permission that pagans might be used as slaves, and black African slave workforces had been used on the Mediterranean islands by the Italians and also in Spain by the Genoese who had moved in to take over the sugar plantations of the retreating Arabs. The Portuguese relied on African slaves to work first their plantations on São Tomé and also, crucially, those of Brazil, the sugar source that dominated the market for about a hundred years from the mid sixteenth century. The Portuguese were not only better organised than anyone else, the Brazilian cane yielded a great deal of sugar and the climate meant it needed no irrigation. Complete state-of-the-art sugar refineries were manufactured in Europe and shipped across the Atlantic to be reassembled; in 1522, one sugar pioneer (a member of the Centurione family) took with him by boat to Brazil not just the metal apparatus for the refinery, but also the bricks. In 1550 there were five sugar plants in Brazil; by 1623 there were 350. The Atlantic ports became the hubs for this new sugar trade as well as for the equally profitable tobacco industry, and Antwerp and then Amsterdam seized the moment. By the 1560s Antwerp was refining more sugar in a fortnight than Venice did in a year, and it financed the expansion of the industry across the Atlantic. At the end of the sixteenth century the Mediterranean sugar trade had effectively collapsed and the traditional producers in India and the Middle East had been forced to reduce their prices to unviable levels.

The Spanish and Portuguese enjoyed a monopoly on the importation of sugar from the Americas through the sixteenth century, and a steady supply and lack of competition led to the price of sugar remaining fairly stable. Strong links were established between the sugar plantations of Brazil and brokers in Amsterdam, London, Hamburg and Rouen. As a result, the confectionery industry was consolidated throughout Europe as a producer of luxury goods that were not, however, inaccessible to those of fairly modest means. After all, sweets can be sold and enjoyed in very small quantities. In 1632 a character in Philip Massinger's play *City Madam* refers to 'the shops of the best confectioners in London', and Bacon in his *New Atlantis* (1626) mentions 'A Confiture-House; where we make all Sweet-Meats, Drie and Moist', which implies that the trade was well established in its own right by this time.

The English, French and Dutch bristled at the Iberian monopoly, and in the first decades of the seventeenth century they instituted semi-official policies of piracy and smuggling in the West Indies. Finally, from about 1630 to 1660, these nations invaded and took control of the most defensible Caribbean islands – the English took Barbados and Jamaica; the French, Guadeloupe, Martinique and St Kitts; the Dutch seized parts of northern Brazil from the Spanish and invested heavily in the new sugar industry of the eastern Caribbean. The Dutch also lent invaluable technological expertise, mainly provided via Sephardic Jews from Amsterdam. Sugar proved to be the perfect crop for the Caribbean islands – it grew far better than tobacco or cotton – and in Barbados by the 1660s the English had established a system of large plantations worked by African slaves that was far more efficient and profitable than the Portuguese model in Brazil. The Barbadian plantation was to become the *modus operandi* of large-scale production in the Americas, an extremely profitable operation that gave rise to the infamous 'triangular trade' of the eighteenth century – European goods to Africa; slaves from Africa to the West Indies; sugar, tobacco and coffee from the West Indies to Europe – which has been covered extensively and in detail elsewhere.

This is not to turn our back on the subject of slavery. The numbers of slaves carried off from Africa to the West Indies at this time makes a disgusting counterpoint to the European orgy of sweet sugar (which the slaves, ironically, never tasted: they were given only the by-product, molasses). During the seventeenth century, the British shipped about 250,000 African slaves in total; in the next century, the average number was 45,000 . . . per year.

But all this was not the fault of sugar or sweets. It was the fault of men. Anti-slavery campaigners, including the poet Coleridge, did their best to stimulate a boycott on the slave-grown sugar by illustrating the link between the luxury of sweetness and the corresponding certainty of human misery. In William Cowper's poem, 'Sweet Meat has Sour Sauce, or, the Slave Trader in the Dumps' (1788), there is the intermixing of the imagery of blood and flesh with sugar that is characteristic of anti-slaving literature:

> Here's padlocks and bolts, and screws for the thumbs
> That squeeze them so lovingly till the blood comes;
> They sweeten the temper like comfits or plums,
> Which nobody can deny.

But Edward Fox and his fellow campaigners were accused by Britain's continental rivals of urging an end to slavery for economic rather than humanitarian reasons, and the British public could not be convinced to give up sugar. The end of slavery was certainly not brought about by what would today be called consumer action.

The European confectionery scene, and its burgeoning new counterpart in North America, was slowly, subtly but decisively altered through the seventeenth and eighteenth centuries by the influx of ever cheaper sugar into the marketplace. The process did not decelerate after the abolition of slavery in the early nineteenth century, as new sugar industries in India, Africa and south-east Asia emerged to take the place of the Caribbean. Sugar consumption in Europe had steadily risen through the sixteenth and seventeenth centuries as the price fell and it became more widely available. Abraham Ortelius remarks in his *Theatrum Orbis* of 1572: 'Whereas before, sugar was only obtainable in the shops of apothecaries, who kept it exclusively for invalids, today people devour it out of gluttony [. . .]What used to be a medicine is nowadays eaten as food.' By 1700 sugar was flooding in from the West Indies. The price dropped sharply at first, opening up new retail markets, and over the next hundred years sugar consumption increased dramatically. Any graph which illustrates this increase is distinguished by an extraordinarily steep and sustained upward curve; in some situations (such as early-eighteenth-century England) sugar consumption doubled within a decade. It even increased during those periods when the price of sugar was rising. The economic and social reasons for England's hearty embrace of sugar have been itemised by Sidney W. Mintz in *Sweetness and Power* (1985), who has examined the changing status of sugar most closely:

Why did the English people become such enthusiastic sugar consumers? Not because of the innate primate liking for sweetness; not because our species is symbolically communicative and builds meaning into all it does; not because socially inferior groups imitate their 'superiors'; not even because people in cold, wet climes supposedly like sugar more than other people. Certain homelier facts seem more persuasive. The diet of the British worker was both calorifically and nutritively inadequate and monotonous. Often working people could not get hot food, especially for their breakfasts and midday meals. New schedules of work and rest, changing conditions of employment, the end of the dependent relationship of agricultural labourer to squire, the development of a putting-out system, then a factory system – these were among the contextual conditions for changes in food habits. It is in their light that the vaunted disposition of people to imitate their betters can be made to rest on a broader interpretative basis.

The nutritive role of sugar, as a provider of quickly absorbed, energy-boosting calories, should not be overlooked in the context of the extreme hardship of many workers' lives as the Industrial Revolution developed. But while it is tempting to subscribe to a view of a self-determining proletariat, choosing sugar for good nutritional reasons, it should be remembered that, unless they are actually starving to death, people are not very good at eating what is good for them because it is good for them. Sugar is sweet and sweetness is nice: that is the main reason why people ate it.

England consumed most sugar. The old habit of sugaring wine provided the precedent for mixing sugar with tea (something the Chinese and Indians never did). There is no evidence of a concerted marketing campaign by traders, retailers or the government aimed at instilling the idea that tea and sugar were inseparable, but this idea became firmly entrenched at an early stage and it is reasonable to assume it was no accident. A healthy home market for sugar, prime product of Britain's colonies, was an insurance policy for the economic health of the growing empire. The link between sugar and tea may have been eroded with time, but the resilience of national food habits is demonstrated by the fact that most of us still unquestioningly take milk in tea today – a practice again unknown in China and India.

The twin commodities of tea and sugar were received with such enthusiasm in Britain that the sugar traders of London, Bristol and Liverpool found to their surprise that it was not necessary or even possible to re-export much of their stock into Europe. The English wanted to eat it all. In the first half of the eighteenth century, only about a fifth of sugar imported to England in any given year was re-exported, and sometimes the figure was as little as 8 per cent. Sugar and tea were usually bought at the same time, about six times as much tea as sugar, from one of the thousands of little shops that were established in town and country in England during the eighteenth century. Many of these 'tea shops' sold little more than tea, sugar and tobacco, plus perhaps coffee and raisins and other dried fruits (sweets did not enter the province of the small shop until the nineteenth century). They were deemed groceries rather than provisions, which were perishable staples. The distinction remained even into my childhood in southern England in the 1970s: the village shop sign advertised, in wavy writing, both Groceries and Provisions. David Davies, a socially minded clergyman, made an acute observation about the exotic pedigree of the basic groceries, sugar and tea, in 1795: 'It appears a very strange thing, that the common people of any European nation should be obliged to use, as part of their daily diet, two articles imported from the opposite sides of the earth.' Davies was well aware that the reasons for this apparently absurd state of affairs were entrepreneurial opportunism, the consolidation of empire, and a little gustatory pleasure.

In other European countries sugar consumption was not as marked, and poor France was least significant in this respect. It could be argued that the British love for sweet things represents the perfectibility of international taste, and that the reduction of sugar consumption in France was a perversion of the palate engendered by excessive use of wine. But that would be the argument of a maniac! How can we know that wine reduces the desire for sweetness? There is evidence that it may in the case of alcoholics, but that is an extreme example. More plausibly, it has been suggested that the French led the way in the post-medieval separation of sweet from savoury throughout Europe because sugar, like other spices, became less of an exotic luxury product. As it became more familiar to the poor, it became less attractive to the rich. It was also the case that the economic and imperial imperative for sugar consumption was less marked in France than in Britain. In *The Culture of Food* (1994), Massimo Montanari points out that by the late seventeenth century, the fashion among the French élites was for 'peasant' foods like chives, shallots, capers, anchovies and mushrooms. Buttery or creamy sauces were preferred over sweetened stocks and bouillons, and herbs from meadow and maquis took the place of exotic spices, which had been imported in bulk since the fifteenth century. Sugar and comfits were omitted from the ingredients list of meat and fish courses. Pepper, cloves and nutmeg were still kitchen essentials, but other spices, such as cinnamon, were left out or relegated to the sweet course, which was placed firmly at the finale of the meal. It is possible that the sweetness of desserts grew more intense, almost as if to compensate for its loss at the earlier stages of the meal, but on the other hand, cheese came to be used as a replacement for the banquet course. Tea, and the sugar that accompanied it, was not as freely available or as popular in France as in England. All this led to sugar being looked upon as an old-fashioned, un-sophisticated gastronomic crowd-pleaser (much as it is today), antique and rather vulgar. In 1691 the Countess d'Aulnoy, dining in Madrid, could not conceal her disgust at a ham 'covered with candies of the sort that we in France call non-pareils [. . .] whose sugar melted into the fat'. Other French travellers at this time were dismayed to see sugar sprinkled on salads in Flanders and Ireland.

But the use of sugar in cookery was slow to decline in many places, particularly in England, and Poland and Germany retained a taste for strongly spiced food. In Britain, the anti-sugar movement in cookery was seen by some as an effete French innovation. William King's *Art of Cookery* (1709) satirised it: 'For what hopes can there be of any Progress in Learning, whilst our Gentlemen suffer their sons at Westminster, Eaton [sic] and Winchester to eat nothing but Salt with their Mutton, and Vinegar with their Roast Beef upon Holidays?' And Mary Ketilby in her cookbook of 1728 wails, 'But so it is, that a Poor Woman must be laugh'd at, for only sugaring a Mess of Beans.' But as if to underline the lowly status of sugar, when the people of Paris rioted over food shortages in 1792, they were not complaining about a lack of bread (or even cake), but of other 'white goods': soap, candles and sugar. France's energetic and prescriptive approach to cuisine ultimately prevailed, and the nation's cooking became the apogee of Western gastronomy. The taste for sweetness, so assiduously cultivated in Britain, had been relegated to juvenile status in international culinary lore, so that Rousseau could pay a backhanded compliment in *La Nouvelle Heloïse* (1761): 'Sweets and dairy foods are the natural favourites of the gentler sex, symbolising the innocence and sweetness that are her most appealing ornament.' The French academies may have signally failed to dictate the progress of language, but fashion in food was easier to influence. This is not to say the French lost a taste for sweetness in its proper place: Diderot himself, king of the *encyclopédistes*, died while reaching for a cherry compote.

Revolutionary America found political inspiration in France, but its sweet tooth was inherited undecayed from Britain. High taxes imposed by the British on sugar imports from the West Indies, which culminated in the Sugar Act of 1760, meant that for their sugar kick Americans had to turn to molasses – a by-product of the refining process, like treacle – and also to maple syrup to some extent. *The Frugal Housewife* (1772) by Susannah Carter contains no sweets, just preserved fruits, tarts, creams and so on, but there are recipes for molasses-based candies in *Miss Leslie's 75 Receipts* of 1837, in which Miss Eliza Leslie of Philadelphia describes candies of molasses, brown sugar and lemon, with optional peanuts or almonds, twisted into sticks. America never lost a taste for it, and when the Rueckheim brothers launched their molasses-covered peanut and popcorn mix, called Cracker Jack, in 1893, they found they had a hit.

Molasses was supplanted by sugar as the national sweetstuff only in the nineteenth century, and it was also the base for the most popular alcoholic drink, rum. The New England rum industry engendered a triangular slave trade of its own: rum to Africa, slaves to the West Indies, molasses back to New England. But consumption of sugar itself among working people in eighteenth-century America appears to have been almost as high as that in Britain. Surviving accounts from the New York and Philadelphia poorhouses indicate that by the mid eighteenth century sugar, molasses, tea and coffee were an important part of the diet of even the poorest people in society. Among the rich and middle classes, sugar and sweets were suitable for special occasions, usually in the form of fruit preserves, conserves or candies, or dry fruit chips made from distilled fruit pulp and syrup. A standard early American cookbook such as *The New Art of Cookery* by Richard Briggs, published in Philadelphia in 1792, contains a chapter on drying and candying, including precise directions on how to cut the fruit aslant to make orange and apricot candies, and a recipe for ginger tablet, made of sugar and ground ginger, to be displayed on a china dish in a single piece.

Through the eighteenth century, sweets became cheaper but the range did not radically change. There were still the comfits, dragées, fruit preserves and candies, jellies, gums and pastilles that had been enjoyed in some form since the Middle Ages, and confectionery manuals of the late eighteenth century contain many of the same recipes as their predecessors of 200 years before. The real change was that more people were able to afford these delicacies, and more people were engaged in making them. Britain – and by extension the English-speaking peoples of the United States, Australia, Canada, New Zealand and the other colonies – was slowly emerging as the third great sweets culture, after those of India and the Islamic empire. Other European countries never lost their taste for sweets, but consumer demand and the confectionery culture did not develop quite as dramatically.

In Britain, through most of the eighteenth century, the confectioner's wares remained speciality foods that were considered a permissible regular extravagance, or an aid to health. They were certainly not casual purchases. The cost of a loaf of sugar may have plummeted, but the price of a box of sweets had not: the confectioners had managed to hold on to the public's respect, and it was still perfectly acceptable to pay a relatively high price for handmade delicacies that were nevertheless made entirely of cheap sugar, seeds, roots or fruits. A good confectioner could make a mint. It was the artistry of the confectioner and the exotic mystery of the confection that ensured the enduring appeal of sweets, coupled with an instinctive and perfectly rational notion that, on the whole, it is simply too much effort to make these things at home. The fact that the sweets and their recipes had changed little over centuries probably led to the idea that confectioners were the keepers of arcane secrets handed down through the generations – the alchemists of sugar. Which of course they were. This romance of sweets, engendered by the presumed rarity of their ingredients and the mysteries of their creation, has never been lost. For Keats, in 'Eve of St Agnes' (1819), sweets are the perfumed embodiments of the East, and a presentiment of lust:

> And still she slept an azure-lidded sleep,
> In blanched linen, smooth, and lavendered,
> While he from forth the closet brought a heap
> Of candied apple, quince, and plum, and gourd;
> With jellies soother than the creamy curd,
> And lucent syrups, tinct with cinnamon;
> Manna and dates, in argosy transferr'd
> From Fez; and spiced dainties, every one,
> From silken Samarcand to cedar'd Lebanon.

Perhaps the sweet which most nearly instils such evocative passions in us today is Turkish Delight (see Lucky Dip, page 50).

The reality of sweetmaking was, of course, more prosaic, although the jargon could be colourful. Take doctors and interfering agents. These are technical terms that refer to certain ingredients added to molten sugar to prevent it losing its transparent lustre through 'graining'. By 1750 French confectioners had discovered that lemon juice was good for this, and British confectioners, perhaps with reference to their trade's association with the medical profession, called the addition a doctor. Later, tartaric acid (from grapes) and glucose syrup were found to be even more effective, and such additives came to be known as interfering agents. The exact science of sugar-boiling was codified in 1698 by the French confectioner François Massialot, who recorded the stages of sugar-boiling and their best application. (This was not Massialot's discovery, he was merely the conduit of hard-won confectionery wisdom.) The correct handling of hot sugar, between about 223 and 350 degrees F (106 and 177 degrees C), is vital to the sweetmaker's art, and the vagaries of cooling times, stirring and the attainment of very high and exact temperatures are the chief cause of the variation in texture and flavour among sweets made by boiling sugar – that is, boiled sweets or hard candy, rock, chews, toffees and caramels. It is truly extraordinary that such a wide range of products – and confectionery certainly displays the widest variation of any category of foodstuff – can be made from the same basic mix of sugar and water, which is heated until a certain amount of the water evaporates, and then cooled quickly or slowly and perhaps kneaded with flavourings (such as milk for toffee) and colouring.

The scrubbed red hands of the confectioner must be able to withstand high temperatures when solidifying sugar is on the slab. Pulled sugar, the basis for rock and all boiled sweets, is kneaded and stretched continually as it cools, either by hand or machine, and as the air comes into contact with it, it acquires its distinctive satiny sheen. In sugar-boiling and handling, the one thing to avoid is crystallisation – except in the case of sweets such as fudge and fondant – and the stage or consistency of the sugar syrup is tested by dropping some of the boiling mixture into iced water and watching how it behaves. This takes skill and fine judgement, and a pan of boiling syrup can be quite a hazard, so home confectioners have generally restricted themselves to preserving or candying fruit and other simple procedures. Unfortunately, whenever the eyes of this international confectionery historian begin to read of the technical aspects of confectionery, they glaze over. To be truthful, I am more interested in eating sweets than making them. So here is a Petrarchan sonnet that delineates the eight stages of sugar-boiling in more condensed if not more palatable form.

> O syrup, when first thy surface is stirred,
> By heat-crazed bubbles pricked out in cool air,
> THREAD you will be, for oozing liqueur or
> FEATHER-made fondant in chocolate interred.
> Thou treacling globe, now appear as a BALL,

> For caramels, fudge, and all there's to chew,
> From HARD BALL to STIFF, make toffees anew –
> D'ye hear the siren confectioner's call?
> Chewier still? At SOFT CRACK I'll try you:
> Nougaty dreams for Arabian nights.
> At CRACK heat it's drops and rock and no goo,
> And pliable sugar for subtle delights.
> Last there is CARAMEL, apples to case,
> Brittle and burnt, but a smile on each face.

The process of change in the confectionery trade was very gradual. The price of sugar had begun to drop by the late seventeenth century, but the role of sweets as banqueting stuff had barely altered since medieval times. An account by John Evelyn of a London reception given by the king for the Venetian ambassadors in 1685 illustrates how sweets, at this time, were still a source of some amazement to the general populace:

> The banquet was 12 vast Chargers piled up so high, as those who sat one against another could hardly see one another, of these Sweetmeats which doubtless were some days piling up in that exquisite manner, the Ambassadors touched not, but leaving them to the Spectators who came in Curiosity to see the dinner &c were exceedingly pleas'd to see in what a moment of time, all that curious work was demolish'd, & the Comfitures &c voided & table clear'd.

In other words, the ambassadors and the other guests stood back to watch the ravening hordes demolish piles of preserved fruits and comfits.

The early-eighteenth-century confectionery manuals, such as John Nott's *Cook's and Confectioner's Dictionary* of 1723 and Mary Eales' *The Compleat Confectioner* (1733), repeat the recipes for preserves, candied fruits and comfits that had been in existence for hundreds of years, but the retail trade became more sophisticated. In the late seventeenth century, the *limonadiers* of Paris, who sold ice cream and confectionery as well as drinks, had begun to create a monopoly for their wares by opening up highly decorated cafés. Procopio dei Coltelli's Café Procope, founded in 1686, was walled with mirrors and hung with chandeliers, its counter piled high with delicious preserved fruits, whipped creams and syllabubs, and neat glasses of ices and sherbets. There was wine, coffee, chocolate and myriad fruit liqueurs to drink. Café society did not exactly translate to London, where more down-to-earth coffee houses and chocolate houses prevailed in the eighteenth century, but the most respectable confectioners' shops were as spectacularly styled as the French cafés, albeit in premises that were much smaller. Confectioners would print elaborate business cards to advertise their wares, and the sign swinging outside the shop would show some exotic fruit – pineapple was the favourite. Women in particular found these shops amenable places to linger and socialise among starched white tablecloths over a coffee or chocolate, and perhaps an ice cream or sweetmeat. The attraction is understandable. By the mid eighteenth century, shopping in London was an extremely glamorous affair, a spectacle of temptation that was continually commented upon by visitors and locals alike. The sumptuous emporia of the West End reflected England's prosperity, founded as it was on a sea trade whose lines of communication had been seared onto the globe by sugar, as hard for competitors to crack as the caramelised carapace of a crème brulée. Even in the provinces, new, brightly lit shops were replacing the older stores and market stalls, their bow windows filled with sumptuous displays that bulged into the street, fat to bursting with riches. England may have been a nation of shopkeepers, but what shops they were!

Daniel Defoe's *The Complete English Tradesman* (1726), a practical-polemical manual, provides the best view of the retail scene in England at the start of this revolution. He bemoans the fact that shopkeepers have to spend so much money on fitting up their shops: in 1710, he reckons it cost £300 to fit up a pastry-cook's shop (which in this case doubles as a confectioner), whereas a few years earlier it would have been £20. Three hundred pounds is a ridiculous sum, but Defoe had a weakness for over-emphasis; his main thrust should be taken seriously. He blames the French for such extravagance, of course, as well as the general public: 'The first inference to be drawn from this must necessarily be, that this age must have more fools than the last; for certainly fools only are most taken with shows and outsides.' He itemises the necessary fitments for even quite a rudimentary shop: sash windows, painted tiles, four tall mirrors, two pairs of candlesticks (one silver), eleven glass hanging lanterns, twenty-five sconces, 'six fine large silver salvers to serve sweetmeats' and twelve table stands for tarts and jellies (three silver). Then there is the expense of painting the shop inside and out, gilding the lanterns and carving the window woodwork. The oven is almost an afterthought. It is telling that Defoe's pastry-cook's shop is also a confectioner's: sweets were available from miscellaneous retail outlets, including milliners. The same is true today: sweets can be found on the counter in various odd shops. In France, the link with baking was more marked: a *confiseur* would come under the jurisdiction of the *pâtissier* in any large kitchen, and the town *pâtisserie* has long doubled as a confectioner.

A clue to the continuing elevated status of sweets in the mid eighteenth century can be found in contemporary tableware. Bonbonnières were dainty little baskets or boxes, usually with lids, in silver or china and designed to contain sweetmeats of various sorts at the banqueting course. Fashionable ceramic manufacturers made them in pairs; the Chelsea factory, for example, produced figures which held comfit baskets aloft. In France, a bonbonnière shaped like a shoe, called a *chopine*, was particularly popular. The medieval *drageoire* had endured, although it was no longer a wooden box according to Joseph Gilliers, author of *Le Cannameliste François* (1751), but a tablepiece made of crystal or green glass, used for displaying 'pyramids of cherries and other small fruits', some of them candied. The centrepiece of a grand banquet course would be a silver epergne, an elaborate piece that supports salvers or baskets on the ends of several delicate arms: an epergne is to the silver-smith what a tiara is to the jeweller. Sweets were still deemed deserving of such presentation, whereas by this time it was not necessary to lock away the sugar from the nimble hands of sweet-toothed servants; small lumps broken from the sugar loaf would be placed in a relatively humble bowl graced by a pair of tongs.

The changing tone and content of confectionery manuals written by professionals in the late eighteenth century illustrates the way the trade in Britain was beginning to react to the ever-increasing demand for cheaper sweets. This was the foundation of the modern confectionery industry. Not all the confectioners bothered with cheaper sweets: the Pall Mall maker Edward Lambert hardly mentions any other sweetmeats except expensive preserved fruits in his *Art of Confectionary* (1745). The celebrated Hannah Glasse also concentrates on recipes for preserved and candied fruit, as well as various creams, jellies, biscuits and other puddings (including the excellent whim-wham, a species of trifle). There is just one generalised recipe for comfits in her *The Complete Confectioner* (1760), and the suggestions for banqueting table layouts at the end of the book specify salvers of fruit (presumably preserved as well as fresh), nuts, 'bloomage stuck with almonds', jellies, creams and ice creams. Very few sweets. A plate of nonpareils makes an appearance in one bill of fare, and the grandest plan suggests a centrepiece distinguished by sweets that is quaintly reminiscent of the old way: 'In the middle a high pyramid of one salver above another, the bottom one large, the next smaller, the top one less; these salvers are to be fill'd with all kinds of wet and dry sweet-meats in glass, baskets or little plates, colour'd jellies, creams, &c. biscuits, crisp'd almonds and little knicknacks, and bottles of flowers prettily intermix'd, the little top salver must have a large preserv'd fruit in it.'

From this evidence, comfits, dragées, gums, pastilles and other sweets appear to have fallen from favour, but these London confectioners might have omitted recipes for such sweets either out of self-conscious deference to what they considered was 'high-class' or because panned dragées and gummy sweets were considered a speciality of foreigners, and not appropriate to the thoroughly modern banquet course, presided over by jellies. Perhaps to fill the dragée niche, *The Court and Country Confectioner* by one Borella – described as an 'ingenious foreigner, now head confectioner to the Spanish ambassador in England' – was translated into English in 1770 and went into many editions. It contains excellent recipes for all kinds of 'bomboons', 'pastils' and dragées – the latter in flavours like violet, caraway and apple. There are useful tips, such as grating your lemon against the sugar loaf to sweeten the rind as you go, and a description of a special tin box with four grates for candying in bulk, as well as some throwbacks to earlier times. For coriander dragées or comfits, Borella advises, 'you keep stirring well your corianders, till you see they are well perled over or rough and grainy like'. This textural distinction dates back to medieval French confectionery.

A continental connection was of some advantage in the eighteenth-century confectionery retail trade, too. One sweet-maker's card read:

D. Negri, confectioner, at the Pineapple, Berkely Sq: makes and sells all sorts of English, French and Italian wet and dry sweet-meats. Cedrati and Bergamot chips, Naples Diavaline and Davalino, All sorts of Biskets and Cakes, fine and common, Sugar Plums, Syrup of lapilaire, Orgeate and Marshmallow, Glumaive or lozenges for colds and coughs, all sorts of ice, fruits and creams, in the best Italian manner.

The 'Italian warehouses' along the Strand in London (most of them owned by Englishmen) were repositories of all kinds of foreign delicacies, not least sweets, which were nevertheless advertised in the popular papers as being excellent value for money, affordable to the 'middling sort' now as well as the rich. And in the provinces by the late eighteenth century, as Hoh-Cheng Mui and Lorna H. Mui show in *Shops and Shopkeeping in Eighteenth-century England* (1989), the number of confectioners in provincial English cities like Norwich, Bristol and York increased three- or fourfold from the 1780s to the 1820s, and confectioners in a city such as Leeds would advertise the delivery of a new consignment of sweets from London in the local evening newspaper (in which they might later be wrapped in the shop). But not all sweets had to be sent from London: there was a growing appetite for relatively cheap boiled sweets, which could be made by anyone prepared to put in the practice and lay out for a copper pan, a few tools of the trade and quite a lot of sugar, which was fairly cheap by then. The casual nature of this cottage industry has meant that official records are non-existent, but it is likely that small-scale sugar boilers, many of them women, were in part-time business by the end of the eighteenth century. Certainly, most villages in Victorian Britain could boast one or two ladies who supplemented their income by sweet- and biscuit-making. The *Oxford English Dictionary* notes that the humbug – a striped, mint-flavoured pulled-sugar sweet with a chewy centre – was known in Gloucestershire in the early nineteenth century, and it was quite possibly invented by a semi-professional sugar boiler (although not necessarily in Gloucestershire): novelty was an important aspect of boiled-sweetmaking, which accounts for the wide variation in boiled sweets invented through the nineteenth and twentieth centuries, a good proportion of which can still be found today.

Sweets made by itinerant traders began to become a fixture at the big town fairs and weekly markets. A fairing, the name for a knick-knack bought or won at a fair, often by young men for girls, is an old term first used to refer to gingerbread or sweets in the 1770s, and by the nineteenth century sweets had become perhaps the most popular fairing of all. Some of them were unique to particular fairs: in northern Ireland, yellowman, a type of brittle and honeycombed toffee made of butter, brown sugar, vinegar, golden syrup and bicarbonate of soda, is specifically associated with the Lammas Fair in Ballycastle, County Antrim, a sheep and pony fair in August. In *Saleable Shop Goods* (1898) by Frederick Vine, a confectioner and baker of Chancery Lane, there is even a recipe for fairings: cakes coated with old-fashioned caraway comfits, which he specifies should be long rather than round, a reference to the shape of some of the medieval originals (which also accounts for the torpedo shape of the modern liquorice comfit, the only sweet actually called a comfit still widely available today).

Perhaps the shifting, mutable, spontaneous atmosphere of fairs makes them good places for snack creativity: the ice-cream cone was invented at a fair, the St Louis Fair of 1904, when Syrian trader Ernest A. Hamwi offered some of his 'zalabia' waffles to a next-door ice-cream seller who had run out of dishes.

Candyfloss is perhaps the only surviving example of a sweet that can really only be bought at fairs, and coincidentally it was launched at the same St Louis Fair as the ice-cream cone. But this pink cloud on a stick, with its bizarre texture, is so large, soft and strange that it might not be a sweet at all. In French it is called '*barbe à papa*' or 'daddy's beard'. What a good idea. More beards should be made of candyfloss. How it is made is a mystery, although it is done right in front of you. It is said it was invented in America in about 1900. I am of the opinion that fairies, friends of the Romany people who run the fairs, are involved in the manufacture of candyfloss, for its genesis is beyond the wit of man or international confectionery historian.

Right on the cusp of the transition of sweets from high-class luxury to everyday purchase is *The Complete Confectioner* (1789) by Frederic Nutt. This book contains information on ice cream, biscuits, wafers, jams, jellies, water ices, preserved and dried fruits, and also a whole chapter on 'drops'. These are simply powdered sugar and lemon juice boiled up, plus flavour and in some cases colour, cooled and stored in papered boxes. They are far humbler than the productions found in sweet manuals up to this point, and indicate a growing demand for sweets as cheaper, more casual purchases even at this, the high end of the profession. Nutt's asides, such as the importance of placing paper over each layer of sweets in the boxes, are those of a professional making observations useful to the retail trade, whereas previously the instructions in manuals had been couched as advice to ladies, or to chefs in private service. Apparently this was not much use to Joseph Bell, 'formerly confectioner to the Prince of Wales and Duke of York', who claims in his *Treatise on Confectionary* (1817) – distinguished by a frontispiece of a lion and unicorn rising up out of a cake – that in his thirty-eight years in the sweetmaking business he has never seen a book used. From his shop in the spa town of Scarborough, Bell sold fancy confects as well as simple sweets like ginger barley sugar drops, nitre barley sugar drops and apple knots (apple and sugar boiled, coloured red, rolled thin, baked, cooled, cut into bootlaces and made into decorative shapes). He also mentions 'rock candies', possibly a first reference to a seaside institution (see Lucky Dip: Rock, page 102). London confectioner James Cox includes similar recipes in his manual of 1822, although any budding international confectionery historian should note that the Siberian crabs he mentions in one recipe are homegrown apples rather than crustacea from cool climes.

Perhaps because of this gradual change in the status of confectionery, the distinction between sweets made in the confectioner's shop and those for sale in the street is commented upon by several high-class confectioners of the early nineteenth century. At the top end of the trade, it was in the confectioner's interest to continue to mystify the profession, to reiterate the fading associations of sweets with exotic lands and luxurious lifestyles. William Gunter was a delightfully pretentious character, whose *Confectioner's Oracle* of 1830 begins with a dream sequence in which the author is led to a massive banqueting table by a witch, where he finds the Earl of Powis and Lady Agar Ellis (valued customers, we can assume) 'indulging their nerves in gustatory rapture' by gorging themselves on his sweets. Then the triumphant Gunter is showered with gold sovereigns and his book goes into a tenth edition. 'It is a remarkable fact', he continues, 'that in this country the art of confectionery has hitherto, for the most part, been surrounded with as many mysteries as the temple of Osiris used to be among the ancient Egyptians, or as the craft of Free-Masonry is at the present day.' Gunter protects his interests by decrying the 'wretched trumpery' that is street confectionery, and also discouraging potential competitors from going into the business of inventing sweets, 'in which last attempt you may injure your health and render your character ambiguous; and instead of being a respectable and thriving professor in Regent Street, Bond Street, St James's Street, or Berkeley Square, you may end your days in a prison after having pined away for years with scarcely the means of keeping body and soul together'. Best leave it to Mr Gunter, then, who appears most congenial in the portrait frontispiece to his book.

Just as benign, to judge from his portrait, is W.A. Jarrin, author of *The Italian Confectioner* of 1820, which went into as many editions as Gunter dreamed about. Jarrin is nostalgic about the old days of confectionery in France, where he was previously employed, and mentions the great and forgotten eighteenth-century artists of spun-sugar table decorations, such as Monprivé, Leccelan and Cocard. 'To make gum paste properly,' he asserts, 'great care and dexterity, much patience, some knowledge of mythology, of history, and of the arts of modelling and design, are requisite – qualifications seldom possessed by the mere pastry-cook.' Jarrin goes on to recount proudly how a two-foot-high paste group that he had made, which featured Napoleon at its centre in the act of sheathing his sword, was praised by the dictator himself at a banquet in Paris in his honour. Napoleon was indifferent to food, and while on campaign subsisted entirely on a diet of roast chicken cooked by his chef at odd times of day and night, but Jarrin reports that the megalomaniac did like food moulded in his own image: 'The Emperor, who rarely noticed anything which ornamented the table, observed his portrait, and, with his characteristic attention to works of ingenuity, was pleased to encourage the artist by his approbation.'

Jarrin's recipes are certainly at the fancy end of confectionery: a giant mushroom made of sugar; spun caramel baskets, containing sugar birds and flowers, that he made for the coronation of George IV; North Pole Candy, hard outside like rock, with a centre of egg white and maraschino: 'They retain their moisture inside, of a beautiful yellow, well tasted, and it is difficult to guess what they are made of.' Not all Jarrin's sweets are quite as delicious-sounding: the one for 'small sausages' – imitation sweet sausages filled with dried apricots and cherries – begins, 'Take some entrails', which refers to real sausage skins. Jarrin was in fact completely out of touch with the realities of the trade. In a new preface to the 1843 edition of his book, he claims: 'I conclude with observing that the art of the Confectioner is absolutely an art administering to pleasure and luxury, and that it requires times of prosperity and abundance, – times in which nobles live as nobles, and in which good taste and liberality walk hand in hand; – such times as existed under Louis the Fourteenth.' This may be true of spun-sugar models and caramel baskets for kings and emperors, liberal and otherwise, but Jarrin affects ignorance of an already thriving street-confectionery scene.

To find out more about the realities of this industry it is necessary to turn to Henry Mayhew, the extraordinary investigative journalist who became obsessed with revealing to the middle-class reading public the truth about life among working people and criminals in mid-nineteenth-century London. He would make repeated forays into the poorest parts of the capital, conduct interviews with people who seemed instinctively to trust him, and return home to his study to dictate his findings to his wife. In the newspaper articles that were collected as *London Labour and the London Poor* (1851),

Mayhew describes a thriving trade in street sales of all kinds of items. The poorest people would have had little cause to enter a shop. Pies, ham sandwiches or a cone of hot peas were popular and cheap meal options purchased on the street, and certain commodities could only be bought from semi-permanent out-door stalls or mobile vendors: Mayhew estimates that catfood and dogfood, for example, accounted for no less than half the total of all street sales in London, about £100,000 a year. (A dog's boney dinner must be fresh, and tins were not yet an option.) His estimate for confectionery sales on the streets of London indicates a relatively healthy trade, when one considers sweets are not something which keeps a person (or a dog) alive: £10,000 on sweets, compared with £31,200 for hot coffee and tea, £19,448 for hot eels, £14,000 for baked potatoes, £11,400 for fried fish, £6,000 for muffins and crumpets, £3,000 for pies and just £42 for ice cream (universally known as hokey pokey, possibly because of the Italian street sellers' cry, 'O che poco!', or 'Oh how little! [it costs]', which the English ice-cream men turned into, 'Hokey pokey, penny a lump, freeze your belly and make you jump!'). Cough drops and other medicinal sweets were considered speciality items and their manufacture was confined to a handful of makers – the patterers of the previous chapter – who sold them only in winter. In his section on 'sweet-stuff sellers' – Mayhew says he never heard sweets or confectionery called by any other name – he mentions 'the several kinds of rocks, sticks, lozenges, candies, and hard-bakes', which are all sweets made from boiled sugar. He notes the popularity of rock and other sweets which could be made of treacle rather than the more expensive sugar, which actually increased in price during certain periods of the early nineteenth century. Of molasses sweets, there was hardbake (toffee), almond toffee, halfpenny lollipops, black balls (presumably boiled treacle balls), the cheaper bullseyes (bi-coloured boiled sweets), and squibs (sweets shaped like asparagus tips). 'Brandy balls', he explains, 'are made of sugar, water, peppermint and a little cinnamon,' designed to warm you up, like a brandy. Rose acid is one of several kinds of transparent boiled sweets, in this case coloured with cochineal (beetles' blood), and barley sugar is also popular. The medieval penides are still very much in favour: pulled sugar sweets in all kinds of shapes and colours. Mayhew adds: 'The flavouring – or "scent" as I heard it called in the trade – now most in demand is peppermint. Gibraltar rock and Wellington pillars used to be flavoured with ginger, but these "sweeties" are now exploded.' (By 'exploded', Mayhew means fallen from favour, not destroyed in some accident involving excessive amounts of bicarbonate of soda.) It would seem that there had been an upsurge in invention among sugar boilers in the early nineteenth century, spurred by increased demand which was unaffected by fluctuations in the price of sugar.

Mayhew says that the majority of the sweetsellers were also manufacturers, and that their parents had generally been bakers or confectioners. The vendors he spoke to asserted that the sweets they were making and selling were exactly the same as those of forty years previously: one of them, a former baker, said that he was thinking of reintroducing a softer sort of treacle toffee called Tom Trot, which indicates that there was probably considerable residual knowledge among the sweetmakers, who knew the selling power of a seeming novelty. Mayhew visited one eccentric confectioner, 'a very intelligent man', who rarely had time to escape his work: 'His room, which was on the second floor of a house in a busy thoroughfare [. . .] was cheerful with birds, of which there were ten or twelve.' This is a scene worthy of Dickens, who himself noted that sweet sellers were even known to work in cellars.

The sweetmakers wrapped their goods in the cheapest paper from the stationer's, or else recycled old books. In one home-based sweets factory, Mayhew observed several volumes of the Acts of Parliament used for this purpose, as well as other books, which the confectioner 'retained to read at his short intervals of leisure, and then used to wrap his goods in. In this way he had read through two Histories of England!' Mayhew counted about 230 sweetsellers trading, of whom twenty to thirty were

Jewish and had a slightly different stock in trade – almond cakes, for example, and 'boolers', thin cakes that contained orange and lemon candies (Jews had been associated with the citrus trade since medieval times). 'The difference', says Mayhew, 'in these cakes, in their sweetmeats, and their elder wine, is that there is a dash of spice about them not ordinarily met with.'

The success of this thriving street trade began to be reflected in the stock of the smarter, shop confectioners, who were also doing extremely well. In a thriving industrial town like Manchester, the confectioners multiplied to become an important part of the retail economy, not just a quaint sideline. The records show that in 1772 there were just two confectioners' shops in the town; this had risen to seven by 1800, forty-one by 1830, and fifty-seven by 1840. Numbers leapt to 119 in 1850. To provide an idea of the relative quantity of these shops, and with apologies for more figures, in the year 1872 in Manchester there were 308 confectioners, 2,716 general shopkeepers, 804 butchers, 741 fruit and vegetable sellers, 473 grocers, 374 bakers and forty-three tea and coffee dealers. Sales of confectionery must have been high, in relative terms.

The British sweet tooth was conclusively consolidated at this time by jam. This cheap and sweet condiment, which generally contained very little fruit, became a staple in working-class households from the 1870s to the late twentieth century, spread on thick slices of bread and butter. Gladstone's removal of the sugar tax in 1874 made a cheap commodity even cheaper (the sugar firm of Tate replaced the sugar loaf with the more convenient sugar lump in the 1880s) and free trade led to an influx of cheap imports and the decline of the refining industry in Britain: in 1864 there were fifty refiners, by 1900 only sixteen. The extraction of sugar from sugar beet – the lumpen *Beta vulgaris*, a blanched relative (second cousin) of beetroot – had been demonstrated in 1747 by Andreas Marggraf, a Prussian chemist who mixed brandy with beet to reveal sugar crystals. Sixty years later, Napoleon attempted to circumvent

Britain's profits from its West Indian plantations and satisfy a sugar-starved nation by calling on patriotic French industrialists to start a sugar-beet industry modelled on the one recently established in Prussia. One Benjamin Delessert duly obliged, and when Napoleon was presented with a beet-sugar loaf at his new plant at Passy near Paris in 1812, he was so overcome that he pinned his own Légion d'Honneur on the breast of the startled factor (whose name, we observe, is an anagram of 'le dessert'). The beet industry that sprang from this source now accounts for about half our sugar; France is still one of the leading producers. These factors led to a sevenfold increase in world sugar production in the first half of the twentieth century, an escalation which no other major crop in history has achieved.

A Victorian confectioner's was an exciting place to be, but by mid century it was no emporium of rare delights. The confectioners' manuals of the time are full of simple sweets, such as lemon and other fruit drops, and peppered with short cuts and cheap ingredients. In *The Confectioner and Pastry Cook's Guide* (1854) by George Read, the instructions for comfit-making, using a comfit pan suspended on hooks above the stove, is appended: 'If they are for common, or cheap comfits, give them occasionally a dust of flour, as you coat them' – thus saving money on sugar. There are acidulated drops, gummy jujubes flavoured with orange-flower water, best bullseyes made from barley sugar mixture (lemon-flavoured), and something called snowy rock or snow: white pulled candy flavoured with lemon or peppermint. These are everyday sweets which smack more of smoggy Sydenham than silken Samarkand. The *New Whole Art of Confectionary* (1837) by Edward Mackenzie (a sweetmaker who worked all over England) contains the only recipe I have seen for the popular patriotic boiled sweets called Nelson's buttons: large drops made of egg whites, sugar and peppermint and coloured rose or pink – probably a gory reference to the hero Nelson's bloodied coat at the Battle of Trafalgar. Other choice sweets made by Mackenzie include paradise twist: boiled sugar streaked with red and white; pulled sugar sweets in the shape of little birds; and gingerbread buttons: very small balls of treacle, oatmeal, butter, candied lemon peel, caraway seeds and cinnamon. They all sound superb.

Conversation lozenges were one fashionable confection which has never fallen from favour. The idea that a sweet might carry a romantic message was born in France or Italy, where bags of dragées had long been used in courtship. Jarrin, in his book of 1820, mentions the New Year's Day bonbons in France, which were contained in envelopes decorated with 'fables, historical subjects, songs, enigmas, jeux de mots, and various little gallantries'. The romantic notes inside Italian Baci chocolates are another version of this. But at some point in the mid to late nineteenth century, British sweetmakers started to make boiled sweets and rock with short messages inside them. These were generally coyly romantic – 'Do You Love Me?' or 'No, I won't ask mamma' – but the temperance movement also got hold of the idea and started improving people's lives by handing out sweets with accompanying printed messages like, 'Misery, sickness and poverty are the effect of drunkenness'. English Lovehearts and American Conversation Hearts are modern versions of these conversation lozenges. The sweets trade was lucrative and respectable, and confectionery schools began to be established: in London, the Ladies' Confiserie Company, for example, or the school of piping and ornamenting on the Tottenham Court Road presided over by the unfortunately named Herr Willy.

In America, the sweets industry had burgeoned in Chicago, a nexus of North American trade and a destination for economic migrants from all over the world. John Mohr opened the city's first candy and cookie factory and store in 1837, selling pralines and sugar wafers among other things, and twenty-two years later Chicago had no fewer than forty-six confectioners making and selling a wide variety of stock, including lemon drops, peppermint candy and canes, rock candy, gibraltars (lemon or peppermint hard candies), liquorice ropes and pipes, and candy corn (then known as chicken feed).

In fact, Chicago's candy industry eclipsed that of New York from the start, and the city saw the founding of the National Confectioners' Association in 1884 by sixty-nine sweetmakers, whose motivation was exactly the same as the medieval spicers' of 700 years before – to set standards and banish adulteration so that customers could rely on their products. Later, big corporations such as Mars and Curtiss set up factories in Chicago, and smaller concerns invented classic American candies that are still on sale today, like the Ferrara Pan Candy Co's Jaw Breakers, Boston Baked Beans, Red Hots and Atomic Fire Balls. Other sweets invented and produced in Chicago include Milk Duds, Jelly Bellies and Tootsie Roll, and the practice of giving sweets out at Hallowe'en was a simple marketing ploy that emanated from the city's confectioners. The large-scale candy retailing trade, an American innovation, came out of Chicago, with Brach's from 1904 and the deliberately old-fashioned Fannie May sweets (which later merged with Fanny Farmer to create a coast-to-coast concern) from 1920. As ever, not all sweets were sold from shops; in the late nineteenth century, so-called candy butchers worked the trains in the United States, selling their wares to travellers. But in both Europe and America it was industrialisation in the form of labour-saving machines that could mass-produce sweets – available from the 1840s – which revolutionised the confectionery business.

The flavour of the early-modern American confectionery scene is captured in Charles W. Popp's *Modern Confectionery* of 1910. This is a no-nonsense trade manual, 'intended for the guidance of practical men, who, working with brains, will be able to produce the best possible results from the materials used'. Popp finished up in Glasgow, but he had worked in Boston, New York, Philadelphia, Denver and Portland, and his manual was a rival to the standard technical work on confectionery, *Skuse's Complete Confectioner*, the first edition of which was published in London in about 1880 and updated every few years or so. These books are sharp and commercial, with none of the aristocratic pretensions, wifely common sense or craftsman's idiosyncrasies of earlier books on sweetmaking.

The importance of machinery is stressed, with *Skuse's* in particular parading detailed drawings of the newest machines, such as the mogul (which can mass-produce chews), tablet pressers, rock choppers, liquorice pellet machines or the delightfully named enrober, still a standard machine in chocolate factories, which creates a curtain of chocolate to coat the 'centres' slowly passing through it. The emphasis is wholeheartedly on mass production, and getting the best value from materials. The number of recipes for caramels in Popp's manual is testament to the popularity of these soft, milky sweets in America, and a huge range is described, with names like Sporty Boy, Nonesuch, Walk-over, Fancy Daisy and Cambridge. The existence of lemonade 'caramels' – of sugar, glucose, citric acid and fruit flavours – indicates that the word was almost synonymous with candy as a whole. Coconut is another favourite flavour, and marshmallows make an appearance (mixed with figs in the case of marshmallow figlets). There is butterscotch, Boston chewing toffee, made with cream, all kinds of gums, pastilles and 'jubes', as well as winter cough drops (with menthol, aniseed and eucalyptus), Jersey beauties (candy canes) and chew-chews or half-hour chews in lemon, strawberry, orange, chocolate and fig.

This is all sugar confectionery. Chocolate and chocolate bars are another matter, and traditionally these two strains of manufacturing do not mix. But by about 1920 on both sides of the Atlantic, the shape of the modern sweets industry had been forged – or rather heated, cooled, stirred and pulled. The world was ready to be enrobed with sweetness.

Lucky Dip

MARSHMALLOWS

There are two kinds of marshmallow in sweets history. The original one was made from the root of the plant called a marsh mallow, and the modern one we all know is made from sugar and egg whites and some sort of gum or gelatin. But marshmallows ancient and modern are united by one thing: their fabulous gooiness.

The marsh mallow plant – Althaea officinalis, or merscmealwe in Old English – common in Europe and Asia, looks like a hollyhock, with pale pink flowers. Its roots produce a sticky, white, mucilaginous substance, so perhaps the white of the root sap and the pink of the flowers is the source of the traditional colours of marshmallows. This marsh mallow sap was used as a kind of gum in northern Europe before gum arabic and gum tragacanth (derived from the bark of Middle Eastern trees) began to be imported in quantities. The medicinal use of marsh mallow, particularly as a cold cure, can be traced back to the eleventh century: during the Middle Ages pieces of mallow root were candied to make mallow suckets, and by the seventeenth century these were being prescribed for urinary problems. But these marshmallows were probably not very nice; at this time, the sweet fell more easily into the province of the pharmacy than the sweetshop.

It was the French who first thought of exploiting the textural possibilities of marsh mallow for its culinary as opposed to medicinal possibilities. Pâte de guimauve, the French name for marshmallow, was made by whipping up egg whites, sugar and the sticky extrusion of the mallow root, to make those familiar soft pillows or lumps, halfway between air and toffee. By the early twentieth century, the marsh mallow itself had been replaced by gelling agents that were easier to obtain, such as gelatin or imported gum, and the United States joined France as the most enthusiastic consumer and manufacturer of this strangely compelling confection. It has a unique texture – part of the reason why one wants to eat a marshmallow is to double-check that such a thing really does exist.

Marshmallow can be enjoyed in a number of ways: in France it is still capable of being considered a relatively sophisticated sweet suitable for adults; in the 1950s and 1960s in America there was a vogue for marshmallow in salads, and American children still love it as a spread on bread (revolting to adults). It is made in various snaky or bouncy shapes; the Balkan states are excessively fond of chocolate-covered marshmallow sweets; Valomilk, the classic American chocolate-covered marshmallow sweet, was accidentally invented in 1931 when a batch of marshmallow was forgotten and it stayed runny; and there is the ever-popular option of barbecued marshmallow, made hot and gooey and burnt on the end of a stick. For me, the finest marshmallow sweets available are Peeps, boxes of bright-yellow, chick-shaped marshmallows that are sold in their millions at Easter in the United States. They are made by Just Born of Pennsylvania, which pioneered marshmallow technology in the 1950s by devising a way of mass-producing complicated marshmallow forms. A Marshmallow Peep is a wonder of finely judged texture, with a slightly crispy skin and a light centre; it is the texture which makes it very difficult not to eat a whole box at one sitting. And of course a Peep is shaped like a little chick, which lends the sweet a certain pathos. This sense of pity for the chick develops only in late childhood, and grows stronger as one gets older and relinquishes the candied callousness of youth.

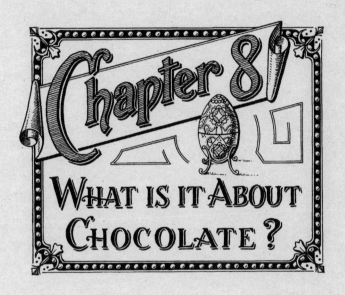

Chapter 8

WHAT IS IT ABOUT CHOCOLATE?

No other sweet excites such extremes of emotion as chocolate, and the emotion it inspires most often is love. A significant minority absolutely adore it, very few of us hate it, and most people struggle to keep their cocoa-lust in some kind of proportion. The very idea of chocolate excites us, and our liking is irrational in two ways: first, the urge to consume is passionate and uncontrollable, like a drug addiction; second, rationing is just not an option.

Chocolate is not like any other sweet. Most confectionery buoys up the spirits and makes us smile: its sweetness is innocent, and our pleasure is, too. With chocolate, however, it is only too easy to form a complicated emotional attachment. This unlikely-looking brown substance, which tastes so wonderful, can excite high emotion and lasting dependency. My own position is this: I like chocolate, but I feel ambivalent about chocolate hype and chocolate connoisseurship, and also about the way women are encouraged to relate to chocolate in modern society. Whenever anyone says the word 'chocoholic', I think 'eating disorder'. So, chocolate is the most complicated of sweets, the most powerful of sweets, and the one that most of us would choose to give up last.

As befits a strange and mutable substance that has taken on many guises, the pedigree of chocolate is not at all straightforward. For the first two thousand years of its history, chocolate could not be eaten. It was a drink; the first solid chocolate bar did not go on sale until 1849. Even then, solid chocolate was not invented and launched with a fanfare, but devised as an expedient way of using up a waste product – excess vegetable fat – that was left over from the manufacture of the cocoa powder used to make hot chocolate drinks. It was not an auspicious beginning, and no one imagined that eatable chocolate would ultimately eclipse a hitherto fashionable beverage.

The history of chocolate is filled with such twists. The first European to come across it, Christopher Columbus, commandeered a Mayan trading vessel in the Gulf of Honduras in 1502. His chronicler described the dried beans of the cacao tree which he found therein as a kind of almond – he apparently did not realise that they could be eaten. The role of these beans was quite unexpected: chocolate was money to the Mayans. Children today love the gold and silver coins that contain chocolate beneath their glittering foil wrappings, but this was real chocolate money. It deteriorated, in a literal sense, so hoarding wealth was not a good idea, and later Spanish commentators noted that this helped keep the Aztec economy fluid. In fact cacao had been in cultivation in coastal areas of Mexico (notably in the Soconusco region) since perhaps the time of the Olmecs (1500–400BC), so to say it was 'discovered' by Columbus is missing the point. It was certainly used as both currency and food by the time of the Mayans, and vessels found at burial sites, inscribed with phonetic hieroglyphs that spell out 'ca-ca-w', have been dated to the fifth century AD. Since cacao grew only in the coastal regions of Mexico, the beans must have been transported thousands of miles to be used as money and as a drink in settlements in the interior.

Chocolate did not remain a South American secret for long. A few years after Columbus, in 1520, Hernando Cortes, leader of the Spanish invasion of Mexico, spent time at the court of Montezuma, king of the Aztecs, and was reportedly struck by the post-prandial practice of drinking golden chalices of chocolate, poured from one vessel to another to create a frothy head. This chocolate, for which there were many different recipes, was not usually sweetened, and a variety of flavours were added to it – chilli pepper, vanilla, allspice and various flower-petal pastes. Honey (which the Mayans are also known to have added) was occasionally used. The beans were sun-dried and then roasted in earthen pots. The shells were removed and the kernels ground on stone over a firebox. Flavourings were added to the resultant paste, and the mixture was patted into cakes and left on banana leaves to cool and harden. To make drinking chocolate, the cakes were broken in pieces, dropped in water and whipped up.

The conquistadors initially thought it was quite unpalatable, so in theory chocolate could have been a delicacy that for ever remained confined to South America (like roast tapir, which the Aztecs adored). But for the Aztecs, chocolate was the most important foodstuff of all. The best Aztec chocolate was an aphrodisiac, it was issued in tablet form to warriors on the march, rich traders coveted it, and it was an important part of religious ritual. It could even be argued that the red dye, annatto, from the achiote plant, which was sometimes added to chocolate and which stained the mouth and lips, was a reference to, or a substitute for, human blood. Both the Aztecs and the Mayans are known to have had a penchant for human sacrifice. One Spaniard, Gonzalez Fernandez de Oviedo, writing in the early sixteenth century, described the fearsome effect of a cup of chocolate: 'The lips, and the part of the face around them, are covered with the foam, and when it has been coloured with annatto it looks horrific because it is just like blood, and when it has no annatto it looks brown, and one way or another it is a dirty sight.' Chocolate seems less innocent in this context. One could conclude that the Aztec association of chocolate with blood, sex, money and fighting is probably more appropriate to a commodity imbued with powerful psychoactive and commercial properties, than the disingenuously infantile identity which has emerged for it in Western culture.

It is not just the human history of chocolate that is strange; the natural history is, too. The cacao tree is a diminutive and agriculturally unreliable tree (it is generally grown beneath a canopy of banana trees, in case the crop fails), and does not have a formal harvesting season: it fruits sporadically all year. It is as if nature cannot get enough of chocolate, either. The seedpods, which look like melons with the weathered texture of a walnut or W. H. Auden, do not hang from the tree, as one might expect: they grow straight out of the trunk or the larger branches, which is an odd sight. Slice open a pod with a machete, and thirty to fifty beans are revealed, clustered like pomegranate seeds and coated in a white mucus that is used to make alcoholic drinks in plantation areas. The beans are dried out, the nibs (kernels) are fermented, dried, roasted and winnowed, and then ground down until they become a liquid known as cocoa liquor. I saw these mysterious nibs at the Ghirardelli chocolate factory in San Francisco, where antique nineteenth-century machines, by Lehmann of Dresden, still make chocolate. As luck would have it, the machines are on display in the ice cream café.

Drinking chocolate became popular throughout Europe in the 1660s, but only after a long period when it was kept as a virtual secret by the Spanish aristocracy and clergy. (When British buccaneers caught a Spanish prize in 1579, sacks of chocolate beans were thrown overboard as worthless, which is ironic, because British seamen later came to consume more chocolate in the form of cocoa than the rest of the nation put together.) In Mexico, chocolate had become so popular with the Spanish colonists that it caused a major scandal in the important town of Chiapa Real, now Cristobal de las Casas, when ladies attending church ignored the repeated requests of the bishop and continued to have their maids deliver hot chocolate to sustain them during mass. As Jean-Anthelme Brillat-Savarin noted in 1825: 'The Spanish Ladies of the New World love chocolate to the point of madness.' Thomas Gage, an English Jesuit in Mexico who drank five cups of chocolate at regular moments through the day, relates how the bishop threatened the ladies with ex-communication, and that when his junior priests tried to confiscate the chocolate in church, swords were drawn against them. The bishop died suddenly shortly afterwards, convinced, on his deathbed, that he had been poisoned.

There has been a rumbling association of chocolate with poison ever since: Pope Clement XIV, who suppressed the chocolate-loving Jesuits in 1773, was purportedly given a poisoned bowl of chocolate in the following year, and the claim is supported by Sir Horace Mann in a letter to his friend Horace Walpole: 'A slow poison was given him by his own confectioner in a dish of chocolate last Holy Thursday at the Vatican [. . .] from the first sip he told the servants that it had a bad taste. Nevertheless, they [the Pope and his confectioner] both continued to swallow their death. A few days after, they both fell ill, and during the whole interval until they expired their symptoms were the same.' The most alarming of these symptoms was that their arms and legs swelled up and their fingernails fell out.

The Spanish colonists were serious about mixing their chocolate: the first book on the subject appeared in 1609. They experimented with various new flavours, such as cinnamon and aniseed, and liked to replace the Aztecs' ground cornmeal (*atole*), used as a thickener, with ground almonds. They also habitually added sugar, which was to become an essential additive to chocolate back in Europe. The frothiness of Aztec chocolate was emulated by means of a swizzle stick, or *molinillo*, which resembles a medieval mace in the curious variety of its design. Later, tall chocolate pots would be distinguished by a hole in the lid to make way for a swizzler, which is perhaps the best way of telling them apart from coffee pots. By the early seventeenth century in Spain, chocolate had become a sweet, rich drink, particularly suited to breakfast. Today, only a few areas in South America (notably Oaxaca in Mexico) and Spain (north-east Aragon and the Basque country) serve up food that harks back to chocolate's old savoury status – dishes such as the Mexican *mole poblano*, which combines chocolate with turkey and chilli.

In the early to mid seventeenth century the irresistible drink was introduced, partly as a result of royal marriages and via networks of monasteries, first to Portugal, then Italy, Flanders, France and soon afterwards England, where chocolate (and later coffee) houses were established as talking shops and neutral environments to talk business. Some of them also became known as hotbeds for the discussion of radical politics, and for this reason Charles II closed them down for a brief period in 1675. Chocolate's radical reputation did not last: by the late eighteenth century in northern Europe it was associated with the corrupt clergy and the reactionary, absolutist regimes of old Catholic Europe – particularly Spain's, of course – and politically progressive thinkers, men of the Enlightenment, tended to favour coffee. (There were exceptions: a young visitor to the ageing Voltaire noted that he ate or drank nothing between the hours of 5am and 3pm except a mocha-like mix of chocolate and coffee.)

The Protestant strongholds of Germany and the Netherlands remained addicted to coffee above all, although intellectuals, including Goethe and Schiller, liked chocolate, too. Indeed, when eating chocolate was introduced, Germany took to it with a vengeance and has ever since remained one of the highest per capita consumers in the world. There is a suitably precise story that the Swiss enthusiasm for chocolate was instigated by the mayor of Zurich, who fell in love with the drink during a visit to Brussels in 1679, and took it home with him. The Portuguese, however, generally preferred tea, no doubt partly a reaction to the predilection for chocolate of its great rival, Spain.

Most of Europe's chocolate supplies were traded through Madrid. On one visit to Spain, Casanova, who was himself very fond of chocolate, complained: 'The Spaniards offer visitors chocolate so frequently at all hours, that if one accepted, one would be choked.' Spanish chocolate drinkers continued to experiment with different flavours – hazelnuts, cloves and musk, for example – and there is even an early reference (1685) to chocolate being enjoyed in solid form: 'The ladies also, and Gentlewomen of Mexico, make little delicate cakes of

Chocolate for daintiness, which are sold likewise in the Shops, to be eaten just as Sweetmeats.' These must have been rather dry and gritty: if they were absolutely delicious, surely they would have been taken up elsewhere?

The Spanish were mad for drinking chocolate with the addition of various flavours, but in the rest of Europe, and in America from about the 1680s, the addition of sugar and vanilla generally sufficed. A fashion for chocolate made with milk as well as water emerged in England (probably not an innovation, but an imitation of a Spanish model), and in Florence the court of Cosimo III de'Medici made jasmine-scented drinking chocolate famous. The Italians were fêted as the most skilled chocolatiers of all, and the northern city of Turin emerged as an important centre of expertise. But the new beverage was always considered slightly suspect. The American academic Barbara Lekatsas writes, in *Chocolate, Food of the Gods* (1997, edited by A. Szogyi): 'Chocolate conquered Europe like an edible form of the noble savage. It was an Aztec Indian version of the Eucharist, an embodiment of deity made available to humans. But more like the nectar of the Greek deities, chocolate had fertility associations, and its aphrodisiac qualities made it quite different from the Christian Eucharist.' Which is an outlandish way of putting it, but captures some of the excitement of chocolate in the early seventeenth century.

As with sugar itself and various other sweets, chocolate was marketed as a substance beneficial to health as well as delicious to taste. In the humoral scheme of things, chocolate was usually viewed as essentially cold and moist, although it was said that it could turn hot as it aged. Many scholars disagreed even with this flexible thesis, arguing that it was always hot. Perhaps the confusion is a reflection of the chemical complexity of chocolate, which is still only slightly understood. In any case, in practice it was the stimulating effects of chocolate (it contains a small amount of caffeine) that gave it a reputation as a cordial and pick-me-up. It could be quite an energiser, and there is no greater advertisement for this quality than the 'quaint and almost unbelievable' fact, revealed by Pamela Parkinson-Large in her history of the knights of Malta, that in the eighteenth century the knights' galley slaves were given cocoa each afternoon, and also a good minestrone soup and huge quantities of bread.

Chocolate was credited with a variety of impressive curative properties: it was first advertised in London in 1657 as 'an excellent West India drink [that] cures and preserves the body of many diseases', and the highly respected physician Sir Hans Sloane was so convinced of its efficacy, after he had seen it given to children in Jamaica, that he gave chocolate his personal seal of approval, to the delight of the manufacturers (Cadbury was making a 'Sir Hans Sloane recipe' cocoa even in the nineteenth century). A French medical treatise of 1685 advanced the idea that chocolate, not ambrosia, was the food of the gods, a notion apparently echoed in the new Latin name given to the cacao plant genus by Linnaeus in 1737: *Theobroma*, or food of the gods. It is likely, however, that Linnaeus, a Swede who was a paragon of scientific rationalism, was not referring to the excitement over chocolate of his own day, as is usually supposed, but drily honouring the place of the bean in Aztec history. Diderot's eighteenth-century encyclopaedia recommends a crumbly lozenge of chocolate as an instant, nourishing breakfast, and Brillat-Savarin in 1825 is unequivocal: 'Persons who drink chocolate regularly are conspicuous for unfailing health and immunity from the host of minor ailments which mar the enjoyment of life.'

In such a case, an early backlash is only to be predicted, and the killjoy Huguenot Dr Daniel Duncan, writing in *The Spectator* in 1712, identified sugar as the demon ingredient: 'Coffee, chocolate and tea were at the first used only as medicines while they continued unpleasant, but since they were made delicious with sugar, they are become poison.' He published a pamphlet in which he inveighed against all hot drinks, claiming, 'We take coffee, tea and chocolate while they're boiling; in which condition they pass through the mouth and the gullet into the stomach, the inner coat of which is lin'd with protruberant tufts, or fibres, which the boiling water burns.' Dr Duncan added that our sense of taste was being damaged by the hot water singeing our 'protruberant tufts'. Perhaps the most ridiculous supposed side-effect of chocolate itself can be found in a letter of 1671 by the fashionable Parisian châtelaine (and gossip) Madame de Sévigné: 'The Marquise de Coetlogon took so much chocolate during her pregnancy last year that she produced a small boy as black as the devil.' Chocolate was evidently too good to be true.

The apothecaries realised that there was money to be made from chocolate as there was from sugar, and chocolate became a basic commodity sold in chemists' shops, ground to order in a chocolate mill. It is worth remembering that this product was still exclusively the powder used to prepare drinking chocolate; eating chocolate was not invented for another hundred years or so. The most entrepreneurial of these medical men focused on chocolate as the way to make a fortune, and several of the pioneers of industrialisation in the early-eighteenth-century confectionery industry – Joseph Fry of Bristol, for example – started as apothecaries. Rudolphe Lindt was the son of an apothecary, and it was said that Philippe Suchard resolved to go into chocolate at the age of twelve, after he had been sent to the local chemist for a pound of chocolate for his sick mother and was shocked to discover that it cost the equivalent of three days' wages for a workman. Soon, more larger-scale chocolate concerns, boasting powered mills, were established in Germany (the Steinhund and von de Lippe chocolate plants), France, Spain and in the United States, where in 1765 Dr James Baker of Dorchester, Massachusetts, backed the concern, initially run by an Irishman called Hannon, that still thrives as the Walter Baker Company. The United States developed a strong liking for chocolate: Boston apothecaries were selling it by 1712, and it was advertised in New York in 1758. Later on in America, eating chocolate came to be sold in grocers' shops and at news stands, as well as in those stores whose name is worth a second look in the context of the medical history of sweets: drugstores.

There were two great revolutions in 1789, one in Paris, and one in Bristol where Joseph Storrs Fry, son of Joseph Fry, invested in Mr Watt's steam engine as a way of grinding his cacao beans. The newly mechanised European chocolate industry slowly developed, with the foundation of a number of companies which survive to this day: Lombart and Pelletier had already appeared in France, Van Houten and Bvloker was established in Amsterdam in 1815, and Pierre Paul Caffarel set up in Turin in 1826. Then there were the firms in French-speaking Switzerland – Cailler at Vevey near Lake Geneva in 1819 (who had learned his trade in Turin), Suchard in 1825, Kohler in 1830, and Sprüngli (later united with Lindt) in German-speaking Switzerland in 1845. But despite the foundation of all these small companies, most of whom made chocolate on their shop premises, chocolate sales were relatively depressed. 'The image of chocolate reached its nadir in the first half of the nineteenth century, when it was typecast as a superannuated and indigestible beverage,' explains William Gervase Clarence-Smith in *Cocoa and Chocolate, 1765–1914* (2000). It was usual practice to thicken the cocoa powder with potato starch, flour, treacle or sago, and even more undesirable additives, such as brick-dust as a colouring, were commonplace. George Cadbury himself described the product as 'a comforting gruel' which was just 20 per cent cocoa: hardly the drink of a modern-day Montezuma.

The biggest single complaint about drinking chocolate was its slightly oily fattiness, a result of the large proportion of vegetable fat in cacao beans. This was deemed detrimental to the delicacy of taste as well as texture, so it was in the interests of the chocolate companies to develop their own superior versions of the product. Efforts were made to isolate the fat content of chocolate by grinding the nibs of the cocoa beans in cocoa liquor as usual, but then pressing out a substance called cocoa butter, a vegetable fat which looks like brownish orange juice, to leave cocoa solids or paste that made pure cocoa powder, an even more palatable basis for a chocolate drink. The discovery of how to do this is usually dated to 1828 and attributed to the Dutch confectioner Conrad van Houten, founder of the company of the same name and the inventor of the screw press later used in the widespread industrialisation of the process. But there are references to the technique dating back to the 1670s, and prototype machines were illustrated in French books of the 1760s, and even in Diderot's encyclopaedia.

However, not one of these divines of confectionery realised that the real value of the technique lay not in the less-fatty cocoa powder, or 'cocoa essence', which was indeed more pleasant to drink, but in the cocoa butter, which was thrown away. Wastage – in this case, up to 30 per cent – is, of course, anathema to any good manufacturer, and eventually in 1847, after false starts by several British firms, Lindt in Switzerland and Caffarel in Italy, Fry of Bristol produced a tasty bar of dark chocolate that was designed for eating rather than dissolving and drinking. This experimental product, which first went on display at a Birmingham trade show, consisted of the cocoa solids, hitherto too dry to be pleasant to eat, thickened with some of the cocoa butter. It made for a palatable eating consistency and also allowed the product to be poured into moulds as a liquid and cooled into a solid. Moulded chocolate, as the trade came to call it, was born: a technical breakthrough which was as important as the new taste and consistency, since it made the product ripe for mass production. Fry's new launch was apparently not deemed exciting enough to inspire imitation by other manufacturers, and was finally offered to the public as a type of 'French' chocolate two years later, a new phase in the sly campaign by British companies to steal back market share from French and Swiss powdered chocolate, which was becoming ever more popular. Given time, this eating chocolate certainly exceeded expectations, however, with sales increasing from nine tons in 1852 to 12,000 tons in 1904.

Cadbury brought out its own version of eatable chocolate a few years after Fry, and the other European firms followed suit over the next decades. In the United States, Walter Baker in Massachusetts was using a Van Houten cocoa-butter press by 1866, which was the year that Cadbury invested in its first press to help speed production. However, as William Gervase Clarence-Smith sagely points out, drinking-chocolate sales continued to outstrip those of eating chocolate even into the early twentieth century. Mechanisation almost completely passed by the chocolate industry in Spain, for instance, where the beans were still ground down by hand on large stones on the factory floor, as they had been since Aztec times, and chocolate retained its primary identity as a drink. The breakfast tradition of chocolate with *churros* (long fried pastries) can be found in a café or two in many Spanish towns today, and the visitor used to pre-sweetened eating chocolate might be surprised to find that one adds sugar to this drink, as one might with coffee.

In the context of the ancient pedigree of most sweets, the bar of chocolate must be viewed as a recent invention, but it would be a hard-hearted international confectionery historian who was not moved by the sight of chocolate bars stamped with the imprint 'Fry', still on general sale today. These bars are not modern versions of Fry's original plain bars, but of the second important innovation in chocolate-bar history: the bar that is not all chocolate. In 1866 Fry launched a dark chocolate bar filled with a mint fondant: Fry's Chocolate Cream. It seems extraordinary that it is possible to buy a Fry's chocolate bar today that is almost identical to the original, and when my eager gaze falls on the familiar navy blue wrapper on the confectionery rack, my heart wells up and I simply have to buy one.

Sales of eating chocolate soared in Europe from the late 1870s until the First World War, and the manufacturing companies expanded their businesses, built new factories and often pursued eccentric company policies (see chapter nine, Real Willy Wonkas). The invention of milk chocolate in Switzerland by Daniel Peter in 1876 is usually hailed as a turning point. Until then, milk added to the eating-chocolate mix was liable to turn rancid and make everything too liquid, but breakfast-cereal magnate Henri Nestlé's invention of powered milk in the 1860s provided the basis for an ideal new ingredient. (Nestlé, yet another chemist, is sometimes erroneously credited as the creator of milk chocolate itself. In fact, as Lindt's company history points out, it was an Englishman, George Page, working at Nestlé's great rival, the Anglo-Swiss Condensed Milk Company, who developed the milk base for Daniel Peter's experiments.)

Milk chocolate did not gain wide popularity for another thirty years or so, however. The real breakthrough in chocolate came a few years later, in 1879, with Rudolphe Lindt's invention of conching, the process whereby liquid chocolate is repeatedly kneaded in a machine armed with wide rollers that are named for their slight resemblance to conch shells but actually look more like old-fashioned garden rollers. This process, which also allows for the addition of more cocoa butter to the chocolate mix, creates the superfine texture and mellow flavour associated with Swiss chocolate today, the result of up to five days' continuous conching. And crucially, it makes for a product that does not need to be crunched up in the mouth, but melts on the tongue in the most delightful way (the trainee international confectionery historian should note that this is due to the unusually low melting point of cocoa butter, at 97 degrees F, just below body temperature).

The public loved this new, smooth, melting chocolate, which Lindt called *chocolat fondant*, and in the late nineteenth century Switzerland surpassed France as the world's most respected and successful chocolate-producing nation. Conching became a vital part of the chocolate-making procedure, and in Switzerland the mysterious science of *chocologie* was established. Confectionery production became a truly international business, with chocolate bars from Britain exported all over the Empire, and Swiss and French chocolate captivating the world and acting as a benchmark for quality. Reassuringly for the rest of us, Switzerland was absolutely bowled over by its own chocolate, and even today sales in the home country far outstrip those anywhere else.

The price of chocolate decreased dramatically in the last twenty years of the nineteenth century, the result of huge cocoa imports, mass production and industrialisation, a wider variety of chocolate bars on sale, and an increase in the amount of disposable income available to working people. Chocolate became an everyday purchase, and it was even issued as rations to the German, British and American armies in the 1890s, for just the same reasons it had been given to Montezuma's warriors. Chocolate was still viewed as a sort of luxury, but one that was in the domain of ordinary citizens. The situation has not really changed today. Sweets are the cheapest luxury we have: a chocolate purchase can seem lavish even if expenditure is low, which is a great selling point. For a time it also became proportionately less appealing to the bourgeoisie and upper classes: Proust, for example, felt chocolate was now too vulgar to serve at teatime.

But if not quite as exclusive, chocolate was perfectly respectable: the temperance movement enthusiastically promoted chocolate because . . . well, mainly because it does not contain alcohol (liqueur chocolates were not invented until the early twentieth century). British Workman houses, or BW houses, which served drinking chocolate, were opened in competition with public houses that sold alcoholic drink, and the temperance movement published guidelines for morality-minded entrepreneurs, describing how to set up and run a successful cocoa house or cocoa room. This is also one of the reasons why several of the biggest chocolate concerns are run by families of Quakers. More recently, the Mormons of Salt Lake City, who eschew alcohol (and tea and coffee), have established a specialisation in fine chocolate.

For many of us, chocolate is a little boring in simple bar form, and the twentieth century saw several important innovations in chocolate confectionery. In 1913, the Swiss chocolatier Jules Séchaud created the technology for making moulded chocolate shells into which fondant could be poured (as opposed to simply dipping hard centres in chocolate) and the chocolate assortment was transformed. 'Combination' bars, or chocolate-covered nut, fruit, toffee, whip, wafer, caramel or fondant bars – which were really just extra-large versions of the types of chocolates found in a chocolate box – were invented at about the same time. The first successful combination bar was America's Clark Bar (1917), still on sale today.

Then there is white chocolate, a product considered so different to normal chocolate that it is illegal to call it chocolate in the United States, where brand names like Chocolate Lover's White Chip and Vanilla Chips are used. When I learned how white chocolate is made, I am afraid I lost all interest in it, and would advise anyone of sensitive disposition who is partial to white chocolate to skip the next few sentences, which describe the process; the end of this potentially offensive passage is marked with ~*@**@*~ for easy visual reference. White chocolate is made from cocoa butter, milk solids, sugar and vanilla – no cocoa solids at all. The texture is there, but the flavour is basically vanilla, with only a faint whiff of chocolate. It was the idea that the principal component in white chocolate is a fat (cocoa butter) that I found particularly revolting. All done. ~*@**@*~ Mocha, another popular variation, is a combination of two South American success stories: chocolate and coffee.

Even in the earliest stages of the modern chocolate industry it was clear that national tastes differed, just as they had with drinking chocolate. It is dangerous to suggest that taste preferences for any food, including chocolate and other sweets, are the result of the climate or geography of a nation, still less race or religion. The most important variables in determining the tastes of nations are the availability of raw materials, and pre-existing food habits. So with chocolate it happened that in southern Europe – where the ready availability of cacao beans meant that drinking chocolate was dark and flavoursome –

brittle eating chocolate with a strong, bitter taste and a minimum of fat and sugar became popular. In countries with important dairy industries – Switzerland, Great Britain and the United States, for example – lighter-coloured, softer milk chocolate was more economically viable and less alien to local palates. Silky smooth Swiss chocolate contains most milk, while German chocolate is the richest, and generally has the highest fat content. Sugar was added to chocolate at levels that roughly accorded with pre-existing taste preferences, which is why most countries have always found British chocolate unpalatably sweet. Even within the same nation, there can be radical differences in chocolate tastes: in the United States, the chocolate favoured on the West Coast, based on the product made by the nineteenth-century Californian pioneers Ghirardelli and Guittard, is lighter and milkier than the East Coast article. Texture – something the food industry unfortunately chooses to call 'mouthfeel' – and to some extent colour will also affect people's perceptions of a particular type of chocolate.

The citizens of every country believe that their own chocolate is 'real' chocolate, and that anything else is an inferior version. The French, Swiss and Italians declare that anything which contains less than 25 per cent cocoa solids is not really chocolate at all, and the British industry narrowly avoided a European Union declaration that chocolate from the United Kingdom, which typically contains about 20 per cent cocoa solids – it is bolstered with cheaper vegetable fats or cocoa butter equivalents (CBEs), plus more sugar, milk and the emulsifier soya lecithin – should not be allowed to be called chocolate at all in European export markets. The other EU nations suggested instead the humiliating appellation 'household chocolate'. The form of words eventually settled upon by the EU was 'family chocolate', which was still extremely galling for the British manufacturers, who argued that the balance of ingredients in their chocolate is a matter of national taste rather than the sign of an inferior product.

I experienced a moment of epiphany while doing vital

research at Chocolate World in Hershey, Pennsylvania. It was a sudden realisation that I really like Hershey chocolate: there is a strong and persuasively genuine chocolatey savour about it, and the grittiness only adds to the impression that the beans are not far away in the experience. The aftertaste is a little odd, certainly, but you get used to it. Perhaps I was swayed because Chocolate World is entirely free (as is the small sample bar you are given on the way in), but I think it was more than that.

Broadly speaking, the best everyday chocolate for any individual is a brand made close to home, or to a specification that suits the national palate. The fact is, a large number of chocolate companies do not even make their own chocolate, but commission specialist manufacturers to provide it to their own recipe. Only the large and extremely well-established companies – the likes of Lindt, Cadbury, Nestlé or Hershey – make their own chocolate; the rest, who are known as 'coaters' in the industry, buy their chocolate mix or 'couverture' from companies such as Barry Callebaut of Belgium or Nestlé, and use it to coat the fruit, fondant, toffee or nut centres of their chocolates. The product is by no means inferior: even a premium chocolate manufacturer like Godiva can be a 'coater'. But while a homegrown chocolate bar is perfect for a snack or post-lunch nibble on a working day, for a treat, a slab of Swiss chocolate cannot be beaten. And for the finest handmade chocolates, one must go to France. When I went on a lone pilgrimage to the celebrated chocolatier Bernachon of Lyon, whose chocolate I like most of all, I stayed for two nights in a small hotel in a side street next to the shop, opposite a large plate-glass window where it was possible to gawk at the action in the kitchens. This made for a bracing start to the day, and my anticipation of this dark, rich chocolate, with a flavour that is imbued with a peculiar clarity of taste, raised (or lowered) me to a state of dazed delirium. As I explained, I am not that much of a chocolate lover, and have the whole thing in perspective.

We are now entering the realm of chocolate connoisseurship – or chocolate snobbery, depending on your outlook. The single most important factor to the epicure of chocolate is the percentile rating of cocoa solids in the bar, usually advertised in large type on the packaging of the bar. Cheap chocolate can contain as little as 15 per cent cocoa solids, while the darkest, bitterest eating chocolate can contain up to 70 per cent. Valrhona, the French company that is the doyen of chocolate manufacturers and employs a full-time tasting panel of ten, will not countenance a product with less than 50 per cent cocoa solids. Anything less is simply not chocolate. It has now become commonplace to hear people praise a bar in terms of its cocoa percentile rating, rather than its taste, which is perhaps missing the point a little. It is as if the bitterness of the chocolate and the absence of sugar is somehow a reflection on the sophistication of the purchaser.

Then there is the question of the bean itself. This is a natural consideration for consumers already well schooled in the concept of coffee bean varieties which have slightly different tastes. But to keep this in perspective: there are only three varieties of chocolate bean. Criollo was the original bean of the Aztecs, and its complexity of flavour is not matched by the hardier and more disease-resistant Forastero bean, which now accounts for perhaps 95 per cent of the world's supply. A third strain, Trinitario, emerged on Trinidad in the eighteenth century as a hybrid between the two, but has not been widely planted in place of the reliable Forastero. The flavours of chocolate grown in different regions are slightly different, and there are myriad variations in taste among the Criollo and Trinitario crops that make what is known as 'fine flavour' cocoa in tiny, blessed pockets of the cocoa-producing belt that girds the earth across the equator – places like Venezuela, Nicaragua, Ecuador and Madagascar. Among chocolate connoisseurs, there is now a vogue for so-called 'grand cru' chocolate, using fine-flavour beans from one area or, in a few cases, a single plantation. At a symposium on flavour at Oxford in 1992, chocolate connoisseur Alice Wooledge Salmon described her experience of experimental batches of single-bean chocolate that she was able to taste at the Valrhona factory:

> The sample from Venezuela tasted a bit smoky, with intense fruit and a markedly 'high-pitched' voice. The Javanese slab was . . . pale red . . . 'blond' . . . citric; while beans from Ecuador justified their reputation as 'distinguished by the scent of orange blossom', yielding chocolate that was also smoky, agreeably bitter though not acid, suffused with coconut and a strong intimation of the soil – un goût de terroir – that had nourished the tree. This was remarkable – and utterly delicious.

Even the major manufacturers carefully monitor and regulate the bean blend used for their standard mass-produced chocolates: British companies have traditionally favoured a Forastero mix dominated by cacao from Ghana, the French opt for the Ivory Coast product and American makers use Brazilian or Dominican stocks.

It was not difficult to find people interested in a chocolate taste test. Four bars were selected from the fine-flavour bean Valrhona range, and the testers had no idea of the make, flavour or cocoa content of the chocolate squares they were given. As with all the best taste tests, I made sure there was ample mineral water (Badoit) for refreshing the palate between samples. First we tried Jivara Lait, the milk chocolate in the Valrhona range, with 40 per cent cocoa content from Ecuadorean beans. The chocolate was described by the eager tasters as 'Swiss', very smooth-textured and soft, with flavours of tea and roses, plus a touch of tannin. It reminded several tasters of Milka, by Suchard. The blurb on the bar mentions 'caramel and vanilla notes', which everyone agreed with in hindsight.

The next bar was Caraibe, with 66 per cent solids from Caribbean beans. The flavour of this chocolate deepened considerably after the first taste, inspiring adjectives like smoky, lapsang souchong, sharp, bitter, woody, with a slightly acid flavour, a granular residue and an exceptionally lingering aftertaste. The notes on the bar suggest it is 'aromatic and long in the mouth, its fruity and barely sweet taste reveals the delicate savours of almonds and roasted coffee'. Everyone got the coffee, but the almonds . . . ? Guanaja was the third bar, with the highest cocoa content, 70 per cent, from what is vaguely described as South American sources. This was most people's favourite, not as bitter, dark and uncompromising as the previous bar, but still with an exceptionally clear and piercing taste, offset by vanilla, and what was described as a strong personality. It is perhaps telling that although this bar seemed to have a particular taste, it was impossible even to begin to dissect it into its constituent flavours. Even the company's own description, with its vague mention of 'floral notes' and a 'powerful, lingering intensity', avoids specifics.

The last bar was an orange bar called Manjari, and everyone commented on how easily the flavour of the candied orange pieces overpowered the chocolate, a strong flavour that is nevertheless easily compromised. Someone said that the chocolate 'goes away' after the first taste. The puzzled brows and middle-distance-gazing during this taste test proved how difficult it is to identify any of the myriad flavours contained in chocolate, very few of which come to the fore on any one occasion. Some of the tasting notes seem pretentious, but with a product that contains hundreds of different aromas, in some ways it is difficult to go wrong as you wildly guess at individual flavours swirling around in your taste consciousness.

Is it all nonsense? There is no doubt that different chocolates have different tastes, but just as listening to stories of people's adventures with illegal drugs is usually indescribably boring, the very enthusiasm of the chocolate connoisseurs can make us suspicious of their motives and wary of their conclusions. Perhaps anatomising chocolate is missing the point of it. Appraisals of wine are more satisfying because there are fewer variables involved, and those there are, such as grape variety, climate and terroir, can be described with clarity. It may still be a mystery why the wine from a particular vineyard is better than its neighbours', but we have enough information to keep us interested. The problem with almost all chocolate products is that the precise provenance of the beans used in the blend is obscure and changeable, and even if such details were known, important variables such as the length of time the beans are left to ferment in the sunshine after harvesting cannot be monitored in practice, since the bedrock of the cacao industry is thousands of small plantations, often in remote areas.

All we are left with is the gourmandising skill of the chocolate connoisseur. So should we take the recommendations of a self-confessed chocolate addict and connoisseur more seriously than those of a casual observer of taste and discernment? Perhaps we should not. This is something to do with the fact that chocolate people seem unusually vulnerable to becoming immersed rather too deeply in their subject, so that their enthusiasm smacks slightly too much of addiction or animal choco-lust.

Those of us who prefer other types of sweets over chocolate love them with a passion but manage to retain some kind of distance – an ironic distance, in many cases. Chocolate people are different to sweets people: for one thing, sweets people love cheap milk chocolate as well as dark, and often prefer it. As long as it tastes nice, they do not care about levels of cocoa solids. Chocolate people care about the ingredients list because they need to ensure that the fix they are getting is of sufficient quality in terms of both chocolate mass and perceived social superiority: part of the reason why premium chocolates are popular with these people is that they are expensive, exclusive and known only to a few. It has to be admitted that this malaise is largely confined to the English-speaking nations, where an interest in food is still viewed as fundamentally embarrassing. In France, Italy, Spain and other parts of Europe, where good chocolate is taken seriously, the professional chocolate-makers, who are usually trained pâtisserie chefs obsessed with maintaining the correct '*mise en point*' of their chocolate, rarely indulge in such panegyrics to cocoa products. The chocolate speaks for itself.

All this may sound somewhat grave and puritanical, but it is really a plea for a sense of proportion with this branch of confectionery. It is not necessary to be an expert to appreciate good chocolate, and if someone truly prefers their Hershey Bar or Cadbury's Dairy Milk over a high-cocoa dark chocolate, it does not make them a peasant. One of the great things about sweets today is their relative cheapness and wide availability, and it seems a shame to compromise their democratic appeal by re-mystifying them with highfalutin' language and spurious expertise. Sweets have until now escaped the tyranny of gourmetism; this is still one of the areas of life where children can be experts too, and I for one would rate a child's sweet recommendation above an adult's.

People do not love chocolate just for its flavour. There is more to it than that, and modern science has certainly not measured up to the task of finding out exactly what that is. There is no doubt that a chocolate bar gives us energy: all that glucose has to go somewhere. And we do know that chocolate is an extremely complex foodstuff, with some 387 separate chemical components already identified, and potentially up to 800 different flavours and scents, to which flavour technicians give generic names like 'volatiles', 'top notes' or 'background notes'. To put chocolate in perspective: wine has about 250 aromatic components, and strawberries 450. The chocolate connoisseur Daniel Quirici reckons: 'Olfactively, ground cocoa beans have the characteristics of many exotic spices, wood essences and aromatic substances, with an abundant variety of fruity, nutty and flowery notes and the coarse fragrance of coffee or the harsh scents of burnt cereals.' It was discovered early that vanilla seems to have the power to heighten the natural flavours of cacao. It also possesses its own charms, as described by Maguelonne Toussaint-Samat in her *History of Food* (1992): 'If some exquisite little goddess of gluttony were to exist, her name would surely be Vanilla, and she would be a delicate, slim, dark creature.' But the goddess Vanilla has a fat little puppy dog of a sidekick called Comfort.

The most basically appealing characteristic of chocolate is

less romantic than any litany of sophisticated epicureanism: it is packed with sugar and fat. There is a palpable sense that chocolate is a rich mixture of good things (although they might not all be good for us in excess) and that makes us feel good, too. Chocolate is rich and affecting, and we consume it as gratefully and greedily as we do any other food. The very idea of chocolate is uniquely stimulating in comparison with other foods: a mildly hungry person might become more excited at the prospect of a bar of chocolate than a dish of hot roast chicken. And when we have gobbled the chocolate we become calm and sated, almost as if we are a different person, although the craving can return again quite quickly. Perhaps this repeated sensual cycle, from extreme stimulation to enjoyable satiation to relaxed serenity, is one reason why chocolate and sex are so readily linked. As with sexual urges, the desire for chocolate can be sudden and almost overwhelming.

Is chocolate addictive? The answer must be: yes, but it is not clear in what proportions this addiction should be attributed to biology or psychology. As with any other food, people can become psychologically dependent on chocolate for a wide variety of reasons, ranging from self-hate to sexual frustration to something as mundane as an entrenched daily routine. Theories about the physiologically addictive qualities of chocolate are centred on the supposed effects of three chemicals with psychoactive properties that are contained in it: caffeine, theobromine and phenylethylamine. We are all familiar with caffeine, which is found in chocolate in small quantities compared with coffee or even tea. The amounts vary, but it appears that a chocolate bar might contain from one twentieth to one fiftieth of the caffeine of a regular cup of coffee.

However, even this small amount should not be discounted, especially in cases where the chocolate consumer is unfamiliar with the drug. In the seventeenth century, pastilles of crumbly chocolate were eaten by Spanish soldiers on night-time guard duty, and several scholars attested to the efficacy of the beverage in all-night writing sessions. If chocolate can have this effect on grown men – beefy soldiers as well as skinny-armed scholars – what must it do to children? Parents often notice that their children become wild-eyed loons when they have eaten chocolate, and this is sometimes attributed to the mysterious evils of the E-numbers: preservatives, colourings and other additives (some of which are quite natural). But surely the most obvious cause of the temporary mayhem is that the children are experiencing a glucose rush, or sugar high, combined with a caffeine kick, which will probably cause more damage to the furniture than to their young brains. In adults, it has been noticed that the effect of caffeine is linked with the cultural background of the drinker: if caffeine beverages are generally believed in a society to be good night-time drinks that help sleep, they will most often have that effect, whereas if they are used as morning or mid-afternoon stimulants, that is the result.

Theobromine is a mild stimulant that acts primarily on the muscles and is found in just nineteen plant species in nature, including tea, coffee and the kola nut. Like coffee and tea, it is a diuretic, in that it stimulates the flow of urine. Theobromine has some psychoactive properties, but there is much debate as to precisely what its effects might be; most likely, an enhancement of general alertness and cognitive skills. Of minerals, chocolate is richest in phosphorus and potassium, and there is a chance that small quantities of magnesium also affect mood, because this mineral stimulates production of the brain's mood-stabilising chemical, serotonin.

The presence of phenylethylamine in chocolate has only recently been confirmed. The effects of this chemical, the release of which is triggered by neurotransmitters in the brain, are similar to those of the better-known brain chemicals called endorphins: that is, elevated or even euphoric feelings of happiness and love. One study claims that the release-mechanism for phenylethylamine is faulty in some people, and that a chocolate binge can help redress an imbalance of emotion. It will probably come as no surprise that the conclusions of limited scientific experimentation on people's attitudes to chocolate have shown that it is overwhelmingly equated with happiness. Could phenylethylamine be released at the very mention of chocolate? Anecdotally speaking, I have noticed that when I introduce myself to someone – at a wedding, say – as an international confectionery historian, they are of course amazed and delighted, eager to quiz me on confectionery and ask about job opportunities as my assistant. But when the subject of chocolate comes up, a change seems to come over them: a slight smile plays over their lips and they seem momentarily distant, as if they are enjoying a private moment of anticipation or memory. Chocolate can cast a strong spell from a distance – to the advertisers' delight.

It must be said that the effects of chocolate are particularly noticeable in women. This is a somewhat sensitive area to delve into, particularly for a male writer, and the first point to establish is that the relationship of women with chocolate is not the result of some inherent female weakness. Men also exhibit cravings for and apparently irrational attitudes towards certain foods or drinks – in their case, alcohol and protein foods, particularly meat. But women have a different cultural relationship with food to men, and that makes all comparisons between the sexes odious. The cultural force of food is, on the whole, far stronger for women than men: when it comes to food, women cannot simply take it or leave it. In *Just Desserts: Women and Food* (1990), Sally Cline writes: 'In our culture women have a complex emotional and symbolic relationship to food. Men do not. Women have access to food in a way they do not have access to power.' To use the language of the man vandalising the top of the Clapham omnibus, chocolate can screw women up.

Many women have a hyped-up relationship with chocolate, caused in part by the advertising and marketing industries, slimming lore and the attitudes of peers. The chocolate bar you hold in your hand is entirely innocent and immediately worthy of consumption, but it would be a mistake to equate its pleasing sweetness with a benignly innocent role in society. Chocolate is marketed as 'sinful', 'naughty', 'tempting' or 'decadent' and restaurants take advantage of this image by concocting puddings with names like 'Death by Chocolate' or 'Devil's Food Cake'. Women traditionally have to be persuaded into ordering a chocolate pudding, and this process of coercion, in which a woman eventually succumbs and submits, can take on a sexual character, to the delight of flirtatious people of both sexes.

The sexual connotations of chocolate are exaggerated in advertisement imagery in order to increase sales. The sexual piquancy of the famous Cadbury's Flake advertisements of the 1970s to 1990s, for example, in which a scantily clad woman eats a crumbly Flake bar in blissful solitude, is generally noted for the obvious phallic imagery of the woman eating the bar itself. But the explicit sexual appeal of the ad in its later incarnations is actually directed at least as much, if not more, towards women, in that it also represents a powerful fantasy of female masturbation. Gift chocolates are, of course, packaged and marketed differently for women and for men. Traditionally, men might get chocolate golf balls or cigars, while women are given beribboned boxes in the shape of hearts, for instance, to emphasise their role as objects of romantic affection, or containers in the shape of fluffy puppy dogs, to create a fantasy of second girlhood. After all, 'What are little girls made of? Sugar and spice and all things nice.' It may be too much to expect the chocolate manufacturers to launch a range of chocolates based on the achievements of, say, Marie Curie (radium creme, anyone?), but the extreme stereotypes that the confectionery industry has always traded in now seem anachronistic – which is not to say they are uncommercial, of course.

In this sustained atmosphere of chocolate hysteria, normally sane women can find themselves conspiring in infantile chocolate fantasies with female friends – sneaking off for cakes, or indulging in mass chocolate binges. Perhaps it is unfair to censure such behaviour; it is harmless enough in isolation, and men are 'allowed' to indulge their regressive tendencies by playing with model railways or becoming obsessed with football. But the cumulative effect of these attitudes on a society's perceptions of women can only be harmful. In this chocolate fantasy world, women become child-like, emotionally uncontrollable and sexually incontinent, as if all the drugs and psychoactive ingredients in chocolates had had their powers magnified a hundred times. To take one striking example, from my own experience, of the transformative power of chocolate: at university, I attended a dinner to celebrate the elevation to don status of a sharp and independent-minded academic, respected by all whom she taught and known for her no-nonsense attitude. Male and female undergraduates alike were astonished by her sudden transformation, when faced with a chocolate pudding, into a giggling, simpering girl. This performance was put on partly for the benefit of her new colleagues (all male) and may have been fuelled by alcohol, but the imbecilic metamorphosis was so striking that eye witnesses still wonder about it, years later. This is an indication of the power of the bean-based mix. To say, 'It's only chocolate', would be to underestimate drastically the biological effects and cultural significance of a complex substance, and would also belittle the suffering of those women who endure alone an obsessive, love-hate relationship with chocolate, scared of seeking help for fear that their addiction might be treated as a joke.

The evidence for physiological dependency or craving for chocolate in women is, of course, hazy and contradictory, as it is in all areas of food science. Current thinking indicates that women crave sugars and fats, for storage, while men crave proteins, for muscle-building value. Chocolate is particularly potent for women because it contains extremely high levels of those sugars and fats. So it appears that nature deals in stereotypes. In addition, the endorphins triggered by the ingestion of fats are, it is claimed, particularly appealing to premenstrual or pregnant women, who usually experience low endorphin levels. Then there is the caffeine, theobromine and phenylethylamine already discussed. This defence of chocolate is enthusiastically expounded by Debra Waterhouse in *Why Women Need Chocolate* (1995), in which she declares: 'Food cravings are Mother Nature's way of informing us that we need to eat a specific food in order to look and feel great!' If we obliterate the image of Mother Nature as some kind of breakfast-television diet guru, we are left with a refreshing take on the notion of 'good' and 'bad' foods, and the idea that it is the attempt to deny certain foods, rather than the cravings themselves, which lead to weight gain. Of course, eating a lot of chocolate will probably make you fat, since chocolate does contain fat (derived primarily from the milk, not the chocolate itself), but it is easy to avoid using chocolate to replace a meal, and even a small amount can satisfy a craving in most cases.

The idea that certain foods are sought out to satisfy hormonally derived cravings is resisted by some women, mainly because of the belief that men do not exhibit similar tendencies. It is felt – correctly – that these animal urges could be interpreted by misogynists as a lack of self-control or emotional instability, so for a woman to admit to hormonal cravings is to admit to weakness. This strategy of denial is understandable, but it does not tally with the latest scientific thinking. Perhaps it would be best for all concerned if some women could be allowed to admit to an honest and intense desire for chocolate, based on legitimate physical needs. Then, women could start to eat chocolate in a sensible atmosphere. It's okay to eat chocolate. Believe me. I am an international confectionery historian. And just to make things fair, I would like to announce that I have discovered, after *no* years of research and having surveyed *no* percentage of the population, a new hormone that can be found in men, called gimmechocaleine, the release of which is stimulated by chocolate consumption, and which increases levels of kindness and finer feelings in the adolescent and adult male.

Lucky Dip

MANNA

Manna is something of a mystery. No one is sure quite what the Bible refers to in its description of a bread of life, miraculously found by the starving Israelites wandering the Sinai Desert: 'And the children of Israel called the name thereof Manna, and it was white like coriander seed and the taste of it was like wafers made with honey' (Exodus 16).

But manna is not a myth: the word has been used throughout history to describe all kinds of real substances, most of them sweet to some degree, and found in nature in circumstances deemed semi-miraculous. A manna is a sweet substance either disgorged by an insect onto a leaf, or exuded by the plant or tree itself. The genesis of the Old Testament story may be traceable to the secretion of a small insect that is left on the twigs of the tamarisk tree in parts of the Middle East. The desert Bedouins still gather this substance early in the morning, before the ants appear, just as the biblical Israelites did with manna. Reportedly up to two kilos of this sticky residue can be gathered in a single morning, and it is made into a purée or halva and stored indefinitely. In Iran, tamarisk manna is shaken off the tree and made into cakes with honey and flour, and in India another tamarisk species is harvested. The Kurds call it helwa-y-gezo. *Perhaps Milton had heard of the phenomenon, for Adam in* Paradise Lost *remarks, 'from off the boughs each morn / We brush mellifluous dews'.*

Then there is manna that is produced by a tree itself rather than insect visitors; Hovenia dulcis, *the Japanese raisin tree, is an example. There are two other types of manna that are candidates for the biblical original. Thorn honey from the camel's thorn,* Alhagi camelorum, *is another effusion from an insect, and it is shaken off the branches. Then* there is the brown lichen called Lecanora esculenta, *which grows on rocks but is sometimes dislodged in high winds. Clouds of this manna have been known to blow into settlements. Is that how the Israelites found their manna? The Syrian Bedouins call this lichen 'earth fat' and make a bread and a type of jelly from it.*

Certain other plants contain other natural substances that give the impression of extreme sweetness, and these have been exploited by indigenous peoples. Paraguayans use the 'sweet shrub', Stevia rebaudiana, *to sweeten their tea: it is thirty times sweeter than sugar, enough to satisfy the sweetest of sweet teeth, and is now being promoted as an alternative to sugar. The miracleberry,* Synsepalum dulcificum, *makes sour things — including lemons — taste sweet, through the agency of a natural taste modifier named miraculin. (Did Willy Wonka name it?) Its major drawback is that it makes absolutely everything taste sweet. One brave nutritionist had a dose of miraculin, and claimed that afterwards, 'sipping hydrochloric acid was like sipping cheap lemonade'. The grape-like serendipity berries of West Africa, shunned by the Nigerians and used with caution by the Congolese, are 1,500 times sweeter than sugar. And the 'miraculous fruit' of the Sudan and Sierra Leone, where it is called* kateme, *contains a sweet transparent jelly that is mixed with bread, fruit, palm wine and tea. This has been traded in Africa since the 1830s, and is the only one of these super-sweet plants which is a viable economic crop: it is now used to make a low-calorie sweetener in Japan, and is added to chewing gum in the United States. Liquorice root, naturally sweet, is more familiar to Westerners, and fresh coconut milk is a staple sweetener of South East Asia. It is boiled down to a treacle and used as sugar in Chile.*

Some trees exude sweetness. The manna ash tree of the Mediterranean is also tapped for a sweet sap that makes syrup, while the date palm produces a liquid which is naturally sweet and can be made into sugar. The Chinese have used the sap of the sugar palm since prehistoric times. Sweetness can also be extruded from maize and from sorghum grass (which was a sweet staple in the Midwestern and Southern states of the United States and is still produced there on a small scale). The sugar maple of North America was the sweet staple of the Native Americans, along with pine sap, and they kindly taught the first European settlers how to tap the trees for their syrup. The Powhatan and the Iroquois steeped fresh cherries in maple syrup as dessert; the settlers later made it into maple sugar and candies. As with wine, there are regional differences in maple-syrup flavour —Vermont is said to produce the best, although that is the sort of claim over which wars are fought. It is a puzzle how and why maples make such sweet sap, but its rich, dark taste, which seems to burn with sweetness, is as beguiling as honey.

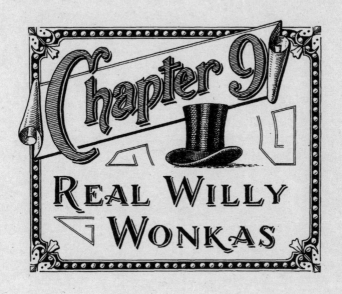

Chapter 9

REAL WILLY WONKAS

Willy Wonka, Roald Dahl's creation, is an eccentric, obsessive, secretive, unique individual, who seeks to keep his dwarfish, chocolate-loving workforce, the Oompa-Loompas, in check through a mix of fatherly love and iron discipline. Gene Wilder's performance as the wild-haired, mercurial sweets genius in the 1971 film *Charlie and the Chocolate Factory* was masterful and definitive, and it matters not that in the book Wonka is diminutive and plump, whereas the purple-coated Wilder was tall and lanky. Wonka spends all his time on new product development, and although his attitude towards children is alternately adoring and aggressive, he seems to be able to tap into their innermost confectionery needs, inventing new lines that are a combination of fantasy, practicality (a quality children greatly admire) and, of course, sugar. Wonka's confectionery innovations include: luminous lollies to eat at night, fizzy lifting drinks that lift you in the air, eatable marshmallow pillows, lickable wallpaper for nurseries, hair toffee (for hair growth), hot ice creams for cold days, square sweets that look round, toffee apple trees, exploding sweets for enemies, cavity filling caramels – 'no more dentists' – fizzy lemonade swimming pools, and the world-famous everlasting gobstopper. It comes as no surprise that Dahl had a lifelong fascination for the workings of the real sweets industry. His portrait of the confectionery manufacturing world is, in certain ways, barely exaggerated: it exhibits that strange Wonka mixture of megalomania, eccentricity, childish delight in sweets, business sense, care for workers, empire-building, marketing verve, secrecy, product innovation and technical exploration.

As a child growing up in Llandaff, Dahl developed a perfectly normal passion for sweets and also the unusually morbid sense of humour that was to entertain his readers later on. For the eight-year-old Roald Dahl, sweets were dangerous as well as delicious. In *Boy* he recalls: 'Pear drops were exciting because they had a dangerous taste. They smelled of nail varnish and they froze the back of your throat. All of us were warned against eating them, and the result was that we ate more than ever.' There was a terrible incident involving the owner of the local sweetshop, the horrid Mrs Pratchett, who hated small boys. The feeling was mutual. When her back was turned, Dahl quite justifiably placed a dead mouse in the gobstopper jar on the counter, and later, when the mortified lady had recovered and paid a visit to the school, Dahl and his accomplices were caned in front of her very eyes by way of revenge. The incident led to Dahl's mother taking him away from the school, which is no small matter for a little boy.

Later, as a public schoolboy at Repton, Dahl took part in taste tests of potential new products conducted by Cadbury: the company would send boxes of goodies out to sixth-form boys, who would write down their reactions by way of exchange for the free chocolate. The early realisation that sweets do not just appear, but are carefully developed, obviously stayed with Dahl into adulthood, as did a sense of the importance of sweets in a child's world-view. His biographer, Jeremy Treglown, noted that he liked to discourse at length on the history of the Malteser (probably dwelling on the way they were conceived as diet sweets, for women only), and sweets and chocolates were always on offer in his home.

Dahl never anatomised his inspiration, but the character of Wonka himself, and his warren-like light-industrial setup, with its pale pink corridors, must have been partly based on the confectionery moguls whom Dahl would have heard about, particularly Cadbury and Hershey, and possibly Mars and

Suchard. The confectionery industry has always attracted more or less eccentric entrepreneurs who think in original ways: it is an extremely tough business, fast-moving and largely dependent on innovation, so anyone who goes in as a manufacturer must be flexible, lateral-minded and able to accept devastating failure as easily as unexpected success. Secrecy is also essential to the industry, since no two recipes for any one sweet are exactly the same, and even if they were, the heating, cooling, pulling and coating techniques vary widely from one factory to the next. Even with modern machinery, much of it comes down to the skills and experience of the confectionery technicians at work in the factory. That is how so many small sweets companies survive: at some point in the past, perhaps even a hundred years ago, great-grandfather perfected a jackpot recipe, and this sweet is for ever after associated with that company alone. No one else can imitate it precisely, and since nostalgic consumers tend to demand the exact same sweet they enjoyed as children, this one line can keep a small company in excellent health. Such emotional attachments with sweets extend even to worldwide brands made by huge corporations. We know that some British people refuse to use the name Snickers, but what they might not know is that Mars is an American company, and that their name came first. But people had formed a personal attachment to the brand Marathon since childhood, and now that relationship was being taken away – as if a parent had remarried and changed their name.

So the confectionery industry is a curious coupling of hard-headed business sense and a high regard for the vagaries of human psychology, that of both children and adults. A good sweets manufacturer is guided as much by instinct and inspiration as by logic and established business rationale. From the start, sweets have attracted peculiar and amusing people. Perhaps this is because it does not pay to take yourself too seriously in the sweets industry: no one else will, no matter how much money you make. Looking through old photographs of moustachioed and bearded Victorian sweets moguls from all over Europe, it is remarkable how many of them have a kindly twinkle in their eye or a half-suppressed smile. Of course there are exceptions, such as the alarmingly stern Jean Tobler, who looks as if his lower body has just been encased in molten sugar, his brow furrowed enough for turnip planting. But bushy-bearded Philippe Suchard looks kind and cuddly, François-Louis Cailler appears gentle and benevolent and Rudolf Sprüngli-Ammann (of Lindt) has a Wonka-esque hair frizz. William Gunter, the irrepressible London confectioner, had himself portrayed for the frontispiece of his 1830 manual sitting in his study surrounded by discarded books, like some absent-minded genius, momentarily distracted. Very like Wonka, in fact.

From the beginnings of the industrialisation of the sweets business, confectionery moguls have pursued their own eccentric policies and fulfilled some extraordinary Utopian dreams, and their unusually high level of social care for workers is well known. This all began with the Quakers in the eighteenth century. Intelligent and respectable young men like Joseph Fry were unable to attend the two English universities, Oxford and Cambridge, which were in the thrall of the Anglican Church. (Also banned, incidentally, were Roman Catholics, Jews, Methodists and other dissenters.) The army was out of the question, because Quakers are pacifists. But a career in business of any sort suited their ethos of hard work, practicality and first-hand engagement with people from all social ranks, and a justified reputation for scrupulous honesty proved extremely useful in their business dealings. The founder of Lloyd's Bank, Sampson Lloyd, was a Quaker, as were the Darbys of Coalbrookdale, pioneers in the iron industry, and a number of other successful businessmen.

Joseph Fry's Bristol-based chocolate business had expanded rapidly from its beginnings in the 1750s, and by 1764 he had agents in fifty-three towns and a London warehouse. Religious belief was not incompatible with an energetic approach to business, especially if one's product could be viewed as an alternative to alcohol, an object of obsessive concern to the church, especially by the mid nineteenth century. The Quakers nevertheless had their dilemmas in the world of business. The ethics of large-scale advertising, for example, caused difficulties early on for Fry, and the company was slow in exploiting the power of a marketing tool that had been developed from the example of pioneers such as the Glasgow grocer Thomas Lipton, who in 1870 had two fat pigs driven through the city streets, their sides painted with, 'I'm going to Lipton's, the best shop in town for Irish bacon'. The idea of metaphorically driving a fat pig through the town — which is, after all, the quintessence of advertising — made the Quakers uneasy, since the aim of the process must be to hoodwink or inveigle the consumer to some extent.

But such qualms did not delay them for long. After the big three confectionery firms — Fry of Bristol, Cadbury of Birmingham and Rowntree of York — had emerged by the mid nineteenth century, they were accused of price-fixing, and of running a cartel based on their brotherhood as Quakers. This relationship extended even to takeovers: in 1935 Fry went into voluntary liquidation, just as one of their creme bars might, but when Cadbury took over, the firm respected and retained the old brand name. But while it is true that there was an unusual level of co-operation, sharing of information and plain trust between the Quaker firms, and that on principle they would not employ anyone currently employed by a Quaker rival (to protect secret recipes and methods), there is no evidence that they sought to monopolise the industry or used aggressive tactics to force out non-Quaker competitors.

In the workplace, the British Quaker confectionery firms pioneered enlightened practices regarding factory conditions, labour relations and the social welfare of employees. These were only much later taken up by all branches of industry, as a result of legislation. The process began informally in the mid nine-teenth century, and in the case of Fry amounted to a reputation for fair play in its dealings with workers, and touches such as the placement of hundreds of potplants in the factory premises. There was considerable emphasis on the family nature of these businesses, with the patriarchal Quakers making great efforts to learn the names of as many employees as possible, and taking an interest in their lives outside the factory. Joseph Rowntree at York, for example, went to some lengths to preserve this personal touch among the management even as the firm rapidly expanded and moved premises, and Rowntree was to be instrumental in the formation of the Industrial Welfare Society. (Seebohm Rowntree later even wrote a book advocating higher pay for all workers.)

But it was the Cadbury brothers who had the greatest ambitions for the welfare of their staff, something which they believed, crucially, led to a more efficient and, ultimately, more profitable business. Cadbury had been a successful purveyor and then manufacturer of drinking chocolate and cocoa powder in Birmingham since the 1830s, but the firm fell prey to the international decline in sales of chocolate in the 1850s and nearly closed down. The situation was turned around after 1866 by the Cadbury brothers, Richard and George, who had introduced a new cocoa press following a visit to the Van Houten factory in Holland, and were thus able to produce a high-quality cocoa powder for drinking and also a new range of eating chocolate made from the plentiful cocoa butter that was a by-product of the process. As the company prospered through the 1860s and 1870s, the Cadburys began to introduce innovative workplace schemes, such as piece-work (in which pay was related to output), half-day holidays on Saturdays, night-school (on company time) for the betterment of younger workers, punctuality rewards and the closure of the factory on Bank Holidays. As time went on, sick pay, pension arrangements, works outings, medical and dental departments and even holiday pay were introduced. Perhaps less popular were the compulsory morning Bible readings, personally conducted by 'Mr George' or 'Mr Richard'.

But the most radical development at Cadbury was the

removal of the factory in its entirety from its city-centre premises in Birmingham to what would now be called a 'green-field site' in the countryside some four miles away. While the Cadburys were certainly concerned about slum conditions in Birmingham (George Cadbury had put his dismay in writing), they must also have anticipated an increase in efficiency and quality of product in the new premises. They may also have been spurred into action after reading press reports about a new state-of-the-art factory built by London cocoa manufacturer James Epps & Co. As if to underline this commitment to high-quality eating chocolate produced in a clean and wholesome new environment, the Cadburys hired a master chocolatier called Frederic Kinchelman, who became universally known as 'Frederic the Frenchman' (except, perhaps, to his wife).

Bournville was the name of the new factory and of the village planned to grow up around it, and when it opened in 1879 workers began to commute in by bicycle or on foot. The new factory was airy, light and spacious, set in fields traversed by the River Bourn. There was a kitchen for the use of workers (a forerunner of the staff canteen), a sports field adjacent to the factory and, for the female workers, a 'girls' garden' and re-creation area that survives in somewhat dilapidated form today. Male and female workers were strictly segregated at Cadbury, and married women were either not accepted or dismissed pre-nuptially, since the Christian ethic decreed that they should stay at home. Women were also paid less than men, a situation addressed by board director Barrow Cadbury as part of evidence to a royal commission in 1913: 'I do not think that I wish to justify it. I simply take it as it is [. . .] we are guided by competition outside.' Which is weak reasoning for a company that prided itself on bucking trends. Photographs in the Cadbury archives show young female workers in the girls' garden reclining gracefully in long white dresses like latterday vestal virgins, which is exactly the image the Cadburys wanted for their 'girls'. Just before she was married, a young woman would be called to the office of one of the Cadbury brothers, given a Bible, a carnation and some kind words, and dispatched into the wide world, jobless. It comes as no surprise that some women endeavoured to keep their engagement, or even their marriage, a secret from the management.

It is difficult to gauge what the early employees at Bournville really thought of the new factory, but judging by reminiscences contained in the archives kept at Cadbury, some of them disliked having to commute out of the city that was deemed bad for their physical health and, by implication, their moral welfare. The old factory may have been unhealthy, but at least it was round the corner. There were no buses to Bournville and although there was a train station a mile away, early trains did not run in the first years of the factory. Many factory workers had to rise before dawn to get to work on time, some of the women became paying lodgers in the sixteen new houses the Cadburys had built for senior workers at the site, and a few of the girls were even allowed to spend their nights in makeshift accommodation in the girls' dining room. This female diaspora apparently caused some upset among the young men of Birmingham.

But according to letters written by ex-Cadbury workers in the 1920s, the first years at Bournville were a revelation: 'It seemed to me to be all holiday and a sort of fairyland factory,' declared one Louis Barrow, and a Lily Houghton recalled, 'We used to go into the lanes and fields and get blackberries, and at one time some very pretty ivy . . . [we] thought ourselves very important going to work by train.' The image of this happy valley was perhaps at the back of Roald Dahl's mind in his description of Willy Wonka's chocolate room: 'They were looking down upon a lovely valley. There were green meadows on either side of the valley, and along the bottom of it there flowed a great brown river.' (Wonka, incidentally, at this point comes up with one of those superficially impressive but basically meaningless statistics that are beloved of all industries. Standing by his chocolate waterfall he announces, 'There's enough chocolate to fill every bathtub in the country.' And who does not desire their bath to be filled with chocolate?)

There is some evidence that Cadbury's new surroundings inspired innovations among the workers, too. The Cadbury archive contains a letter from Cephas Edwards, who remembered a man named Pendleton who was 'always bursting with big ideas', and in 1880 had a 'brainy idea' for a jack-in-a-box chocolate-assortment box. 'On opening the lid a grotesque figure shot up, offering the surprised owner a chocolate cream stuck on a needle point.' More fun was to be had in the factory's spacious new workrooms. According to Mr Edwards, one of the younger male members of the Cadbury dynasty was shocked to enter the girls' work room to discover six girls hanging upside-down by their heels from one of the beams.

The Cadburys certainly did not sanction such frivolity, but instead encouraged workers to direct their energies into wholesome activities, particularly sport. There were football, hockey and cricket pitches, tennis and squash courts, a bowling green and two swimming pools (one for men and one for women, naturally). One of the very first Bournville workers, a William Cooper, concluded, 'The atmosphere of Bournville of early days was decidedly a religious atmosphere', and even into the late twentieth century some Cadbury workers maintained that anyone who attended chapel on a Sunday would be in line for quicker promotion. Walter Pickard, who worked as a clerk at Bournville in the 1890s, recalled a typical day: 'On arrival at the office we attended a short prayer meeting at 9 o'clock at which we sang a hymn and listened to a brief address by Mr Richard or Mr George Cadbury. At about 11am the clerks took a cup of cocoa or coffee at the kitchen bar. The midday meal was managed by clubs known as Beef Clubs, some of which were quite noted. In the afternoon jugs of tea and lemonade were served on the desks, presumably to stay [sic] off exhaustion until teatime. On the whole a very comfortable sort of day.' The comfort continued into the evening for anyone staying on to work overtime: there are misty-eyed accounts of George Cadbury personally distributing biscuits to his loyal, hard-working employees.

The Cadburys' ambitions for their workers did not stop at the creation of a state-of-the-art workplace; they wanted to give them somewhere to live, too. From 1895 the village of Bournville took shape, a prototype garden city based on an Arts and Crafts vision of rural England. It is possible to take an informative tour of the village by minibus today, and it is remarkable how the original layout has been preserved. Unlike the bleak rows of identical terraced houses built for workers in Britain's cities, the Bournville houses, which are attractive and of high quality, were clustered in small, informal groups, with generous gardens, front and back. The Bournville Village Trust issued a booklet to all newcomers to the village, filled with rules and regulations about keeping one's property tidy and the garden in good order, and even extending to moral recommendations, such as not drinking alcohol on Sunday and the benefits of single beds for married couples. In Bournville you can find a village green, a post office, a bank, almshouses and an ornamental clock, but no public house, unlike the rest of England. To paraphrase T.S. Eliot, it is an unreal village. Today's company literature advances the idea that the Cadburys developed the land for housing in order to prevent property entrepreneurs spoiling the atmosphere of the village, but of course the company could have bought the land and simply left it as green fields.

It is telling that the company initially had some difficulty finding tenants for their new houses. The reason usually given by employees was that they were too expensive, but the over-bearing presence of the company in every area of a worker's life may have had something to do with it. Was it not enough that these people were working all day for Cadbury? Did they also have to be grateful and pious and clean and clean-living, playing cricket on Cadbury pitches, eating at long trestle tables in the dining room like schoolchildren (as employees still do), attending Cadbury churches, even living in Cadbury houses? One worker's letter mentions that the empty houses attracted occupants only when the fruit trees in the gardens began to mature. Ironic, that Cadbury workers should be tempted by fruit in a garden.

Then there was the dilemma of the Boer War chocolate: in 1900 Queen Victoria wrote to George Cadbury requiring that the company manufacture special Christmas tins of chocolate for soldiers of the British Army on the frontline in southern Africa. Cadbury wrote back, politely declining the suggestion on account of the opposition of Quakers to wars of any kind. Queen Victoria immediately sent a virtually identical letter. This made it clear that this was not a royal suggestion but a royal order, and Cadbury took the pragmatic way out, consulting with Fry and Rowntree and agreeing to produce between them 100,000 unbranded tins of chocolate for the soldiers. The provenance of the chocolate was kept quiet, and the Quaker confectioners did not desist in their vocal opposition to the war: George Cadbury even paid for the printing of a million anti-war leaflets.

The occasional incompatibility of Quaker moral ideals with business pragmatism also emerged over the issue of slavery. In the late eighteenth century, Joseph Fry had been a prominent abolitionist, and the Quaker confectioners continued to voice their antipathy to all such inhumanity. Over a century later, when a newspaper article was printed suggesting that slavery was endemic in the cacao plantations of Portuguese West Africa, and that Cadbury knew all about it, the company decided to sue. Reports of the 1909 court case make sorry reading, as venerable, good-hearted old Cadburys take the stand and parade their complete ignorance about working conditions in the plantations. It was true that Cadbury knew nothing of working conditions in Africa, and the company won the case. But it was awarded just a farthing's damages. Despite its outspoken stance about workplace abuses in Britain, Cadbury had not made any attempt to check up on conditions in the plantations which supplied its own cocoa. Of course, the situation in the chocolate industry as a whole is, in practical terms, almost exactly the same today, which is less forgivable (see chapter ten, Bad Candy).

But it feels churlish to find fault with the vision of the Cadburys at Bournville – theirs may have been a tyranny, but at least it was benevolent, which certainly could not be said of most nineteenth-century industry. George Cadbury organised an exhibition in 1906 to highlight the plight of workers in sweated industry – terrible conditions and low pay – and at Bournville the company instigated a system of works committees in 1905 and later democratically elected works councils (one for women, one for men) that oversaw health and safety. The Quaker approach to meetings, in which consensus is sought regardless of how long it might take, made for harmonious if slow-moving industrial relations. Labour unrest was anathema to the Quakers – in some sense they would have failed in their mission if it arose – and the system was designed to circumvent this possibility as much as possible. If the management had found themselves in direct confrontation with their workforce, they would have been morally compromised and temperamentally nonplussed. But this cosy setup, the format of an act of collective worship inappropriately applied to a business environment, meant that negotiations, and particularly pay negotiations, were always skewed in the company's favour. Full unionisation was duly established in 1918 with the active support of the Cadburys. Indeed, Edward Cadbury was concerned that his workers might be too comfortably off to want to join the union, noting that one of the benefits of unionisation would be that workers who left the company to go elsewhere would be able to contrast conditions, 'And this enlightened discontent is the soil in which trade unionism will flourish.' It is almost inconceivable that any modern executive, Quaker or not, would say such a thing.

It is a curious aspect of manufacturing history that the large-scale confectionery industry as a whole in Europe became possessed of unusual idealism in the late nineteenth and early twentieth centuries. (It also happened, to a less marked degree, in the United States, where the New England Confectionery Company, or NECCO, introduced a profit-share system for workers as early as 1906, and life insurance in 1920.) The way forward had been shown in the first years of the nineteenth century by pioneer Utopian socialists like Robert Owen, who demonstrated, crucially, at his New Lanark cotton mills, that enlightened management practices could go hand in hand with higher profits. The confectionery moguls were not radicals who described themselves as socialists – their impulse was generally religious rather than political – but they were nevertheless remarkably forward-looking in their treatment of the workforce.

In Britain, the Cadburys' example was picked up by fellow Quakers Rowntree, who built their own model village at New Earswick, near York, in 1902. At Serrières in Switzerland, the Huguenot Philippe Suchard, or 'Papa Suchard' as he became known, pioneered the concept of health and accident insurance for workers as early as 1876. There were baths and a kindergarten at the factory, and the company offered free holidays to workers and their families in an Alpine chalet purchased for the purpose. From the 1860s Suchard slowly expanded the 'Cité Suchard', with houses for workers, some buildings with minarets (reflecting Suchard's eccentric fixation with the East) and even an alcohol-free restaurant called 'Tempérance'. The French manufacturer Menier was also known early on for its paternalistic social policies (houses, school, a bank and a library for workers from the 1870s) and actively publicised the joys of its modern factory at Noisiel, known as 'the cathedral' – the first multi-storey iron-framed building in France, decorated inside with tiles in flower and cocoa-bean patterns. Rudolf Sprüngli beautified his new factory in lakeside Zurich with a park, complete with serpentine walks, a fountain and arbour; and Jean Tobler in Berne was one of several confectionery magnates who eagerly embraced the new vogue for 'scientific management' devised in 1911 by the American theorist F.W. Taylor, in which the health of the workers and the factory environment was prioritised. Tobler also provided an Alpine holiday retreat and built workers' houses in the countryside outside Berne. The factories themselves were certainly not dark satanic mills, and presented a pleasant and optimistic façade to the outside world. In Switzerland, the leading chocolate factories were clustered on the banks of Lake Geneva in picturesque locations, and even the Tobler factory in the centre of Berne is a handsome building, which has now been refurbished as a popular library for university students.

But philanthropy was always accompanied by efficiency in these developments: Papa Suchard may have been kindly, but he was also one of the most successful early exploiters of the advertising medium, introducing cards in the wrappers of his chocolate bars before the cigarette industry did, and running tours of the lake next to the factory on his steamer *L'Industriel* as an imaginative way of securing customer loyalty and reinforcing brand awareness. It should also be remembered that when they instituted these patrician policies, the chocolate manufacturers concerned were making pots and pots of money. In time, good industrial relations, perks for the workers and exemplary factory conditions became synonymous with good management practice, and worker loyalty and contentment came to be viewed as excellent ways of maximising efficiency of production. The startling success of the chocolate companies was enhanced, not held back, by their social policies.

However, these business considerations may have eclipsed the religious or philanthropic impulse quite early on, something the chocolate magnates would not have liked to admit. More than in other industries, it was in the management's interests to keep their workers relatively content, because confectionery manufacture is an extremely hands-on operation, and the finished article, though mass-produced, is supposed to be a luxury comestible. It is desirable to foster employees who take pride and care in their handicraft, while working as speedily as possible. Any industrial action or – heaven forbid – adulteration of the product by a disgruntled worker could result in a scandal that would cause sales to plummet and public confidence to disappear.

International competition between the manufacturers may

have further intensified the chocolate companies' eagerness to respond to a perceived notion among consumers that the goodness of the product was somehow linked with the goodness of the company. By this token, if the company did manage to secure a kindly reputation, its sales would inevitably increase. Healthy sales implied that there was no reason for the manufacturers to doubt the wisdom of this philosophy, although later companies (such as Mars) successfully bucked the convention by concentrating on the qualities of individual brands and obscuring the identity and culture of the parent company. However, this idea that a company can have a personality is no longer controversial today – indeed, it is a linchpin of brand strategy – so perhaps the confectioners were ahead of their time in this, too.

Milton Snavely Hershey was responsible for the most ambitious and overweening empire-building ever conceived in the confectionery industry. Hershey was a barely educated entrepreneur from Pennsylvania, a descendant of immigrants of Pennsylvania Dutch stock who had come to America in the eighteenth century. This community of hard-working Germans and Swiss originates from the mountains (the 'Dutch' came from a misunderstanding of 'Deutsch'); they are Mennonites, an Anabaptist sect related to the more famous Amish, although they do not follow the same uncompromising way of life and in fact have quite a strong culinary tradition, based on a doctrine known as 'the seven sweets and seven sours'. The religious similarities between Hershey and the Quakers across the Atlantic end there, however. Hershey's father, who split with his mother when he was a child, was described by contemporaries as an atheist, and Hershey himself had nothing to say on the subject of religion; there were no explicitly religious overtones to his philanthropic activities. Hershey left school at the age of seven. He had trouble reading throughout his life (which sometimes led to embarrassment) and he never lost his suspicion of academics and 'clever' people. It appears that in place of a formal education, a fearsome business ethic was inculcated in Hershey at a young age by his mother, and when he showed little interest in farming, she instead had him apprenticed to a local confectioner and ice-cream maker. The young Hershey is generally described as a 'failed businessman', since by the age of 29 he had presided over the slight rise and precipitate fall of no fewer than three sweets businesses – in Philadelphia, Colorado and New York. However, his later success would indicate that the main problem in the early days was indeed the lack of investment he complained about. He managed to obtain several loans from an aunt (one rather desperate begging letter from this young man in a hurry inelegantly demands that the money be sent 'at once'), but it was not enough to establish a consistently high volume of goods and turnover. Hershey's later strategy, of concentrating on a small number of well-known brands, mass-producing them and distributing them as widely as possible all over America, justified his early philosophy of saturation sales to create massive product awareness. Hershey thought big from the outset.

His business breakthrough came not with chocolate, but with caramels. The Lancaster Caramel Company, which Hershey formed in the 1880s, did sterling business through its leading product, Crystal A Caramels. Pennsylvania is dairy country, and the milk needed for the sweets was plentiful and relatively cheap. However, to finance this company Hershey had had to resort to borrowing money from an employee, one Henry 'Lebbie' Lebkicher, who continued at the firm for years, a nagging reminder that Hershey had not always been successful. (It is never a good idea to embarrass the boss, even as a result of a good turn, and not surprisingly Hershey maintained an increasingly distant relationship with Lebbie, finally firing him, the story goes, after he built a row of identical houses for employees – Hershey wanted them all to be different.) The caramel business thrived internationally after 1887, when a British businessman was engaged to find markets for the sweets in Europe. Then, on a visit to a Chicago trade fair in 1893,

Hershey saw a chocolate-making machine made by Lehmann of Dresden and, enamoured as he always was by novelty, he immediately bought it. Hershey began making milk chocolate to his own recipe and using it to coat his caramels. His long-time business associate, the sales and marketing director William Murrie, went on the road to sell them. In 1895 Hershey began to manufacture plain chocolate bars, and at the turn of the century he made the remarkably bold decision to sell the caramel company (for a million dollars) and move into chocolate alone. It proved a masterstroke, and by 1904 Hershey had built a new state-of-the-art chocolate factory in Derry Township, just two miles from his birthplace, distinguished by the two tall, thin chimneys that were to become famous across America. The town which grew up on the hills round the factory, renamed Hershey in due course, began to take shape by about 1910 with the laying out of Trinidad Street. More streets named after cocoa plantation regions were added to the chocolate town, and Chocolate Avenue (with streetlamps shaped like Hershey Kisses) was established as the main thoroughfare. It is not clear to what extent Hershey was inspired by the example of Bournville or other industrial villages, such as the Lever brothers' Port Sunlight (Hershey was not the sort of person given to writing or even dictating his memoirs), but a 1903 edition of the *Harrisburg Independent* reported that the new town was to be 'patterned after those in England'. The first houses built in Hershey were intended for executives and key workers (as was the case at Bournville), and they still stand today on Chocolate Avenue and at the eastern end of town, decorously screened from envious eyes by groups of mature specimen trees. The houses built for regular factory workers were fairly large, detached, individually styled properties, while High Point, the mansion Hershey built for himself and his wife Kitty, was modest – especially compared with the edifices constructed by the likes of his millionaire contemporaries such as the Du Ponts or the Rockefellers – and accommodated just three servants. Hershey never became pretentious, and in many ways stayed a poor farm boy at heart. With the proviso, of course, that he was a quite extraordinarily rich poor farm boy.

The level of Hershey's philanthropy has been somewhat mythologised by the company. Nearly everything in the town of Hershey was conceived as a way of making money. Europeans, however, should remember that this is itself a moral imperative in the entrepreneurial culture of the United States, where the Quakers' brand of religious paternalism would perhaps have been viewed as patronising and suspect, an insult to the independent working man. In a watercolour of 1916, Hershey looks like a pretty, busy little town with lots of green space. Today it is no such Utopia, but a relatively charmless and alienating place, its public and company buildings spread out over a wide area and isolated from each other along hilly roads criss-crossed by power lines. What unites Hershey with Bournville is an enveloping odour of chocolate and a pervasive sense of unreality. The focus of the town is unequivocally the factory, rather than a village green or town square, and Dahl's description of Wonka's factory also fits Hershey's:

> And it wasn't simply an ordinary enormous chocolate factory, either. It was the largest and most famous in the whole world! [...] And what a tremendous, marvellous place it was! It had huge iron gates leading in to it, and a high wall surrounding it, and smoke belching from its chimneys, and strange whizzing sounds coming from deep inside it. And outside the walls, for half a mile around in every direction, the air was scented with the heavy rich smell of melting chocolate!

From the earliest days Hershey was developed more as a tourist attraction than as a place to live. The Hotel Hershey, a magnificent hilltop edifice in the style of a Spanish hacienda, still caters for the high-end tourist (today's guests can enjoy 'exquisite therapies and personalized programs' including a whipped cocoa bath or a chocolate fondue body wrap), while a campsite and numerous cheap hotels in and around Hershey struggle to cope with the influx of summer visitors. From the 1910s to the end of the 1930s, Hershey presented to his employees and the paying public a golfcourse, zoo, ice rink, Chinese-style ballroom, cinema, 'Venetian' theatre, American Indian Museum, restaurant, department store, huge outdoor swimming pool, gardens and amusement park. Today Hersheypark, the descendant of that first amusement park, is probably the main visitor draw and an attraction of national renown, so the boss's instinct about the town was right, at least in terms of making money. According to the recorded testimony of one of the waitresses of the 1920s, Hershey liked to dine alone on simple food in his own restaurant at the park, ostentatiously smoking his post-lunch cigar in his own time.

There were various other amenities available to Hershey workers, such as a school, hospital, gym, five churches and a community centre with library, but the single biggest philanthropic gesture Hershey made – perhaps the biggest ever by any industrialist – was to establish the Milton Hershey Industrial School, a place where orphans and poor boys (or economically disadvantaged boys, as they are now called) could be educated. The school was started on a small scale in 1909, apparently at the suggestion of his wife Kitty, who never had children. Three years after her death in 1915 at the age of just forty-two, Hershey made a breathtakingly generous decision: to place his entire personal fortune, some sixty million dollars, in trust for the school. Hershey did not advertise his largesse, and the story only leaked out five years later, when it hit the front pages of the *New York Times*. Hershey's boarding school duly established itself as a first-class institution – with a few eccentricities, such as the compulsory hand-milking of cows every morning, a practice abolished only in 1990 – and many of its intake, who are selected regardless of race or religion, have gone on to Ivy League universities and impressive careers in business and politics. Ex-pupils are officially discouraged from joining the company, but the various Hershey boardrooms have seen several old boys, and perhaps they might come to see some old girls, too, since the school went co-educational in the 1970s.

Through the Depression era Hershey was able to boast of full employment for his workers (albeit at reduced hours and pay), and the amusement park and swimming pool were opened free of charge to a jaded public. Projects requiring large amounts of manual labour, such as a new railroad and sports arena, provided employment for hundreds of workers. But Hershey himself, who left the day-to-day running of the business to Murrie, had been spending a lot of time in Cuba, where in 1916 he had created a smaller version of his Pennsylvania chocolate town: Central Hershey, near Santa Cruz de Norte, sixty miles east of Havana, complete with school, workers' houses, high-sided sidewalks to cope with sudden floods, an electric railroad and baseball diamond. The economic imperative here was the company's sugar supply, which had been threatened in the First World War and could now be provided by 65,000 acres of company-owned cane plantation. Hershey envisaged lucrative tourism as a diversification at his Cuban town, too: a hotel, golf-course, country club and even a racetrack were built to attract visitors. Hershey sold its Cuban concerns after the Second World War, and with the revolution in 1959 the sugar mills went into public ownership. (The dilapidated Cuban Hershey still stands today, renamed Camilio Cienfuegos, the old Hershey manager's home now serving as a dining hall and meeting facility for refinery workers.)

Hershey's retreat to Cuba or into his experimentation labs in Pennsylvania meant that he had lost touch with his workforce and the changing world of labour relations since the Depression, and in 1937 he was completely unprepared for a lightning strike organised by activists from the Congress of Industrial Organisations, or CIO, and the newly formed United Chocolate Workers of America. 'Trouble in Paradise' or 'Sour Milk at Hershey' ran the newspaper headlines, while the 79-year-old Hershey simply could not understand why a proportion of the community of employees which he had nurtured was now turning against him. It went completely against the grain of the Hershey tradition. The strike was one of the most important early instances of industrial action in America, it caused bitter divisions among the workforce, and it ended in violence and recrimination.

There is some evidence that Hershey had been targeted by the trades union movement in order to show that no employer, no matter how enlightened by reputation, could ignore the power of an organised workforce. Henry Ford had been antagonistic towards the unions, saying he would never allow them in, and workers occupied his St Louis factory in one of the first sit-down strikes in the United States. But the union had been officially recognised at Hershey just a few months before the strike. The rhetoric of the leading shop steward, 'Red' Loy, and the substance of several of the union's grievances – the collection of union dues direct from staff paychecks, a closed shop, and the exemption of union officials from the seniority rule (first in, first out, during periods of layoff) to prevent victimisation – imply that to some extent the union was flexing its muscles. This was the start of the age of the teamsters. On the other hand, the union was protesting about inconsistent rates of pay in different areas of the factory, and also working conditions: the heat in the mill room could rise to 120 degrees F and workers were forced to move between very warm and very cold rooms, with the consequent danger of pneumonia. Perhaps the main problem was the prevailing atmosphere of paternalism in Hershey, which had seemed outdated since the 1920s at least and more akin to feudalism to many workers. The pugnacious Hershey had not enamoured himself to the workforce by his (occasional) habit of instantly dismissing workers whom he deemed slapdash, and also by incidents such as the day he climbed aboard a public streetcar in Hershey to inform commuting workers, in his unexpectedly high-pitched voice, that anyone not using the company's own trolley service would be fired.

In the event, some 500 members of a workforce that fluctuated between 2,500 and 3,000 chose to strike. They occupied the chocolate plant at midnight and instigated a shift system for the pickets, allowing only the company foremen to stay behind to guard the machinery and against fire. The strikers leaned out of the windows or stood on the roof and sang their song – 'Glory, Glory, Chocolate Workers!' – or good-naturedly called out to anyone in the street below. Unionised steel workers staged sympathy demonstrations outside the chocolate factory. It did not take long for 'loyal' Hershey workers to organise a parade to demonstrate their sympathy with the company, and when Hershey saw it from behind the curtain in his mansion, where he was ensconced in silence on the advice of his lawyers, he enquired whether they were the strikers. When he heard that the parade consisted of loyal employees, he reportedly broke down in tears. But that story came from a company source; according to aural testimony in the Hershey Community Archive, a good proportion of the Hershey work-force wanted nothing to do with either side in the dispute. Perhaps the dominant mood among the workers was one of ambivalence about both the company and the union. The paradox of paternalism had reached crisis point at Hershey. The Oompa Loompas had finally turned.

The strike quickly assumed national importance, and within days the Senate had voted seventy-five to three that the Hershey action and all other sit-down strikes were illegal. The 'loyal' workers held a rally in the Hershey ice rink (the company museum today) in which they resolved to attack the plant. According to eye witnesses, as the men ran down Chocolate Avenue towards the factory, some of the women present tried to stop them while others looked on in tears. The precise identity of the men who stormed the factory is unclear. There were probably a good number of dairy farmers involved – these were not Hershey employees, but their livelihoods depended on milk sales and thousands of gallons were going sour; 'the cows weren't striking', as one newspaper put it. Several ex-employees mention that the company shipped in 'heavies' from Philadelphia to help break the strike, and one particularly honest testimony describes how the Hershey Estates men – the electricians, plumbers, welders and carpenters – were informally told they had to help break the strike or lose their jobs. Armed with farm implements, ice-pick handles, baseball bats, lead pipes and weapons made in the company workshops, the strikebreakers smashed windows and broke down the doors of the factory at both ends and charged in. The pitched battle lasted just twenty minutes, but it was bloody. Both sides were armed. Some fifty people, mainly strikers, were injured, half of them hospitalised, and it was surprising no one was killed, given the weaponry and the ferocity of feelings. The factory floor was slippery with blood, and the fighting spilled out onto the smooth lawns around the building. Some strikers escaped by jumping out of windows and fleeing, and some tried to hide behind machines or in storerooms, but they were weeded out and forced to leave the factory in small groups with their hands in the air. Once outside, the strikers were taunted by the crowd, showered in coal and ashes, and kicked and punched if they showed any resistance or refused to salute the national flag (which the union had earlier lowered in preference to its own). Several testimonies in the Hershey archive recount the hysteria among the 'loyal' workers gathered outside the factory, and the shame of individuals who found themselves attacking people who had been workmates a few days earlier.

A vote by the Hershey workforce a few days after the strike went against the union (about a third of employees abstained) but the company nevertheless began to negotiate, the striking workers were reinstated without questions, and joint picnics were organised for farmers and Hershey employees in an attempt to heal the rift. The unionised workers could sing,

It happened one night in dreamtown and we can't forget it as
  yet
We were kicked and clubbed out of the factory, but what gain
  did the rioters get?

but Hershey's chocolate town would never be the same again, and the whole country knew it.

Which was excellent news for Mars, Hershey's old adversary. The rivalry had begun in 1924, when Frank Mars and his son Forrest launched the Milky Way in an effort to displace the Hershey Bar as the nation's number one chocolate bar. The Milky Way – later recreated as the Mars Bar in Britain and elsewhere – was one of the first really successful 'combination' chocolate bars; that is, it was not just a slab of pure chocolate but contained a filling. Its unique selling point was that it was huge compared with a regular chocolate bar. Frank Mars was delighted that a Hershey Bar looked so skinny in comparison with a chunky Milky Way, since the chocolate, which was the most expensive part, was used only as a coating. Mars followed up with another combination bar, Snickers, in 1930, and it met with similar success. Forrest Mars later claimed that he, not his father, invented the Milky Way, explaining that he got the idea while drinking a chocolate malt drink, and suddenly realised that a candy bar could be marketed as a food as well as a treat. But it is difficult to know the truth.

Forrest had a strange relationship with his father. After his parents divorced when he was five, Forrest saw nothing of Frank Mars for twelve years. Their unexpected reunion occurred in strange circumstances. The 18-year-old Forrest was working as a marketeer for Camel cigarettes, travelling the country with a small team and organising promotional stunts. In Chicago his flyposting activities landed him in a police cell and his father turned up out of nowhere to bail him out. The older Mars asked his enterprising son to join his business, which had only recently taken off for him after some twenty years of scraping a living as a wholesaler and manufacturer in towns all over the United States. The Yale-educated Forrest displayed a genius for business and presided over the building of a state-of-the-art factory in Chicago, but his expansive style was not compatible with his father's more dogged approach, and finally, in 1932, Frank unceremoniously kicked him out of the company after an impasse concerning their export ambitions.

Forrest took his family to Europe and, to start with, tried to forget all about confectionery. He went into the shoe-tree business, of all things. But within months he had been drawn back into the world of chocolate, and he decided it was time to learn about the product first-hand, for reasons he disclosed in a video-recorded interview towards the end of his life: 'You can hire lawyers, you can hire accountants, you can hire advertising men or financial types. But if you want to get rich, you have got to know how to make a product. And you aren't going to hire anybody to make a product for you to make you rich. They'll only make it for themselves.' Forrest took this view of human nature with him to Switzerland to learn about chocolate for a few months, working incognito (as Hershey had apparently done in the 1890s) at the Nestlé and Tobler factories. 'I was an hourly paid guy,' Forrest recalled. 'They didn't know who I was. I just told them I was an American, and the factory manager didn't care. All he cared was whether I knew anything about candy.' Forrest never made that mistake in his own factories, where secrecy was and is a priority.

With his new-found knowledge, Forrest went to England – principally because he could speak the language – and, alarmed at the cost of manufacturing space in London, he travelled out to Slough, about twenty miles west of the capital. Here Forrest set about perfecting the recipe and organising the manufacture of the bar that would become the Mars Bar – really a sweeter, richer version of the American Milky Way, designed to suit the British palate. Another bar called Milky Way was later launched in Britain, consisting of the fondant mix alone. Whenever a British person becomes over-patriotic about confectionery, it pays to remind them that the 'real' Mars Bar is in fact a 'real' American Milky Way. (On the other side of the Atlantic, it can be salutary for jingoistic sweet-eaters to learn that the KitKat, one of the best-selling bars for decades in the United States, and apparently as American as apple pie, was invented not in New York but at Rowntree in 'old' York, in the north of England.)

Forrest began to take boxes of Mars Bars up to London on the train from Slough to hawk them around tobacconists' and other small shops. This big new 'American' bar was an instant success, and from these beginnings Forrest built up a company to rival that of his father, creating Uncle Ben's Rice (and Uncle Ben himself) and inventing the unmeltable M&Ms along the way – with the help of Bruce Murrie, second son of the Hershey president: Mars & Murrie = M&M. Eventually Forrest was able to wrest control of the parent (literally) Mars company away from the family of Frank Mars' second wife, and he set about remoulding the Mars company culture in his own image: hardworking, obsessed with quality, fanatical about detail and consumed with a desire to keep everything firmly behind closed doors. The *Washington Post* journalist Joël Glenn Brenner, author of *Chocolate Wars: Inside the Secret Worlds of Mars and Hershey* (1999), has managed to find out more about the secretive setup at Mars than anyone else, and she neatly summarises Forrest's first priorities in 1964, when he finally took control of the company he saw as his destiny:

> Forrest ripped out the executive dining room, fired the French chef, tore down the office walls, stripped the oak panelling and sold the art collection, the rugs, the stained glass and the corporate helicopter. He then increased salaries 30 per cent, replaced fixed annual compensation with incentive pay and handed each associate a time card.

Mars became the company it is today, renowned for excellent rates of pay, a flat management structure, bereft of perks at senior management level, low on meetings and high on secrecy and isolation from the rest of the industry. So perhaps it was simply ahead of its time. According to Brenner, Forrest Mars expected all his employees to act and think as he did: to worry about 'scuffmarks' on the chocolate bars and the formation of the letter M on each and every M&M, and reject anything that was less than perfect; to taste the dogfood and catfood which has long been a somewhat unfortunate but extraordinarily lucrative sideline of the company; to forgo, if you are an executive, a personal assistant and do your own photocopying; to clean every nook and cranny of every machine; to talk to people rather than write memos; and to reveal absolutely nothing about the company to outsiders. A generous payscale – there are six grades at management level, and no variations in between – and clarity about job expectations from the start apparently offset the pressurised atmosphere at Mars, where employees talk about being paired up with colleagues who are in line for a similar level of promotion, and then placed in a more or less openly competitive situation to see who does best. One ex-Mars employee who had worked on the factory floor told me how impressed he was by the fact that when the Mars brothers came to visit the plant, they always quietly queued up in line with the other workers in the canteen. That is the Mars style. The company has various community initiatives at its eighty-plus factories worldwide, but it makes no philanthropic gestures on a Hershey scale. Its mission is to make money and to smash the competition. Nevertheless, the secrecy around the company, and the unique and uncompromising corporate culture, give Mars a slightly cultish flavour. Its website talks about quality as the number-one priority – 'time after time, without deviation' – and a section called 'freedom' pontificates that 'profit is the key; profit allows us to remain free', which is a strange, obscurely idealistic way of justifying the perfectly legitimate business goal of making money.

Willy Wonka also craved the freedom to be creative with his confectionery, but he never had to worry overmuch about profits. Wonka's world, as envisioned by Roald Dahl, was an only slightly distorted mirror image of the real world of the chocolate magnates. The strange thing is, the eccentricities of the big companies percolate through the whole confectionery industry, which is still peppered with small- to medium-sized family firms, obsessed with secrecy, hidebound by their own history but always on the lookout for the next big thing in sweeties. Confectionery is a sharp-end business, but the imaginative kick that comes with eccentricity has made it one of the most fast-moving, unusual and exciting industries of all. In the world of international confectionery, only the fittest sweets survive.

Lucky Dip

CHEWING GUM

First, a confession. I do not like chewing gum. It is my only sweets blind spot. The problem is not based on snobbery about the admittedly some-what bestial habit of chewing away like a stolid bovine, but in the way the flavour of the sweet is less than intimately amalgamated with its agent. Put another way, I hate the way the flavour of chewing gum goes away, leaving you with a ghost of a sweet, a limp husk that lingers in the mouth, bereft of taste and even of sugar, unswallowable (as any schoolchild or competent doctor knows, the ingestion of chewing gum causes instantaneous death through the gumming up of the alimentary tract) and difficult to dispose of without causing misery to others – gum removal from public areas is a growth industry.

It was decided long ago that language is what separates man from the beasts; chewing gum, on the other hand, reunites us with the animals because it not only prevents us from talking properly but renders us meditatively dull and insensible, like beasts in their worst moments. All other sweets elevate mankind; chewing gum alone diminishes him. Bubble gum is another matter. Bubble gum is exceptionally fine, because it is bright pink and you can blow bubbles with it – which colour and which action immediately sets the blower apart from the animal king-dom. But spent chewing gum lurks in the mouth like some detached oral appendix, useless. And it is grey – whoever heard of a grey sweet? It is a disgrace.

Primitive cultures are united in their preference for chewing sub-stances like betel nuts, sassafras twigs, chicle and spruce resin; anthropologists say it indicates dietary deficiency and a desire to deceive the body into thinking it is receiving nourishment. In medieval Europe, beeswax from honeycombs served as a kind of chewing gum, and candlewax has long been favoured by the poor: John F. Dulles, Eisenhower's foreign policy guru in the 1950s, was once caught eating candlewax at a formal dinner by a forthright lady. 'I know it's awful,' he apologised. 'But I just love to chew candle grease. I've been doing it all my life.' The compulsion to chew without the pleasure of flavour is clearly difficult for the ignorant and weak-willed to resist, but just as with religion, evidence of an ancient propensity for something does not make it desirable or naturally judicious.

Chewing gum as we know it was invented in 1871, when Thomas Adams, a New York photographer and general entrepreneur, had almost finished experimenting with a ton of chicle (latex from the sapodilla tree) which the exiled Mexican general, Antonio de Santa Ana, who led the attack on the Alamo during the Mexican Civil War (and held a state funeral for his amputated leg), had brought to America with him, intending to find a commercial use for it. Adams had taken up the general's challenge and in his warehouse in Front Street, New York, he had experimented with making rubber tyres, toys, masks and boots from the chicle. To no avail. It had not occurred to him that there could be a business proposition in the fact that the South Americans were fond of chewing it, just as the native Americans used lumps of spruce resin, which had served as the basis for the existing Maine-based American gum industry (which had recently turned to flavoured paraffin wax-based gum as a cheap substitute). At a company dinner in 1944, Adams' grandson gave this version of the story of the invention of chicle-based chewing gum:

After about a year's work of blending chicle with rubber, the experiments were regarded as a failure. Consequently, Mr Adams intended to throw the remaining lot into the East River. But it happened that before this was done, Thomas Adams went into a drugstore at the corner. While he was there, a little girl came into the shop and asked for a chewing gum for one penny. It was known to Mr Adams that chicle, which he had tried unsuccessfully to vulcanise as a rubber substitute, had been used as a chewing gum by the natives of Mexico for many years. So the idea struck him that perhaps they could use the chicle he wanted to throw away for the production of chewing gum and so salvage the lot in the storage. After the child had left the store, Mr Adams asked the druggist what kind of chewing gum the little girl had bought. He was told that it was made of paraffin wax and called White Mountain. When he asked the man if he would be willing to try an entirely different kind of gum, the druggist agreed. When Mr Adams arrived home that night, he spoke to his son, Tom Jr, my father, about his idea. Junior was very much impressed, and suggested that they make up a few boxes of chicle chewing gum and give it a name and a label. He offered to take it out on one of his trips (he was a salesman in wholesale tailors' trimmings and traveled as far west as the Mississippi). They decided on the name of Adams New York No. 1. It was made of pure chicle gum without any flavor. It was made in little penny sticks and wrapped in various colored tissue papers. The retail value of the box, I believe, was one dollar. On the cover of the box was a picture of City Hall, New York, in colour.

This flavourless gum, marketed with the words 'snapping and stretching', was, of course, an instant success, and in 1884 Adams introduced a liquorice-flavour gum, the famous Adams' Black Jack. Four years later, and the inventive Adams was selling gumballs from vending machines in New York subway stations. By the end of the century, the chewing gum industry was thriving, with brands such as Chiclets, Dentyne (the 'dental gum') and pepsin-enhanced Beeman's competing with Adams' products. In 1891 Thomas Wrigley Jr arrived in Chicago from Philadelphia, set on selling soap. At first he offered baking powder as a free incentive to his new clients, and when he found that the gift was more popular than the soap, he switched to selling primarily the baking powder, with chewing gum as the incentive. When the chewing gum proved more popular than the baking powder, he switched again and never looked back. Wrigley's Spearmint gum and Juicy Fruit were launched in 1893, and the company quickly grew to dominate the industry through the personable salesmanship and business acumen of its founder.

Since then, chewing gum sales have not stopped growing, and lucrative new markets in India, China and Eastern Europe are now being enthusiastically exploited. Perhaps the greatest trick yet pulled by chewing gum is the way it has become accepted as a healthy product, in its sugar-free guise somehow capable of keeping the teeth clean rather than causing them to decay. The infiltration of this sweet into the health-food culture was complete when Colgate launched its first chewing gum product in October 2001.

Chapter 10

BAD CANDY

Sweets are bad for you. That is the unequivocal message from the health establishment nowadays. Sweets are something to be slightly ashamed of, to be scoffed secretly or else scoffed at. In the past fifty years, scientists have linked sugar (and therefore sweets) with heart disease, diabetes, obesity, anaemia, hyperactivity, arthritis, cancer, osteoporosis, mental illness including schizophrenia, menstrual cramps, scurvy, hair loss, varicose veins, impotence, drug addiction, suicide and criminality. Oh, and haemorrhoids. But the science is very fuzzy. The effects of food on the body are complex and variable, and in truth barely understood beyond the chemical level – in this sense nutrition is perhaps more akin to psychology than any other branch of science – but many of the scientists in this sphere, as elsewhere, do not like to admit incomplete knowledge. The results of isolated experiments are advanced or appropriated as likely indications of the root causes of massive public-health problems, but most such experiments are necessarily conducted across small samples of people from single food cultures, and the results often directly contradict other studies. And there are massive discrepancies between the dietary guidelines of neighbouring countries, and these guidelines change all the time. As we shall see, the grand total of commonplace diseases which have been conclusively linked with sugar consumption is . . . one: tooth decay. This is not sugar propaganda, but scientific fact, acknowledged by nutritionists and even by sugar's worst enemies. But sugar is still demonised in the mind of the public, stereotyped as a foodstuff that is as detrimental to health as saturated fat (which itself, as the professor of nutrition at Harvard pointed out in 1995, is far from conclusively linked with heart disease).

There is some historical precedent for the suspicion of sugar. Although European medicine from the thirteenth to the eighteenth centuries was overwhelmingly persuaded of the beneficial effects of sugar and syrups derived from the Arabic pharmacopoeia, there were sporadic voices of dissent. The early sixteenth century saw a rash of anti-sugar sentiment – from the physicians Miguel Serveto and Leonhard Fuchs, for example, and the respected alchemist Paracelsus, who was suspicious of its too-liberal usage by 'swill-makers who do an idiot's job by mixing drugs with sugar and honey'. Paracelsus did not deny sugar's medicinal usefulness in certain cases, however, whereas Joseph Duchesne, in *Le Pourtraict de la Santé* (1606), took a less circumspect view: 'Beneath its whiteness, sugar conceals a profound blackness, and beneath its sweetness lurks a harsh corrosiveness, as bad as that of aqua fortis. From it one can even derive a solvent capable of dissolving gold.' More cogently argued reservations about sugar appeared a hundred years later, in early-eighteenth-century London, with Thomas Willis's speculations about the link between sugar and diabetes, the disease he had just identified. This led to a frenzied attack from one Dr Frederick Slare, a 67-year-old physician and sugar fanatic, which took the form of *A Vindication of Sugars Against the Charge of Dr Willis and Other Physicians, and Common Prejudices: Dedicated to the Ladies* (1715). Slare says that he habitually adds two ounces of sugar to a pint of wine, takes sugar snuff, uses sugar to treat sores, and even brushes his teeth with a sugar toothpaste. He includes two inspiring case studies that back up his enthusiasm:

A friend: 'He was a litle lean Man, who us'd to drink much wine in the Company of strong Drinkers; I asked him how he was able to bear it? He told me, that he receiv'd much damage in his health, and was apt to be fuddl'd before he us'd to dissolve Sugar in his Wine, from that time he was never sick, nor inflam'd, nor fuddled with Wine; but if he chanc'd to be in a place where he could not have sugar (which seldom happen'd) that he suffer'd much, had a Head-ach, and was feverish after it. He usually drank Red Wine.'

The Duke of Beaufort's personal physician, a letter: 'Bristol Nov 3 1714. The Great Duke of Beaufort, grandfather to the late, died of a fever in the 70th year of his age; was opened in the presence of Dr Hay, Dr Wincle, Dr Baskervile and myself. All the Viscera were as found in a person of 20. Never troubled with coughs, and his teeth firm. His chaplain, Mr Hopkins, and his secretary, Mr Crow, told me, that for near 40 years he had used near a pound of sugar a day, in his sherry, chocolate and sweetmeats, which he did eat constantly after dinner. I asked the housekeeper, Mrs Grymes, and she said, That he did at least take that quantity daily; and would mention the English proverb

That which preserves Apples and Plumbs,

Will also preserve Liver and Lungs.'

But the dissent over sugar would not go away: Brillat-Savarin, who loved sugar himself, noted in 1825 that 'some said that it heated the blood, some that it attacked the lungs, other that it was a cause of apoplexy'. Meanwhile sugar consumption kept increasing through the nineteenth and into the late twentieth century, considered a pleasant energy food that was fundamentally harmless, and also an emblem of affluence.

So, despite a few isolated flashpoints of sucrophobia, sweet things were innocently enjoyed in all cultures for some two millennia. With improvements in refining, the very whiteness of sugar was held up as evidence of its benign purity, and the likes of Rousseau lauded it as an entirely natural, unsullied product. Then suddenly, in the 1970s, the young science of nutrition got into its stride and we began to be told that sugar was the cause of all kinds of health defects, from diabetes to heart disease to obesity. Scientists vilified sugar as a useless source of 'empty calories', and health 'gurus' successfully promoted the idea that anything with sugar in it was somehow corrupted. This simple idea proved to be potent enough to become entrenched in the minds of both the medical profession and Western consumers, who are now highly suspicious of sugar in all its forms (although the fact that they are eating more and more of it just goes to show how useless the anti-sugar strategy has been).

The turning point was the publication in 1972 of *Pure, White and Deadly* by John Yudkin. The anti-sugar lobby had found its champion (or rather, the champion had found his audience). Yudkin was the first professor of nutrition at London University, and he hated sugar. In the first chapter of his book he writes: 'I hope that, when you have read this book, I shall have convinced you that sugar is really dangerous.' His last chapter is called 'Why Sugar Should be Banned', but the title of the book says it all. In his publications and lectures, Yudkin promoted the idea that sugar was linked with heart disease. But he did not stop there: he went on to add a host of other ailments until one gained the impression that sugar was nothing less than a deadly poison. However, as the historian Harvey Levenstein observes in *Paradox of Plenty* (1993), Yudkin's lecture tours of the United States and elsewhere were part-funded by the egg industry. His research was favourably looked upon by the lobby because his focus was exclusively and obsessively on sugar, rather than the saturated fats in dairy products and meat which are now considered more serious threats to health. (The British Heart Foundation's lifestyle advice today is: 'Too much saturated fat from red meat, biscuits, cakes, chips and dairy products can clog up your arteries and put a strain on your heart.' The prescription is for more vegetables and starchy foods, less salt and alcohol and just three eggs a week. Sugar is not mentioned at all.) Today, *Pure, White and Deadly* reads like a bad eighteenth-century polemic. The author's fixation on sugar and obsessive personal distaste for it reduces him to the level of a crank. The fact that Yudkin accused scientists who disagreed with him of being addicted to sugar did not stop his work being discredited – of his many works, only a book about slimming is cited in the capacious bibliography to the current standard reference work, *Nutrition: A Reference Handbook* (1997), by Yudkin's successors at the University of London. But the damage had been done. It was now open season on sugar and sweets. A lone nutritionist with a grudge, a marketable idea and a taste for fame can change a nation's eating habits, and Yudkin's theories received a huge amount of publicity. Perhaps his anti-sugar crusade was especially seductive in those puritan-influenced societies, like America and Britain, where sensual pleasure tends to be linked with moral downfall.

One of the most potent ideas to emerge in the post-Yudkin anti-sugar free-for-all was that sugar caused mental excitement. One expert suggested that people should not be allowed to drive a car after ingesting a certain amount, and in 1979 the conservative American politician Dan White, who shot San Francisco mayor George Moscone and his gay supervisor Harvey Milk, was notoriously successful at his trial in his use of the 'Twinkie Defence'. White's lawyers argued that an excess of sugar from Twinkie bars had sent him over the edge, and he was convicted of manslaughter rather than murder. Sugar was first linked with hyperactivity at this time, and parents became convinced that their children's bad behaviour was the fault of sweets, soft drinks and cakes. It does not seem unreasonable to suppose that children might experience a 'glucose rush' after eating sweets, and – anecdotally – many parents are sure it does have this effect, but sugar has not been linked with the medical condition called hyperactivity. (One experiment into the proposition found that the children tested were not affected by sugar to any great degree – in fact, the one thing that made them calm down and behave was their parents leaving the room.) Then, in 1975, came a modest essay in the *American Journal of Nursing* by a scientist called B.F. Feingold, which suggested a link between artificial colours and flavourings – vital in most sweets, of course – and hyperactivity. This tentative hypothesis, made more than a quarter of a century ago, has not been converted into clinically proven fact, but the idea that 'E Numbers' and other additives cause children to go wild is nevertheless accepted as truth by the general public. The innocent playground of sweets had mutated into a hostile jungle, filled with strange and unlikely dangers.

The prime nutritional fallacy that has arisen from the anti-sugar diatribes is the idea that sugar makes you fat. The truth is, fat makes you fat. Nutritionists today are clear on this. Sugar is a simple carbohydrate that is quickly converted into glucose energy in the bloodstream, and if a lot is being ingested, it is true that a certain proportion might be squirrelled away and stored as fat. But mainstream nutritionists (as opposed to people selling diet books) do not advocate a reduction in carbohydrate intake to induce weight loss. They say that in our diets it is the saturated fats in dairy products, meats and fried foods which cause most of the problems (and ostensibly raise cholesterol levels, although that is unproven). By this reasoning, the most unhealthy thing about a chocolate bar is the amount of full-fat milk in it, not the sugar: eating lots of chocolate bars will probably make you fatter, whereas eating boiled sweets will not – a simple message that is more or less a revelation to most people. But it is unlikely that the demonisation of sugar will simply evaporate, and sales of chemical sweeteners such as sodium saccharine and aspartame are sure to remain buoyant (despite the discovery of a link between cyclamates, formerly one of the most popular sugar alternatives, and cancer, which led to its ban in Britain and the United States).

The end result of the swirling cauldron of nutritional claim and counter-claim is that sugar is generally considered to be as bad for you as saturated fat. Some nutritionists and health lobbies have decided not to disabuse us of this fallacy – indeed, they promote it – because they have correctly deduced that people prefer high-sugar diets to healthier foods. In a sincere effort at improving the eating habits of the general populace, they have developed a strategy of frightening consumers away from sugar, in the belief that somehow they will be lured on to healthier foods as a matter of course. It is a desperate measure, doomed to failure, fundamentally dishonest and morally reprehensible, but most public-health organisations pursue it as unwritten policy. To take just one example, in 1999 the Washington-based Centre for Science in the Public Interest (CSPI) published a press release which stated, 'If you're drinking soda pop instead of low-fat milk or orange juice, or eating a candy bar instead of a piece of fruit, you're missing a chance to cut your risk of osteoporosis, cancer, or heart disease.' This apparently straightforward argument is deeply casuistic. It does not actually state that candy bars cause cancer or heart disease, but it does suggest they contribute to risk, because eating a candy bar fills you up and therefore makes you unable to eat the healthier sorts of food that just might prevent you contracting these diseases. The nutritionists will argue that they have not actually stated any falsehoods in pronouncements like these, but the effect of their words – and it is the intended effect – is to link sugar and sweets with specific illnesses in people's minds.

I am no apologist for the sugar companies – I do not believe them either. Their rhetoric equates sugar with purity and goodness; they promote the idea that white table sugar is pure and entirely natural because it is 99 per cent sucrose. But the product has gone through a lengthy refining process, and its 'naturalness' refers only to its chemical purity. Even manufacturers of off-white, less-refined sugars are guilty of exaggeration, claiming that their product is 'unrefined' and therefore retains the natural goodness of sugar, when the nutritional difference from table sugar is nominal (the taste is different, however). The sugar industry also funds research into nutrition, just as the tobacco industry did with cigarettes. This work is usually carried out by 'independent' scientists, but it is now believed that interpretation in these circumstances is sometimes fatally compromised because of an irresistible and involuntary bias in research teams towards the interests of funding bodies (although most scientists furiously contest this).

As consumers we are innocent civilians, taste-damaged in a savage war between entrenched enemies. We are refugees from this culinary meltdown, scurrying round our supermarkets in ignorance and dismay, feeling bad when we buy things we really like, and cajoled and manipulated when we buy more expensive and sometimes more unpleasant 'healthy' versions of our desired foods. Food morality is another modern complication, whether it is ethical farming issues, like veal crates or depleted fish stocks, or lifestyle choices such as vegetarianism or whether to buy free-range and organic to support the suppliers, and decisions made on this basis are often justifiable and even honourable. But does every food choice have to be a moral choice? Labelling is usually trumpeted as the best way for consumers to exercise choice, allowing them to examine the small print on packages to discover precisely what is inside, but perhaps this just encourages more food neurosis among the public. Some of us may relish the idea of looking at sweet wrappers and adding up calories and being constantly aware of what it is we are ingesting, but not all of us. Sweets are partly an act of escapism, and worrying about death hardly enhances the experience.

This policy of attacking sugar and sweets does not fundamentally improve people's diets; all it does is spoil an innocent moment of pleasure, a balm amid the stress of life. I am not suggesting that sugar is wholly good and that nutritionists are all misguided – to be fair, most of them state the chemical facts and leave the food propaganda to others. And there is no doubt that people can eat sweets for the wrong reasons – boredom, loneliness, anxiety, guilt – and end up by abusing them. It is just that the public-health argument has been made too forcefully against sugar. After all, sweets can also be good for you: they contain glucose energy, they taste nice, they are easily digested, they cheer you up and they can play an important part in both our social and private lives. The benefits of sweets are more psychological than physical, but these positive aspects are never mentioned by the medical establishment and used to balance the so-called ill effects. Our bodies are treated more like auto-mobiles than temples. If we really believe sweets are so bad, surely we would never eat them?

The result of all this nutritional perversity is that children grow up with ideas about 'good' foods and 'bad' foods, associat-ing them with punishment or reward. This can store up problems for the future: mentally labelling foods is central to the warped logic of people with eating disorders. But sweets are almost always treated in this way. No one is saying that children should be allowed to eat as many sweets as they want, at any time, but a more relaxed approach would make everyone happier and healthier. Most parents will want to ration their children's sweets, but it would be better for their psychological health if sweets were given joyfully, as an expression of love, rather than grudgingly and disapprovingly. Sometimes it seems that parents derive a perverse satisfaction from banning or demonising certain foods, because they feel they are taking some positive action in protecting their children, regardless of whether it is doing more harm than good. I was banned sweets as a child, allowed only ten pence worth on a Saturday, to be eaten straight after lunch. And look what happened to me! I still hide sweets. As it stands, parents are encouraged to treat sweets as a life-or-death issue, and children grow up with wonky notions that no Wonka can put right. So give children a break, and give them back their sweets.

The authorities would do better to leave sugar alone and address poverty as the root cause of poor diet in many people – rather than hectoring people with scare stories – and to encourage the teaching of cookery and understanding of fresh ingredients in schools. The only way to encourage healthier eat-ing is to make sure it is more enjoyable eating, to give people the will and the skills to make their own good food. And to make the ingredients necessary for this kind of food affordable.

Of course, it would be easier for me to argue the case if I was thin. But I am not thin. I am fat – not really fat, but quite fat. If I was sitting across the table from you, you might listen to the argument and then say, 'Oh yeah? Take a look in the mirror, sunshine.' The argument is fatally undercut by girth. It may also be that my medical defence of sweets is further compromised by the fact that I have written a book extolling their virtues. As John Ring put it in *A Treatise on the Gout* (1811): 'Amid the joys of wine, and the shouts of the Bacchanals, the still voice of reason is not heard; the sober dictates of discretion are disregarded; and the friendly warnings of the physician are either totally forgotten, or treated with ridicule and contempt.' And yes, I suffer from gout, too.

But the fact is, the only common disease that has been conclusively linked with sugar is tooth decay. (There is also a rare form of reactive hypoglycemia – a condition commonly associated with alcoholics – which can be triggered by a high-sugar diet; it prompts the release of insulin, lowering blood sugar and causing confusion and personality change.) As the huge American governmental study called *Diet and Health* (1989) concluded in its section on sugar: 'Sugar consumption (by those with an adequate diet) has not been established as a risk factor for any chronic disease other than dental caries in humans.'

Tooth decay itself should not be passed over lightly, however. As the son of a dentist, how could I? The disease called dental caries occurs when easily fermentable carbohydrates, including sucrose, create the nutrient base which allows bacterial microorganisms such as *Streptococcus mutans* to thrive. These bacteria dwell in an acid which erodes tooth enamel and creates cavities and dental caries. My new dentist was admirably calm when I told him I was an international confectionery historian (his assistant giggled), but he did not try to ban me from eating sweets. I clean my teeth, and they are in quite good condition; I have three fillings. What he did say was that current thinking dictates that it is best to eat sweets all in one go – whole packets at a time – rather than keep them in contact with the teeth for extended periods. Greed is good, my dentist seemed to be saying. This suits me, because I tend to wolf sweets down quickly.

But sweets are not the only culprit with tooth decay: starchy foods like crisps have been identified as at least as bad, and possibly even worse, and unsweetened as well as sugary breakfast cereal and even bread also trigger acid attacks on the teeth. After all, they are all easily fermentable carbohydrates, and their unfortunate tendency to cling to the teeth is as bad for dental hygiene as it is for personal grooming. The fine teeth of some Oceanic peoples has led to the suggestion that chewing raw sugar cane is actually good for teeth, because it contains calcium sucrose phosphates that harden the enamel (these beneficial compounds are lost in the refining process, however). And some of the substances given the chemical name of sugar-alcohols have been proven to inhibit dental caries; one of them, commercially manufactured as Xylitol, has such pronounced properties in this respect that it is used in sweets marketed as 'tooth-friendly'.

The low social status of sweets is perhaps their most potent adversary. As sugar became a cheap, staple food through the nineteenth century and its luxury status was forgotten, sweet foods began to be associated with the poor more than the rich. Today, the medieval status of sugar as the food of kings and the aristocracy has been reversed: the poorest people eat the most sugar (and the most fat). Those who consider themselves to be individuals of taste and discernment assiduously avoid sugar in all but its most expensive and exclusive forms ('bitter' chocolate is desirable, since its sweetness is tempered and thus made sophisticated). A taste for sweet is seen as infantile, old-fashioned or low-class: only the lowest of the low would favour a sweet German wine over a crisp, dry sauvignon blanc. In *The Taste of America* (1989), Karen and John Hess reveal their distaste for an average fellow American (as seen on television) and her defence that she gives her family sugar-rich processed foods because they say they 'taste good':

When she says 'taste good,' she simply means 'taste sweet'. If she is a typical American, and she sounds like one, her very first mouthful of nourishment was a synthetic, sweetened bottle formula; she was weaned on starchy baby foods loaded with sugar and monosodium glutamate, and she grew up on soda pop, candy, corn flakes, ketchup-doused hamburgers, and instant coffee.

Why does everyone have to eat well? Is it really to make them happier, to save tax dollars in healthcare and welfare, or is it to avoid offending the sensibilities of the elite? It may be difficult to swallow, but for many people, junk food and candy bars are among life's greatest pleasures.

The suspicion of sweetness is reflected in language. It is as if the very pleasure of sweetness means there must be something wrong with it, hence the duplicity of 'sugared words' and Shakespeare's 'Things sweet to taste prove in digestion sour.' Slang words for sweets themselves, particularly children's sweets, are synonymous with 'rubbish' in several languages. In the north-east of England, the word for sweets is still kets or ket, which also means trash, and 'humbug' meant nonsense for at least half a century before it was appropriated as the name for a sweet. Sweet words like candy, marshmallow, saccharine and confection are often employed to describe something as insubstantial, shallow or dishonest. In medieval France, the practice of bribing or softening up judges with gifts of sugared almonds became known as 'paying in spices', and even today '*payer en espèces*' is slang for paying in cash. There are examples everywhere: Tristan Tzara, theorist of the Dada movement, proclaimed, 'Morality is the infusion of chocolate in the veins of all men', and a Tennessee Williams short story called 'Hard Candy' is an unedifying tale of an old sweetmaker who propositions a boy in a cinema with candy and then expires. Sweet imagery is freely linked with pornography and lowlife in literature: in my library research, calling up a book called *Candy* from an archive, unseen, could as easily produce a steamy novel as a children's book.

From here it is but a short step to abduction and murder, and the potent image of the child-molester or child-killer tempting children with gifts of sweets. The extremely frightening child-catcher in the film of *Chitty Chitty Bang Bang* (1968), with his lollipops and his lockable cart, or the fairytale witch of the Gingerbread House, are cautionary tales about the power of sweet temptation. One hopes they might be of some use. In 1989 a Colombian man called Daniel Barbosa admitted to the killing of seventy-one young girls in Ecuador. He had used sweets to lure his victims, and it was a stray fingerprint left on a sweet wrapper at a crime scene that led to his arrest (Barbosa was killed in prison in 1999 by a cousin of one of his victims). Horror books and movies abound with such imagery – as in *Candyman* (1992), itself based on an urban legend, with a hook-handed monster, and faceless visions like 'Candy Cane', a psychotic truck driver in the teen-trash movie *Roadkill* (2002). There is nothing new in this duplicity of sweet meaning – 'candyman' was a term of abuse in Newcastle in the mid nineteenth century, after itinerant sweetsellers took money to act as bailiffs and forcibly eject striking miners and their families from their homes.

Stories and rumours about specific sweets have a tendency to be gruesome. Roald Dahl recalled how a friend's father, one Dr Thwaites, told him and his friends that liquorice bootlaces were made from rats' blood. He explained how rat-catchers took the rats to the factory and put them, 10,000 at a time, into a huge vat where they were mashed up into a rat stew. This was then pressed into a giant rat pancake which was divided into boot-laces. 'It didn't stop any of us except Thwaites from buying liquorice bootlaces,' Dahl observed. There is no evidence that this delightful rumour gained wider currency, but plenty have. For instance, the idea that marshmallows contained 'glue' made from boiled-up horses, or the potent late-1970s urban myth that Bubble Yum bubble gum contained spiders' eggs (or sometimes legs), which was the reason why it was so soft. That story was so widely believed in America and Britain that the company even took out advertisements designed to reassure children (and parents).

This penchant among sweets consumers for a frisson of horror has been exploited by the manufacturers, not just in conventional horror imagery, but in more ghastly ways. Kelly-in-a-Coffin, a sugar baby in a coffin, was a well-known sweet in the late nineteenth century, when infant mortality was more a part of life. Morbidity sells: a sweet called 'hangman's noose' is mentioned in an 1895 trade list, and in 2002 the British Prime Minister was questioned in Parliament about the sale in Glasgow of sweets called Freekee Drops, which resembled bloodstained syringes (it was reported that children were mimicking injecting themselves with drugs). Even Jelly Babies harbour a dark secret. The first jelly baby was born in 1864 at Fryer's, a Lancashire sweets firm. It was the invention of an Austrian immigrant confectioner called Steinboch (known as 'Springbok' locally), and the name he coined, and the name Jelly Babies were initially marketed under, was 'Unclaimed Babies'.

The other famous baby-orientated sweet has an even un-happier legacy. The Baby Ruth is one of the best-loved old American candies, a chocolate-covered caramel and peanut bar launched in 1921 by the Curtiss Candy Company of Chicago. It was quite common for companies to appropriate celebrities' names, with or without permission, and the launch of the bar coincided with the first flush of fame for Babe Ruth, the great baseball player. The bar itself was not new – it had previously been called Kandy Kate, so the name Baby Ruth must have initially derived from the theme of girls' names. You can imagine the brainstorming session, and the sudden realisation that the new name that had popped out of nowhere contained the added bonus of an association with a baseball star. There can be no doubt that the celebrity connection was conceived as the bar's main selling point, but the company did not approach Babe Ruth for endorsement, and was careful enough to vary the name ever so slightly from Babe to Baby. The bar was aggressively marketed (thousands were given away free) and competitively priced at just five cents, and it was a big success.

Babe Ruth himself was understandably piqued at this use of his name (or nearly his name) and formed his own company, the George H. Ruth Candy Co., planning the launch of a product called the 'Babe Ruth Home Run Bar'. At this point the Curtiss Candy Company sued for breach of copyright, claiming that Babe Ruth's own bar would be 'passing itself off' (in legal parlance) as their own.

To justify this, someone at Curtiss made a claim which the company must have regretted ever since. It was said that the bar had nothing to do with Babe Ruth and was in fact named after the young daughter of President Grover Cleveland, who was the darling of the White House back in the 1890s. It was said that Ruth Cleveland had visited the Curtiss factory in its early days, and that the bar was named in recognition of this (somewhat dated) association. If this was an off-the-cuff remark, or even a flippant lawyer's tactic, it backfired. Ruth Cleveland died of diphtheria in 1904 at the age of 12, more than a decade before the company was founded. She could not have visited the factory. The story sounded more like a sick joke than a charming anecdote, but for years the company stuck to this unlikely story – that the Baby Ruth bar was named after a long deceased president's daughter rather than a fashionable baseball player – presumably to avoid retrospective litigation. Only recently has the company coyly acknowledged its association with the history of baseball. Presumably the name is safe now.

The mildly subversive side of sweets can be seen in the enduring popularity of sweet pipes and tobacco made of liquorice, and of packets of sweet cigarettes. The latter even have their own historian, who maintains an extensive website on the many different sweet-cigarette brands, past and present, many of which aped real cigarette brands. Of course, sweet cigarettes are no longer allowed to be called 'cigarettes' – they have to be sold as 'candy sticks'. There was outrage in the United States in 2001 at the launch of a mint-flavoured cigar that contained real nicotine. Some sweets are plain nasty, like the Freak Sweets assortment of the 1920s, in which chocolate-covered onions, gherkins and cheese were included among the normal centres. Burning hot chewing gum and peppermints are still a jokeshop favourite. And in 2001 a Ukrainian company shocked the world with the launch of 'fat in chocolate' – pure pork fat encased in chocolate. This was really a self-referential joke about the national snack of salted pork fat, called *salo*, but an American news agency reported: 'A bar tasted [on] Tuesday was very sweet, while the fat filling retained some of its saltiness. The fat had the gooey texture of overcooked pasta.'

The misunderstanding of other countries' sweet tastes has formed the basis of a whole website – bad-candy.com – whose name I have borrowed as the title for this chapter. Bad Candy's writers produce extremely long and usually funny essays about the disgusting taste (to them) of sweets from around the world. On one level it smacks of cultural imperialism of a particularly unedifying nature, but the great redeeming feature of the site is its humour.

Rude sweets are another embarrassing confectionery side-line. German marzipan makers excel in crafting pigs and other animals engaged in sexual acts, and various firms make humorous items such as chocolate penises. Wilson's, an old Lake District Kendal mint cake company, has embarrassed itself in this way (and perhaps saved itself, in the process) by branching out into a spectacularly vulgar range that includes Chocolate Snotty Noses (with green fondant), Dinosaur Dollops, White Chocolate Maggots, Cowpats (fudge), Seagull Droppings, Rabbit Droppings, Donkey Droppings and something called Zoopoo. Wilson's is not alone: the venerable American company of Necco has launched Sour Stinky Feet (green) and Hot Stinky Feet (orange) with the tagline, 'toe-rific candy'. Snotshots are a successful line invented by a small Irish company, and I gazed with wonderment at a photograph, in a confectionery magazine, of the three jolly men who run the outfit and dreamt up this delight. What a strange business they are in.

But the doyen of rude sweets is Rolf D. Schwartz, a New

York-based confectioner who makes all kinds of sweets and cakes in 'erotic' or biologically explicit shapes. I arranged to view his book, *Backwerk der Lüste* (1984), or 'Bakery of Lust', in the British Library rare books department, where they made me sit at a special desk and gave me the book concealed in a large cardboard folder. Here is an exact transcript of the notes I made on that occasion.

> This is special material! Special desk. Feels terribly naughty.
> Author runs 'The Erotic Baker' in New York; 3 branches; 117 Christopher St, 001 212 989 8846. Cakes and sweets, carefully made e.g. willy emerges from banana. Horrible, vulgar. Lots of willies and breasts, sperm rendered with icing. Vaginas and pubic hair; vagina on a stick; a cake with seven erect willies pointing up from it inscribed 'Good luck Olga!' What's the story there?

The Marquis de Sade would perhaps have enjoyed Herr Schwartz's wares. The old voluptuary loved sweets all his life, especially chocolate, and when he was imprisoned in the Bastille he gave his wife precise instructions regarding his chocolate, marshmallow and candied fruits order from his favourite shop. According to one biographer, at his death De Sade owed more to the pâtissier-confiseur and the fruiterer than could be raised from the sale of all his books, clothes and furniture. It was sweets that got De Sade into the worst scrape of his career. This was a sorry episode in a backstreet room in Marseilles involving his manservant and some prostitutes, but it was elevated to the status of a high-society event in contemporary gossip:

> [De Sade] gave a ball to which he invited many people and for dessert gave them very pretty chocolate pastilles. They were mixed with powdered Spanish fly. Their action is well known. All who ate them were seized by shameless ardour and lust and started the wildest excesses of love. The festival became an ancient Roman orgy.

This is what De Sade would have wanted, no doubt, but it is not what actually happened. According to his biographer Francine du Plessix Gray, De Sade produced his gold-rimmed crystal candy box in the dingy hotel room and encouraged the prostitutes to eat pastilles of Spanish fly, or cantharides. These pastilles were coated with aniseed-flavoured sugar, which De Sade hoped would increase their flatulence and so enhance his coprophilic gratification. The prostitutes were respectable girls, and very shocked, but eventually did what they were told. The problem was, De Sade became somewhat overexcited and made them eat far too many of his pastilles (the maximum dose was two pastilles in twenty-four hours), and one of the prostitutes experienced agonising intestinal pains and vomiting. The orgy had gone badly wrong, De Sade was reported to the police for attempted murder by poisoning, and the trial remained a millstone round his neck for years. The moral of this story is clear: do not overdose your prostitutes with flatulence-inducing aphrodisiac sweets.

Accidental poisoning was a serious problem with sweets in the nineteenth century. The new market for a cheaper product led many confectioners to cut corners and incorporate alternative ingredients in place of more expensive substances. Colouring was the main area for such substitution, with mercury, arsenic and lead among the noxious substances employed. There was a case of arsenic poisoning through sweets in 1850, discovered after two girls fell ill having eaten sweets purchased in Petticoat Lane, London. Sand or even powdered glass was used to bulk up sugar supplies, and cocoa was commonly adulterated with brick dust. But that was not all: in 1851 the *Lancet* published its analysis of fifty commercial cocoa powders and found that 90 per cent of them contained fillers such as starch, animal fat, red and yellow ochres, red lead, vermilion, sulphate of lime and chalk. One of the best sources of information on this subject is Frederick Accum's *A Treatise on the Adulterations of Food* (1820), in which the author states:

In the preparation of sugar plums, comfits, and other kinds of confectionery, especially those sweetmeats of inferior quality frequently exposed to sale in the open streets, for the allurement of children, the grossest abuses are committed. The white comfits, called sugar pease, are chiefly composed of a mixture of sugar, starch, and Cornish clay (a species of very white pipeclay).

He goes on to allege that the colour green in sweets usually comes from copper, and red from red lead. (Accum also relates a story about a school in Richmond where poisonous custard was served. Cherry-laurel leaves had been used instead of almond essence, and a boy and a girl were rendered unconscious for ten hours. Such effects might sound mild to those familiar with school custard.) These scandals led to a gradual improvement in the quality of cheap confectionery in the latter half of the nineteenth century.

Even when high-quality ingredients are used, they can still be dangerous to factory workers exposed to large quantities of them over long periods. Skin diseases are most common – chocolate dermatitis, sugar dermatitis and grocer's itch. Then there is silicosis from inhaling sugar, as well as simple tooth decay from the factory atmosphere, citric acid burns for orange- and lemon-peelers, and vanillism, an allergic reaction to vanilla that makes one's eyebrows fall out. And that is before you get anywhere near all that flailing machinery. A sweets factory can still be a dangerous place, and even in 2002 a Pennsylvania worker drowned after falling into a chocolate vat.

Sweets can mask the flavours of poisons. William Maynard, the teetotal Methodist minister who invented wine gums, committed suicide with a cocktail of chemicals, plus peppermint. A sweetmaker to the last. One would have thought that the famous bitter-almond flavour of cyanide would have made marzipan or sugared almonds the perfect vehicle for it. But it seems no discerning murderer has taken advantage of this so far: arsenic has always been the favourite poison, anyway. This is what poisoned Mary Dunning and her family in Delaware in

1898. Mary – the daughter of a congressman – was sent a box of chocolate creams postmarked San Francisco, with an accompanying note that read only: 'Love to yourself and baby. Mrs C.' Mystified as to the donor, Mary – who was pregnant – nevertheless shared them that evening with her sister and her two children, as well as two lady callers. All of them were very ill overnight, and Mary and her sister died a few days later. It transpired that 'Mrs C' was 'Mrs Curtis', real name Cordelia Botkin – the lover of Mary's husband, who had just been jilted by him. She had bought the arsenic on the pretext of cleaning a hat, and simply painted the chocolates with it.

More innocently, sweets can mask the smell of cigarette smoke or alcohol: in the speakeasies of the Prohibition era in America, clove chewing gum was routinely handed out to customers as they left. And Henry Mayhew quotes one mid-nineteenth-century London sweetseller:

> I've known women, that seemed working men's or little shop-keeper's wives, buy of me and ask which of my stuffs took greatest hold of the breath. I always knew what they was up to. They'd been having a drop, and didn't want it to be detected. Why, it was only last Saturday week two niceish-looking and niceish-dressed women, come up to me, and one was going to buy peppermint-rock, and the other says to her: 'Don't, you fool, he'll only think you've been drinking gin-and-peppermint. Coffee takes it off best.' So I lost my customers.

Sweets and medicines can be easily confused, and it is the same with drugs – illegal drugs. The nicknames given to drugs often echo or even replicate the names of sweets, to emphasise their recreational and far-from-innocent nature, and this tendency is most marked in the case of Ecstasy. I first came across this in the early 1990s when I was offered something called a Rhubarb and Custard by a pale-faced urchin in a night-club. 'It will make you mental,' he said. And it did. Rhubarb and Custard became my favourite type of Ecstasy as well as my favourite sweet. The capsule versions were even colour-coded like the sweets: one half red, the other half yellow. I also tried Love Heart pills and Blackjack pills, and heard about versions called Lemon and Lime, and Parma Violets. Glucose is often used to adulterate illegal drugs, as is sugar, and this may be why amphetamine, or speed, often tastes slightly sweet. In fact this cheap, old-fashioned drug is generally dabbed with the fingers, just like sherbet powder. But no Ecstasy pill tastes like a sweet − it is bitter, rather than sugary. The names of sweets were used to market this drug because of their association with childhood innocence, which is the state to which people who take Ecstasy aspire.

This infantilist streak was extended into clothing and accessories for a brief period in the late 1990s with the 'candy ravers' of clubs with their penchant for inflatable or cuddly toys, fluorescent clothes, glitter make-up, light-up sticks and aerosol-squirt string. The 'candy' refers to Ecstasy. The movement has been further developed in the United States, where the candy ravers or candy kids scene is an Ecstasy-based subculture developed by young people in their teens and early twenties, most of them living in suburban areas. Candy kids dress in brightly coloured, outsize versions of children's clothes, adorned with acres of fake fur (sometimes homemade from deconstituted soft toys) and huge trousers. They carry backpacks full of toys and the kind of useful accessories children take to school − crayons, bottles of water and miniature fans (to prevent dehydration and overheating). Of course, they also carry Class A drugs. The sweet of choice is chewing gum, as it is for all Ecstasy users, because the drug induces muscle hyperactivity in the form of teeth grinding, which can cause ulcers and wear down the molars (so this 'candy' hurts the teeth, too). Popular candy-kid candies are childhood favourites like gummy bears, Sweet Tarts, Pez, Starburst and Twizzlers. Ecstasy pills with candy names include Skittles and Golden Ticket, but new ones are launched all the time. Probably the only alteration made to most 'new' Ecstasy tablets is the name, but candy-raver websites include reviews of new products. One such webpage is designed to look just like a child's pink fluorescent plastic notepad, which makes the enthusiastic references to pills containing pressed heroin all the stranger.

If the big shift in attitudes to sweets from the 1970s on was based on nutritional and personal-health revelations – or, what sweets are doing to us – the main development in recent years has been an awareness of political morality – or, what the sweets industry is doing to the world. The growing suspicion of the motives and methods of multinational corporations has been well documented elsewhere, and in the world of sweets, the most dramatic example of an apparent failure of corporate morality has been the Nestlé débâcle. This Swiss conglomerate is one of the biggest food companies in the world, with more than 450 factories, and it owns all kinds of brands: to take just one sector, both Perrier and San Pellegrino are Nestlé-owned. The company also makes millions from its sales of powdered baby milk, and it was its policy of promoting this product in Third World countries that first got it into trouble in the late 1970s. The problem is, powdered baby milk needs to be mixed with water and put in a bottle, and in places where the water supply is contaminated and sterilisation is impossible, there is a risk that babies might catch diarrhoea and other water-borne ailments. Diarrhoea is a tummy bug to the West, but it is a significant cause of infant death in the developing world. The World Health Organisation estimates that 1.5 million infants die each year because they are bottle- rather than breast-fed, and in January 1981 the WHO ratified its International Code of Marketing of Breastmilk Substitutes, which more than twenty countries have subsequently implemented and at least twenty more enforce to some degree. In an effort to encourage breast-feeding instead of bottle-feeding, this initiative instigated a ban on all advertising, marketing and promotion of powdered baby milk. Nestlé had been roundly criticised for the way it seemed to be trying to persuade mothers to use bottled milk through various 'health education' initiatives. A consumer boycott on Nestlé products organised by groups such as Baby Milk Action had helped focus attention on the issue, and in 2002 this was still in place – despite claims from Nestlé that such criticisms are 'years out of date'.

In Britain, it used to be quite easy for sweets lovers to boycott Nestlé products. There was the extremely nice Milky Bar, admittedly, but otherwise just things like the ultra-boring Crunch wafer bar. It is hardly in the spirit of a boycott, but now that Nestlé owns Rowntree it is much harder. Sweet lovers are faced with forgoing KitKat, Smarties, Aero, Lion Bar, Polo, Fruit Gums, Fruit Pastilles, After Eights and Quality Street. Even Perugina, makers of Baci, is owned by Nestlé. When I saw that Nestlé were marketing sweets under the Willy Wonka trademark, I was incensed that this great name had been appropriated for commercial exploitation. I thought about writing to Nestlé masquerading as Timothy Wonka, a bitter-lemon drinks manufacturer and estranged son of Willy, to demand they desist using the name. But some Wonka sweets are nice; I am particularly fond of Nerds, which are hard little pink and green granules, like strawberry and lime gravel.

I tried with the Nestlé boycott. God, I tried. But in my lust for sweets I kept forgetting about it at the moment of truth. And if you only remembered the boycott when you were halfway through a sweet, what were you supposed to do – throw it away? It was as if a cloud of unknowing enveloped my head whenever I approached a sweets stall; I became mesmerised and morally miniaturised. The turning point came one afternoon in the ticket hall of White City tube station in west London. I had just bought a Milky Bar and started eating it when I remembered the boycott – too late, as always. That was when I decided that it was pointless for me to continue try-ing with the boycott. It was just too hard. Anyway, it could be argued that it is a little out-of-date now – the direct action did its job twenty years ago, but today the powdered-milk com-panies know to tread warily and are constantly monitored by pressure groups, charities and government agencies. How can a boycott help the situation, except as revenge by obsessed activists against a target corporation? It could also be argued that if one decided not to eat products made by companies with blemishes on their records it would be very difficult to find anything to eat at all. (Except maybe Ben & Jerry's Ice Cream – they look like nice guys, and a diet of ice cream would not be so bad.) But those clever arguments were not the real reason for my stopping the boycott. The real reason was my own weakness.

An even bigger moral issue affecting the sweets industry today is chocolate and slavery. This came to a head in April 2001 with a news report about a 'slave ship', the *MV Etirino*, thought to be carrying up to 250 children to the West African country of Ivory Coast, where it was rumoured they were to be put to work on the cacao plantations. There have been many eye-witness accounts of child slavery and slave-dealing in the region, but this story hit the headlines because of the exciting chase-and-rescue element, as the ship was tracked across the ocean, and because of the involvement of children. As it turned out there were about forty children on board the ship, and there was no evidence that they were going to be sold into slavery. However, the story focused attention on the issue of slavery in West Africa, particularly in relation to the chocolate industry. Subsequent news coverage revealed to the world a well-established slave trade, in which children were sold to 'brokers' by poor families in – particularly – Benin, Burkina Faso, Cameroon, Ivory Coast, Gabon, Nigeria and Togo. These children are sometimes as young as five, although eight and upwards is usual.

The practice has semi-respectable roots, in that education has traditionally been organised through the extended family system, so families are used to entrusting children to others who might live some distance away. However, the practice has developed into a full-blown slave trade, with markets, dealers and buyers who are eager to purchase children, usually for domestic service in wealthier households, but also to work in shops and on market stalls, for purposes of sexual exploitation and for manual labour on cacao, coffee, rice and maize plantations. In 1996 one illegal market discovered in Lagos, Nigeria, was found to be full of malnourished children aged between seven and seventeen years old, and the Ivory Coast town of Abidjan has a famous child-slave market called the Marché du Plateau, where wealthy local women buy their 'helpers'.

The cacao plantations of Ivory Coast are thought to harbour up to 15,000 child slaves taken from neighbouring countries, mainly Mali. There was a tradition of immigrant labour on cacao plantations, in which workers stayed on farms during the harvesting season and returned home after they were paid. But it is thought that low cacao prices and deregulation of the market have made farmers unwilling or unable to pay their workforce, and some of them have resorted to coercing children into slavery. In April 2001 the BBC reporter Humphrey Hawksley filed a report from a town in Mali where children are regularly kidnapped and taken to the cacao plantations. The going rate is about $30 each. One escaped slave told him: 'I might have got out but there are thousands of children still over there. It's definitely slavery. The kids have to work so hard they get sick and some even die.' Other recorded testimony runs: 'After one year you don't get money. If you ask for your money, you don't get money and you are beaten.' There are also accounts of savage beatings of attempted runaways. The director of Mali's Save the Children Fund, a charity working to end these abuses, said: 'People who are drinking cocoa or coffee are drinking their blood. It is the blood of young children carrying six kilos of cacao sacks, so heavy that they have wounds all over their shoulders. It's really pitiful to see.'

The policy of the global chocolate industry has been to studiously ignore evidence such as this, presumably because if nothing is known about the subject, nothing has to be spent remedying it, and no sales would be lost through bad publicity. The official line has always been shock and outrage at the

discovery of slavery and abuses, quickly followed by protest-
ations of complete ignorance, assurances that their own supplies
are slave-free, and attempts to deflect focus away from chocolate by noting that coffee and maize plantations also use slaves.
At the most respectable end of the chocolate industry – among
those who sit on committees and organise conferences for the
trade associations – there has been a sense that slavery is not
really their problem, because no large, respectable chocolate
company would knowingly buy cacao from plantations using
slave labour. A company like Cadbury – which sources its cacao
from Ghana, where there is far less slavery than in Ivory Coast
– believes that its chocolate is slave-free. But just as the chocolate companies say that it is impossible, practically, to monitor
the million-plus small plantations which contribute to the
cacao yield (an obstacle which they believe effectively exoner-
ates them from responsibility), so it is impossible for them to
state categorically that every single cacao bean used for their
bars has been harvested by adult, free, fairly-paid workers. You
cannot profess ignorance and provide guarantees in the same
breath.

Slavery truly is the skeleton in the closet of the chocolate
industry. And it took the non-story of the Ivory Coast slave ship
to cause that skeleton to clatter out and onto the floor in
front of the world's chocolate eaters. I went for a high-level
meeting with John Newman, director of the Biscuit, Cake,
Chocolate and Confectionery Alliance (BCCCA) in London.
Mr Newman is a very nice man, if suspiciously thin and fit-
looking (does he never touch his own supply?), in a crisply
ironed short-sleeved shirt. There was a plate of chocolate
biscuits; I had three and Mr Newman had one. I asked about
the slavery issue, and Mr Newman explained how it was shocking and must be stopped, and how none of the BCCCA's
representatives, or its members' representatives, had ever seen
any evidence of slavery in West Africa. Then I asked Mr
Newman about the 1909 Cadbury libel case, which was all
about slavery in West Africa, when the chocolate industry

denied all knowledge of its existence. Cadbury won that case, and indeed, the Quaker management at that time may have been so out of touch that they genuinely knew nothing. But how can the industry expect to get away with the same excuse today? Mr Newman expressed mild surprise that I knew about the Cadbury case, and referred me to the new industry policy of setting up co-operatives in the plantation areas, so everything can be properly monitored. The rationale of the chocolate-company boardrooms might have been:

We cannot get away with ignoring this any longer. We are in the business of making money from chocolate bars, but consumers need to be reassured our product is slavery-free. Otherwise, we could be hit by a consumer boycott. Slavery in West Africa is not our problem to sort out. The best we can do is ensure transparency when it comes to our own business, and make sure our own supplies are from plantations that are demonstrably free of slavery and child labour. As for the situation in the rest of the region, outside our own monitored co-operatives – sorry, we may have helped create the plantation system through our actions over the past century and more, but we have never officially acknowledged slavery, child labour and other abuses, and it is not in our interests to start accepting any responsibility for it now.

Good old Quakers. It has taken almost a hundred years and a headline-winning news story about a possible slave ship to force the chocolate industry into something like meaningful action. But at least it has now acknowledged the slavery problem as its problem, to some degree. A coalition of European and American chocolate organisations, government agencies, consumer groups, anti-child labour and anti-slavery groups has been formed to combat slavery in the cacao plantations of West Africa. This at least does not look like it will be an industry whitewash. In an open letter on the subject, Larry Graham, president of the (US) Chocolate Manufacturers Association and

National Confectioners Association, outlines the plans for the Ivory Coast plantations:

> The pilot programs will focus on workplace conditions, trafficking and migration, social protection and education, strengthening community focused organisations (cooperatives), technology transfer, and trade and information systems to help farmers improve cocoa quality and yields, which in turn will lead to increased income from their cocoa trees.

Whatever they decide to do, I do hope the chocolate industry sorts this slavery problem out. I don't think I could cope with a chocolate boycott.

Lucky Dip

MY TOP TEN SWEETS

1. Rhubarb and Custards (Bond's). *Sublime balance of sour fruit and creamy custard.*

2. Mystery Violet Sweet. *I have not yet discovered a sweet that captures the fragrant beauty of violets, so it must live in the imagination for now. The closest thus far are the chocolate violet creams from Charbonnel et Walker of London.*

3. Barfi. *Rich, milky, multi-flavoured Indian sweet, like soft fudge but refreshing rather than cloying.*

4. Liquorice Allsorts (Bassett's). *Spectacularly beautiful.*

5. Fine chocolate by Bernachon of Lyon. *Complex flavour, not too bitter.*

6. Fry's Chocolate Cream. *A slight snap from the crystalline centre speaks volumes.*

7. Turkish Delight. *Rose flavour, preferably from the Egyptian Bazaar in Istanbul.*

8. Pine-nut caramels (El Caserio). *Wonderful texture and flavour in this old Spanish recipe.*

9. Creme Egg (Cadbury's). *Another design classic; enormously satisfying to devour.*

10. Vichy mints. *These chalky tablets are the ultimate refreshing sweets, made in the French town.*

Chapter 11

THE HIMALAYAN GOBSTOPPER

As I gazed at the bright blue Chinese pickled raspberry 'sweet', which I had just spat out in disgust and which was now gently bobbing in my lavatory in the Holiday Inn Chinatown in San Francisco, it occurred to me that babies are born without any teeth, let alone sweet ones: our preferences for particular types of sweets are learned rather than innate. Every nation has its own peculiar sweet tooth, and this is why sweets from a different part of the world can taste absolutely horrid, worthy of being spat out, even to someone who considers himself a gourmet of international confectionery. Individuals from the same taste culture have different physiological levels of personal liking for sweetness, but the range of sweet tastes which they are potentially able to enjoy is broadly the same, the result of a similar gastronomic upbringing. Thus, in some cultures, such as the Chinese, sweetness is sharpened with terrifying sourness; while in others, such as the Arabic, a piercing, uncompromised sweetness is enjoyed, leavened by the bitterness of coffee; and in still others, like the Indian, there is a unifying flavour tone – in that case, rich milk. So it can be that although foreign sweets can sometimes taste odd or unpleasant, a person who is unhappy about the sweets made at home, and even admits to a lack of a sweet tooth, can go to another part of the world and find a spiritual sweets homeland. This chapter is a rollercoaster ride through the sweets of the world, certainly not exhaustive, but intended to provide a revealing snapshot of the different sweet tastes of most regions.

Globalised sweets companies and a growing taste for Western-style sweets have not yet subsumed the traditional taste preferences of cultures – there is a clear distinction between traditional sweets and modern ones, but also new sweets have been developed that are fascinating hybrids between the old and new styles. Flavours sound similar but are not similar: American cherry is not like German cherry, and while the flavour of coconut is based on the desiccated version in Europe and the United States, this would be completely unpalatable in South-east Asia, where sweets based on the taste of fresh coconut milk are made. International chocolate-bar brands and versions of Western-style sweets are found everywhere, so to avoid repetition I will assume their presence is accepted and omit them. The aim here is to describe sweets that are in some way peculiar to a region, or sweets which are just peculiar.

THE ENGLISH-SPEAKING PEOPLES

The world's dominant sweets culture is that of the English-speaking peoples, in economic terms at least. By the 1840s in Britain, the price of sugar matched its status as an everyday commodity, and this, coupled with an increase in disposable income for a large swathe of the population, led to an increased demand for quality sweets. Until this point, there had been a clear distinction between high-class sweets, either imported or handmade by fancy old-fashioned confectioners, and the cheap articles concocted since the turn of the century by artisans with copper boiling pans in city basements or by working women at their stoves in country cottages. But a new type of sweet was emerging, made by a new type of confectioner, and the key was machinery. The invention of new gadgets, particularly in the powerhouse of mechanical innovation that was London, allowed mass production of good-quality, uniform, dependable and affordable sweets, packaged and branded with the name of the manufacturer rather than sold loose on the street or from the market barrow. Some of the old sweets could be made by the new machines, but there were many new product innovations during the mid to late nineteenth century.

Henry Weatherley, author of *A Treatise on the Art of Boiling Sugar* (1864), provides the most revealing insights into this period of transition. 'Bonapartes Ribs, Gibraltar Rock, Ellecampane, and many of the old sweets which were the favourites of a past generation have disappeared from the London shops,' he explains, 'and their place taken by various other goods of a much more difficult nature.' These sweets include 'the Loggets or Cushies of the eastern part of the kingdom; the Tom Trot or ButterScotch of the north; the Humbugs or Lollys of the south; the Suckers and Hardbake of the west', although he says that toffee and hardbake (a brittle toffee, often with nuts) are the most popular sweets everywhere. Lemon barley sugar, according to Weatherley, is 'one of the oldest sweets, this and acid drops were formerly the only boiled sweets that the old city houses made. Tringhams on Holborn Hill, now Moores, used to be a very great attraction thirty years ago, to see the barley sugar made in the shop.' Weatherley notes that on a visit to Paris in 1848, he was surprised to find only high-priced bonbons on sale in the shops, and just one itinerant boiled-sweetmaker in the streets (compared with several hundred in London). This is a revealing aside, because it illustrates the cultural difference that had already emerged between Britain – and by extension its former colonies – and continental Europe. The demand for sugar products was such in the English-speaking nations that an industry developed with an emphasis on mass-produced, cheap sweets, and novelty, entrepreneurial flair and fluidity in the market, whereas in Europe the old tradition of artisan-sweetmaking, using unchanging ancient recipes, prevailed.

So the British sugar confectionery industry flourished through the nineteenth century, and it was focused on the cities with refineries: London and the west coast ports such as Bristol, Glasgow and Liverpool. An Andean peasant can distinguish between 300 types of potato, and it came to pass that a British person with peasant tastes could distinguish between a similar number of different boiled sweets: pear drops, bonbons, sherbet lemons, bullseyes, humbugs, chocolate limes, West Indian limes, jazz balls, lemon crystals, cherry balls, fishes, Tom Thumb drops, jujubes, gumdrops, wine gums, pineapple chunks, cola cubes, cough candy, horehound tablets, aniseed twist, rhubarb and custard, sherbet pips, Everton mints, coltsfoot rock, paradise twist, black bullets, snowy rock, dolly mixture, rosy apples, clove balls, acid drops, barley sugar, army and navy, aniseed balls, Jap (coconut sweets), pineapple rock, mint imperials . . . the list goes on. Then there are all the variations on toffee, fudge (including operas, even nut operas), butterscotch, nut brittle, liquorice, gums, pastilles, rock, marshmallow, coconut ice and more, plus regional specialities like Kendal mint cake (crystalline), Pontefract cakes (liquorice) and Scottish tablet (hard, sugary fudge). Even today there are strong regional preferences in Britain, and a Midlands boiled-sweetmaker told me at the Cologne sweets fair that people from neighbouring counties have completely different likes and dislikes. Chocolate, meanwhile, developed along singular lines everywhere, as we have seen; if Britain can be said to excel in any one area of chocolate it has to be bittermints, particularly the high-class after-dinner creams and thins produced by the likes of Bendick's of Mayfair and made affordable in the inimitably packaged After Eights. These chocolate mints are a delightful curiosity in other countries, and are the only chocolate that the Swiss *chocolatiers* seem to envy.

Sherbet is a strange phenomenon, one of the most nutritionally unjustifiable and gastronomically obscure foodstuffs available to man (or child). Named after the Middle Eastern drink, which does taste ever so slightly fizzy in its zesty sweetness, sherbet is made from sugar, flavouring (usually lemon), colouring, bicarbonate of soda and either malic or tartaric acid, which is what makes sherbet fizz when moistened. The first recipes for fizzy sherbet powder appear in the mid nineteenth century (1864 is the earliest reference I have seen), and it would appear it was conceived as a cheap version, or an exotic echo, of the real sherbet fruit cordials (again, mainly lemon) that had been shipped to Europe from Turkey and the Middle East since early medieval times. Sherbet was a cheap, locally made version of these expensive imported fruit cordials, preserves and conserves, just as Victorian boiled sweets were. Persia has been the source of so many culinary ideas that it is perhaps worth mentioning the slim possibility that this English sherbet was inspired by a delicacy called *ghahut*, a kind of dusty nut sherbet made of roasted chick pea powder and sugar. In her brilliant book about Persian cuisine, *New Food of Life* (1992), Najmieh Batmanglij recalls: 'As children we loved ghahut. The best way to eat this snack is to take a handful, tilt your head back, and then pour it into your mouth.'

Which is exactly how brave children eat fizzy sherbet, of course, although the sherbet dip (using a lollipop) or sherbet fountain (a liquorice stick) are equally efficacious and preferred by daintier children, such as myself. It is also possible that this type of powdered sherbet was originally intended as a base for a mock version of the drink – just add water. Children have always made drinks from their 'kali', as it was often called, and there is an admittedly obscure precedent in *Classic Russian Cooking* (1861) by Elena Molokhovets, the Mrs Beeton of Russia, in which a recipe for 'sherbet' consists of a pound of sugar and the zest of five lemons, either boiled with water and made into a hardened syrup, or else amalgamated into a sherbet-like paste, and taken with tea. But enough of possible sherbets. Real sherbet is widely used in modern confectionery, and forms the basis for all sorts of famous fizzy sweets, such as flying saucers, Sweet Tarts and Refreshers. It is indeed the fizz that makes them whizz.

The masters (mistresses, really) of sweetmaking in the British Isles are the Scots. It is far from clear why Glasgow, Edinburgh and the Scottish Borders should have seen an explosion in sweet creativity in the late eighteenth and nineteenth centuries, but that is what happened. The Scots had for centuries been assiduously cultivating their famous sweet tooth, first by the old tradition of taking the bees to the heather on the moors in summer, to improve the flavour of the honey, then with the Scottish embrace of sugar in the sixteenth century. Edinburgh's first confectioners, termed 'sukkermen', are mentioned in the city records for 1503, and in 1587 the provost and bailies of the city set up a table in the High Street to give out bread, wine and sweets to celebrate the accession of James VI. Two years later, to celebrate the king's marriage, the authorities bought twelve boxes of sweets to scatter among the people. There appears to have been a street confectionery scene in Glasgow and Edinburgh from some time in the late eighteenth century, when tablet, toffee and what the Scots call hard boilings were sold by the so-called 'sweetie wives', who went by names like Candy Kate, Sweetie Annie, or Taffie Knott – although there were sweetie husbands, too: an itinerant candyman named Coltart made a famous aniseed sweet (possibly related to the Scarborough rock firm of Coulthart?), and Greenock, formerly Port Glasgow, boasted a celebrated male sweetmaker by the name of Ball Allan, inventor of cheugh jeans, a chewy toffee with cloves, cinnamon, pepper and ginger.

The port of Greenock was known as 'sugaropolis' because from the 1760s it was the destination for thousands of tons of West Indian sugar, and in its heyday in the late nineteenth century several dozen refineries lined its busy streets. They filtered their sugar with bullocks' blood and were exceptionally prone to burning down. Tate & Lyle closed the last Greenock refinery in 1995, and when I visited the town one rainy October day it was depressing: the lowering skies and evident poverty among magisterial civic buildings and windowless warehouses, in a place that had once been rich but has now shrunk economically, too small for its grandiose architectural clothes. Some of the larger edifices were actually boarded up, and all around were reminders of its past, including a fine museum which displays proud reminders of the port's sugary prosperity, as well as curiosities such as a great winged insect found inside a bag of sugar in 1882, its body the size of a chipolata. Several of the grandest Georgian residences near the museum are now dental surgeries, and chandeliers can be spied inside, brightly twinkling in pain-filled waiting rooms, once pleasure-filled drawing rooms where silver salvers glittered with sugar-frosted fruits.

In the Scottish Lowlands, the sweetie wives, some of whom opened shops, and the itinerant 'candymen', who sold sweets from barrows or trays hung round their necks at fairs, developed a range of wonderfully named sweets that are peculiarly Scottish: curly andra was an old-style coriander comfit (curryander becomes curly andra), and its offspring curly murlies or curly doddies were mixed comfits with an aniseed savour, a speciality of Dundee. Claggum or clack are sticks of treacle rock (also known as teasing candy); oddfellows, soft lozenges made in Wishaw, come in delicate colours flavoured with cinnamon, clove and rose geranium; mealie candy contained warming oatmeal and ginger – the porridge of sweets; gundy is hard toffee flavoured with aniseed or cinnamon; and starrie rock, made in Kirriemuir of golden syrup, was supposedly invented in 1833 by a blinded stonemason. Scottish tablet, rich and crunchy, a crystalline fudge, is a very old sweet, and orange, rose, cinnamon and ginger versions are included in the first Scottish cookbook (1736); it is mentioned even earlier as 'taiblet for bairns [children]'.

Edinburgh rock, the most celebrated sweet of the capital, was accidentally invented by Alexander Ferguson, universally known as 'Sweetie Sandy'. He was born in Doune, Perthshire, in 1798, and took to sweetmaking early, as F. Marian McNeill relates in *The Scots Kitchen* (1929):

> As a boy, Sandy used to concoct sweet-smelling, bubbling liquids in old tins and disused pans in the parental outhouses. So singular a hobby aroused the wrath and scorn of his father, a joiner and skeely craftsman; but Sandy refused to desist, and eventually left home to learn the business side of his chosen

craft with a confectioner in Glasgow. Thence he removed to Edinburgh.

Once in the capital, Ferguson set up a successful confectionery business, but he hit upon his master recipe only when he allowed some of his rock to go soft in the warmth of the factory. He ended up with the chalky, delicately flavoured, pastel-coloured delicacy still made by Ross of Edinburgh today (Ferguson's closed in 1985). In *Traditional Foods of Britain* (1999), Laura Mason suggests that Ferguson may have been dissembling about the accidental nature of his invention, instead building on an old sweetmaker's practice of deliberately allowing rock candy or penides to 'grain' and go soft. Stories of accidental invention are good marketing tools for confectioners, which is probably why they abound. Whatever its provenance, Edinburgh rock was internationally fêted, and it is indeed a unique experience: a smart, plain little stick with a chalky appearance and texture, which goes pasty in the mouth. It comes in delicate fruit flavours – and also a somewhat shocking ginger – that pleasingly linger about the eater. Apparently even the mere aroma of Ferguson's factory, in Melbourne Place, could arouse raptures among fans of Edinburgh Rock. Witness John W. Oliver's poetic paean:

> Quelle est cette odeur agréable
> That's wafted on the air?
> The perfume of Arabia
> Cannot with it compare.
> What makes the crowds to Melbourne Place
> With wide-stretched nostrils flock?
> It's Ferguson who's boiling up
> His Edinburgh rock.

For those of us who adore them, the mecca for boiled sweets is the Scottish Lowlands. My favourite sweetshop, Casey's of Edinburgh, where I get to go just once a year, and which does not entertain ideas of mail order, has a wide range of these hard and flavoursome, brightly coloured boilings, which are all made on the premises. Casey's sherbet lemons are the tartest and fizziest available (which is a compliment), but they are not particularly Scottish. No, the real Scottish sweets are articles like soor plooms ('sour plums'), bright green balls, originally from Peebles and Galashiels, that are indeed delightfully sour, from the amount of tartaric acid in them. They were supposedly invented to celebrate a 1377 skirmish, when Scots lads surprised an English raiding party feasting on – guess what? – sour plums. That story is ridiculous, even in the annals of sweets-invention stories, but soor plooms happen to chime with the international craze for sour sweets, and if well marketed surely they could take on the world.

The sweetie wives of many Borders towns created their own speciality, and some of them are still on sale today. Berwick, the ultimate Border town, historically half English, half Scottish, has the beautiful Berwick cockles, chalky mint sweets with delicate pink striations. Jeddart snails are made of dark brown toffee, with a peppermint taste; they were supposedly invented by a French prisoner-of-war during the Napoleonic period, and that could explain the snail shape, which was popular in eighteenth-century French confectionery. Hawick balls, once known as taffy rock bools, are minty, cinnamony humbugs associated with rugby, while Moffat Toffee, hard and dark with golden stripes, has a taste all its own. Needless to say, the recipes for all these sweets are deadly secret. In Scotland, hard boilings are particularly associated with church (or kirk, correctly), since they help one to focus one's absolute and undivided attention on the minister's sermon.

Sweetmaking was not just left to the professionals. F. Marian McNeill quotes from what she describes as 'an old booklet on cottage cookery':

In rural districts in Scotland candy-making is a regular adjunct to courting. It draws together all the lads and lasses round for miles, and the fun and the daffing that go on during the boiling, pulling, clipping, cooling, are, both lads and lasses declare, worth the money [. . .] A few of the lasses club their sixpences together, a night is set, a house is named, and, of course, the young men who are socially wanted are invited to lend a hand and a foot, too, for dancing is not an uncommon adjunct to such gatherings.

You wonder how many sweeties actually got made on these occasions. Such parties are reminiscent of the taffy-pulling gatherings traditional in Wales (where it was called taffi, which perhaps led to the Welsh nickname 'Taffs'), England and also the United States. But perhaps America's sweets tradition is descended more directly from the Scottish rather than the English or any other model. Terms such as candy, as opposed to 'sweets', taffy rather than toffee, and the figure of the candyman are all most likely of Scottish derivation. Of course, American candy has since been influenced by scores of immigrant cultures, but in the early days, American candy books, recipes and products have a certain Scottish flavour.

The influences at work on the early cuisines of America, Australia, Canada and New Zealand were many and various, but since most of the first settlers were British, the core food culture was that of Britain, with French recipes reserved for the fanciest occasions in the wealthier households. As Waverley Root declares of these countries, during a discussion of ice cream consumption in his definitive *Eating in America* (1976): 'All of them, it is pertinent to point out, [are] joint heirs with ourselves of the dubious eating habits of the British Isles.' A major part of that dubious inheritance is a sweet tooth. In America in the eighteenth and early nineteenth centuries, sweets and confections were similar to some of those being made across the Atlantic in Britain, mainly fruit conserves and preserves, and especially candied chips made of fruit pulps. The enterprising settlers made use of the indigenous fruit and berries, and especially the nuts, in their candies, but on the evidence of early recipe books and household manuals, cooks concentrated on puddings – mainly fritters, creams and fruit tarts – rather than fiddly sweets.

Comfits and other technically demanding specialities do not appear to have survived the journey from Europe, and re-emerged only in the late nineteenth century. Sweets are not mentioned at all in the dessert section of Susannah Carter's *The Frugal Housewife* (1772), and Richard Briggs's *New Art of Cookery* (1792), a popular compendium, concentrates on drying and candying fruits almost exclusively, although the instructions he does give – precisely how to cut fruit aslant to make orange and apricot candies, for example – indicate that he was writing from first-hand experience and not merely lifting recipes from earlier sources. Briggs also includes a recipe for ginger tablet, to be displayed in a single piece on a china dish, which is more evidence of the Scottish inheritance of American confectionery.

By the mid eighteenth century, sugar consumption in the United States was high, perhaps even comparable to that of Britain (available figures are inconclusive), but it was mainly employed to sweeten drinks, to make rum and in cooking, for pickles and sauces. Molasses was an important part of the diet, both for the white settlers who could not afford sugar all the time, and for the black slaves, for whom it was one of the 'three Ms' of the diet: meat, meal and molasses. By about 1800 there was an amateur and cottage-industry confectionery culture, as there was in Britain, and molasses figures in it. In her no-nonsense *75 Recipts*, dated 1837, Miss Eliza Leslie of Philadelphia includes a recipe for molasses candy, with brown sugar, lemon and optional peanuts or almonds, twisted into sticks. Yellowjack was a pulled molasses candy from New Orleans. Molasses is still used as a base for candies in the United States, and not just in nostalgic hangovers such as the Mary Jane chew, from Massachusetts. This last also contains peanut butter. Peanuts were to become the favourite candy ingredient in America – besides their deliciousness and interesting texture, they were cheap, locally grown and plentiful.

Americans invented many other candies. In the South, there was divinity (similar to nougat, with nuts and glacé cherries); nut brittles; the pecan pralines of New Orleans and Louisiana, made and sold by Creole women called pralinières; Texas pralines; the walnut confections of West Virginia; and the bourbon balls of Kentucky: chocolate, crushed vanilla wafers, pecans, corn syrup and bourbon. The African-American slaves made their own candies of crushed sesame seeds and molasses (possibly a throwback to the popularity of sesame in Africa). In the far north, Vermont maple syrup was the basis for rich candies that seem to burn hotly with sweet flavour. Sugar-on-snow may not be a sweet exactly, but it sounds good in Helen and Scott Nearing's description in *The Maple Sugar Book* (1970): 'The thick syrup, when poured out in trailing spoonfuls, is a delicious concoction, fragrant and flavoursome, chewy and ice cold. There is nothing quite like it in the way of sweets.' It was developed through the practice of using snow to ascertain the temperature of the maple syrup, which is traditionally boiled up at the end of winter. Pulled candy, or taffy, became something of a national pastime in America, repeatedly draped over a hook in the kitchen and left to stretch, and by the mid nineteenth century caramels – the softer, creamier version of toffee – had become established as a national sweet, and there were scores of variations. Later, well-loved commercial caramel brands were launched like Slo Pokes, Cow Tales, Sugar Babies and Sugar Daddies, and caramel is still an American favourite. Saltwater taffy is perhaps the most evocative old American candy, and was actually made with sea water, for the tang, in its original incarnation, although table salt is used in later recipes.

By mid-century, there was plenty of room for pretension on the tables of well-to-do New Englanders, and *The Cook's Own Book* (1864), by 'a Boston housekeeper', includes fancy French desserts, compotes, cardamom and caraway comfits and – most revealingly – no fewer than eleven recipes for cinnamon sweets, including dragées and 'pastils'. Cinnamon is a peculiarly popular candy flavour in the United States, and its spicy hot savour makes something like the cinnamon Tic-Tac (which was released to general bemusement in Britain in the 1980s) perhaps the closest modern equivalent to the medieval comfit. Certainly the unique popularity of cinnamon in America, together with other spicy flavours, can be traced back to medieval Europe via the Scots liking for strong flavours in sweets. This is one area of European culture that Americans can claim to have safeguarded, while Europeans let it go.

The modern sweets industry began in America in 1847, when Oliver R. Chase, a Boston confectioner, patented the first American candy machine, a lozenge cutter. There were perhaps forty mid-sized candy firms in the country at this time, most of them based in New York, Philadelphia, Boston and Pennsylvania. Young & Smylie, for example, later incorporated as Y&S, famous for its Twizzlers liquorice products, was founded in 1845. Mechanisation gradually revolutionised the scene: Oliver Chase and his brother Edwin founded Chase and Company the same year as their invention, and three years later they devised a machine for pulverising sugar. By 1866 they had developed their patented Lozenge Printing Machine, for making the romantic conversation candies which had been such a hit in Europe, and then they invested in new steam-driven machines, which decisively accelerated production. By the time of the Centennial Exposition in Philadelphia of 1876, twenty candy firms were able to exhibit their wares made with specialised high-tech machinery. Chase and Company later formed the core of the New England Confectionery Company, or NECCO (famous for their deceptively brightly coloured menthol wafers (1901), an acquired taste), which is still going strong in Boston and can therefore claim to be the nation's oldest candy company.

As the industry grew, more candy outfits were established further west, in Pennsylvania, the Midwest and particularly in Chicago, which was ideally placed as a hub for the import of a wide range of candy ingredients, and of course for export opportunities. By the middle of the century, Chicago had a thriving sugar-confectionery scene; the Goelitz candy dynasty, which later reinvented itself as Jelly Belly (1976) with the pragmatism of the successful sweetsmaker, emigrated from Germany and started in Chicago in 1869. William Luden, later known for his cough drops and Fifth Avenue Bar (1936), began boiling up sugar in his mother's kitchen in Reading, Pennsylvania, in 1879, and in 1886 David Clark began making candy in two backrooms in Pittsburgh. As we have seen, the Clark Bar (1917), a chocolate-coated peanut butter crunch, was the world's first really successful 'combination' chocolate bar, made in a special small size for American troops in the First World War, but a hit when it went on sale to the public at five cents. (So the Clark Bar was a hit because it was small; the Mars Bar was a hit because it was big. Who can tell when it comes to candy?) August Goetze, who later created Caramel Creams, started up in Baltimore in 1895, and Leo Hirshfield produced America's first wrapped penny chew, the chocolate-flavoured Tootsie Roll, in New York in 1896, three years after the launch of liquorice Good & Plenty by the Quaker City Confectionery Company of Philadelphia (which is therefore the oldest branded candy still on sale in the United States). By the turn of the century, machines that could individually wrap candies were available – an early model was named the Oliver Twister – and this led to a surge in the production of such cheap sweets for children. It was discovered early on that brightly coloured wrappers helped sell them.

The candy makers multiplied to satisfy America's apparently insatiable sweet tooth, and the 1920s and 1930s were a particularly productive period. Butternut (1916) and Cherry Mash (1918) had been early candy-bar successes, but it was the Clark Bar that broke the mould by introducing sweets to the troops: suddenly it was acceptable for grown men to eat candy bars. Then Mars launched a series of classics, including Milky Way (1923) and the Three Musketeers Bar (1932). Snickers (1930), named after a favourite horse in the Mars stables, built upon the success of early peanut products such as Goo Goo Clusters (1913), Goldenberg's Peanut Chews (1922) and Reese's Peanut Butter Cups (1928) to become America's number-one candy bar, then as always. Distinguished entrants in the world of boiled and panned (hard) sweets include Life Savers (1912); Boston Baked Beans (1930s), sugar-coated peanuts; Tootsie Pops (1931), the lollipop Kojak favoured; cinnamon Red Hots (1932), Starburst Chews (1960) and Lemonheads (1962). Candy canes, particularly the Cris Cringle brand introduced in the 1950s, have remained popular in the United States, when they faded from view in Britain. These are associated with Christmas, of course, while traditional Easter candy in America is the chocolate Easter bunny (rather than the Easter egg). A specialist seasonal candy company like Palmer of Pennsylvania will manufacture a bewildering variety of chocolate bunnies: big ears bunnies, professor bunnies, biking bunnies, magic bunnies, builder bunnies, and even Tropical Fruit 'n' Chewy Bunnyettes. This company has also started producing a chocolate crucifix for Easter, which might prove useful in warding off the spectral host of candy witches, vampires, pumpkins and Frankensteins illustrated in its own catalogue for America's trick or treat Hallowe'en ritual.

The sweets industry has detected that seasonal associations and invented traditions can be extremely profitable. The more romantic occasions of Valentine's Day and Mother's Day can be marked with a bunch of red lollipop roses, and for Thanksgiving a brightly wrapped chocolate turkey might seem more appropriate. I really like the look of these turkeys. Today, M&M Mars and Hershey control 70 per cent of the candy-bar market in the United States, with Snickers, peanut M&Ms, Reese's Peanut Butter Cups, KitKat, the Hershey Bar, Milky Way and Twix leading the way. The top three brands all contain peanuts.

Coconut is a flavour of choice in Australia, and this is clearly linked with the hairy nut's superabundance in South-east Asia and Australasia. Mint is also popular, a taste imported from

Britain along with the sweet tooth, which has been undiluted by the hot weather (contrary to scientific expectation). In the early days of colonial Australia, the food element of an itinerant worker's swag was called a sugar bag, which reflected the importance of the commodity. Australia had its own 'sugaropolis', Mackay on the Queensland coast, succinctly described by one 1879 arrival: 'The wharves were stacked with sugar, the sheds full of sugar, the wagons on the road over-flowing with sugar and wherever you looked sugar cane fields.' The most famous old Australian candy company was Mac Robertson, established in Fitzroy, Victoria, in 1880 by a 19-year-old Scot called Macpherson Robertson. He began making sugar candy in the bathroom of the family house, which remained the core of the factory even as it expanded, eventually employing 2,000 staff and making seventy lines of confectionery and chocolate. The habitually white-suited Robertson placed a 123-foot-long neon sign on the factory roof, and boasted of the way 'purified cold air is brought to play on every chocolate' to prevent them melting. Mac Robertson was bought by Cadbury in 1967, but not before it had launched Australian favourites such as Violet Crumble (chocolate-covered honeycomb) and Minties. Other classic Australian sweets include White Knights (chocolate-coated mint toffee) from Nestlé, Jaffas (little chocolate oranges) from Cadbury, Menz Crown Mints, Castlemaine Rock, Fizzoes, Pollywaffles (a chocolate-coated, marshmallow-filled wafer bar), Freddo Frog chocolate bars, Cherry Ripe cherry-and-coconut chocolate bars and Caramello Bears. Australia is also unique in its enthusiasm for musk-flavoured sweets, notably musk Lifesavers and musk sticks.

The first white settlers in New Zealand had at least one thing in common with the Maori peoples – a sweet tooth – and the explorer Thomas Brunner, who lived with the Maoris in the 1840s, reported his delight at being given fern root moistened with treacly brown sugar crystals from the pith of the cordyline, or cabbage palm, 'a similar relish to gingerbread'.

The Maoris also made chewing gum from the puha stalk, flavoured with resin from the lemonwood tree. The sweet flesh of the wood-boring huhu grub is still eaten by the adventurous, including one Barry Crump, according to David Burton in *200 Years of New Zealand Cookery* (1982): 'Barry Crump recommends that they be roasted on a shovel placed over hot embers, then bitten off below the head. They taste similar to peanut butter.' I must invite this Barry Crump over. New Zealand shared with Australia an obsession with baking, plus a passion for pavlova, and their 'gems' were little pastries made in special 'gem irons'. But there were also sweets, such as hokey pokey (golden syrup toffees) and slugs, a West Coast speciality: vanilla and sugar sweets rolled in coconut, with a date in the middle. Today, Cadbury, which has long had a presence in New Zealand, looms large in the confectionery scene.

A sweet-eating history of the English-speaking peoples would be incomplete without reference to Canada and South Africa. Canada boasts an impressive array of maple-syrup candies, and also homegrown brands such as Neilson Jersey Milk chocolate. But the big European companies control the market, albeit with some brands unique to Canada, such as Caramilk from Cadbury and Nestlé's Coffee Crisp. Among white South Africans, the British inheritance is reflected in the popularity of Cadbury and Nestlé products, while the Afrikaans sweet tooth is mainly indulged in baked goods, such as the light biscuits called *banket* and *koeksusters*. The homegrown Beacon chocolate-bar company makes popular brands such as New Look (nougat, caramel, nuts), T.V. (coconut and puffed rice) and Swing (peanuts and caramel), but recently the domestic industry has been threatened by European imports.

INDIA

The biggest revelation during the writing of this book has been my discovery of the milk sweets of India. This has turned into a full-blown love affair: I have developed an occasional craving for Indian sweets that is stronger than for any other type of confectionery, which – in case this needs clarifying – I consider a great enhancement to my quality of life. As we have seen, India was the home of the first great sweets culture, and these products remain utterly unique in the pantheon of world confectionery. My familiarity with Indian sweets is based solely on items such as *barfi*, perishable chunks of soft, fudge-like material made by continual stirring and reduction of milk kept at just below boiling point, subtly flavoured with cardamom and other spices, and textured with rice, grain or pulse flours. The rich, cool, moist texture of *barfi* – the word descends from *barf*, meaning snow – makes it irresistibly refreshing and satisfying, although it seems to hurt my teeth in a way other sweets do not.

Besides *barfi*, the best-known Indian sweets (or halwa) are *sandesh*, a Bengali sweet made of *chhana* (curdled milk) and sugar rather than syrup; *rasogolla*, a syrupy sponge; *jalebi*, spirals of crisp, delicate batter which release rosewater when bitten; *gulab jamun*, solid balls of *chhana* in rosewater, in which the outside stays firm but rosewater seeps inside; *laddu*, a range of spherical sweets made with cereal or pulse flour and sometimes milk; and halwa itself, which is basically semolina and ghee, flavoured with nuts and spices (although there are also Indian halwas which use fruit, vegetables or flour as their base, and flavours stretch to carrot, beetroot, pumpkin, marrow, banana, egg, almonds, walnuts, pistachio, cashew, raisins and cardamom). Simple jaggery or gur – unrefined cane sugar – is a popular sweet in itself, aromatic, brown, chunky and variously textured. But every region of India has its own specialities and flavour predilections: chewy halwas, crisp nut brittles, syrupy pastries and creamy milk sweets decorated with gold and silver leaf.

There are hundreds and hundreds of Indian sweets, and while many of them are associated with specific events, such as marriages, Diwali and other Hindu festivals, they are also used simply as gestures of good hospitality. Indian sweets are eaten at any time: they are as suitable as an official pudding as they are an unofficial snack. They are in a confectionery universe of their own, every one a variation on a variation, which makes for an almost impenetrable taxonomy. The Western international confectionery historian feels like a satellite cut adrift amid the twinkling delights of the Indian sweets universe, confused but happy. In Kerala in the south, for example, the Christians use rice, jaggery and coconut to make sweets like *unda* (coconut balls), and in Hyderabad the speciality is *badam-ki-jali*, latticed sweets of ground almonds. In some areas, cereal crops are the basis for sweets – the revered and strangely crumbly *Mysore pak*, for example, of sugar, chickpea flour and cardamom. In the north, the sweets of Bihar, called *mithai*, tend to be dry, whereas the *mishti doi* of Bengal are usually deep-fried, syrupy pastries. But there are exceptions to exceptions to exceptions.

The last reliable staging point in the history of Indian confectionery is the Mogul Empire of 1526 to 1707 (the first Muslim sultans are recorded at Delhi in about 1206). The *jalebi*, a descendant of the Arab *zalabiya*, is first mentioned in a Jain work of 1450, and in *Indian Food: A Historical Companion* (1994), K.T. Achaya quotes the poet Annaji's description of about 1600 of a sweetmeat shop in Kannada:

> For those who cannot command these delicacies at home the sweetmeat shop offers a variety of delights. There is karajjige, a sweet made from maida flour; athirisa fried in ghee; urad-based vadai; idlis as fair as the moon; sweet sesame balls; obattu garige, round as the earth, made of wheat or rice flour and jaggery, flavoured with lemon and fried in ghee; chakli; delicious strands of pheni; jilabiya, looking like plant stems, or rods of nectar; manoharada, fried globes held together with jaggery; and halundige, cakes of fine rice powder with milk and sugar.

Perhaps more decipherable for the Western reader are the experiences of Sir Thomas Roe, ambassador to India from 1615 to 1619. On his travels one prince gave him a gift of 'five cases of sugar candy dressed with muscke' and a big loaf of sugar, and he relates how when he fell ill the king, Jahangir, sent him 'a fat hogge, the fattest I ever saw' from Goa, which arrived at his lodgings at midnight with a message that 'since it came to the king it had eaten nothing but sugar and butter [ghee]. I took this as a sign of favour, and I am sure in that court it is a great one.' It takes a true diplomat to respond with good grace when a great fat pig comes knocking at the door at midnight when one is on one's deathbed. (I am not suggesting that this pig itself should be considered some kind of living, meaty sweet, merely using the story to illustrate the esteem with which sweetness is held in the Indian tradition.)

The British were less genteel 250 years later, at the height of the Raj, when they studiously ignored much local cuisine, including the sweets, and endeavoured (and generally failed) to teach their cooks how to make plum duff and other stalwart British steamed puddings. The leading cookery writer of imperial India, 'Wyvern' of the *Madras Mail* (Colonel Kenney-Herbert), produced a book called *Sweet Dishes* (1881) which consisted of Puddings Class I, Puddings Class II and Puddings Class III, all of which were British or European. That stiff upper lip was obviously petrified with sugar. This book, or the Madras Club, was the place to turn when cravings for Genoese *tambale* became too much in the tropic heat. The only pudding the Indian cooks mastered was a type of crème caramel, which became such a fixture on the menu that the British nicknamed it '365'. There is one surviving sweet that celebrates Anglo-Indian harmony during the Raj period: *ledikeni*, a species of *gulab jamun* that was originally named after Lady Canning, wife of the viceroy, who happened to be extremely popular – Lord Canning had suppressed a police mutiny – when a famous sweetmaker called Bhim Chandra Nag hit upon a new recipe. It is not recorded whether Lady Canning ever ate a Lady Canning. Probably not.

The only serious attempt at codifying Indian sweets in their infinite variety has been made by Anil Kishore Sinha, an Indian academic and author of *Anthropology of Sweetmeats* (2000), published in New Delhi. Dr Sinha says that most famous Indian sweets were invented in the late nineteenth century by professional sweetmakers; for example *rasogolla*, a type of sponge sweet in syrup, was created in 1868 by an employee of Nobin Chandra Das of Sitabuti, and fifty years later his son Krishna Chandra Das invented *rasamalai*, flat *chhana* (curdled milk) patties in milk, which are sold tinned under the famous KC Das label. Dr Sinha gets under the skin of the sweets from his native Bihar, noting how the sweetmakers stress the importance of the mineral content (particularly sulphur) of the local water (something which Wilson Deyermond at Penguin Confectionery in Carlisle also mentioned) and the way sweets can be localised for all sorts of reasons: in a village called Maner, for example, the *laddu* recipe – at least a hundred years old – depends on a special large and heavy sieve with very fine holes called a *chanauta*, an implement unique to the village and made only by two local blacksmiths. Dr Sinha has researched far and wide: 'In Gohanna, in Sonepat district [in Kashmir], it was found by the author and his friends while conducting fieldwork in October 1999 that very large jilebis were sold as a very popular item at one shop. These jilebis were about 1.1in in diameter and weighed from 250–400gms.' Dr Sinha's *jilebi*-measuring fieldtrips sound like fun.

West Bengal and Bangladesh (East Bengal) are the hotbeds of Indian sweetmaking, as Aroona Reejhsinghani points out in *Indian Sweets and Desserts* (1979):

> The Indians have an unparalleled sweet tooth which, in some parts of India, especially in Gujurat and Maharashtra, is evidenced by the custom of beginning a meal with a sweet. But it is the Bengalis amongst all the communities who beat everybody in consuming sweets. They sometimes take only sweets for a meal. They serve sweets for all important festivals and ceremonies, at which sweets are eaten in massive quantities.

This Bengali habit of eating only sweets for a meal is a first in world cuisine. I once had a sit-down three-course ice-cream banquet in the Häagen Dazs restaurant in Leicester Square, but never an all-sweets banquet. Bengal's milk sweets probably developed from the common practice of thickening and condensing milk, to produce what is called *kheer*, as a way of preserving it. But curdling milk for sweets is peculiar to Bengal, as Dr Sinha points out:

> These chhana sweets are Bengal's contribution to the Indian universe of sweets. In other parts of India, sweets are either of the halva category or based on kheer thick enough to be solidified. This is probably because for a long time people believed that 'cutting' the milk with acid to make chhana is a sin. Krishna, whose idyllic pastoral childhood among the cowherds of Brindaban has been the subject of a large body of poetry in central and northern India, is depicted as a mischievous boy stealing butter and cream, but never chhana.

K.T. Achaya believes that the religious justification for these Bengali curdled milk sweets, based on the *sandesh*, is that the sweetmaker does not allow the milk to stand and curdle naturally by itself, which it would be a sin to consume, but instead deliberately encourages the process. Sweets made of curdled milk might not sound very nice, but they are, and such theological problems do not bother the modern Bengali sweets consumer, who can choose between concoctions like the syrupy *pantua*, *chamcham*, *rajbhog* and the homemade *malpo*, round fennel-seed dumplings in syrup, of which Chitrita Banerji, author of *Bengali Cooking* (1997), says, 'there is nothing like the surreptitious pleasure of quickly eating a malpo in the middle of your day's work when you are sure nobody is looking'. Many Indian sweets are seasonal; in northern Bangladesh, for example, a popular summer speciality is *kanchagolla*, made of mangoes and milk.

The social importance of Indian sweets is reflected in their names, which usually refer to their shape but can also take the form of greetings. The word *sandesh* originally meant 'news', because sweets would accompany any messenger, and the Bengali word *tathya* (enquiry) has also come to mean 'presents of sweets'. There is a theory that in ancient times *sandesh* was deemed a suitable gift for anyone because it contains no cereal crops, and thus would not have been touched by those of a lower caste. *Sandesh* are made in all kinds of shapes – flowers and shells are popular – and are sometimes encased in a hard sugar coating. Sweets are consumed at the end of a visit, too, in the old Bengali custom of *mishtimukh*, or sweetening the mouth of guests before they leave. And sweets can be offered to vegetarians as an acceptable alternative to meat or fish being eaten by other guests. Other customs revolve around the associations of sweets with specific situations, such as journeys beginning on particular days (*jaggery* is best for Tuesdays, for example), and *sandesh* are prescribed to the ill. A marriage is a signal for some serious sweetmaking: the prosperity of a family is partly judged by the length of the *bhiyan*, the number of days before a wedding or festival that professional sweetmakers are employed in a household. Chitrita Banerji, a cookery author who is unusual in that she shows no embarrassment about sweets, recalls such occasions from her childhood:

> Apart from the mishti doi, ordered from one of the famous Calcutta sweetshops, the other sweets were all made by hired cooks who never minded when I slipped upstairs and stood watching their activities, and inevitably grinned when I reached out a greedy little paw for a surreptitious handful. I will never forget the fresh taste and fragrance of those sweets, still hot from the huge karai. Nothing tasted half as good when bought from the shops.

The autumn festival of Durgapuja is one of the biggest in the Bengali calendar, and lasts for three days. Women offer humble sweets to the female goddess Durga, and at the end, friends and relatives visit each other's houses. Banerji notes: 'They must be offered sweets, which cannot be refused – I have seen even diabetics put fragments into their mouths to honour the custom.' Sweets are bound up with Hinduism not just during festivals such as Diwali (where the goddess Lakshmi or – in Bengal – Kali is honoured with sweets, and sugar statues of the deities are on sale) or the more minor, localised festivals like Chaitra-Purnamasi, when mothers with sons are given a ritual jug filled with *laddu*, but also in everyday religious lore. The clearest description of this can be found in *Indian Sweet Cookery* (1979) by Jack Santa Maria:

> Puja, the private act of daily worship, is central to Hindu life. Among such things as incense, flowers and fruit, sweets are an important part of the offerings made to the god, goddess or Chosen Ideal of the worshipper. Indeed, the worshipper's idea of the sacred is said to reside in the centre of a sea of nectar, the thousand petalled lotus where the individual self – atman – and the cosmic self – brahman – are seen as one. This union is frequently compared to the taste of honey or some divine nectar. Sometimes the same image is described as a beautiful city to be found on a jewelled island which is itself set in an ocean of sweet milk. This nectar gives its name to the special offering and libation made by the priests. It is used to bathe an image or object during the puja. This nectar – amrita – is usually made from five ingredients such as honey, milk, ghee, sugar and water and is known as panchamrita. It is sometimes used to wash the feet of holy men. In this special offering are found the basic ingredients of all Indian sweets and the essential reason for using them.

In Hindu sacred scriptures it is said that the gods and goddesses are like children in that they like simple offerings, including sweets and cakes, since spiritual enlightenment is linked with sweetness. Sweets offered up to the gods as symbolic sacrifices are called *bhoga*, and when they have been ritually 'accepted' by a deity they are blessed and become *prasad*, the god's sacred leftovers, which can be bought and eaten by worshippers and pilgrims. The minor god Ghaninath is worshipped on Saturdays with offerings of rice, fruit and sweetmeats, which are afterwards eaten by members of the household. Vinayaka, an elephant-headed god, is particularly associated with sweets: one eleventh-century statue shows him tasting sweets with his trunk from a jar which he holds in one of his four hands. The goddess Lakshmi also loves sweets (especially *motichur laddu*), as do Ganesh and also Vishnu, in his various incarnations.

Just as Christian nunneries and monasteries became sweet-making centres in Europe, many Hindu temples have their own special sweet – for example, the Vishnu temple at Srimushnam has a sweet prepared from the root *korai* which is said to be liked by Varaha, the boar incarnation of Vishnu; and at the great Thirupati temple dedicated to Lord Venkateshwara, up to 70,000 special *laddus* are made every day, for selling to pilgrims, by a team of thirty cooks.

Sweets are an important part of the personal diet of a devout person, too, since many of them represent the quality of *sattva*, or harmony, and can nullify the effects of foods with too much *tamas* (inertia) or *rajas* (activity). In the Hindu ethos, there are six qualities to food – sweet, sour, salty, bitter, pungent and astringent – and they must be in balance to ensure the eater, the food and the universe are in harmony. All foods, including sweets, are revered in Hinduism, because food is one of the principal conduits for communication with the deities.

Indian sweets are not the explicit preserve of the Hindu religion, however. Many of them have their roots in the Moghul Empire, and *kheer* sweets, *laddu*, *jalebis* and *barfi* belong as much to Muslims and members of other faiths, and also people of no faith in India's officially secular society. Sweets are really too good to be captured by religion; who needs an after-life when you have got sweets? Specific Indian Muslim sweets include the fried wheat-vermicelli confections called *phirni* and *seviyan*; Parsis (Zoroastrians descended from ancient Persians) have *sev*, a sweet fried-noodle dish; Sikhs specialise in halwas, and eat special wheat versions at engagement ceremonies and cremations;

and sugar is one of the foods recommended by Buddha.

Pakistan, as might be expected, shares India's obsession with sweets, and the country has developed a relatively industrialised confectionery scene, with big companies such as Candyland (maker of jelly shooters: guns made of jelly), the toffee firm BP Industries and Corals Confections of Lahore (which markets 'go-stoppers'). At the ISM in Cologne, I met with Jalaluddin J. Marani of Pearl Food Industries, who let me sample Kashmiri Gold, his version of the *paan* traditionally used to freshen the mouth after a meal. This beguiling mix of coconut, little sugar-coated seeds, small shards of rock and nuts was quite delicious, beautiful to look at and texturally fascinating, and only just missed inclusion in my top ten favourite world sweets (see Lucky Dip, page 327).

Since so many Indian sweets are perishable, and made to private recipes for a local clientele, they are usually the preserve of professional sweetmakers working from shops, rather than mass-produced in factories. The number of such private sweet-shops has fallen in recent years, but a typical town might have up to a dozen establishments, each boasting its own speciality and commanding its own devotees and regular customers. As is usual in India, the profession is organised according to caste. There are two principal castes of sweetmaker, the halwai and the moira – who can be either Hindu or Muslim – and they are considered eminently respectable. R.V. Russell, author of *The Tribes and Castes of the Central Provinces of India* (1916), says of the sweetmaker: 'His art implies rather an advanced state of culture, and hence his rank in the social scale is a higher one. There is no caste in India which considers itself too pure to eat what a confectioner has made.' This is vital for someone who supplies sweets for weddings, say; in fact, the halwai caste is so pure that even a Brahmin can take water from their hands without the need for a purification ritual. This being India, the structures of these castes are labyrinthine: in Bihar, for example, there are four halwai castes and eight sub-castes, and these sub-castes can have up to fifty sections. Some castes change their vocation – the madhunapit are Bengali barbers turned confectioners – and of course caste members rarely follow their specified trades nowadays. In practice, many modern sweet-makers do not belong to the revered halwai castes, and they encourage customer loyalty with practices such as distributing free boxes of sweets to regulars during Diwali. Recently there has been an influx of Western sweets into India, particularly chewing gum, but the addictive quality of traditional Indian sweets is evinced by the fact that there are more Internet sites devoted to them than for any other type of sweet, and these sites are both copiously illustrated and exhaustive. As the site for Kaleva Sweets says: 'We feel that through Kaleva, we should give everyone a chance to eat sweets. We feel sweets add cheer and that extra zing to your life.'

THE ARAB WORLD

We have covered the sweets culture of the English-speaking peoples and of India; the third constituent of the great trium-virate of confectionery cultures in history is the Arab world. We have seen how Iran was the cradle of the cuisine of the Muslim peoples, and there remains a certain homogeneity in its sweets, which are principally pastries along the lines of the ubiquitous baklava, Turkish delights (*lokoum*), nut brittles, and halvas (a term which covers a wide variety of cereal-based sweets, as well as non-cereal versions such as the sesame halva that is most familiar to Westerners). But of course there are many regional variations in the Middle East and the Arab world.

In Iran itself, a national dish is the *ghotab*, a pastry which can be either sweet or savoury. In its sweet form it is filled with a sweet green-almond paste. In *Entertaining the Persian Way* (1988), Shirin Simmons remembers how 'the whole family would join in the preparation, and great play was made of who could achieve the best original shape. I can still recall the scent of the spring flowers, the singing of the birds and the sound of the old-fashioned gramophone playing in the background.' *Toot* are ground almonds, sugar and cardamom moulded to look like fat white mulberries, with a little slither of pistachio as the 'stalk', and *halva berenji* is a white halva made with basmati rice. Nuts are vital to Iranian cuisine: hazelnut sweets are given for engagements, almonds are used in a saffron toffee called *sohan-e-asali*, and a variation on sugared almonds (*noghl*, served as tiny shards in Iran) is *badam sookhteh*, shredded almonds caramelised in sugar and eaten as hot blobs. Among Iran's pastries, the light filo confections called *goosh-e feel* (elephants' ears) – delightfully named in both languages – are worthy of mention (horses' ears are smaller versions), and among several fudges perhaps *ranginak*, date fudge decorated with walnut halves, is most typical. Sweets and biscuits play an important role in Iranian custom and religious ritual. Gift boxes are customarily given to people either arriving or about to leave, given the charming name *did-o-baz-did*, or 'sweets to come and go'. Baklava and sugared almonds are among the seven sweets (the rest are really cookies) placed on the table for luck at New Year (*No Rooz*), celebrated at the spring equinox. Sweets also figure largely at weddings: the groom pays for sweets to be made in the bride's house, including sugared almonds and *nabat* (sugar crystals), and during the ceremony itself the couple place sugared almonds in each other's mouths.

Syria is famed for the lightness of its pastry sweets, such as *kol wa shkor*, filled with nuts and bathed in rosewater or orange-water. Candied walnuts and stiff fruit pastes, or leathers, are also popular, and Syrian *helva*, named *mamounia* after its supposed ninth-century inventor, Caliph Al-Mamun, is eaten warm for breakfast, with cinnamon. A number of modern sweets companies have opened in Syria since the 1940s, and chewing gum is extremely popular, although there are other specialists such as the Ghraoui Caramel Factory, Ramzy Licorice and Cristal, which makes simple bagged toffees and menthol sweets. Coffee has emerged as a popular flavour. Lebanon specialises in little pastries like *borma*, in a twist shape, and *aysh el-saraya*, or 'bread of the seraglio'. The pistachio is the favourite nut of the Lebanese, and it is used in the national version of baklava.

Jordan also has a thriving sweets-and-black-coffee scene, and companies such as Zalatimo Brothers of Amman (founded 1860) make baklava, *kunafa*, *awama* and other syrupy pastries to general acclaim. Further south, Saudi Arabia gleefully indulges its obsession with dates, which the country's date-marketing service associates with a wide range of healthful effects, from curing vertigo to increasing sex power ('eat a date on a date' could be a slogan for them, or maybe even 'make a date with a date before you go on a date'). Chewing gum and little wrapped chews are also popular now, as they are throughout the Arab world, and high-end chocolatiers are even making inroads in this market, as refrigeration becomes a standard feature in more shops. The United Arab Emirates boasts a serious chocolate-bar outfit, Tiffany, whose Quanta subsidiary makes Desire, Crispy and Break, which are copies of Mars Bar, Nestlé Crunch and KitKat. Oman has also spawned some Western-style sweets companies, such as Sweets of Oman, which makes chocolate bars, chocolate-filled toffee eclairs (its speciality) and toffees under the brand names Chiko and Royale. More traditionally, Yemeni women enjoy a snack called *ksu*, which is baked sweet potato or pumpkin, eaten with coffee and a mix of spices – ginger, cinnamon and sugar.

But of all Middle Eastern countries, Turkey has the best reputation for its sweets. The *pastane* is the place to buy Turkish sweets, whereas a *muhallebici* specialises in light, milky puddings such as *sutlac*. There is Turkish Delight, obviously, and also all the romantic variations on baklava. These are particularly evocative in Turkey, and they can imbue a roadside café with all the promise of the harem, from the simple baked *kadayfi*, or shredded-wheat pastry, to the *lokma*, or deep-fried pastries, such as *kadin gobegi* ('lady's navel': small golden rounds with a hole in the middle), *gozleme* ('glad eyes'), *saray* ('palace') and *dilber dudagi* ('sweetheart's lips'). Turkish *helva* is semolina-based, flavoured with nuts (usually almonds), raisins and spices; the disc-shaped *kara topak helva*, of sesame and hazelnuts, is traditionally given after a death. Other traditional Turkish sweets include *acibadem kurabiyesi*, baked almond chews, and *kesme bulamaci*, a spicy confection made of bulghur wheat, cloves, cinnamon and hazelnuts, cut into squares. It is said that at the Topkapi Palace in the mid eighteenth century, six types of *helva* were made by six chefs, each with his own team of a hundred apprentices.

Superfine marzipans (pistachio and almond) are another Turkish passion, rarely appreciated by foreigners, and candied chestnuts or marrons glacés are a speciality of the town of Bursa, made by old companies such as Kafkas. Gaziantep in southern Turkey is famed for its cuisine, and *antep suarzesi*, or bird's nest pastries, are its unique contribution to Turkish sweets; the respected firm of Güllüoglu, which moved to Istanbul from Gaziantep in 1949, trades on the town's reputation, and has now branched out into chocolate products as well as baklava and *lokoum*. Big companies like Saray, Erden and Cici mass-produce Western-style sweets for the home market, and Turkey's very own manufacturer of popping candy (known as Space Dust or Pop Rocks elsewhere) goes by the name of Shoogy Boom.

The traditional *helva* of Egypt is *basboosa* – diamond-shaped, delicately scented, flavoured with coconut and served with tea, although in the rest of North Africa couscous is usually a base for *helva*. Similarly *kishik*, which is a savoury dish of barley and yoghurt elsewhere, is blended with honey to make a sweet in Egypt. Sweetness plays an important role in the spicy-sweet *tagines* of Morocco, although here as elsewhere in the Middle East, fresh fruit is the preferred dessert. In all Islamic countries, sweets play an important part in Ramadan, with halva often being used as an energy food to break the fast at nightfall. In Morocco as Ramadan approaches, the doughnut sellers begin to make aromatic, sesame-based halvas instead.

CENTRAL AND EASTERN EUROPE

Russia's indigenous sweets culture is based on fruit, and across eastern Europe and the Balkans one finds the custom of presenting a guest with a saucer of jam or compote and a little spoon, to eat with a cup of tea. In Russia this is called *varen'ye*; in Serbia, *slatko*; in Romania, *dulceata*; and in Greece, *gliko*. Preserved fruits in honey and, later, sugar syrup, sometimes enriched with brandy, form the basis of the Russian sweets tradition. Vegetables and nuts are also treated in this way, as in old sweets such as walnuts in syrup, and lettuce stalks or radishes preserved with ginger. According to R.E.F. Smith in *Bread and Salt: A Social and Economic History of Food and Drink in Russia* (1984), the first Russian sweet was made from the honey of wild bees, mixed with berry pulp and dried in the sun to form a kind of jelly or pastille; the author says it is still made in this way in Bashkiriya. *Kissel* is Russia's own form of fruit jelly, which varies in consistency from runny to stiff, and can thus be treated as a dessert or a sweet.

Russia's first sugar refinery was established in St Petersburg in 1723, and sugar was imported in considerable amounts via Archangel in Siberia from this time. Sweetmeats had been enjoyed by the rich for a century at least, but they became widely popular among the middle classes through the eighteenth century. An English traveller in Russia in the 1830s described how picnicking Russians were served blueberry tarts and steaming cocoa (it was said that Peter the Great had brought back the recipe for chocolate with him from Holland). Halvas, syrupy *babas* and *lokoums* also have a role in Russian confectionery, thanks to the incorporation of the Mongol khanates into the Muscovite state under Ivan the Terrible (who once had a dessert made in the form of the Kremlin — the best bits must have been the domes). But fruit sweets held sway, and in the nineteenth century dessert often consisted of fresh fruit, Russian champagne and fruit pastilles, dragées or chocolate. Puddings tended to be both fruity and milky, and are still the specialities of Byelorussia (White Russia), which led the nostalgic cookery author Marie Alexandre Markevitch, in her *The Epicure in Imperial Russia* (1941), to produce the most outlandishly patriotic confectionery theory ever conceived. She makes an elaborate comparison between Russian cuisine and that of the Vikings, commenting on the 'fabulous appetites and refined cuisine' of both cultures, and pointing up similarities between Norman and Russian cuisine – principally the predilection for cream.

In the more down-to-earth and correspondingly less entertaining *Classic Russian Cooking* (published in many editions from 1861 to 1917), Elena Molokhovets includes recipes for apple sweets, made with egg whites and almonds, gooseberry and cranberry sweets, and also gums flavoured with cinnamon, rose or lemon oil, or mint. One curiosity is her mint 'mushrooms', with stems dyed with saffron and caps of chocolate.

The more extravagant regions of confectionery were understandably suppressed under the Communist regime, and the Russian liking for fruit preserves had to be satisfied by tinned fruit. But the chocolate industry survived. One company, Krasny Oktyabr, founded by a German businessman in Moscow in 1867, found itself renamed State Confectionery Factory No. 1 in 1918. It continued to turn out good chocolate (brands like Zolotoy Yarlyk and Mishka Kosolapy) even during the Second World War, when aeroplane parts were made in the factory, side by side with special chocolate bars for the air force, while the company's sister factory in Leningrad made sugar confectionery, jellies, marshmallows and dragées. Both concerns are thriving today. Other well-known Russian makes are Novosibirskaia of Siberia, Konfi in the Urals and Ptichye Moloko, makers of fine chocolates. In recent years new companies have tried to exploit the market: Korkunov, founded in Moscow in 1999, packages its hazelnut chocolates in the most old-fashioned boxes of all. Muscovites are also partial to roasted nut candies called *grilyazh*, *zefir* (marshmallow) and sesame crunch bars, as well as a full range of those fruit preserves, syrups and compotes.

One of the most venerable companies of the old Soviet regime was Kalev, in what is now Estonia. This company's roots go back to 1806, when it was established in Tallinn by a marzipan master in a shop that is still open (Café Maiasmokk, if you are in the area). Kalev was in fact a 1940s Soviet amalgamation of all the city's sweetmaking companies, but today it still specialises in handmade marzipan figures, chocolate and caramels (chewy chocolates are a recent innovation), and it even opened its own company museum last year.

The traditional sweet of the Ukraine is apple *pastila*, a type of paste or jelly made with egg whites, a sweet popular across eastern Europe in various forms; quinces are used in Moldavia. Today, Ukraine boasts some thirty confectionery manufacturers, such as Svitoch, the largest chocolate concern, several companies backed by the likes of Kraft and Nestlé, and specialists like Pokc, which makes lovely-looking lollipops that were displayed in lit-up revolving cases, like watches in a jeweller's, at the Cologne fair. In Georgia and Armenia, a type of walnut brittle, made with honey, called *gozinake*, is popular, and also *churchkhela*, an elaborate hazelnut sweet confected with fermented white grape juice (*pekmez*) and sugar. The local baklava contains walnuts.

Armenia is burdened by the most patriotic cookery writers of all, who seem to insist that almost all foods were invented in their native land. Armenian sweetmakers really do specialise in *bastegh*, stiff fruit pastes or leathers that are hung out to dry in sheets like washing, and *soudjuk*, walnuts strung on threads and dipped in liquid *bastegh* and left to harden. *Yelag bastegh* is a strawberry version, a sugary pulp mix left to cool in the sunshine for a day in a thin layer in a tin lined with clingfilm; by the next morning it should be dry enough to peel off in a single piece. Threads, sheets, tins, clingfilm: those Armenian sweetmakers don't make it easy for themselves.

Fruits and nuts dominate the whole of Eastern Europe – that is, in terms of its sweets. They can be found lurking deliciously in many regional halvas, and also in chocolate. Karuna, a Lithuanian brand, comes with whole hazelnuts or crushed hazelnuts – take your pick – and Ruta, an old Lithuanian caramel company, fills its caramels with fruit. Milky caramels are also a speciality of Latvia – the best known is Gotina, or 'little cow', which is popular in Poland – and Laima, the leading brand (once famous in the USSR), makes more than fifty types, in many fruit flavours, as well as a range of chocolate bars to suit local tastes: Cirks is filled with pumpkin seeds, Laiks with sunflower seeds, and Serenade is 'hazelnut crumbs in apricot and apple jam and chocolate'. Rum-flavoured chocolate is also something of a penchant in eastern Europe, and the alcohol aspect did not prevent its inclusion in the Hungarian sports bar, Sport Szelet – 'This great tasting chocolate bar will energize you throughout the day!' (Just be careful where you throw that shotput.) There has been a long tradition of fine sweetmaking in this vein in Hungary; in his *Confectioners Oracle* (1830), William Gunter mentions the fact that bonbons ('very beautiful and diaphanous' candied spheres) are made with liqueurs. As well as their famous pastries, Hungarians share a liking for creamy sweetness with the Russians, and the nation's creamy Christmas bonbons, *szaloncukor*, are exported to homesick Hungarians all over the world.

Jewish food has been informed by the cuisines of at least eighty cultures, although at first sight it can appear more akin to Middle Eastern models than anything else. Jews have a reputation for a sweet tooth, but the sharing of sweets and biscuits appears to be inevitable in any close-knit community with an advanced culture of hospitality. The reputation could also stem from the association of Jews with the sugar trade, particularly in Antwerp and Amsterdam, and in the sugar-refining businesses of Poland and Russia. Jews have also been associated with the trade in citrus fruit since medieval times, and with marzipan production. Sweet things are associated with several Jewish rituals – apples in honey for Rosh Hashanah, for example, or the practice of putting sweets under newlyweds' pillows among Sephardic Jews. Passover sweets include *ingber*, or carrot candy, and *tayglach*, ginger sweets.

Far, far from the Middle East, Poland is nevertheless an outpost of halva, baklava, nougat and marzipan (this last made at

Kaliningrad on the Baltic coast). Vera Levai includes a recipe for the popular homemade Polish honey nougat, in *Culinary Delights of Eight Countries* (1985), that is so simple that I will break my rule of having no recipes in this book. Take half a litre of honey; boil until brown. Mix in 600 grammes poppy seed. Allow to cool. Poland is also known for its fancy pre-Soviet chocolates and sweets, which are enjoying something of a renaissance. Chopin chocolates, Delfina pralines (named for a beautiful nineteenth-century châtelaine) and the less romantic chocolate-covered prunes are all popular, as are the famously delicate vanilla and sesame halvas made by the Warsaw firm of Wedel, founded in 1851 (and now owned by Pepsi-Cola). The central and eastern European mania for cakes and biscuits is reflected in Poland in a wide range of chocolate-covered wafer-type bars, such as Prince Polo crunchy waffles and the huge number made under the JM brand since 1989. The prognosis for the confectionery business in the former Soviet states is good. For example, S.C. Excelent, a Romanian firm, makes toffees under the brand name Pitic, and – ignoring the quality of the translation, which it is not my intention to ridicule – the priorities espoused in its mission statement are spot on:

> Excelent toffees ARE NOT luxury goods made specially for the 'elite' but are designed for everyone's taste regardless the age. Children of all ages, buy these items for more than 40 years when we start producing them. What we are thinking about our products is not enough, tastes and preferences of consumers are vital in our decisions making (wideness of the range, variety of taste, shape of the sweets we have been producing). Excelent toffees have 5 variants as follows: milk (nourishing); fruits (fresh taste of fruits); cocoa (energising); coconut (exotic sensation); mint (refreshing taste).

In the Balkans, runny marshmallow is favoured, in incarnations such as the Serbian Munchmallows. There are several well-respected confectionery firms still going strong in the former Yugoslavia: Pionir was founded in Subotica in 1917 and makes a huge range of sweets and chocolates, and the Croatian firm Kras, started in Zagreb in 1911, makes fine chocolate under the Dorina brand, as well as nougat, toffees, cherry sweets and all kinds of biscuits. Long, sausage-shaped sweets, sliced thin like salami, are a traditional sweet of the region, either chocolate-covered marzipan, or a confection called *rolat*, which is dried figs rolled out like pastry, filled with almonds or walnuts, sugar and lemon juice. In Bosnia and Serbia, mashed up prunes are mixed up with rum or brandy, nuts and sugar and made into sweets called prune balls or prune dreams. (Who would dream of a prune?) Throughout the Balkans, fruit is stewed, thickened, rolled into balls, dipped in nuts or perhaps chocolate or rum, and served up as a sweet. Macedonia has its own fruity sweets called *retselia*, as well as local baklava, and modern companies such as Europa make fruity toffees and caramels in the popular regional flavours: orange, lemon, strawberry, currant, apricot, cherry, blackberry, raspberry, apple and honey.

Halvas are made everywhere from India to Poland, but the Balkans display perhaps the widest range in the smallest geographical area; they seem to come in every flavour and consistency, from the hard, bar-like halvas of Serbia, often covered with chocolate, to halvas made of wafers, chocolate and nuts, to the *soyhuke* of Albania, a walnut halva made with cornflour that has the consistency of Turkish Delight. Then there is the halva of Bulgaria, which is really just rice and syrup. Bulgaria is home to some singular sweets which do not utilise that country's famous rosepetals, such as carrot balls (*bonboni* of Morkovi) and *kolivo*, a powdery wheat sweet with hazelnuts and sultanas, reserved for funerals, when it is eaten in spoonfuls at the graveside.

This is called *koliva* in Greece, which of course has its own world of halvas, based on semolina, sesame seeds and almonds, made in consistencies to suit every occasion. Not all these halvas are marketed as old-fashioned delights: the Haitoglou brothers of Thessaloniki package their range in sleek black boxes with subtle typography. As well as a full-range of syrupy, baklava-style pastries, the Greek taste for sweets extends to *pasteli*, a traditional sesame and honey brittle regarded as an energy sweet, and also a variety of wafer-style sweets and bars; one of the most popular types is known as a Viennese wafer, with a vanilla or nut filling. Chocolate-covered halvas, filled with cherries, raisins and nuts, are very popular, and the Greek facility with chocolate is reflected in the number of Belgian chocolate houses with Greek origins – Leonidas and Daskalides are famous examples.

THE EAST

On the far side of Russia, in the easternmost regions of the former Soviet Union, the sweets of states such as Uzbekistan and Tajikistan are positively oriental, and Azerbayjani cooks indulge their obsession with continual variation of recipes with sweets as with other dishes. Turkish and Persian influences are particularly evident in this confectionery culture. The same is true of Afghanistan, crisscrossed with ancient trading routes, which boasts some delightful variations, such as a milky wheat halva, the custom of eating *jalebis* after fish (they are often on sale at adjacent stalls in markets), the Indian-influenced *sheer payra*, made with milk, nuts and cardamom, and the extra-ordinary 'silk kebab', *abrayshum kebab*, which is made by rolling up egg threads and sprinkling them with syrup.

China's best-known sweet is the White Rabbit mint chew. But this is a relatively modern innovation; there has never been a great sweets culture in China, and nearly all the street food – *xiaochi*, or small foods – are savoury things like pork-filled buns and *wontons*. Many Chinese sweets take the form of sour fruit pickles, which look sweet to Western eyes but are actually extremely strong and lip-pursingly astringent – hence my lavatorial experience after a foray into the many pick 'n' mix shops of San Francisco's Chinatown. The Chinese sweet tooth, such as it is, is largely satisfied by cakes, both modern and traditional – and of course this narrative must eschew cakes. But there are straightforward sweet foods served in China, too, according to Frederick J. Simoons' *Food in China* (1991): most unusual is a candied version of the gelatinous nest of the swiftlet, which is generally found in bird's nest soup but gets sugar-candied for weddings. The roots and seeds of lotuses and mung beans are favourite munchurian candying candidates, as well as the more parochial oranges, almonds, walnuts and coconut chunks.

Recently, the global sweets companies have identified China as a potentially huge new market, but their first inroads have been unsuccessful, partly because cheap imitations of Western sweets are launched almost as soon as the real thing hits the shelves, but also because research into regional tastes has not been carried out, and the importance of local contacts in retailing underestimated. Chinese companies have been springing up to cater to local tastes; Erko Foods of Guangdong, for instance, makes a disarmingly wide range of marshmallow products with liquid centres, in flavours from grape to coffee. And Kimberli is responsible for perhaps the finest handpainted and moulded lollipops on earth, from a superbly expressive, purple-coated vampire to a chubbily charming bumble bee.

The sweets of Tibet are few, and a good proportion are simply imported from India – *shekara* (the general term for Indian sweets), *jeril* (toffee) and *burangarma* (squares of Indian *gur*, or unrefined sugar). But Tibetans do make some sweets, including cubes of condensed yak milk, which are dried out and then strung on a thread to make a garland (as Turkish Delight is in Iran). *Tasoma* are yellow sweets made from sugar syrup, and the national halva is called *yola*, a pastry with cardamom that originated in India. But it is rice pudding (*desil*) rather than sweets which provides most sweet satisfaction in Tibet.

Taiwan is crazy for fruit jelly sweets, which come in small, sealed, cone-shaped plastic containers, a little like the individual portions of jam served in hotels. Eating one of these for the first time is a disconcerting experience, because the little portion of jelly pops out with a gentle glooping sound and reveals itself to be stiff, wobbly and dripping with a sugary mucus. It must be eaten all in one, however, and reveals itself as amazingly delicious, like a heightened version of eating real fruit in terms of both texture and flavour. Small chunks of fruit lurk inside these cold, densely flavoured and strangely refreshing globules, which are made in flavours such as mango, lychee, papaya and melon. They are extremely popular all over South-east Asia, and in Taiwan the ABC brand, for instance, has a huge range.

Sweetened, sticky rice forms the basis for a great many sweets in China and south Asia. In Burma, for example, a sticky purée of rice, peanuts, sesame seeds and coconut (called *htamane*) is cooked up in a huge pot and divided to make sweets for weddings and festivals. Such rice sweets are often eaten with green tea rather than as a snack or for dessert.

Rice is also important in the aromatic world of Thai sweets (*kanom*), with coconut as the almost universal flavouring. Most of these sweets are variations on *khao niew mamuang*, sticky rice flavoured with coconut and perhaps mung beans, served on a piece of banana leaf with a dollop of some fruit purée on top and garnished with toasted sesame seeds. Mango, lychee, banana and jackfruit are enjoyed, plus of course the ubiquitous coconut cream. These sweets are popular street food, and can be made to order in the flavour of choice by the vendor, and even heated up in cold weather. Scent is important to Thai sweets lovers, and jasmine is a popular addition to the sugar syrup used in sweetmaking; sweets are sometimes left next to scented flowers overnight, or placed beside aromatic candles. Egg-yolk sweets are in a class of their own: *foi thong*, for example, are golden threads of egg yolk cooked hard in a sugar syrup flavoured with jasmine. Then there are the fruit jellies, made with *agar* (from seaweed) as a thickening agent. One Thai sweet, *kanom sam kloe,* which translates as 'three friends', are balls of coconut, mung beans and sesame seeds and sugar, fried in batter. They are generally reserved for weddings, and fried in little batches of three or four. It is said that if the balls stick together while frying, the wedding is off to an auspicious start; if one ball floats off in the oil, the couple will be childless; and if all three separate, disaster will follow. Not surprisingly, cooks make up a specially thick batter to encourage cohesion between the balls, and if necessary toothpicks are used to secure them.

Further east, coconut and fruit are important sweets ingredients in Vietnam and Laos. All kinds of fruits and vegetables are candied, particularly at New Year; everything from sweet potato to melon. Cambodia, however, has less of a sweet tooth, preferring acid and sour flavours. Korean sweets are based on steamed rice and honey, and rice cakes might be filled with bean paste, chestnuts or dates. The modern Lotte brand makes marshmallows called Chocopie and Dream Cakes, as well as ginseng chewing gum and chocolate-coated sunflower seeds. Milkiness returns to Malaysia, usually in confederacy with coconut and fruit (as in the celebrated coconut *dodol*), and firms catering to national tastes, such as Goodfood, produce delicacies such as lotus-flavoured candy for kids, sold in flower-shaped containers.

In the islands of Indonesia, coconut is again used in sticky rice-based sweets, but mixed with spices or local flavourings – *onde-onde* are bright green sticky rice cakes rolled in coconut, which derive their colour from a fragrant leaf called *daun pandan*. Coconut and rice also rule in the islands of the South Pacific, although there are anomalies, such as the blue-green coconut candy of Fiji or the popular peanut bars of Papua New Guinea. In Samoa, chiefs are given *poi* – not steak and kidney *poi*, but a kind of milkshake drink of mashed banana, coconut and citrus leaves, the Samoan equivalent of Aztec chocolate.

Japan, needless to say, exists in a world of its own when it comes to sweets, although like many aspects of Japanese culture, its sweets can be traced back to Chinese precedents, transformed with wondrous artistry by the unique Japanese sensibility. The spread of Buddhism in the eighth century led to a great deal of interaction between China and Japan, and the first sweets were called *kajitsu*, or Chinese fruits. By the tenth century they had become known as *wagashi*, from *wa*, meaning Japan, and *kashi*, fruit. These first sweets were simple mixes of rice and fruit, and contained no sugar or even honey; their fruity, energy-giving properties may have been valued by the vegetarian Buddhist priests. Later, Japanese sweets became an essential adjunct to the tea ceremony, the sweetness of sugar off-setting the startling bitterness of the green tea (which is pounded in front of you until it resembles bright green milk-shake). In *A Taste of Japan* (1985), Donald Richie makes the lovely observation that traditional Japanese tea-ceremony sweets are designed to appeal to all five senses: the shape and colour to the eye; the poetic name to the ear; the delicate smell to the nose; the texture to the mouth; and of course the taste. It has taken a refined culture to produce it, but this is a paradigm applicable to sweets everywhere.

Traditional *wagashi*, known as *namagashi*, are steamed or left uncooked, and have as their base ingredient moist, pounded rice, called *mochi*. The simplest *mochi* sweets are just balls of pounded white rice; these are associated with purity and the New Year, and celebrities such as sumo wrestlers get involved with high-profile rice-pounding ceremonies at this time. Japanese children are encouraged to look at the moon and find a rabbit pounding *mochi*. These simple sweets are often given as offerings at Shinto shrines, and as with the Hindu temple sweets, they are eaten by worshippers once the deity has symbolically accepted them. In the best Shinto tradition, *mochi* are associated with money, and like wealth they can be difficult to swallow all at once – every year a few people choke to death on them. Most *mochi* sweets are flavoured with *an*, a delicate paste made from sugar mixed with red or white azuki beans, or perhaps chestnuts, sweet potato or other vegetables and fruits. These are made in hundreds of shapes and colours, many of them related to the seasons or beautiful regional features. The most sophisticated versions are little parcels folded with the precision of origami, arranged with the grace of *ikebana* (flower-arranging) and marked with subtle crests of leaves or flowers to indicate their seasonal attributes. Traditionally, *mochi* are square in Tokyo, and round in Osaka and Kyoto.

These sweets are sold in old, high-class shops such as Toraya in Tokyo, which caters to the royal family, and Mannendou in Kyoto, with its speciality *kome dango*, a skewer of three rice cakes coated with white bean paste and seaweed, each one subtly different. Shops like this are decorated with hanging scrolls, stone basins and flower arrangements, with smart uniformed staff and possibly a side room through a paper screen with traditional *tatami* (soft reed) mats.

But most *wagashi* today are jolly, colourful items mass-produced in moulds – subtle pastel shades are anathema to the Japanese sweetmaker and *wagashi* seem deliberately naive, appealing to a particular sentimental streak in Japanese people.

Cherry-blossom time (*sakura*) is a fine time for sweetmaking, when the *sakuramochi*, rice-flour buns, are made in pinks and whites in flower shapes by machines in shop windows; the outside is made of crisp rice flour, to keep the shape, and the whole is wrapped in a fragrant, almost minty, pickled cherry leaf. In autumn, red maple leaves are a popular theme, although in a sweet such as *kozue no aki*, the sweetmaker uses all the colours of the leaf – bright green, yellow and pink, all at the same time, a bright and beautiful combination (and, incidentally, botanic-ally possible). Another autumn sweet is *kikugoromo*, in the shape of a chrysanthemum, like a fat wonton. A winter delicacy is *yukimochi*, a *mochi* ball covered in powder of *korimochi* (frozen and crushed *mochi*) so it looks like a delectable snowball. Jellied sweets made from *agar* (yokan) are also popular, especially in summer, and a gorgeous sweet at this season is *kokeshimizu* (moss in stream): pale green cubes of cool, mottled jelly. A funny jelly sweet is *wakabakage*, little imitation goldfish trapped in cubes of clear jelly.

Perhaps the most popular *wagashi* of all is the *manju*, a simple floury bun stuffed with bean paste. These can be bought in immaculate presentation boxes (it is always a surprise to find how few sweets are actually inside) and make good gifts when visiting other people's houses, an occasion when a present is compulsory. When I spent time in Japan in the late 1980s, the agreed value of such a present was the equivalent of £5, and many of the beribboned *manju* or *mochi* boxes were priced accordingly.

The Portuguese influence in southern Japan from the end of the sixteenth century is reflected in the sweets called *namban-gashi*, or 'southern barbarian sweets', which is rather hard on the Portuguese. These sweets are fascinating to the sweets historian in that they are oriental transmogrifications of the egg-yolky sweets of Portugal. Nagasaki was the centre of this interchange, and numerous Portuguese sweets have been assimilated into the local dialect, such as the spongey cakes called *bolo*, rendered *maruboro* in Japanese, or *bolo de Castella*, *kasutera* in Japanese. Other more recent Japanese sweets are known as *higashi*: *rakugan* are sweets made with sugar and soy or rice flours, moulded in different shapes, and in the nineteenth century, candied citron and sugar-glazed beans joined the Japanese foreign sweets legion. There are deep-fried Japanese sweets, too, including *karinto* (deep-fried dough) and *yama-imo no ame-daki*: fried yam slivers dipped in sugar, then soy, coated in sesame and left to cool. More conventional sweets are *hakkato* (peppermints) and *shogato* (ginger candies).

The Japanese talent for strangely assimilating foreign in-fluences is in full flow in its selection of Western-style sweets, or *yogashi*, the products of an industry which began in earnest in 1899 with the founding of the Morinaga sweets company, later joined by Meiji, the other big player in this sphere. These companies make serious caramels. Everyburger has always been my favourite Japanese sweet, a funny little biscuit that looks just like a tiny cheeseburger, right down to the sesame seeds on the bun; the 'burger' itself is chocolatey paste. Everyburgers – or 'Eberrybeggaro', as they are pronounced – are indeed shaped like every burger. Another classic is Pocky, biscuity sticks with chocolate- or strawberry-dipped ends, although recently I have developed a taste for the aptly named Hello Panda, biscuity sweets with a liquid centre in a box which sports a truly goofy yet strangely adorable panda.

SOUTH AMERICA

Across the deep Pacific, the sweets of South America owe much to the colonial legacy. In Brazil, the eggy Portuguese influence can be tasted in *quindao*, the custardy sweets flavoured with coconut that are standard fare, but the most famous single *docinho* or sweet has got to be the *brigadeiro*: balls made from condensed milk flavoured with cocoa powder which are a must-have at children's parties. These are named after Brigadier Eduardo Gomes, a famous air force commander who ran for election in 1945. The brigadier was tall, dark and handsome, and his campaign was focused on female voters; one slogan reportedly read: 'Vote for the Brigadier! He is single and handsome.' The adoring women in the brigadier's camp invented the brigadier sweet as an election gimmick and fundraiser, and after the brigadier's political career foundered (he lost the election to an army general) the sweet named after him lived on.

Dulce de leche – rich, runny caramel, sold in jars – is a classic sweet flavour in South America, available everywhere in different forms (it is called *cajeta* in Mexico). I have a special Uruguayan supply that is delicious mixed with homemade vanilla ice cream. *Dulce de leche* in sweet form, called *alfajores*, is hugely popular in Argentina, where the healthy market for sweets is also reflected in the products of the giant Arcor corporation, which has resisted competition from foreign multinationals. Well-known Argentinian sweets brands include ShotShots, which are Argentine M&Ms.

Chews, toffees, mints and lollipops are produced by modern sweets companies across South America, from Confiteca in Ecuador to Noel in Colombia. Chewing gum is a big seller right across the continent, a throwback to the ingrained chewing habit in the indigenous cultures of South America.

Venezuela and Ecuador are magnets for chocolate companies, because the subtle and sought-after Criollo variety is grown here; Nestlé and Nabisco have big interests. There is a famous sweet made in the Ecuadorean town of Baños called *melcocha*; this is pulled candy hung from a hook in the usual way and allowed to elongate, but also beaten against the door.

But it is Mexico that has the most highly developed sweets scene in this part of the world, perhaps because of the sheer numbers of sweet-crazed nuns and monks who have lived there. The makers of the original 'convent' *dulces* may have disappeared, but their legacy survives in the fine confectioners who specialise in candied fruits, and quince and guava pastes. These often depend on locally available produce; for example, the towns of Irapuato and Zamora sell crystallised strawberries, while in the industrial area around Monterrey in the north, *dulce de leche* candies (made of goats' milk) are a speciality. *Penuche* is Mexican fudge with nuts, successfully exported to the United States. Down in the Yucatan, coconut is used extensively, as in *coco melcochado*, coconut in dark caramel brittle, and the corrosive flesh of the cashew fruit (*maranon*) becomes sweetly edible when preserved in syrup. In her *Mexican Regional Cooking* (1984), Diana Kennedy describes Dulces de Celaya, an old Mexico City sweetshop founded in 1874 and still in the same family:

> One window is usually filled with crystallised fruit – whole sweet potatoes, thick slices of pineapple, rich, dark-red watermelon, hunks of the whitish chilacayote with its black seeds, and whole shells of orange peel. On the other side are the gaznates – cornets of a thin, fried dough filled with a pineapple and coconut paste; thin triangles of almond turron between layers of rice paper, and thick discs of chocolate ground on the metate [basalt slab] with almonds and sugar and perfumed with vanilla and cinnamon. Inside the shop those that specially catch my eye are the small, brilliant green limes stuffed with coconut; almond paste miniatures of earthenware milk pitchers about one inch

high, a mamey with a piece of its light brown skin curled back to display the rich, salmon-pink fruit inside; or the papaya, also in miniature, with a slice cut out of it to see the flesh and small seeds inside. There are large rectangular jamoncillos of Puebla decorated with pine nuts and raisins; the acid-sweet tamarind candies from Jalisco and small fudge-like rolls covered with pecan halves from Saltillo.

The Day of the Dead (celebrated on 1 and 2 November) heralds some bizarre sweets behaviour in Mexico, aimed at pleasing the souls of dead children and babies. Alongside the grisly papier mâché ornaments sold by roadside vendors are a wide array of sugar models of skulls, coffins, skeletons, bones, tombstones, wreaths and assorted scary figures. This is not a new tradition, as a letter written in 1841 by Frances Calderón de la Barca shows:

Last Sunday was the festival of All Saints; on the evening of which day we walked out under the portales [. . .] to look at the illumination, and at the numerous booths filled with sugar skulls, etc., temptingly ranged in grinning rows, to the great edification of the children [. . .] The old women at their booths, with their cracked voices, kept up the constant cry of 'skulls, niñas, skulls!' – but there were also animals done in sugar, of every species, enough to form specimens for a Noah's ark.

Today, the shops and makeshift stalls sell everything from anatomically correct rib and thigh bones, to frightening images of souls in purgatory – all in creamy white sugar decorated with icing, with cherries for eyes, or else moulded from chocolate. A slightly less disturbing sweets tradition occurs at Christmas parties in Mexico, when blindfolded children take turns swinging a stick at a sweet-filled papier mâché animal, called a *piñata*. The modern sweets industry is massive in Mexico, with scores of companies. Recent curiosities include a beer-flavoured lollipop from Dulces Beny of Jalisco, and tamarind lollipops from the likes of Ronny Productions. These last are extraordinary: first, a dark and caramelised taste, like toffee apple, but lurking underneath a granular substance that is exceptionally sour from the tamarind and unbelievably hot from the chilli. To say these are an acquired taste would be something of an understatement. Hot sweets imported from Mexico – such as Scorned Woman Jalapeño Fudge or Hola Pop! hot lollipops – are currently a bit hit among American schoolchildren.

The legacy of slavery has also had its effect on the cuisine of Central and South America. In the Caribbean, nut brittle made of sesame seeds, or wangla nuts, were formerly popular, as they are in Africa. The exciting contrast of sweet and sour or sweet and hot has traditionally been exploited by the slave and slave-descended population in ginger candies and pawpaw or tamarind balls, rolled in sugar. In Jamaica, ginger root is best harvested in December and January, hence its traditional popularity at Christmas back in Britain. Fruit 'cheeses' or pastes made of guava or mango, sprinkled with sugar and sliced up, are extremely popular, a taste which can be traced back to the earliest days of the West Indian colonies. Thomas Trapham, in *A Discourse on the State of Health in the Island of Jamaica* (1679), warns of the dangers of icy drinks: 'and lest such at sometimes should chill the stomach too much, the Spanish custome of eating candid warm Fruits and Roots after such draughts may be esteemed reasonable, such as candied limes, oranges, ginger, marmalade of Guavas, quiddimes or Citrons to be taken in little quantities'.

Different islands boast different sweets specialities – St Lucia has *tuloons*, of coconuts and sometimes nuts, and Jamaica adores peppermint. In *Traditional Jamaican Cookery* (1985), Norma Benghiat looks into this tradition:

> Not many years ago, both in the city and country areas, candy vendors were to be seen everywhere with their showcases full of striped red and white peppermints, sugar or grater cake and

other sweets [. . .] I was told that one had to pay to be initiated into the art, and, once learned, it was a closely kept secret [. . .] For example, no new person was allowed into the area of candy-making once the operation had started. If anyone in the group had to leave suddenly for some reason, but had to return later, this person must look into the saucepan before departing. Some lime juice must be sprinkled round the table on which the candy would be worked, to get rid of smells. This, I think, was also intended to ward off spirits or the evil eye.

This liking for mint is reflected in KC Dinner Mints, one of the bestselling lines of the leading Caribbean sweet company, KC Candy of Trinidad and Tobago. These unpretentious sweets, sold in humble bags, journey thousands of miles with West Indian people as they travel the world, a comforting reminder of home.

AFRICA

Africa has not had a developed sugar industry, historically, and its paltry sweets legacy has developed piecemeal. Aside from fresh and dried fruits, pieces of sorghum or sweet cane have long been chewed in many African cultures and go by many names. Ethiopia has *tej*, its famous alcoholic honey-wine, but the preferred African flavours are bitter and what has been unappetisingly described as 'sour/musty'; there is no dessert or sweets culture. Fruit is sometimes eaten, or a kola nut is chewed. It is a great shame that the grubs and insects eaten in some African countries are covered in salt and never sugar. In West Africa, coconut is a popular flavour, but the peanut brittle bar called variously *kanya* or *kayan* or *kanyan*, made of peanut butter, ground rice and sugar, is most typical, and one of the few true sweets of Africa. Fried sweetened dough balls can be found everywhere, called *oorah* in Sierra Leone, for example, and *togbei* (sheep's balls) in Ghana, where they are brightly coloured for weddings. Doughnut-type sweets with names like *puff-puff* and *chin-chin* are widely available as street food. The Portuguese influence in Angola and Mozambique has encouraged a sweet tooth, particularly for egg and milk sweets and desserts, and coconut puddings and candies are commonplace. *Kashatas* are moist coconut sweets that are extremely popular at teatime in Uganda and Tanzania. The modern industry is expanding rapidly in Africa: Cadbury has opened a plant in Swaziland, mainly supplying South Africa, and a Nestlé-backed chocolate factory in Ghana (a country known for its cuisine) makes an excellent product. The heat is a problem with chocolate, of course, and African companies concentrate on unmeltable jellies, marshmallow and nougats.

EUROPE

Most sweets ideas have seeped up to Europe from the south. Sicily has been a nexus for confectionery lore since the Arab occupation in the ninth century, and many of the sweets of the island bear a marked resemblance to Arab precedents, with dried fruits and almonds in abundance. For example, the Sicilian version of *torrone* called *cubaita* (from the Arabic *qubhayt*) is made with sesame and cut into diamonds, in the tradition of Eastern lozenges. (Only Andalusia can be said to be as close to Araby as Sicily in its sweetmaking.) The craft of marzipan modelling has become Sicily's own, and shops display gorgeous assortments of fruit and vegetables, and even sandwiches or salamis in marzipan, as well as (for some reason) pigs wearing bowler hats. The nuns of the Convent of Eloise at Martorana are said to have invented marzipan fruits – which are known as *frutta di Martorana* – as a practical joke on a visiting archbishop: the fake fruit was hung from trees in the garden. One of the first references to this speciality is in a letter dated 1402 in which King Martin of Sicily ordered a large amount. Marzipan fruit-making developed into a veritable artform, practised by nuns and professional confectioners alike, to the wonderment of visitors, like one Gastone Vullier, writing in 1897:

Most marvellous of all is the fruit that they exhibit, such as figs just opened from which a crystalline drop is oozing, little strawberries, pears, bananas, walnuts with the shell broken so the inside is visible, roast chestnuts sprinkled with a faint trace of ashes; nor do they forget the vegetables. There are entire collections of peas, of fava beans, of artichokes, of asparagus; I even saw some snails! And all this in almond paste: the shell of the snails and that of the walnuts are sugar and melt in your mouth, like real sweets. The imitation is of an amazing exactness.

Sugar statues, *pupa di cena*, are another old Sicilian speciality (largely obsolete elsewhere), and they are now made in the shape of celebrities, ballerinas, cowboys, Disney characters or religious figures. These sugar statues are mentioned in an account of a noble wedding of 1574, which reflects the importance of sweets in Sicilian life at this time:

The entertainments of this day consisted of diverse dances performed by the Ladies with the Knights, which were opened by the groom and the bride. Said dances were interspersed with pauses for a most excellent refreshment of sweets, brought on in this order. There appeared at one end of the corridor, through a door that leads to the rooms of the Palace, milord the Marchese della Favara with 25 gentlemen, each carrying a bowl of silver, full of comfits and diverse sorts of fruit with sugar statues adorned by banners of silver and gold with the coats of arms of the bride and groom, upon these followed milord the Conte di Raccuia with 25 other gentlemen and as many bowls; then came milord the Conte di Cammarata with the third formation, and finally milord the Marchese d'Avola; and these four masters of ceremony were also accompanied by cup-bearers with pitchers of drinks.

Palermo's city accounts of the sixteenth century show that important guests were always showered with sweets on their arrival in the city. Later, in the seventeenth and particularly the eighteenth centuries, the nuns and monks in the monasteries on the island – many of them quite luxurious – found a creative outlet in sweet- and pastry-making. A number of these sweets have sexual connotations, so it is possible to speculate whether sweetmaking provided an outlet for urges besides creativity.

The nuns of Santa Trinità del Cancelliere, founded in 1190, were all women of aristocratic birth, and their speciality, a pastry filled with apricot paste, called *fedde*, bore a remarkable resemblance to female genitalia. The nuns replaced the design in the nineteenth century. In her essential essay 'The Waning of Sexually Allusive Monastic Confectionery in Southern Italy', June di Schino suggests that many of these sweets reflected pre-Christian fertility rites and customs practised at agricultural festivals – a *prucitanu*, for example, is a type of Sicilian biscuit apparently shaped like female genitalia – although perhaps the best-known example, the breast of Saint Agatha, is explicitly Christian (and still made by the nuns at the Monastery of the Virgins of Palermo). This is not a sexy object at all, but a reference to the awful martyrdom of Saint Agatha, who had her breasts cut off and died clasping a green olive branch. She is always depicted holding a severed breast on a plate. In her honour, the nuns make 'virgin's breast cake', and there is a local breast-shaped cassata with cherries for nipples. The virgin's breasts of the nuns of the Monastery of Itria di Sciacca are custardy cakes with chocolate and *zuccata* (candied pumpkin). I wonder whether the classic Italian ice-cream pudding, the bombe, is a version of the breast of Saint Agatha? The monasteries began to close down in the late nineteenth century, and according to Mary Taylor Simeti, author of *Sicilian Food* (1989), only one convent in Palermo, staffed by elderly nuns, still makes pastries. You order through a grate, the pastries come round to you on a wheel, and you leave the money in their place.

Italians do not make much of a distinction between sweets and biscuits, and very often something described as a sweet turns out to be hard, baked and most certainly a biscuit.

Indubitable sweets are *confetti*, silvered or silver-blue sugared almonds that are traditionally thrown at weddings and festivals. The old firm of Confetti Crispo, of Vesuviano, near Naples, specialises in these traditional dragées. The candied fruit of Genoa and Milan is famous, although isolated artisans such as Cascina San Cassiano in Piedmont also produce wonders. *Torrone* is another Italian speciality, and each maker produces its own variation; Quaranta, for example, makes wonderful multi-coloured nougat cakes, studded with hazelnuts, figs, cherries, orange peel and so on. This company also makes another Italian favourite, nut brittle, which is simply caramel poured over nuts. These are made in round cakes or sold in bar form: *nocciola* (hazelnuts), *mandorla* (almond), *arachidi* (peanuts) and *sesamo* (sesame). The Italian chocolate taste favours the hazelnut style immortalised in the *gianduja* of Turin, a tale of two creaminesses: the fibrous creaminess of mashed Piedmontese hazelnuts, and the creaminess of rich milk chocolate. In the mid nineteenth century, the firm of Caffarel developed its own rich and smooth, bite-sized concoction larded with hazelnuts: *gianduiotto*. Hazelnut is also the flavour for Italy's most famous commercial chocolate brand, Baci of Perugina (made in Milan). It is embarrassing to point out, but these *baci* (kisses) are also shaped like breasts, with a hazelnut as a nipple. Baci has perhaps the most effective sweets packaging in the world, a superb deep blue and silver scheme and a wide variety of containers, from tubes to tins. All are designed with Milanese flair, and the temptation to add colours is resisted at all times except Christmas, when a special smattering of red might appear. On top of this, each sweet contains a love note in four languages. An Italian masterpiece.

All the Mediterranean islands came under some kind of Arab influence in the early medieval period, and several – such as Cyprus – developed important sugar-cane industries. Cypriot sweets have a distinctly Arab flavour, with various nut brittles, almond sweets, baklava and halva. Specialities include Cyprus walnuts, candied whole and served to guests with a glass of water, and *kaloprama* (meaning 'good thing'): moist semolina and almond cake, dripping in syrup, which is eaten as a sweet by children.

Maltese nougat, *qubbajt*, comes from the same Arabic root as the Sicilian version, and other sweets unique to the island are clearly Eastern in origin, notably *qaghaq tal-ghasel*, Christmas treacle rings with a filling of syrup, cloves and citrus peel. Maltese toffee, clear and golden, is made for fiestas.

There is a rich, Arab-derived almond inheritance on Majorca, with sweets like *amargos* (baked almond balls) and the Christmas delicacy called *coques de torro*, marzipan wrapped in rice paper.

Mainland Spain's confectionery landscape is indebted to the Arab invaders who settled there and assimilated, the last of whom, Boabdil, left in 1492. (I once ate an *île flottante* in Granada which had been poetically named 'Boabdil's Dream', a much better name for this average dessert.) So Andalusia was the last stronghold of the Arabs, and it is a hotbed for little almond cakes and pastries (like *polvorones* and *mantecadas*) made in the *pastelerías*. Almond flour is often used instead of regular flour in cakemaking. These shops are principally bakers, but they and the *bombonerías* also produce sweets such as *tocinillo de almendra*, or nut brittle. Toledo is famed for its marzipan and Valencia makes *guirlache* (chopped almonds, sugar and lard, cooled and cut into strips), but the Spanish sweet to end all sweets is of course *turrón*, or nougat. The manufacture of this sticky, nutty, eggy brick of pleasure has been centred since at least the fifteenth century round the almond groves in the mountains north of Alicante, near the town of Jijona. Here, a dozen or so old firms, such as Turrones José Garrigós, Sirvent Selfa and Castillo de Jijona, now make *turrón* industrially, with the focus on the traditional Christmas market. Round-the-clock production proceeds from May to December.

The 'garden almonds' or '*jarden*' almonds (hence their name, Jordan almonds, in the United States) arrive ready-peeled at the factory and are toasted for an hour. Then they are pulverised in machines called *boixets*. A big vat of honey, sugar and egg white is mixed, and the chopped almonds are added in different proportions depending on the type of *turrón* being made. Traditionally, the owner of a large estate in Spain would have had *turrón* made up to an old family recipe and distributed it to the estate workers or villagers; today, the last job of the year in a *turrón* factory is the manufacture of a special *turrona la piedra*, perhaps with hazelnuts and dusted with cinnamon, just for the employees (who are presumably sick of the taste of normal *turrón*).

Catalonia as a whole has a very ancient sweets tradition; Barcelona's first pastry shop is recorded in 1382 and in his fifteenth-century cookbook, Platina praises the Catalan sweet-makers for their Lenten confectionery. In *Catalan Cuisine* (1989), Colman Andrews states that 'there are at least fifty traditional associations of specific sweetmeats with specific holidays in the region'. Most of these are almond-based pastries or marzipans, although candied fruit and pine-nut pastries and sweets are also made. The pine-nut is a superb and (outside Spain) under-used confectionery ingredient. Sugar-coated pine-nuts are a Spanish delicacy, and the gloriously chewy and luxuriant texture of these divine pellets is exploited to the full in the pine-nut toffees made by the Navarra firm of El Caserío.

Spain is far from fixated on the past in its confectionery, however. Chupa Chups, the Barcelona-based lollipop specialists, are world leaders, exporting to 170 countries and tailoring flavours accordingly. There has been a liquorice Chupa Chup for Holland, root beer for America and *tarte tatin* for France; the new Max size has a gummy centre. I purchased a huge and heavy cola-flavoured Chupa Chup lolly, the size of the head of a partially grown gorilla, which I intend to use on any intruders in my house. Space Dust, or Pop Rocks popping candy, was popularised in the late 1970s in Spain, by an incredible Barcelona company called Zeta Espacial. This sweet is quite unnerving to eat: it really feels as if the little granular pieces of candy in your mouth are alive, as they pop about and almost hurt the roof of your mouth and tongue. It feels illegal. The slightly scary nature of this sweet led not only to its success as a worldwide craze, but also to various urban myths, such as the one about the kid who ate a dozen bags and then exploded. In America this kid even had a name: Little Mikey, the boy in a series of television adverts for LIFE breakfast cereal. It was (and still is) widely believed that in real life the too-cute Little Mikey ate six bags of Pop Rocks followed by six cans of Pepsi-Cola and then exploded. The makers of Pop Rocks, General Foods, battled the myth by taking out advertisements and writing to school principals, but Pop Rocks were taken off the market in 1983. Little Mikey was in reality an actor called John Gilchrist who did not explode but instead grew up to become an advertising manager for a radio station. Surely popping candy is quite safe, as the manufacturers say. Isn't it?

Zeta Espacial, which had to design and build its own machines to make its popping candy in its remarkably anonymous-looking factory, explains the mystery of its product:

> Popping candy is small pieces of hard candy that have been gasified with carbon dioxide under superatmospheric pressure. When this candy comes in contact with moisture these small pieces release the gas to give off a lasting sensation of action as well as unique cracking and crackling sounds. In a child's mouth this means fun!

'Gasified with carbon dioxide under superatmospheric pressure'! – Willy Wonka could not have put it better. Zeta Espacial's product is the Holy Grail of sweetmakers: a novel idea that is also a stunning commercial success. The company's products, which now include Hair Fashion Pop Rocks for girls and a Magic Fizz 'paint your tongue!' with paintbrush version, are now exported to sixty countries. The pleasure of the pop prevails.

Egg leads the way in Portugal, particularly the yolk. As in the rest of southern Europe, the monasteries and nunneries were the prime sweetmaking centres, and every ecclesiastical establishment had its speciality, usually with symbolic religious overtones. Breast-shaped sweets are again popular, and *papos de anjo* (breasts of angels) made from sugar and jam, mixed with egg and cinnamon and baked, were made at nunneries in Beja, Amarante, Viseu, Mirandela and on the Azores. A wide range of local ingredients is employed in Portuguese sweetmaking, from the candied plums of Elvas, to the eggy-filled almond sweets (*doces de amendoa*) made in fruit, fish and vegetable shapes in the Algarve. Then there are the *nozes de Cascais*, made in the seaside town near Lisbon – walnut halves laid on balls of almond paste and caramelised – and Setúbal, south of Lisbon, is famous for both its oranges and its homemade candied orange peel, although the town's *laranjinha* sweet is actually mashed carrot boiled up with the pith of oranges and sugar, which is then shaped like an orange.

Potato is an ingredient in a few Portuguese sweets – it is mixed with almonds in Benavente, and sweet potato is used on Madeira to make the unfortunately named *Fartes de Batata*. But egg rules Portuguese sweets. Famous examples are the *bolos de ovos de Viseu*, made with seven ounces of sugar and fourteen egg yolks (which is pretty eggy), moulded as balls, cylinders or pyramids, browned under the grill and left to stand for two full days to firm up. The *bolos de Dom Rodrigo* of the Algarve are usually left to the professionals because they are extremely fiddly to make: first, a nest is spun from threads of egg yolk and sugar, which is easy to say but probably next to impossible to do. This is filled with a mixture of egg yolk, almonds, sugar and cinnamon, and the whole thing is then dunked in hot syrup. Each *bolo* is put in a foil wrapper with the ends twisted, so that no syrup is lost.

Moving northwards, the sweets of France are perhaps the most delicately flavoured and carefully made in the world. The old skills and techniques of the eighteenth- and nineteenth-century sweetmakers have not been lost, and the *pâtisserie-confiserie* of many a town or village makes its own speciality. These sweets tend to be richer and more strongly flavoured than the mass-produced varieties that are now the norm, as suitable for adults as for children and sold in dainty packages done up with ribbons, or smart boxes and tins. These sweets are not consumed casually, as a matter of course, but valued as an official branch of cuisine. They are perhaps a little poncey compared with the democratic sweets of other countries, but their quality is undeniable.

Dragées, or sugared almonds, are standard here as across the whole of continental Europe and the Middle East, and used in a variety of ways at christenings and weddings. I did some research into these customs but ultimately found them slightly boring, so – as Baedeker said of Cambridge in the first edition of his guidebook – we shall omit them. French sugared almonds themselves are quite the best, to my taste, just crunchy enough and delicately perfumed with various flavours; this perfume is the key to a good sugared almond: it should infuse the nut. The French variety called *cailloux du gave* look like river pebbles with a marbled finish. Pralines in their original form are entirely French; that is, whole (and later, historically, crushed) almonds boiled up in thin caramel to make a delicious crunchy confection used in a variety of ways. The other use of the word praline, meaning a filled chocolate (usually with a soft chocolate centre) is a Belgian and German interpolation. There is a persistent story that the word praline derives from the Duke of Plessis-Praslin of the late sixteenth century, whose cook is said to have invented the recipe. One wonders what this cook was called. The pralines of Montargis are most celebrated, and the chocolate-covered Charlestines of Nancy, the Jacquelines of Dion and the Forestines of Bourges are all esteemed versions.

French boiled sweets are a long way from the merry, galumphing – and cheap – British varieties. The standard type is the *berlingot*, a triangular tetrahedron of secretly flavoured, pulled sugar candy with jolly stripes and crimped ends (cut with scissors, or a *berlingotière*). *Berlingots* have been made all over France since the nineteenth century, although their spiritual home is Carpentras. Nantes disputes this claim, however, arguing that there is no proof of the Carpentras *berlingot*'s medieval origins, and that the Nantais version, which is smaller and plain white, was definitely invented in the reign of Louis XVI. I have not had leisure to look into this.

Barley sugar is an ancient French as well as English sweet, originally made with a sugar syrup infused with barley water, and the most traditional version in France is the *sucre d'orge* that was made by the Benedictine nuns of Moret-sur-Loing from the seventeenth century. When the nunnery closed, Napoleon employed an ex-nun called Felicité to keep him supplied (so the story goes). *Sucre d'orge* is still made at Moret, either in the shape of a *berlingot* or in a rod shape; there is a secret ingredient, *poudre de perlimpinpin*, the composition of which is said to be known only by one person. These sweets are intoxicatingly rich, with the merest hint of lemon. Another type of barley sugar is made at Lille, *p'tits quinquins* – variously flavoured, acid sweets named after a nursery rhyme.

Nancy is the home of bergamot, that musky, perfumed manifestation of a fruit that is halfway between a pear and a lemon, encapsulated here in the incomparable *bergamotes* of Nancy, which come in an attractive yellow box and are a superb afternoon pick-me-up. It is a flavour that cannot be replicated. Nemours has its poppy-flavoured *bonbon au coquelicot*, invented in 1850, and Cambrai has its *bêtises*, or 'sillies', sticky yet brittle mint candies invented in 1880 by a young confectioner whose grandmother berated him for wasting his time. Brittany makes *coquillages*, multicoloured boiled sweets shaped like shells, as well as various sweets with soft centres.

At the more commercial end, Barnier of Rouen is perhaps the best-known boiled-sweetmaker, and a tray of their lollipops is often positioned near the cash till in a *pâtisserie-confiserie*. The French tradition of panned sweets is epitomised by Flavigny, which makes a range of small aniseed balls with different outer flavours; Agatha Christie's favourite was violet. Flavigny does not have a monopoly: a company called Avolas of St-Gély du

Fresc makes pure white dragées that come in a very stylish white package.

Provence and the Auvergne are well known for their candied fruits, and the town of Apt is a centre of the craft. But these and fine fruit pastes, covered in sugar and cut in squares, can be found all over France. Marrons glacés, candied chestnuts, are a speciality of the Ardèche. Gums are surprisingly scarce in France now, given the country's historical facility with the genre in the eighteenth and nineteenth centuries, although traditional marzipan and almond pastes perfected at this time have not waned in popularity. *Calissons* are a speciality of Aix-en-Provence, diamonds of fresh almond paste with a hint of orange and melon, topped with white icing. Other French marzipans are the versions made by the nuns of Issoudon, simple squares and triangles of superfine, caramel-coloured marzipan, and *les crottins de Sancerre*, white-chocolate-coated almond pastes flavoured with orange that look like little cheeses. Lyon, that gastronomic centre, has a variety of sweet marzipan versions of the *quenelle*, a type of steamed pike sausage in its official incarnation, as well as *coussins* (cushions) that are generally made of bright-green marzipan. Toulouse is the world centre of violets, and candied violet petals are a speciality, although I have always found the range of violet sweets here disappointing. (Admittedly I have a mania for violet.)

Caramels are something of a secret passion in France, since they are not readily associated with that country but sell well everywhere. *Les chuques du Nord* are a popular variety of coffee-flavoured caramels, invented in 1887, as are *verités de la palisse*, soft caramels with hints of fruit flavours. Chocolate-covered versions are perhaps best of all, such as the soft and expensive Négus brand in their black tin, Le Charitois of the Loire, and Kanouga of Bayonne. American saltwater taffy is not the only sweet to utilise seawater: there are several companies making salty caramels in the saltwater marshes of Brittany, at Noirmoutier and the Isle de Ré, principally; these come in jaunty blue and white tins with a maritime flavour that matches the sweets inside. Until you have eaten one of these sweets, you would not believe that salt and sugar could be such a satisfying pairing. One of my favourite French sweets is the smart rectangular mint that is the speciality of Vichy, and my after-dinner regime often includes biting down on one of these gentle powdery mints, which also come in a delightful lemon flavour. Montelimar means nougat, of course, a softer, chewier version than Spanish *turrón* or Italian *torrone*, which better emphasises the textural contrast between nougat and nut. Jean Durand's *Le Nougat de Montélimar* (1994) informs us that the first factory in the town, Michel Fils Cadet, was established in 1770, and the business has thrived since then. Enormous cubes of nougat are sometimes made for exhibitions, and in 1930 one factory even made a nougat zeppelin. The brotherhood of nougat makers, La Confrèrie du Nougat, was established in 1988, and Monsieur Durand and his cronies wear robes and nominate a grandmaster. As they would tell you, real Montelimar should be made with lavender honey.

Belgium is famed for its chocolate above all, which is creamier and softer than other national types. But its sweets story does not end there. Fruit jellies and pastes made of fruit, sugar and apple pectin are a national speciality, and arguably eclipse even those of France in their quality. Companies such as Confidas make up lovely boxes of assorted fruit jellies and the en masse effect of all those translucent coloured cubes, plus the anticipation of biting into them, is superlative. *Sugarbonen*, or sugared almonds, are again popular for many occasions, but Belgium's sweetmakers have a flair for originality, too. At the Cologne sweets fair I talked to the owner of Confiserie Thijs, who was knowledgeable and passionate about his fine lollipops – including a trademark chocolate-covered nougat type – and also to the inventor of coconut marzipan, who has been making his signature product in the shape and colour of carrots since 1973, under the brand name Cocomas. The Cuberdon is a remarkable Belgian sweet, a dark purple or black pyramid, hard on the outside but possessed of an extraordinary liquid centre inside, whose perfume fills the nostrils on biting. The gradation of texture is equally amazing and highly satisfying, although the family who make them say that the sweet's eight-week shelf-life has always been a problem. Twin Sweets is a Belgian company but very much on its own planet. Initially, I found them on the Internet, and could not understand who they were, what they made, or how they remained solvent. Twin Sweets specialises in what looks like sticks of rock, made in one shape only, thrillingly marketed in giant, normal and small sizes. Their stand at Cologne confirmed this suspicion.

The Netherlands glories in liquorice (see Lucky Dip, page 72), but there are other special Dutch sweets. *Stroopballetjes* are a kind of soft toffee made with treacle, and chocolate is made into capital-letter shapes so you can buy initials for friends. Droste's chocolates are a national institution, and very good. Lonka makes caramels, Hirsch produces lollipops and Rademaker's signature product are its *hopjes*, coffee candies. Chewy Mentos are a Dutch product. But most Dutch of all are the Wilhelmina peppermints made by Fortuin Dockum. These substantial mints were invented in 1842 – and they look like it. Decorated with a bust of the queen, they feel like currency; perhaps they should be used as Euros, in the same way cacao beans were used as money by the Aztecs?

Germany consumes vast quantities of sweets of all kinds. Its most noted confectionery product is marzipan, although in recent years firms led by Haribo have spearheaded the international popularity of gummy sweets, which have been enjoyed in Germany since the 1920s. German marzipan is light yet rich, and the production is centred on Lübeck, particularly the dominant brand, Niederegger. Marzipan comes in many forms in Germany, from salamis to imitation hams. In Bayreuth, the products of Funsch, a large novelty marzipan concern, are enjoyed by the local populace – the ring of the nibblers – and the full range can be appreciated in the company's encyclopaedic catalogue, which segues from marzipan models of just-married couples, to ladybirds, red roses, a bug in bed, mice with cheese, hedgehogs, computers, potatoes, bananas (forty to a tray), fruits, Bratwurst and pigs doing almost anything. Frischmann is a similar concern, with better quality models. The *Edelmarzipan* of Dresden is chocolate-coated, and Ewald Liedtke has made toasted marzipan products since 1809. These golden toasties in squares and rounds have a delicate foretaste, followed by an intense and sustained almond flavour, with none of the cloy or bitterness that sometimes accompanies marzipan. German chocolate companies include Halloren (founded in 1804), Ritter, Sarotti, Alpia, Schogetten and Dreher, and the important firm of Katjes makes fruit gums and chews as well as its classic liquorice products. Wafer bars and creamy chocolate fillings (like Duplo from Kinder) are particularly popular.

Switzerland is not just chocolate, either, although you might think so when confronted with a towering wall of different bars in an average Swiss sweets department. Swiss confectioners excel in carefully made bonbons using natural ingredients, such as the caramels from Klein, or the celebrated herbal sweets made by Ricola. Similarly, Austria is not all tarts. We have already touched on the phenomenon that is Pez, and aside from malty caramels called Milchmalz and Blockmalz (also popular in Germany), Austria boasts the Mozart ball, a marzipan-filled chocolate ball wrapped in a portrait of the composer. Niemetz of Vienna also manufactures a famous marshmallow bombe called the *Schwedenbombe*.

If this really came from Sweden it is more likely to have been filled with liquorice, for the whole of Scandinavia has a taste for it. Perhaps the most traditional Swedish sweet is *polkagrisa*, pulled candy in red and white stripes, flavoured with peppermint and . . . vinegar. But in recent years Sweden and indeed all Scandinavia has consumed sweets made by the massive Finland-based Leaf corporation (which produces Chewits), although Marabou is also an important contender. Ahlgrens Bihar are one of Sweden's favourite sweets, shaped like a Bugatti sports car, in white, green and pink.

Denmark has the honour of regularly coming top in per-capita ratings of national sweets consumption, followed by Switzerland, Germany, Ireland and the United Kingdom. Not far behind are Belgium, the United States, Austria, the Netherlands and Sweden, followed by France. It is difficult to explain Denmark's pre-eminence, impressive though it is. With the exception of Anthon Berg chocolates, the country does not produce any sweets of international note; rather, it appears to eat all the sweets that come its way, like a whale consuming krill.

Norway has a penchant for marzipan, especially at Easter, and its Freia chocolate brand produces bars called Quicklunch, for those hikes round the fjords, and Non-Stop chocolate. Norwegians are also proud of their ultra-creamy milk chocolate. Much of Scandinavia's confectionery emanates from Finland. Cloetta Fazer controls about a quarter of the market with bars such as Fazer Blue milk chocolate (1922), Dumle (toffee, 1960), Geisha (hazelnut nougat, 1908), Marianne (mint, 1949) and Wienernougat (1904). Leaf produces bars such as Tupla, which has the same colour scheme as a Mars Bar but contains cracked almonds in the mix, and the bestselling Lauantaipussi ('Saturday bag') assortment for children.

Iceland is exceedingly fond of sweets, again mainly liquorice but also curiosities such as Buffalo Bites, chocolate-covered marshmallows, from Mona Confectionery, and the Olsen Olsen chocolate-covered marzipan bar. Opal is the major Icelandic boiled-sweets player.

THE PHILIPPINES

That is the world of sweets. Except for the Philippines. Which I have left until last because it is so extraordinary. The Philippines is a group of 7,107 islands in South-east Asia, about the size of the British Isles in all. It has absorbed culinary influences from East and West – principally Chinese, Spanish and American; Indian and Arab in the Muslim south – and plays host to at least eighty ethno-linguistic groups. But it has also devised an unparalleled vocabulary for describing food in all its gradations of sourness, bitterness and sweetness. *Manamisnamis*, or the 'hidden sweetness' of some seafoods and fruits, is the most prized flavour of all, as described by Gilda Cordero-Fernando in *The Culinary Culture of the Philippines* (1976): 'Manamisnamis is a very delicate taste which connotes a touch of sweetness without the use of sugar. The flesh of a crab is manamisnamis, as is newly-boiled shrimp and just-pickled vegetables.' The sweetness of coconuts is similarly appraised, and only coconuts which are ripe, or *makapuno* (full up), are considered good for sweetmaking. There has long been a sweet tooth in the Philippines: when Magellan landed here in 1521, his chronicler Pigafetta reported that the natives 'presented a gift of various foods all made of rice, some in leaves made with rather long pieces of sugar loaves, others like tarts with eggs and honey'. Rice sweets remain a part of the Philippines confectionery culture, whereas most other sweets can be traced back to the Spanish inheritance. The Philippines developed economically after Manila was opened to trade in 1814, and coffee, sugar and coconut were exported. The province of Pampanga became associated with sweets, and also the quiet town of San Miguel de Mayumo (*mayumo* means sweets in the Pampango dialect).

Bibingka are the traditional, brightly coloured baked-rice sweets of the Philippines, associated with festivals and family times. They are made from rice, coconut, sugar and egg, cooked in a clay mould. Slices of white cottage cheese or salted egg are added halfway through cooking, and they are served hot, with ginger tea. Since *bibingka* are cooked right through, from top to bottom, over a charcoal fire (a galvanised sheet placed on top equalises heat), *bibingka* is also the term used when people from all levels meet to discuss affairs. *Puto bumbong* is a special Christmas *bibingka* made in churchyards, ready for people leaving church: it is made from a sticky rice that is naturally purple, cooked over a fire in narrow bamboo tubes that are set up like a row of test tubes. The resulting long, thin, chewy purple cylinder is dipped in sugar and coconut. (The food historian of Hawaii, Rachel Laudan, has suggested that *bibingka* may have originated in Goa, and the Hawaiian *mochi* which are supposed to be Japanese could in fact be descended from *bibingka*.) There are other rice sweets. *Nilupak* is made of rice communally ground in a rice mortar, which is a good opportunity for flirting; there are many regional varieties, like green banana, young coconut or sweet potato. *Palitaw* is made of ground rice formed into tongue shapes (hence its other name, *dila-dila*) which is boiled and then rolled in sugar, coconut and sesame seeds. *Espasol*, often sold by the roadside, is rice flour cooked in coconut milk, sweetened, made into cylinders, dusted in rice flour and wrapped in white paper.

The Chinese presence in the Philippines is reflected in sweets such as *carrioca*, caramelised balls of glutinous rice, stuck three at a time on a bamboo stick; the superbly named *bitchu-bitcho*, a cylinder of dough deep-fried and rolled in sugar; and *ampaw*, puffed rice stuck together with syrup and cut in rectangles. But the Spanish tradition has had more influence, especially in *pastillas*, cylinder- or bar-shaped sweets made of milk and nuts. The *pastillas de leche*, or milk sweets, are most popular, sometimes with the addition of rind of dayap (a fragrant native lemon) or egg and cheese. *Pastillas de ube* are made with jam from yams. Yam jam? Wonders never cease in the world of sweets. There is great debate as to whether the yam jam should be perfectly smooth or slightly grainy, thus giving a true sense of the vegetable. For festivals, *pastillas* are decorated with long tails of brightly coloured paper, cut into intricate patterns with scissors and sometimes displaying messages that hang down over the edge of raised-up plates.

Empañaditas are small versions of the beef-filled Spanish flour *empañada*, stuffed instead with honey and nuts or perhaps custard. *Turron* is another Spanish speciality transferred to the Philippines, although here a cashew nut version is popular.

Preserved fruits are also given a special Filipino treatment: santol fruit, *suha* (pomelo), *kundol* (wax gourd), lime, tomatoes, breadfruit, *guyabano* (soursop) and *dayap* are etched with incredibly complex designs using a sharp knife. According to Gilda Cordero-Fernando, the *suha* is the best fruit for this treatment: it is picked before it is ripe, the rind removed and the fruit discarded. It is carved, placed in several changes of salt water, then pressed, thoroughly dried and then cooked in syrup. A skilled old lady is able to carve intricate flower designs on a hundred rinds a day, which makes three and a half jars. An *abrillantada* is a carved miniature version of a whole fruit made from pieces of that particular fruit – apple, pear or guava – with a real leaf attached. A version favoured by poorer families is made of coconut paste rolled in sugar. Another cheap everyday sweet is the banana cue, cooked in brown sugar and stuck on a bamboo stick or rolled in a leaf. These are sold by vendors at the roadside and near supermarkets.

The Philippines even had its own chocolate culture. The Chinese dominated the trade, and traditionally an oriental trader would call and grind up the chocolate to the customer's specification (as in Spain). Guests would expect to be served a cup of chocolate, and a host would employ a subtle code to indicate to the servants how much precious chocolate to use: 'chocolate . . . eh' was *espeso*, thick, and whipped in pure carabao milk; 'chocolate . . . ah' was *aguado*, meaning watered-down.

The Philippines is a nation that contains a world of sweets, a fitting end to this world tour of confectionery. My personal 'sweets museum', overflowing from a dozen bags and suitcases, contains sweets from all round the world, collected, sent or brought back from foreign climes, or else purchased by mail order. It is amazing how very few of these sweets are unpalatable. The sweet tooth truly does unite us.

But I never found that Himalayan gobstopper.

EPILOGUE

In which the author advances a personal and philosophical
justification for sweet-eating based on the writings of
Epicurus

Why eat sweets? It is incontrovertibly true that they can rot the teeth, and many adults decry sweet-eating as an infantile habit. After the hiatus of adolescence, young people emerge blinking into the strip-lit glare of the newsagent's or drugstore, wondering what kind of new relationship they should construct with the sweets that are laid out so temptingly before them. Most of them do not leave behind their liking for sweets with their dollies and model cars, but decide to suppress their appetite because sweets are seen as one of those childish things to be put away if one wishes to be taken seriously in the world.

But I would argue that as we grow older we should eat more sweets, rather than fewer sweets. For my authority I turn to Epicurus, the fourth-century BC Greek philosopher who presided over an open-air community of philosophically-minded men and women in Athens, a kind of commune which was known as The Garden. Epicurus is caricatured today as a hedonist who advocated the pursuit of pleasure above all else, but this is not an accurate reflection of his philosophy. It is true that Epicurus maintained that in the pursuit of the good life, pleasure is the guiding principle: 'Pleasure is the beginning and end of the happy life [. . .] For we recognise pleasure as the first good innate in us, and from pleasure we begin every act of choice and avoidance, and to pleasure we return again, using the feeling as the standard by which we judge every good.'

But Epicurus's philosophy is not a hedonistic calculus: he

advocates moderation in such things, because his definition of pleasure is simply the absence of pain, mental or physical, and true happiness is happiness of the mind rather than the body. A simple pleasure like the removal of the pain of hunger through a meal of bread and cheese is equal to that of a gourmet dinner in the same circumstances. The pleasure of fine food is only a variation of this basic pleasure of satiation, not a fundamental improvement on it. Pleasure is not the same thing as luxury.

In practice, Epicurus valued friendship above all else, and advocated a quiet life with no public responsibility (a scandalous idea to the civic-minded Greeks). In his philosophy, there are no moral absolutes and no such thing as natural justice, only a social justice that is dictated by the self-interest of the majority. Epicurus maintained that the only point of personal morality is that it produces pleasurable feelings in the do-gooder. This could be seen either as a fundamentally selfish code of behaviour, or simply as an unusually honest way of looking at the world and how people behave in it.

But what has this got to do with sweets? Epicurus does not mention them; I am appropriating his ideas for my own ends. It seems to me that Epicurus's principles are a useful guide to constructing a way of life that celebrates pleasure as the route to happiness, while also embracing the virtues of moderation.

Sweets fit into the Epicurean world-view in a number of ways. First, there is no doubt that they are a pleasure, and they actively improve one's life. A sweet can remove mental pain, even if we do not notice it. Epicurus points out that the moment of transition between pleasure and pain can be difficult to discern, so at the end of a long day, we might be dimly aware that we have had a bad day or a good day, but be unable to itemise the events which have contributed to the final balance. It is my belief that sweets can just tip the balance in favour of happiness, and that is partly why people like to eat them. Sweets can make us happy.

But they are also humble pleasures. Brillat-Savarin declared, 'The discovery of a new dish does more for the happiness of mankind than the discovery of a star' – which may be true, but sweets do not aspire to such heights. They are incidentals: small, cheap and usually quick; they are often eaten in ones and twos. Sweets can feel like a luxury, but they are not really much of an extravagance. They provide a modicum of stimulation of the senses but do not intoxicate; they give pleasure but harm no one.

Sweets are also the embodiment of Epicurus's idea of the variation of pleasure. They can remove a mental pain by providing a little patch of pleasure over it, a psychological Bandaid of sweetness, and continual sweet-eating might well prolong this effect without altering it. But Epicurus was entirely in favour of experiencing pleasure in all its variety, even if its depth remained unchanged, and encouraged the exploration of the sensual variety of life. It is as if sweets, in all their flavours and textures, are tailor-made examples of this principle of the variation of pleasure.

Finally, there is friendship. Sweets are made for sharing, and they can be used to shore up relationships or make new friends. Epicurus would say that the motivation for sharing out sweets must always be self-interest, but I am not so sure. Perhaps they bring out the best in us sometimes. With sweets, you can quickly and easily improve other people's lives, as well as your own.

Fancy a rhubarb and custard?

BIBLIOGRAPHY

Achaya, K.T. *Indian Food: A Historical Companion*. Oxford University Press, 1994.

Adamson, Melitta Weiss, ed. *Food in the Middle Ages*. London. Garland, 1995.

Anonymous. 'The Pontefract Liquorice Industry', in *Petits Propos Culinaires*, no. 39, 1991.

Apicius, Coelius. *The Roman Cookery Book*, translated by B. Flower and E. Rosenbaum. London. Harrap & Co., 1958.

Arberry, A. J. 'A Baghdad Cookbook', in *Islamic Culture and Hyderabad Quarterly Review*, Jan/April 1939.

Austin, Alma H. *The Romance of Candy*. Harper & Bros, 1938.

Ayrton, Elisabeth. *The Cookery of England*. London. André Deutsch, 1974.

Ayto, John. *Diner's Dictionary*. Oxford University Press, 1993.

Bailey, Cyril, ed. *Epicurus: The Extant Remains*. New York. Limited Editions Club, 1947.

Barthel, Diane. 'Modernism and Marketing: The Chocolate Box', in *Theory, Culture and Society*, no. 6, pp. 429-38, 1989.

Belasco, Warren J. *Appetite for Change: How the Counterculture Took On the Food Industry*. New York. Pantheon Books, 1989.

Bell, Joseph. *A Treatise on Confectionary*. Newcastle, 1817.

Bender, David A., and Bender, Arnold E. *Nutrition: A Reference Handbook*. Oxford University Press, 1997.

Blégny, Nicolas de. *Le Bon Usage de Thé, du Caffé, et du Chocolat*. Paris, 1687.

Bober, Phyllis Pray. *Art, Culture and Cuisine: Ancient and Medieval Gastronomy*. University of Chicago Press, 1999.

Bode, W.K.H. *European Gastronomy*. London. Hodder & Stoughton, 1994.

Boeser, Knut, ed. *The Elixirs of Nostradamus* [1552]. London. Bloomsbury, 1995.

Brenner, Joël Glenn. *The Chocolate Wars: Inside the Secret Worlds of Mars and Hershey*. London. HarperCollins Business, 1999.

Brewer, John, and Porter, Roy, eds. *Consumption and the World of Goods*. London. Routledge, 1993. Includes important essays by Carole Shammas and Sidney W. Mintz.

Brillat-Savarin, Jean-Anthelme. *La Physiologie du Goût*. Paris, 1825.

Brown, Catherine. *Scottish Cookery*. London. Drew, 1989.

Brown, Catherine. *Scottish Regional Recipes*. London. Penguin, 1983.

da Canal, Zibaldone. *Merchant Culture in Fourteenth-Century Venice*. State University of New York, 1994.

Chang, K. C., ed. *Food in Chinese Culture*. Yale University Press, 1977.

Chinn, Carl. *The Cadbury Story*. Studley. Brewin Books, 1998.

Cholmeley, Henry Patrick, ed. *John of Gaddesden and the Rosa Medicinae*. Oxford. Clarendon Press, 1912.

Clair, Colin. *Kitchen and Table*. London. Abelard-Schuman, 1964.

Clarence-Smith, William Gervase. *Cocoa and Chocolate, 1765–1914*. London. Routledge, 2000.

Cline, Sally. *Just Desserts*. London. Deutsch, 1990.

Coady, Chantal. *The Chocolate Companion*. London. Apple, 1995.

Coe, Sophie D., and Coe, Michael D. *The True History of Chocolate*. London. Thames and Hudson, 1996.

Crossley-Holland, Nicole. *Living and Dining in Medieval Paris*. Cardiff. University of Wales Press, 1996.

Dalby, Andrew. *Siren Feasts, A History of Food and Gastronomy in Greece*. London. Routledge, 1996.

Dalby, Andrew, and Grainger, Sally. *Classical Cookbook*. London. British Museum Press, 1996.

Daniel, Albert R. *Up-to-Date Confectionery* [4th edn]. London. Applied Science Publishers, 1978.

Daniels, John, and Daniels, Christian. 'Sugarcane in Prehistory' in *Archaeology of Oceania*, 1993.

Davidson, Alan, ed. *The Oxford Companion to Food*. Oxford University Press, 1999.

Deerr, Noël. *The History of Sugar*. London. Chapman & Hall, 1949.

Driver, Christopher, ed. *John Evelyn, Cook: the Manuscript Receipt Book of John Evelyn*. Totnes. Prospect Books, 1997.

Duncan, Daniel. *Wholesome Advice Against the Abuse of Hot Liquors* [translated] London, 1706.

Emmison, Frederick George. *Tudor Food and Pastimes*. London. Ernest Benn, 1964.

Fieldhouse, Paul. *Food and Nutrition, Customs and Culture* [2nd edn]. London. Chapman and Hall, 1995.

Fitzgerald, Robert. *Rowntree and the Marketing Revolution, 1862–1969*. Cambridge University Press, 1995.

Flandrin, Jean-Louis, and Montanari, Massimo, eds. *Food: a Culinary History from Antiquity to the Present*. Columbia University Press, 1999.

Furnivall, Frederick J., ed. *Early English Meals and Manners*. London, 1868.

Galloway, J. H. *The Sugar Cane Industry*. Cambridge University Press, 1989.

Goody, Jack. *Cooking, Cuisine and Class*. Cambridge University Press, 1982.

Hagen, Ann. *A Handbook of Anglo-Saxon Food*. Pinner. Anglo-Saxon Books, 1992.

Head, Brandon. *Food of the Gods* [cocoa history]. London. R. Brimley Johnson, 1903.

Heiser, Charles B. *Seed to Civilisation: the Story of Food.* Harvard University Press, 1990.

Henisch, Bridget Ann. *Fast and Feast: Food in Medieval Society.* Pennsylvania State University Press, 1976.

Hess, Karen, ed. *Martha Washington's Booke of Cookery*, New York. Columbia University Press, 1981.

Hess, John L. and Hess, Karen. *The Taste of America.* New York. Penguin, 1977.

Hieatt, Constance B., and Butler, Sharon, eds. *Curye on Inglysch* [Cookery in English]. Oxford University Press, 1985. Contains the Treatise of Walter of Bibbesworth.

Historicus [Richard Cadbury]. *Cocoa: All About It.* London. Sampson Low & Co., 1891.

Huggett, Jane. *The Mirror of Health: Medieval Food, Diet and Medical Theory, 1450–1660.* Bristol. Stuart Press, 1995.

Hunting, Penelope. *A History of the Society of Apothecaries.* London. Society of Apothecaries, 1998.

James, Alison. Essay on confectionery, in *Sociology Review*, vol. 38 no. 4, 1990.

Jeaffreson, John Cordy. *A Book About the Table.* London, 1875.

Jones, Howard. *The Epicurean Tradition.* London. Routledge, 1989.

Khare, R. S., ed. *The Eternal Food: Gastronomic Ideas and Experiences of Hindus and Buddhists.* State University of New York Press, 1992.

Kittler, Pamela Goyan, and Sucher, Kathryn P., eds. *Cultural Foods, Traditions and Trends.* London. Wadsworth/Thompson Learning, 2000.

Lane, Frederic C. *Venice, a Maritime Republic.* Johns Hopkins University Press, 1973.

Levenstein, Harvey. *Paradox of Plenty: A Social History of Eating in Modern America.* Oxford University Press, 1993.

Levey, Martin. *Early Arabic Pharmacology.* Leiden. Brill, 1973.

Logue, A. W. *Psychology of Eating and Drinking.* New York. W. H. Freeman, 1986.

Lucretius. *De Rerum Naturum*, translated by Ronald Melville. Oxford University Press, 1997.

McGee, Harold. *On Food and Cooking.* London. Allen & Unwin, 1984.

McIntosh, Elaine N. *American Food Habits in Historical Perspective.* London. Praeger, 1995.

McNeal, J. U. *Children as Consumers.* London. Lexington, 1987.

Marín, Manuela, and Waines, David, ed. *Kanz al-fawa.* Beirut, 1993.

Mason, Laura. 'Rock', in *Petits Propos Culinaires*, no. 49.

Mason, Laura. 'Sherbet', *in Petits Propos Culinaires*, no. 35.

Mason, Laura. *Sugar Plums and Sherbet.* Totnes. Prospect Books, 1998.

Mason, Laura. *Sweets and Sweet Shops.* Princes Risborough. Shire, 1999.

Mason, Laura, with Brown, Catherine. *Traditional Foods of Britain.* Totnes. Prospect Books, 1999.

Mayhew, Henry. *London Labour and the London Poor.* London, 1851.

Mintz, Sidney W. *Sweetness and Power: The Place of Sugar in Modern History.* London. Penguin, 1986.

Montanari, Massimo. *The Culture of Food.* Oxford. Blackwell, 1994.

Morton, Timothy. *The Poetics of Spice.* Cambridge University Press, 2000.

Morton, Timothy, ed. *Radical Food: the Culture and Politics of Eating and Drinking, 1790–1820*. London. Routledge, 2000.

Mui, Hoh-Cheung and Mui, Lorna H. *Shops and Shopkeeping in Eighteenth-Century England*. London. Routledge, 1989.

Needler, Raymond. *Needlers of Hull*. Beverley. Hutton, 1993.

Ohrnberg, Kaj, and Mroueh, Sahban, eds. *Kitab al-tabikh*. Helsinki. Finnish Oriental Society, 1987.

Opie, Iona, and Opie, Peter. *The Lore and Language of Schoolchildren*. Oxford. Clarendon Press, 1959.

Orton, Anne. *Tudor Food and Cookery*. A. Orton, 1985.

Packard, Vance. *Hidden Persuaders*. London. Longmans, Green, 1957.

Perry, Charles. 'Moorish Sugar', in *Spicing Up the Palate: Oxford Symposium on Food and Cookery*. Totnes. Prospect Books, 1992.

Perry, Charles. 'The Taste for Layered Bread among the Nomadic Turks and the Central Asian Origins of Baklava', in *Culinary Cultures of the Middle East*, ed. Sami Zubaida. University of London, 1994.

Peterson, T. Sarah. *Acquired Taste: the French Origins of Modern Cooking*. Cornell University Press, 1994.

Platina. *De Honesta Voluptate*. ed. Mary Ella Milham. Tempe, Arizona, 1998.

du Plessix Gray, Francine. *At Home with the Marquis de Sade*. London. Chatto & Windus, 1999.

Pullar, Philippa. *Consuming Passions: A History of English Food and Appetite*. London. Hamish Hamilton, 1970.

Push, and Scott, Mireille. *The Book of E*. London. Omnibus, 2000.

Race, Margaret. *The Story of Blackpool Rock*. Blackpool. M. Race, 1990.

Rebora, Giovanni. *Culture of the Fork: A Brief History of Food in Europe*. New York. Columbia University Press, 2001.

Regan, Geoffrey. *Lionhearts: Saladin and Richard I*. London. Constable, 1998.

Richie, Donald. *A Taste of Japan*. Tokyo. Kodansha, 1985.

Rinzler, Carol Ann. *The Signet Book of Chocolate*. New York. New American Library, 1978.

Roden, Claudia. *The Book of Jewish Food*. Knopf, 1996.

Root, Waverley and Root, Richard de Rochemont. *Eating in America*. New York. Morrow, 1976.

Rowntree, Benjamin Seebohm. *The Human Factor in Business*. London. Longmans & Co., 1921.

Rozin, Elisabeth. *Blue Corn and Chocolate*. London. Ebury Press, 1992.

Sayer, Chloe, ed. *Mexico, the Day of the Dead, an Anthology*. London. Redstone, 1990.

Schaeffer, Neil. *The Marquis de Sade: A Life*. London. Hamish Hamilton, 1999.

di Schino, June. 'The Waning of Sexually Allusive Monastic Confectionery in Southern Italy', in *Disappearing Foods*, Oxford Symposium on Food and Cookery, 1994.

Schivelbusch, Wolfgang. *Tastes of Paradise*. New York. Pantheon Books, 1992.

Schneider, Norbert. *Still Life*. Cologne. Taschen, 1994.

Schwartz, Rolf D. *Backwerk der Lüste*. Dortmund. Harenberg, 1984.

Scola, Roger. 'Food Markets and Shops in Manchester, 1770–1870', in *Journal of Historical Geography*, no. 1, 1975.

Scully, D. Eleanor, and Scully, Terence. *Early French Cookery*. University of Michigan Press, 1995.

Scully, Terence. *The Art of Cookery in the Middle Ages*. Woodbridge. Boydell, 1995.

Seaton, Meg. *Sweets*. Published in conjunction with an exhibition at the Whitechapel Gallery, London, 1973.

Sheridan, Richard B. *Sugar and Slavery*. Eagle Hall. Caribbean Universities Press, 1974.

Sinha, Anil Kishore. *Anthropology of Sweetmeats*. New Delhi. Gyan Publishing House, 2000.

Skuse, E. *Skuse's Complete Confectioner*. Several editions, from 1880s.

Smith, Chris, Child, John, and Rowlinson, Michael. *Reshaping Work: the Cadbury Experience*. Cambridge University Press, 1990.

Smith, R. E. F. *Bread and Salt, a Social and Economic History of Food and Drink in Russia*. Cambridge University Press, 1984.

Sombart, Werner. *Luxury and Capitalism*. University of Michigan Press, 1967.

Steiner, Jacob. Research published in *Taste and Development: The Genesis of Sweet Preference*, ed. J. M. Weiffenbach, Fogarty International Centre Proceedings, no. 32, 1977; and *Food Acceptability*, proceedings of the Society of Chemical Industry Symposium at the University of Reading, 1987, ed. Thomson, Elsevier Applied Science, 1988.

Steingarten, Jeffrey. *The Man Who Ate Everything*. London. Headline, 1998.

Symons, Michael. *One Continuous Picnic: A History of Eating in Australia*. Ringwood. Penguin, 1984.

Szogyi, Alex, ed. *Chocolate, Food of the Gods*. London. Greenwood Press, 1997.

Tannahill, Reay. *Food in History*. London. Eyre Methuen, 1973.

Tomlinson, Richard. *A Medicinal Dispensatory, Containing the Whole Body of Physick* [translation of Renodaeus]. London, 1657.

Toussaint-Samat, Maguelonne. *History of Food*. Blackwell, 1992.

Tracy, James D., ed. *The Rise of Merchant Empires: Long-Distance Trade in the Early Modern World, 1350–1750*. Cambridge University Press, 1990.

Traeger, James. *The Food Chronology*. London. Aurum, 1996.

Trease, George Edward. *Spicers and Apothecaries*. 1959.

Treglown, Jeremy. *Roald Dahl*. London. Faber and Faber, 1994.

Wagner, Gillian. *The Chocolate Conscience*. London. Chatto & Windus, 1987.

Waines, David. *In a Caliph's Kitchen*. Riad El-Rayyes, 1989.

Walvin, James. *Fruits of Empire*. Basingstoke. Macmillan, 1997.

Waterhouse, Debra. *Why Women Need Chocolate*. London. Vermilion, 1995.

Weatherley, Henry. *A Treatise on the Art of Boiling Sugar*. London, 1864.

Wheaton, Barbara Ketcham. *Savouring the Past, the French Kitchen and Table from 1300–1789*. London. Chatto & Windus, 1983.

Whittaker, Nicholas. *Sweet Talk*. London. Victor Gollancz, 1998.

Wilkins, John, Harvey, David, and Dobson, Mike, ed. *Food in Antiquity*. University of Exeter Press, 1995.

Williams, Cecil Trevor. *Chocolate and Confectionery* [3rd edn], London 1964.

Wilson, C. Anne. *Food and Drink in Britain*. London. Constable, 1973.

Witteveen, Joop. 'Rose Sugar and other Medieval Sweets', in *Petits Propos Culinaires*, no. 20, pp. 22–8, 1985.

'Wyvern'. *Sweet Dishes: A Little Treatise*. Calcutta, 1881.

Yudkin, John. *Pure, White and Deadly: The Problem of Sugar*. London. Davis-Poynter, 1972.

Zubaida, Sami, and Tapper, Richard, eds. *Culinary Cultures of the Middle East*. Tauris/University of London, 1994.

INDEX

INDEX

INDEX

A SELECTED LIST OF NON-FICTION TITLES AVAILABLE FROM BANTAM BOOKS